THE MAKING OF MODERN WOMAN

THE MAKING OF MODERN WOMAN: EUROPE 1789–1918

LYNN ABRAMS

An imprint of **Pearson Education**

London · New York · Toronto · Sydney · Tokyo · Singapore · Hong Kong · Cape Town
New Delhi · Madrid · Paris · Amsterdam · Munich · Milan · Stockholm

PEARSON EDUCATION LIMITED

Head Office:
Edinburgh Gate
Harlow CM20 2JE
Tel: +44 (0)1279 623623
Fax: +44 (0)1279 431059

London Office:
128 Long Acre
London WC2E 9AN
Tel: +44 (0)20 7447 2000
Fax: +44 (0)20 7240 5771
Website: www.history-minds.com

First published in Great Britain in 2002

© Pearson Education 2002

The right of Lynn Abrams to be identified as Author
of this Work has been asserted by her in accordance
with the Copyright, Designs and Patents Act 1988.

ISBN 0 582 41410 5

British Library Cataloguing in Publication Data
A CIP catalogue record for this book can be obtained from the British Library

Library of Congress Cataloging in Publication Data
A CIP catalog record for this book can be obtained from the Library of Congress

10 9 8 7 6 5 4 3 2 1

Set by 35 in 11.5/14 pt Garamond
Produced by Pearson Education Asia Pte Ltd
Printed in Malaysia, PA

The Publishers' policy is to use paper manufactured from sustainable forests.

CONTENTS

———◆———

LIST OF TABLES AND FIGURES

——— ◆ ———

ACKNOWLEDGEMENTS

◆

This book is the culmination of a decade of my own teaching and research on the history of women in modern Europe, and the product of several decades of immensely rich and stimulating writing by other women's historians who have made the lives of European women more tangible, and a little better understood. My debt to the work of others is enormous. The corpus of women's and gender history, especially for the nineteenth century, is now so great that the task of those who try to synthesise this body of material is likely to produce a partial and incomplete vision of the experiences, the roles and the struggles of those women who helped to make European history. I should like to pay tribute to the work of feminist scholars of European women who have contributed to the reshaping of the historical agenda. Hilary Wilkey, former editor at Longman, urged me to embark on this road. I would like to thank her for encouraging me to write this book. I hope the final product is what she envisaged.

I have many debts of gratitude. I first starting teaching European women's history while at Lancaster University between 1990 and 1995. Penny Summerfield was at that time – and still is – my mentor, and her enthusiasm for, and practice of, women's history is motivating and inspiring. At Glasgow University, the students on my women's history courses have always been critically engaged and intellectually challenging. In particular, my special subject class of 1996–97 forced me to think hard about feminism and women, and many of them have gone on to emulate the ambition and drive of their heroines from the past.

A number of friends have carried out the unpaid work of commenting on various drafts of the text. My thanks are extended to Eleanor Gordon, Elizabeth Harvey, Deborah Simonton, Megan Smitley and Perry Willson. My neighbour Moira Lawson, sustained my writing by many acts of traditional female reciprocity – although my cucumbers never did seem like a fair exchange for her cream cakes. My deepest thanks are to Callum Brown. He read my words so many times and so immersed himself in European women's history, he deserves the equivalent of a 'motherhood medal'.

Acknowledgements

This book is dedicated to my paternal grandmother, Grace Abrams (1900–2000), and my maternal grandmother, May Jay (born 1911), both of whom, in their different ways, are the reason why women's history remains a history to be written.

INTRODUCTION

—— ◆ ——

MAN'S WORLD, WOMEN'S NARRATIVES

'It is evident,' wrote a young Scot, Marion Kirkland Reid, in 1843, 'that if woman is a responsible being, there must be a limit to her submission and obedience to man.'[1] Reid in her book *A Plea for Woman* urged women to recognise the 'system of depression' which stunted their education and their claim to full and equal participation in civil society. 'Notwithstanding the comparatively happy lot of woman in this country,' she said of Britain, 'we think it pretty clear that even here she is harassed by needless trammels.' Looking back fifty years, Reid noted the advances in women's condition since the Enlightenment and the French Revolution. Yet, she was aware of the distance still to be travelled by women on the road to equality: 'Why should we rest contented with the advances we have made, instead of looking earnestly forward to those improvements which are still before us?'[2]

This book covers a century of immense significance in the history of women. It starts with the French Revolution, when European women first became aware that their subordination to men was a product of a concerted ideology that could and should be challenged by their own counter-ideology. It ends with the victories of first-wave feminism, notably women's suffrage, in the shadow of the First World War. In between is a century and a quarter when modern womanhood was constantly being debated and challenged. It is a period when women like Marion Reid discussed, wrote and changed ideas about themselves to an extent before unseen, looking back with little regret and forward with great optimism. This self-reflection was a product of unprecedented tension. This was caused on the one hand by massive structural and ideological change – intellectual, scientific and political revolution, nation-state formation, and industrialisation and urbanisation. On the other hand, there was an evolution of new ideas about woman's nature and her role – ideas about women as wives, mothers, lovers, workers and feminists. There were seemingly contradictory and at times deeply disturbing messages for nineteenth-century women to negotiate whilst seeking to survive immensely profound social and economic change.

Much of the story of this book concerns how changing ideas about sexual difference between women and men informed women's experience in the home, in the workplace and in the world of politics, and about how these ideas were subsequently used by women to claim the privileges previously restricted to men. It is a story comprising much struggle but rather slow yet incremental achievement. Woman's suffrage was achieved or imminent in most countries by the end of the book in 1918, and this seemed for many to be a winning tape – a talismanic success that marked a conclusion to first-wave feminist struggle. Yet we know, a century later, that the vote fell far short of changing women's position in society. There had to be a second wave of feminism from the 1960s which challenged hitherto almost unimaginable and untouchable fundamentals of women's identity. It is in the light of this knowledge that we approach European women's history in 'the long nineteenth century' from 1789 to 1918.

At the beginning is the French Revolution of 1789 which started Europe's serious engagement with Enlightenment ideas on human equality and the rights of man. At the outset, the Enlightenment and the French Revolution both seemed to offer the possibility that women might be included in the body politic as equals with men. The language of rights and of citizenship enthused radical women to begin to argue for an elevated role for women and the rights – civil and political – that followed. But in all the pronouncements of the predominantly male thinkers of the Enlightenment, there was singularly no gifting of these rights to women – even as a hypothetical right. Rights were for men, and it was left to women themselves over the succeeding decades to appropriate the language and the legacy of the Enlightenment's intellectual ferment, and to seek amends for the vast democratic deficit the *philosophes* left to women. The story of European women is dominated by this struggle to achieve the equality denied them by the Enlightenment. The fact must be faced that European nations granted human rights of legal independence to emancipated slaves and most working-class men before it was granted to women. This was ironic of course because it was women who played the key role in the movement to end slavery. Nonetheless, it is legitimate to see women's rights as something attained during this period as women slowly achieved something akin to the status of full European citizenship. It is an optimistic historical view of the century as one of more or less constant women's progress towards emancipation.

There is a radically different approach. This view interprets the nineteenth century as witnessing a decline in women's status and opportunities. This decline resulted in part from the failure of the French Revolution to deliver on women's rights, but more importantly it was in part the product of the rise of a Europe-wide ideology that placed women in the home. This was called the ideology of *separate spheres* which specified that women should inhabit the sphere of the home and men the sphere of the world (of work, politics and play). The women's element of separate spheres is referred to as *domestic ideology*, and it is seen as becoming an ideology of imprisonment for many women. For most of the period, European culture witnessed the language of domesticity and of separate spheres predominating over that of women's rights and pervading the world of work, of politics and of intellectual life.

So powerful was domestic ideology that radical women could not simply reject it. They had to struggle – not always with total success – to find a language which resolved the tensions between domestic ideology and the notion of women having rights. The resolution for many first-wave feminists of the nineteenth century was the concept of 'equality in difference' – the notion that women were equal to men because they possessed different qualities. 'The ground on which equality is claimed for all men is of equal force for all women,' Marion Reid argued on the one hand in the middle of our period, 'for women share the common nature of humanity.' Yet on the other hand she appealed to women's 'purer, clearer, less embarrassed reason – of a judgement more disentangled from political prejudices' than that of men. This supposition of difference between the sexes – of fundamental difference between male and female in relation to minds, moral construction, capacities and roles – was the Enlightenment's legacy to European women. This notion of difference was to dictate so much of what women experienced, and was to endure with remarkable vigour in European consciousness. As a result, it generated a continuity between the eighteenth and twentieth centuries which shapes much of this book, and which draws upon what is now a very influential 'narrative of continuity' in women's experience.

If historical continuity is a female-led experience, historical change is traditionally seen as a male experience. Few centuries witnessed such profound and manifold transformations as the nineteenth, transformations that are characteristically portrayed in history books as man-made. Men make economies, discover science, make inventions, fight wars, form governments, explore far-off places and write books. Framed by the two 'watershed' events of the French Revolution and the First World War, the era is packed with the major events that have provided the bread and butter of the traditional history of the nineteenth century: the revolutions of 1789, 1830, 1848 and

1917; European and overseas wars (from the Napoleonic and Crimean to the Great War); the pinnacle of European imperialist expansion in Africa, Asia and the world's island groups; the rise of the Enlightenment, liberalism, Marxism, Darwinism and eugenics; and the industrial revolution, world economic growth, urbanisation, and transformation in the structures of most European societies. No European state escaped these currents, though the impact might vary from place to place. No century features more prominently in the current-day perception of the past, shaping our nations, their boundaries and constitutions, and giving most European nations their official heroes – Napoleon, Nelson, Wellington, Bismarck, Garibaldi, Mazzini, Parnell, Kossuth and Masaryk. Historians and sociologists regard this period as creating our modern society, modern politics, modern nations, modern boundaries and economic systems.

That is the normative story of Europe from 1789 to 1918, and it is a highly male one. Women are more or less absent from that story because they are associated with continuity, the 'female' aspect of history – the unchanging home with the wife, mother, daughter and cook at its helm, experiencing those unceasing reproductive functions of birth and rearing. According to the majority of mainstream histories of the nineteenth century, the lives of women stayed much the same, largely unaffected by the so-called historical watersheds and having negligible impact themselves on the motors of historical change. In this simplistic and blinkered view, male and female represent change and continuity, the yin and yang of conventional historical narrative. A 1998 student textbook on the history of one European nation during the nineteenth century actually confined women to one paragraph and had the gall to state that 'they had remained in the background during much of the country's changing history'.[3] Despite four decades of intense historical scholarship on women's lives during the nineteenth century, the grand historical narrative has men resolutely filling the stage, with women merely cheering – or shouting angrily – from the sidelines.

CHANGE AND CONTINUITY

Why are women restricted to playing cameo roles in these grand narratives of European history? And how do historians who focus on women's history tackle these assumptions about the gendered nature of change and continuity? One obvious explanation for women's exclusion is that they were not the diplomats, the generals and the politicians. It was men who were the fighters, legislators, thinkers, and, if the traditional narrative is believed, they were the makers, inventors and sole breadwinners too. However, there are other reasons for exclusion. In the words of one chronicler of women's lives: 'There is no doubt that the plot of women's history is no less complex than that of men's. But we may assume that time as lived by the female part of humanity does not pass according to the same rhythms and that it is not perceived in the same way as that of men.'[4] This proposition has been eagerly taken up by women's historians whose writings testify to this perceived difference in the way women experience time.

In place of a standard chronological framework structured by major political events or wars, historians of women have often taken the female lifecycle as the prime organising principle of their works. It is an approach especially attractive to historians of women since it encourages the examination of the relationship between 'historical time' and 'individual time'.[5] The first half of Olwen Hufton's magisterial history of women in early modern Europe moves from marriage through motherhood to widowhood; Bonnie Smith's survey of European women since 1700 opens with the story of a marriage, an approach which creates a personalised account of three centuries of women's lives.[6] The result has been that women's historians of the post-Enlightenment period have written alternative historical narratives using different measurements. In the Anglo-American literature, one such narrative – dubbed Golden Age to Separate Spheres – has achieved considerable status, in part perhaps because it sits comfortably alongside mainstream explanations of historical change and does not threaten to undermine dominant accounts.[7] This alternative narrative is exemplified by Davidoff and Hall's *Family Fortunes*, an influential study of the English middle classes in the formative capitalist period. The narrative goes something like this. Women enjoyed considerable freedom, status and 'authentic function' during a 'golden age' for women in the seventeenth and early eighteenth centuries. This age came to an end when, in the late eighteenth and nineteenth centuries, the capitalist industrial economy arrived with an ideology of separate spheres which placed women in the home and men in the world of work, politics and war. This caused women's power in society to decline, constrained their ambitions, almost imprisoned them in their homes, denied them freedoms in leisure, recreation and enjoyment, and denied them access to accumulated capital and the status and power this conferred. Women were restrained by domestic conceptions of their femininity by which they were, after 1800, being judged in terms of their piety, purity, submissiveness and spiritual motherhood. Whilst disabling in one sense, this ideology became within middle-class circles a cult of domesticity and 'true womanhood' which, ironically, gave women a sense of special destiny. Women felt morally superior in this industrial civilisation, propagating a separate woman's culture centred on the church, the home and philanthropic endeavour. This it is argued gradually evolved into a proto-feminist consciousness, empowering women by their own moral action within the home. In this way, a different chronology seems to be created for the writing of women's history.

However, one feminist scholar, Judith Bennett, argues that this is not really a new chronology at all, but merely an accommodation to the male historical narrative: 'we have synchronized transformations in women's status with major historical turning points, even though we have found regress for women in the midst of seemingly progressive historical change.'[8] Women's historians, argues Bennett, are reluctant to shake off the traditional periodisation of European history even when women's experiences do not fit that framework. The recognised historical turning points remain male, she says; women's historians have merely chosen to interpret their impact differently (and usually in a negative way). As a result, there is a view amongst some women's historians that the ideology of separate spheres has been used merely to explain women's exclusion from the formative political and economic processes of the nineteenth century, and not to provide a truly alternative women's narrative.

The most obvious alternative women's narrative is that of continuity: that women of all ages until the late twentieth century experienced essentially the same subordination to men in work, play, politics and leisure, and were confined to the duties of home and motherhood. Recent trends in women's history have certainly preferred to stress the continuities in women's experience and status over the *longue durée* – continuity over centuries when other historians would look at change. In this narrative the traditional watershed events such as revolutions and wars recede from view, to be replaced by the apparently timeless experiences of one half of the population: marriage, childbirth, work, widowhood. It is this willingness to rethink traditional periodisation that marks women's and gender history as a transformative discipline. Here the emphasis is on long-term structural changes – such as the transformation of the economy – rather than immediate or revolutionary change. In this approach, evident changes in women's experiences mask underlying and fundamental continuity. Judith Bennett has written of a patriarchal equilibrium which, for centuries, has sustained women's subordinate status despite the very obvious changes that happened in women's lives.[9] Olwen Hufton acknowledges that, for three centuries, 1500 to 1800, 'everyone who survived the birth process . . . was a lifelong hostage to the constraints imposed by economic circumstances and belief patterns and was socialised into a set of values, visions, ways of doing things, dependent on class.'[10] Early modern historians have quite convincingly argued that continuity is the more accurate characterisation of women's position over at least three centuries. Most importantly, they deny that there ever was a golden age for women in the past, showing that women's subordination and oppression were as evident in the feudal and neo-feudal worlds of 1000 to 1500 as they were under capitalism and industrialisation thereafter.[11] Moreover, Amanda Vickery has forcefully argued that the separation of spheres between men and women was a constant in history, and not a creation of the late eighteenth and early nineteenth century middle classes. Women, she says, were always confined to the home whilst men dominated in the world outside. In her support, historians of women's work have recently stressed the continuities in terms of the proportion of women in employment, in the types of work undertaken (low skilled, low status, low paid) and the sectors in which women were to be found. Women's experiences may have changed, but their status remained much the same.

Yet, the historian is inexorably drawn to change. It would be strange if she did not make special claims for her particular period of interest (thus implying change from the period before). It is a natural product of being a historian. In any event, as Bennett concedes, historical change is more fun than continuity.[12] This book argues for the necessity of embracing both change and continuity. The narrative of this book accepts the historian Amanda Vickery's call for a less heroic chronology, and sympathises to some extent with her rejection of separate spheres as the quintessential organising principle of men's and women's lives in this era. Nevertheless, the nineteenth century was heralded by fundamental ideological and economic shifts which took most of the century to work through.[13] There were manifest changes to women's experiences during the period, and some of these changes were quite sudden. It would be a dereliction to ignore them. The status quo was disrupted by the French and industrial revolutions on a number of levels – ideological, political, economic, financial, cultural and personal – across much of Europe. Even if we allow for the virtues of the continuity narrative, the narrative does come to a stop in Europe in the twentieth century (largely after 1950) when women won new powers, rights, liberties, and self-identities. That change in women's experience started sometime, and it started in the nineteenth century – not for all women, not all at the same time, and not everywhere, but nevertheless change there was.

The way this 'big change', the liberation of European women, began in the nineteenth century is not at all straightforward. It is complex and seemingly contradictory. We explore in this book how the Enlightenment constructed a woman's distinctive nature in terms of home, motherhood and piety, not in terms of skill, ability, reason and worldly ambition. We shall see how this dichotomy between female and male spheres had a profound impact on women's experiences and opportunities. Women endured constraints from men and from themselves upon their education, their employment opportunities and the possibility of an independent existence from men. But, at the same time, though very slowly, the pervasiveness of this domestic ideology also underpinned the ways in which women themselves started to engage with politics. The construction of female difference began to be used as a strength by women to stake a claim to a greater share of power. In short, women of the period themselves acknowledged the distinctiveness of separate spheres to their era, and exploited it as it had never been exploited before (or possibly since): using the domestic piety and morality of the respectable woman to stake a claim to social power. They brought the principles of their domestic world to the forefront of politics and social change. If for no other reason, it is because our sisters in the nineteenth century acknowledged the distinctive power of separate spheres that we, too, as historians of their experience, must acknowledge its distinctiveness then and its positive role to them.

WOMEN'S AGENDA

Women's history not only focuses attention on chronological issues of change and continuity. It also changes the historical agenda. One of the great contributions of women's history has been the introduction of new topics to the agenda – reproduction, motherhood and sexuality for instance. This asserts the significance of the personal in historical understanding, and in this the role of women's bodies – their functions, opportunities, exploitation and exuberance – is an important aspect of the unfolding story ahead. This is reflected in many of the early chapters of this book where we look not only at how women were perceived as mothers, for instance, but also at how they experienced it.

But women are not just bodies. They are also part of the grand narratives of Europe. Women were on the barricades, they were killed by bombs, they stood on political soapboxes, and above all they worked – in industry, commerce, mining and shops. Women's history changes the agenda *within* these narratives. By focusing on the personal as it relates to the social, by thinking about the political importance of representations of sexual difference, women's historians and historians of gender relations have begun the process of rethinking some of the grand narratives of European history in the nineteenth century. As Joan Scott has reminded us, 'gender is one of the recurrent references by which political power has been conceived, legitimised, and criticised.'[14] The formation of nation-states, for example, is now seen as more than a mere political, diplomatic and economic achievement. It is seen as a gendered process whereby moral as much as geopolitical borders were policed, and national identities forged with symbols of masculinity and femininity. The era of mass politics encompassing the rise of 'popular' political parties is in many respects a misnomer when one remembers that the citizen was, until the very end of the century, male, and the disenfranchisement of women was often justified by their nature. Gendered understandings of the ways in which ideas about sexual difference are used in the labour market have altered our understanding of the industrial revolution, of the organisation of production and of the emergence of the labour movement.

Thus, a woman's eye view of the nineteenth century would not, in all likelihood, be solely concerned with those traditionally 'essential' female spheres of activity like the home and motherhood. Neither would it focus solely on the long march of women from political and legal subordination to some measure of equality – although, of course, the story of women's rights activism and organised feminism does have a prominent place in the narrative. Rather, women's perspective on the past must include the interaction between ideas about women (and men) and the ways in which these ideas are put into practice in all realms of human activity.

This book, then, aims to place women squarely within the traditional grand narratives of the nineteenth century in order to reflect how the agenda within them is being changed by women's historians. The nineteenth century as the bourgeois century, as the age of revolution and as the age of empire are three of the narratives that must be re-evaluated according to the agenda of women not merely as onlookers but as participants in the political and economic upheavals of the age. The nineteenth century was not a man's world. Women were at the very centre of the century's defining developments: they were revolutionaries on the barricades and protesters demanding bread and justice; they were workers in the fields and in the factories helping to fuel Europe's industrial revolution. Likewise women were deemed essential to the emergence of the nation and the consolidation of empire – as mothers, educators and minders of the hearth. However, we should bear in mind that on the human scale, at the level of the individual woman, change was mostly gradual and unremarkable. The macro perspective which presents the nineteenth century as a series of overlapping and cumulative revolutions conceals the reality for ordinary people. For most women, change could be measured in terms of the number of children born and how many survived compared with their mother's generation; in terms of the nature of work opportunities on offer; in terms of the kind of marriage relationship expected and experienced; in terms of access to wealth, power, and political and civil rights. And in these terms, for the majority of women, the continuities outweighed the changes.

The book examines the lives of European women both in terms of their own lifecycles and within a broader social, economic, intellectual and political framework. It does not present an alternative history of the nineteenth century – all the traditional turning points are featured – but rather a history of that period from a woman-centred perspective. This inevitably means making some hard decisions about prioritising certain experiences over those traditionally included in historical surveys. Just as historians have traditionally used high politics or ideological trends to chart the period, I use women's experiences and a gendered perspective to structure this account of the nineteenth century. In this sense I follow the entreaty of Gianna Pomata who has argued that: 'Nowadays a women's history textbook should not be written either to legitimate women's history as a separate field or to pursue the objective of an integrated and unified notion of historical knowledge. It should be written instead simply to reflect, with unavoidable partiality, that multiple, non-unified vision that is emerging from current research.'[15]

There is also a methodological issue to be considered: should women of the nineteenth century be regarded as victims or agents? The historian of women who adopts the perspective across the *longue durée* gets herself entangled in a perpetual spiral constituted by two interwoven strands. The first concerns how far 'events' – political, ideological, economic, social – impacted upon the lives of women; the second concerns how far women themselves influenced the course of those events. This tension between *passivity* and *agency* sits at the heart of any study of women's history, and it lay at the very centre of early feminist analyses of women's condition and the potential for change. For Marion Reid, whose voice we heard at the beginning of this chapter, the conundrum was at the heart of the feminist agenda: women first of all have to recognise their position and then act as agents to shape their own lives. Most non-gender historians who attempt to include women in their grand narratives tend to see them as acted upon – women are included as passive vessels in a historical landscape that has already been determined. Certain 'important' or 'significant' events such as the French Revolution retain their pride of place; women are added on as extras, cheering from the sidelines or engaging in spontaneous riot. Nothing these women do changes the story substantially. Women's historians, on the other hand, have attempted to put women at the centre of history as agents in historical change. Historical currents are shaped by women's agency. The question 'what difference did it make?' is no longer posed in a sceptical frame of mind, as numerous women's historians have demonstrated: the difference was fundamental. A good example is that of the industrial revolution in England, where women's historian Maxine Berg and others have shown that high productivity at the technical sharp-end of industrialisation by low-waged labour – women and children – fuelled unprecedented economic growth.[16] The industrial revolution simply could not have happened so quickly or so successfully without female labour. So, women were agents not passive victims in nineteenth-century Europe. They were not led kicking and screaming to the barricades – they went themselves.

There is no longer any excuse for ignorance about the position and experience of women in the states of northern and western Europe. Women's history is vibrant there, whilst our understanding of women in the southern European states is growing, especially as materials become available to the English-speaking world. Anglo-American historians have always pursued a keen interest in Russian women, but the relatively slow emergence of women's history in the east European states has meant that research is only now reaching the public domain. As an historian of Germany and of Scotland, my feet are planted firmly in north-west Europe. My perspective is informed by my knowledge of the western European pattern of development and my immersion in the watershed events of modern European history. The narrative I write is driven by the experiences of the most economically and politically advanced states on the understanding that most of Europe was affected by similar economic and political trends, if at different times and different speeds. No country was left untouched by the eighteenth-century intellectual revolution or the nineteenth-century industrial revolution. Yet, at the same time, it is important to give voice to the experience of women at the geographical and social periphery of the advanced economies. In any work of women's history, then, there are various categories of analysis as well as gender to be deployed: geography, economy, ethnicity, religion and social class. Each affects the experiences of women in Europe.

But in looking at such factors, one of the findings of this book is that centre and periphery were not as far asunder as the historian may be accustomed to think. It is not so much the differences but the similarities of women's experiences across the varied European landscape which has been the most striking feature in compiling this work. Notwithstanding differences of religion, geography and geology, climate, political regime and stage of economic development, women from the west of Ireland to the Urals were subject to similar pressures in their personal lives. They experienced similar patterns of work, and the ways in which they challenged their subordinate status bear a remarkable likeness. The differences are of degree rather than of substance and, more often than not, the differences between women are regional, that is within countries, rather than between them. Not all states were as industrialised as Britain by 1900, but most contained regional pockets of intense industrial development, usually specialising in one sector. Conversely, much of Britain, and especially the western and northern peripheries, retained an agrarian character so that the women of the far north of Scotland had more in common with other women in the Nordic countries or the fishing villages of northern Spain than they did with their sisters in the textile mills of northern England.

The agenda of women's history is therefore far from simple. Women's history does not, cannot and should not stand apart from the rest of the historical agenda. Women were central to every aspect and every event of European history from 1789 to 1918. To be a historian of Europe, you must think about the history of women and what light it throws upon the whole experience of the continent.

THE BOOK'S STRUCTURE

The book is organised in three Parts. Part I , 'Imagining woman', discusses how woman was conceived of and represented in cultural terms: how she was constructed as an ideal woman (and also her opposite, an anti-ideal woman) in the discourses of the philosophical, medical, scientific and religious worlds. In this, the Enlightenment was paramount in this period, for though it may not have had an immediate impact on women (in terms of conferring new rights, for instance), its ideas did shape attitudes towards women and women's conception of themselves until the twentieth century. These representations or discourses on women are vital territory for the women's historian, for they lay the basis for all manner of political and legislative enactments concerning women, for how men regarded women, and for how women themselves constructed, negotiated and changed their own identities.

Part II of the book focuses on women's experience and status within the family and the community. For the vast majority of European women in this period, their lives revolved around their immediate family and around social and economic relations within the community. Though this may be seen as the characteristic issue defining women's subordination from which feminists, for example, sought liberation, it is within these interconnected spheres that women, paradoxically, possessed greatest autonomy. The domestic sphere was a context of both subordination and the springboard for ideas about liberation, and this part of the book looks at these contradictory issues as they were experienced in respect of marriage and motherhood, community networks, sexuality, and paid and unpaid work.

Part III discusses women's explicit engagement with what has been called the public sphere. Here, in the world of domestic and imperial politics, the labour movement, and in organised feminism, women participated in the public face of the nineteenth century. They participated in various guises – as revolutionaries, nationalists, missionaries, strikers and feminists. It is here in the public sphere that, with hindsight, we have come to judge the freedoms of women. In the final chapter, I reconsider the event traditionally identified as marking both the end of the nineteenth century and the watershed in European women's long march to freedom – the Great War. I ask whether total war really was such a turning point, when the constraining gender ideology of the nineteenth century transformed into the liberation of the twentieth. The answer, like the story that precedes it, is complex, but it is at heart a story of optimism.

Part I

◆

IMAGINING WOMAN

Chapter 1

◆

BODY, MIND
AND SPIRIT

A woman's identity and her experience are influenced, in part, by the ways in which she is 'constructed' by others. This means that the language used to describe her and what the ideals of womanhood and femininity should be, are just as important for her experience of life as the economic and social structures that surround her. To understand the structures of womanly life we must appreciate the construction of the woman. Part I of this book is concerned with this. We look at how woman and her role were imagined by philosophers, scientists, writers and women themselves in the late eighteenth and early nineteenth centuries. Constructions of that abstract concept 'woman' – her body, her mind and her role – were all important in helping to determine how she was treated in European society. At the same time though, women both negotiated and challenged these constructions through their everyday actions and their writings.

So much of the verbal construction of our modern world began with the Enlightenment. For many historians of the modern period it is the eighteenth-century Enlightenment which signals a turning away from the darkness and superstition of the early modern period and an awakening in the light, symbolised by rationality, science and knowledge. Centring on France, but extending across most of Europe from Edinburgh to St Petersburg, and lasting some seventy years, the Enlightenment was at its essence an intellectual, philosophical and scientific investigation into the human condition and the physical world, characterised by a desire to apply fresh observation to old ways of thinking. Old shibboleths were opened up for discussion and subjected to reasoned debate. Enlightenment writers and thinkers addressed the 'science of man': the human condition, family, marriage and gender relations. This movement or set of ideas acts as a convenient frontier between early modern and modern Europe, between the old regime and the new.

The Enlightenment also constructed modern woman. But the merits of this construction are double-edged. It left an ambiguous legacy for women. There is a danger in drawing a line between Enlightenment belief in individual natural rights and arguments for those rights to be applied to women. As Jane Rendall remarks: 'the heritage of the Enlightenment to feminists and their opponents is an extraordinarily confusing one.'[1] The revolutionary potential of Enlightenment thought on such diverse subjects as marriage and the family, individual citizenship rights, political thought and natural law nevertheless stopped short of challenging the fundamental relationship between the sexes. Sexual difference was rethought but not undermined or rejected; inequality was questioned and reworked but not discarded. For every writer who raised the possibility of women's emancipation, he or she was outnumbered by those who sought to justify or even reaffirm existing inequalities and sexual difference. Some, like Montesquieu, managed to combine a belief in woman's natural weakness with calls for her independence and greater gender equality, but most intimated that woman's nature inclined her towards passion and irrationality, her mind dominated by her biology. The truly revolutionary writings of those *philosophes* who dared to suggest the unthinkable in terms of women's status were marginalised, not least because the question of the relationship between the sexes was more a by-product of debate about the nature and source of difference than a discrete issue. The French mathematician and philosopher the Marquis de Condorcet (1743–94) questioned the absurdity of the exclusion of women from citizenship rights, and the Prussian Theodor Gottlieb von Hippel (1741–96) similarly demanded that women be granted equal political, educational and professional rights. In one sense, Enlightenment thought turned traditional ideas about woman's nature inside-out: although woman was ascribed a new elevated status in the family (as wife and mother) and by extension within society, her role was still, if not even more, tightly defined. And the privilege of citizenship was not extended to women. European society was not ready to consider female citizenship rights. It much preferred the language of gender difference to that of equality which threatened stability in the home and in the body politic.

It would be careless to disregard this philosophical revolution on account of its apparent irrelevance to women. Women did have an Enlightenment.

All women were affected but some actively engaged in and benefited from this unprecedented opportunity to challenge accepted ways of thinking. Some participated in the intellectual ferment, hosting salons for intellectual sociability and debate and providing a space where women could 'think for themselves'. In London, Elizabeth Montagu (1720–1800) became known as the pioneer 'blue stocking', so-called because she permitted this apparel in the place of the more formal black silk at her literary gatherings. In Paris, Madame du Deffand and Madame Necker, and in Berlin Rahel Levin Varnhagen (1771–1833), hosted gatherings of intellectuals helping to create a culture which encouraged independent thought.[2] Women also contributed to the realm of scientific and mathematical knowledge. The physicist Laura Bassi (1711–78) and mathematician Maria Agnesi (1718–99) both rose to prominence at the University of Bologna, although there were many more whose contribution was never properly acknowledged, or at least not by their contemporaries. The Anglo-German astronomer Caroline Herschel (1750–1848) discovered a comet in 1786 but was only recognised much later for this work of assisting her brother William.

For most women, however, the Enlightenment impacted in other ways. They participated even more than men in the explosion of literature and the dissemination of knowledge. Women's literacy rates, especially in urban parts of Protestant Europe, rose faster than those of men. In Amsterdam for example, two-thirds of women could read in 1780 compared with only one-third in 1630.[3] Although female literacy rates as a whole still lagged behind male, many more women could consume the debates about gender relations in newspapers, broadsheets and ballads and could contribute to those debates through the pages of novels and journals. 'We women think under our coiffures as well as you do under your wigs', insisted the female editor of the Parisian *Journal des Dames* in 1761. 'We are as capable of reasoning as you are.'[4] The range of contributions was enormous, from the poetry of Austrian Gabrielle Baumberg (1766–1839) who used her writing to express her belief that the convention of marriage was stifling women's expression of sexual desire, to the writings of English republican Catherine Macaulay-Graham (1731–91), an early advocate of education for girls.[5] In Britain, Eliza Haywood's (1693–1756) contributions to the first periodical written by and for women, *The Female Spectator*, published between 1744 and 1746, both addressed the difficulties faced by women within a system that defined their role in such restrictive ways and advocated a 'life of the mind' as compensation for subordination to a husband. Women's lack of education was disabling, argued Haywood:

Why do they call us *silly Women* and not endeavour to make us otherwise? . . . For while we live in a free Country, and are assured from our excellent *Christian* Principles that we are capable of those refined Pleasures which last to Immortality, our Minds, our better Parts, are wholly left uncultivated, and, like a rich Soil neglected, bring forth nothing but noxious Weeds.[6]

And then there were the novels of countless female authors, amongst them Jane Austen (1775–1817) and Sophie von La Roche (1731–1807), featuring heroines who experienced all the contradictions and constraints for women at the end of the eighteenth century. Women were talking, writing and reading about themselves in ways they had never done before. Woman was in her own thoughts.

Certainly the intellectual shifts wrought in terms of citizenship and politics by the Enlightenment and the French Revolution had less direct impact than those in the realm of science, medicine and culture. The end of the eighteenth century signalled a change in the ways in which woman was imagined, for good and for bad. These changes were mediated through debates about woman's body and the relationship between the body and the mind, and in turn the relationship between mind and body and a woman's role in the family and society. Moreover, a new concept of female piety and domesticity was to emerge as a central plank of nineteenth-century idealised femininity, and it had a profound impact on the image of woman and the ways in which women experienced their lives. These shifts did not affect all women equally or at the same time, yet, by the end of the nineteenth century there were few places where Enlightenment thought, however diluted, had not reached.

THE BODY

The Enlightenment construction of woman started with her body. The body is an appropriate starting point for a study of nineteenth-century woman because the body, and more especially reproductive biology, was used to underpin a broader reconception of woman's nature and role. The physical differentiation of women from men was thought to account for the moral and social differences between the sexes. Different gender roles were determined by different bodily function, but it was the female body that came to bear an enormous interpretive weight. As Rousseau so memorably put it: 'The consequences of sex are wholly unlike for man and woman. The male is only a male now and again, the female is always a female . . . everything reminds her of her sex.'[7] For woman, experience could not be independent of her physical function.

The belief that women were enslaved to their bodies has been a historical constant. The words of one sixteenth-century German Protestant speaking of women 'inextricably caught in the snares of their own biology, enslaved to a sexuality which destroyed their reason and unbalanced their health' anticipates the much later nineteenth-century assertions equating women's physical with their mental weakness.[8] What had changed in the intervening centuries was, first of all, the fact that women's bodies 'in their scientifically accessible concreteness . . . came to bear an enormous new weight of meaning'.[9] The second change was a new conviction on the part of the medical profession that the body (and implicitly the mind) of woman could be medicalised, pathologised and controlled.[10]

Until the seventeenth and eighteenth centuries, the classical idea of woman's body prevailed. According to this model of the male and female body, and more especially of the reproductive organs, formulated by Galen in the second century CE, the female was essentially the same as the male, her sexual organs were the mirror image of his only they were located inside the body. Thus the ovaries were equivalent to the testes, the vagina to the penis. 'Turn outward the woman's, turn inward, so to speak, and fold double the man's, and you will find the same in both in every respect.'[11] This 'one-sex model' of humankind was not equal. It prioritised the male or normal sex; the female was the lesser sex, a variation on the norm, lacking the strength or heat of the male and thus imperfect. Stories of women transmogrifying into men when placed under duress abounded. One apocryphal tale from the sixteenth century featured a female swineherd who, upon chasing a pig, jumped a ditch and promptly developed male genitalia on account of the vigorous activity and the generation of heat from the exertion. Such stories attest not only to the belief in the transmutability of sex but also to the idea of a sexual hierarchy because, as the seventeenth-century story-teller said: 'Nature tends always toward what is most perfect and not, on the contrary, to perform in such a way that what is perfect should become imperfect.'[12]

In this pre-Enlightenment conception, the woman was seen not merely as weaker in body but also as weaker in mind. A woman's body was unstable. She had no control over her own body, it was said, because of the demonic struggles contained therein. This instability was most powerfully manifested in the image of the wandering womb: women who experienced fits or 'hysteria' were said to be suffering from a condition in which the womb roamed around the body as a result of the failure to put the womb to its rightful use. Thus, psychological complaints were explicitly linked to physical changes in the body. Woman's mind was, therefore, unstable, unable to reason. 'Her mind and judgement is as variable and as fickle as the weather,' stated a husband of his wife in 1713.[13]

By the middle of the eighteenth century things were changing. The one-sex model of humankind was being replaced by the 'two-sex model' which stressed not the similarities but the differences between the sexes. The female reproductive organs were no longer seen as imperfect versions of the male forms, but as distinct in their own right. Thus the early modern gender hierarchy predicated on male heat and strength and female coldness and weakness (a male model of bodily form and female imperfection) was superseded by gender difference based on distinct anatomies with specific functions. The Enlightenment, and specifically the medical and scientific investigations of the anatomy and physiology of sex, caused this reassessment of ideas of sexual difference. The discovery that women's bodies were not the inverse of men's – that they had a smaller frame, a broader pelvis and completely different reproductive organs – propounded the concrete reality of sexual difference. Now there was no in-between, no possibility of uncertainty. And, in theory, the old hierarchy which subordinated the female to the male body could be discarded as the differences between the two were clear for all to see. Yet, in the eighteenth century, writers used the body and physical difference more than ever to explain and legitimise cultural and political inequality. Indeed, whereas before 1700 a woman's status might have been signified by cultural signs such as the long hair of the virgin and the covered head of the married woman, now sex determined identity and destiny. Scientists and doctors played a central role in the rethinking of gender; their discoveries based on natural law rather than religious belief or metaphysics, served to bolster the new conception of male–female relations. Women's anatomical difference was said to be natural: their finer nerves made them more sensitive than men; their smaller frames made them more childlike; their reproductive cycles made them prone to mental disturbance; their smaller skulls and brains made them unsuited to mental exertion.[14] Women's bodies may have become more fixed in a scientific sense but little had changed in the perception that women were enslaved to their bodies in ways that men never would be. The scientific and medical revolution, far from breaking down sexual stereotypes, served to reinforce them.[15]

Woman, according to the men of the Enlightenment, was not, as previously imagined, an imperfect man, but a completely different creature.[16] It followed that whilst a man might be unencumbered by his body, his sex, a woman could never be free of hers. For woman, body and mind were as one. Her mind was in thrall to her physical being. The consequences were twofold. Firstly, the theory that a woman's mind was innately connected to her reproductive function helped to justify the theory of separate spheres – the translation of sexual difference into social and economic difference comprising the belief that woman was fitted for the private or domestic sphere and the male for the public or civic and political arena. Secondly, the mind–body continuum helped to legitimise the use of the female body as a battleground for a variety of knowledges or discourses. By the end of the nineteenth century the female body had been transformed in popular discourse from a wild, untameable symbolic entity containing demons and unknown forces, into something that could be medicalised, invaded and controlled. The modern (female) body, then, was a sexualised body which determined identity and destiny.

The new Enlightenment understanding of women's bodies did not result in the liberation of women from physical and mental limitations. In fact the female body increasingly became a site of struggle – not of demons as in the early modern period, but of doctors and scientists who attempted to usurp women's functional and metaphysical understanding of their own bodies. There was a gradual shift from a privileging of a woman's own understanding of her body which relied upon sensation and what might appear as superstitious or ritual practices, to interpretations legitimised by scientific knowledge and the application of reason. Before the rise of men of science, women relied upon what might be described as a sensation-based bodily knowledge. For example, only a pregnant woman would know when quickening had occurred, the moment when an expectant mother could feel her baby move, indicating the birth of the soul. From the end of the eighteenth century the medical profession began slowly to take possession of women's bodies, expropriating what had previously been areas under the control of women themselves based on visual or sensual apprehension. Thus the interpretive authority shifted from she who experienced the bodily sensations to he who observed the symptoms. What had previously been regarded as a 'private reality under the skin became a public affair'.[17] Women's 'natural' functions were identified as specific causes of ill-health. The female body became a public space.[18] Whilst nature continued to exert its hold over woman, now medical men believed they could actively intervene: nature as female was to be 'unveiled, unclothed and penetrated by masculine science'.[19]

'Woman is woman by every part of her being and not uniquely by her uterus . . . woman is all maternity.'[20] Thus stated the French doctor Bernutz in 1874, a statement which bears all the hallmarks of an ideology which defined woman in terms of her sex. By the second half of the nineteenth century the belief amongst the medical and scientific communities that the reproductive system was the key to understanding woman's physical and mental peculiarities was pervasive. Womanness was inscribed on the body so there was no escape. Woman was depicted as a slave to her own body, its monthly cycle, its specific reproductive functions, its secretions. Across Europe, doctors elaborated the theory of women's inherent disablement. The French doctor Michelet memorably commented that menstruation rendered woman 'not only an invalid, but a wounded one' for 15 to 20 days out of 28.[21] In Germany, another remarked that 'every month for several days she is enfeebled, if not downright ill.'[22] Pregnancy and childbirth were similarly regarded amongst the medical community as pathological conditions. Indeed, it has been said that for many women, most notably those amongst the middle classes, ill-health became a way of life.[23] Even the menopause offered no respite – despite the belief that the end of a woman's fertility symbolised the end of womanhood – since, according to one specialist, 'many women [who] may have passed through the trials of puberty and child-bearing without serious nervous disorder, will break down at menopause.'[24]

However, not only was a woman's reproductive function regarded as a determinant of her physical well-being, but her mental state was also said to be derived from her sex. Menstrual cramps aside, at this time of the month a woman was prone to a 'mental state varying from a slight psychosis to absolute irresponsibility', according to one Parisian medical man in 1890.[25] What doctors termed the sex-specific character of women's physiology predisposed her to mental illness and nowhere was this demonstrated more starkly than in the diagnosis of 'nervous disorders' including 'hysteria', anorexia nervosa, nervous excitability and other such neurological disorders which appeared to constitute an epidemic amongst middle-class women by the second half of the century. At the same time the belief in the inherently sick state of woman was buttressed by an ideology of femininity which restricted women's role and opportunities and which told women they would become ill if they tried to escape their destiny.

The false notion of a female disease originating in disorder of the uterus was known to the ancient Egyptians. By the eighteenth century, though, the seat of this nervous disorder was seen as both neurological and uterine, so that by the nineteenth century hysteria was a diagnosis uniquely ascribed to the middle-class woman who suffered not only from the physical constraints of her sex, but also from the cultural constraints of idealised femininity. Hysteria was a diagnosis that incorporated a multitude of symptoms – fainting, palpitations, suffocation, dizziness, tiredness, speech disturbance as well as acts of defiance and independence – all were seen to be signs of uterine disorder in a woman. The cause, according to the medical men, was the failure to follow the path nature had intended. Thus, a woman deprived of male company – the abstinent woman – was prone to developing the hysteric personality as was the educated woman, the woman who strove for independence. In Paris in 1880 it was authoritatively stated, 'where young ladies of the lower classes and the petite bourgeoisie are educated beyond their social standing, hysteria is very frequent.'[26] Women who harboured 'overexalted dreams', who craved mental stimulation, women who thus threatened to destabilise gender roles were prime candidates for the diagnosis.[27] The cure, according to those doctors who chose to specialise in female nervous complaints, was either marriage and children or complete rest and deprivation of any sensory stimulation. Isolation in a darkened room without reading matter or visitors, a diet of pappy food, regular body massage and an absence of exercise was the recommended treatment for a woman who was experiencing a struggle between her body and her mind. The rest cure supposedly lulled the mind into a state of languor and total submission so that in time, the patient would accept her assigned role as dutiful wife and mother. For some women, though, this treatment was more insufferable than the symptoms it was supposed to cure, tipping them closer to madness as a consequence of deprivation of any mental stimulus.[28]

Hysteria was not the only supposed female malady said to derive from uterine disorder. Madness or lunacy and anorexia nervosa were similarly defined as conditions arising from the sex of woman. However, feminist historians have rightly drawn attention to the symbolic and literal meaning of such conditions. Notwithstanding the physical reality of these complaints exacerbated by restrictive corsets and heavy clothing, lack of exercise and a diet which induced anaemia, it is clear that the propensity of women to such disorders was also induced by a certain way of life. The lifestyle of some middle-class women almost predisposed them to sickness, and their sickness determined their way of life. Deprived of education, mental stimulation and economic independence, and forever exhorted to conform to an ideal of femininity which exalted a pale, sickly, languid beauty, illness became both a vindication and a cry for help. Anorexic girls, argues Elaine Showalter, 'paraded physical starvation as a way of drawing attention to the starvation of their mental and moral faculties.'[29] The inherent sickness of woman was both accepted by her and used as a means of rebellion against a rigid and restraining social role. It is doubtful, as some have suggested, that women (or their advocates) deliberately feigned hysteria and other nervous disorders as a defence in prosecutions for a whole range of crimes from shoplifting to murder. But the belief that women were suggestible, weak and prone to uncontrolled acts in moments of temporary insanity resulted in hundreds of women in the late nineteenth century being judged sympathetically by the courts.[30]

Women were caught in a double bind. By 1850 the belief in the relationship between the brain or mind and female sexuality was so strong amongst the medical fraternity that if a woman escaped a nervous disease she was liable to be warned of the danger of succumbing to gynaecological complaint. Diseases of the reproductive system, argued physicians, were almost certainly caused by women's emancipation. Excessive stimulation, education and public activity caused atrophy of the reproductive organs; in other words it unsexed a woman. Likewise, a disorderly woman, a woman whose behaviour did not conform to the feminine ideal, might be considered a candidate for invasive surgery. From the 1860s onwards, clitoridectomy (surgical removal of the clitoris), ovariotomy (removal of the ovaries) and hysterectomy (removal of the uterus), were carried out by gynaecologists as cures for masturbation, lunacy, and other so-called nervous complaints.[31] Ironically, gynaecological surgery desexed a woman but in the process it controlled her, brought her within the bounds of appropriate behaviour. The English doctor Isaac Baker Brown became infamous for his surgical procedures which exerted the power of the doctor over the woman's body and mind. A typical case was that of Mrs O upon whom Brown commenced treatment in 1862. 'She had been ill ever since marriage, five years previously; having distaste for the society of her husband, always laid upon the sofa, and under medical treatment', wrote Brown in his case notes. 'Evidence of peripheral excitement being manifest, I performed my usual operation [clitoridectomy]. She rapidly lost all the hysterical symptoms which had previously existed.'[32] Mrs O went on to deliver two children and regained a 'robust health'. For Brown and his followers such operations rendered women 'tractable, orderly, industrious, and cleanly.'[33]

So far, we have been talking about perceptions and understandings of women's bodies – discourses – but not about women's own experiences of their bodies. It is necessary to know how the body was imagined and talked about in the past as a framework for understanding how women experienced their own bodies. Yet, as Lyndal Roper has reminded us, 'Sexual difference is not purely discursive nor merely social. It is also physical.'[34] The body has always been important for feminist historians for whom it is not merely a discursive construct but 'a feminist site of lived experience that serves to ground agency and resistance, to give it concrete origins'.[35] However, how can we know how a nineteenth-century woman experienced her own body at a time when few women expressed their physical experiences in writing? How do we deal with the tension between how a culture imagines a body and actual corporeal experience? Barbara Duden argues that in pre-modern western society, women understood their bodies by interpreting their own bodily sensations; thus they would 'know' when they were sick or pregnant by observation. Even in nineteenth-century Saxony the notion of the wandering womb was still current: 'Womb, you rascal, get the hell back to your own house' – suggesting that medical advances had not penetrated all that far into the popular psyche.[36] Before 1800 there existed a female culture which strongly influenced reproductive practices; and after 1800 or thereabouts, this female world was powerfully superseded by male doctors and surgeons. Women's bodies have always been a matter of public concern and a range of community and legal constraints competed with women's own interpretations of their reproductive functions.[37] But in the early modern period the balance was tipped towards women.

In the modern era, then, visual signs were prioritised over sensation and thus the interpretation of bodily experience shifted from the individual to the observer, often a male doctor.[38] This transformation, writes Isabel Hull, 'did more than simply undermine women's relative autonomy over their bodies, it changed the manner in which a modern person's sense of self . . . is organised.'[39] In pre-modern infanticide cases a woman carrying an illegitimate child might convincingly deny her pregnancy to others and to herself, despite visual evidence to the contrary. It was generally understood that a missed period was not a sure indication that a woman was with child; a swollen stomach could be interpreted as the result of a cyst, clogged blood or a wandering womb. By the modern era the visual sign of a physical condition and a doctor's confirmation of a pregnancy overrode women's assertions to the contrary. Medical knowledge became privileged as proof in a court of law over women's word. When Robina Ritch was legally indicted for suspected concealment of a pregnancy in 1903 in northern Scotland, it was necessary that the prosecution included a doctor's evidence. The doctor did not merely rely on Robina's appearance – swollen abdomen and ankles – his examination detected that her 'womb could be felt contracting and relaxing' and his stethoscope 'revealed foetal heart beats 132 per minute'.[40] With a male doctor's evidence there could be no doubt that Robina had been with child.

Historians of women tend to approach the history of women's bodily experience through the stages of the lifecycle – youth and adolescence, marriage, motherhood and old age. It is a valid framework although it tends to perpetuate the belief that women are little more than their reproductive systems.[41] However, although it is undeniable that medical science has had a major impact upon women's experience of themselves as women, it is necessary to move beyond the notion that women were innately sick, since it is plain that the vast majority of European women did not experience their bodies in this way. For the rural and urban working classes and the poor, the notion that menstruation was a disabling experience must have been laughable. Pregnancy and childbirth, although undoubtedly debilitating and dangerous for some, were dealt with as natural occurrences in a woman's lifecycle. Illness was a luxury few working women could afford; the economically active woman had no time to be an invalid. Working-class women were rarely diagnosed with the symptoms of hysteria. On the other hand, a combination of religious ideology and superstitious practices did influence the ways in which these women understood their bodies. Some popular beliefs had meaning in an uncontrollable world little affected by modern science and rational thought. Taboos associated with pregnancy were especially strong at a time when pregnancy and childbirth were fraught with danger. Prohibitions on pregnant women consuming particular foodstuffs such as seafood, green salad, and even milk, were common in Spain. Everywhere pregnant women tried to avoid looking at certain animals for fear they would cause the baby to be born with a deformity. Birthmarks on a baby were attributed to the mother touching certain objects or having contact with a dead person or developing food cravings. If a pregnant woman looked at the moon her child would be born a lunatic; if she had intercourse during menstruation she would bear a monstrous child.[42] These beliefs can be seen as part of a female knowledge – women's ways of knowing – which aided women's control over their pregnancy in an age when stillbirths, infant defects and maternal mortality were frequent enough to present a real fear. The words of one Alsatian proverb, 'heaven stays open nine days for the woman in childbed', indicates the prescient fear of death following the delivery of a child.[43] In the religiously prescribed practice of 'churching' (*les relevailles* in France, *Muttersegen* in Germany), a woman recently delivered of a child went to church as soon as possible because she was regarded as unclean and liable to bring bad luck on any household she entered. This continued as a popular practice until the middle of the twentieth century in the Church of England and Catholic churches in Britain and France. Although in religious terms a purification ritual, it was also a celebration of the woman's survival of childbirth and her return to everyday life and as such became a female social occasion which gave thanks for a woman's life and fertility rather than emphasising the impurity of her body.[44] Reproductive ill-health was undoubtedly, then, a key factor in women's corporeal experience but not the only one. Amongst the working classes, women were more likely than men to succumb to chronic diseases such as tuberculosis. Breast cancer was a scourge even in the nineteenth century and as a consequence of years of childbearing accompanied by hard physical labour it was said that women aged prematurely. In a Baden village in 1900, peasant women were routinely said to be worn out.[45] Most European women continued to experience and interpret their bodies according to their own knowledge and understanding of physical sensation. But the emphasis on sex difference was bolstered by the scientific elaboration of ideas about social or cultural difference. Sexual difference was thus translated into separate spheres, or the idea that men and women were destined by nature for separate roles in public and private life.

CONSTRUCTING FEMININITY

If male physicians led the reimagining of women's bodies as objects of science in the nineteenth century, other professional men joined in with the reimagining of women's social role and identity. Both sets of ideas affirmed the connection between a woman's body and nature and entangled her in a set of interconnected ideas which served to delineate the ideal (and natural) female role. These constructions of femaleness and the womanly role were formulated by church leaders, philosophical writers, political thinkers, educationalists, novelists, scientists and professionals, and they reached their apotheosis in the nineteenth century. Jean-Jacques Rousseau is the Enlightenment thinker who expounded most authoritatively on the nature of the sexes:

> In the union of the sexes each alike contributes to the common end, but in different ways. From this diversity springs the first difference that may be observed between man and woman in their moral relations. The man should be strong and active; the woman should be weak and passive; the one must have both the power and the will; it is enough that the other should offer little resistance. When this principle is admitted, it follows that woman should be made for man's delight. If man in his turn ought to be pleasing in her eyes, the necessity is less urgent, his virtue is in his strength, he pleases because he is strong.[46]

This observation acutely summed up the widespread belief in the direct connection between sexual difference and social function. It is Rousseau

– writer, philosopher, educator and not least eccentric – who, in his two widely read novels, *Julie, ou La Nouvelle Heloïse* (1761) and *Émile* (1762), is widely credited with popularising the ideologies of domesticity, romantic motherhood and what is now described as separate spheres. But it was not until the early nineteenth century that the elaboration and multiplication of discourses on gender roles and especially womanhood became a sacrosanct element of European culture.

What has become known as the ideology of separate spheres, incorporating the separation of male and female roles, the division between public and private and the formulation of domestic ideology, was almost certainly a creation of the industrialising societies of western Europe and not the creation of one man – Rousseau. Undoubtedly many of the strands which go to make up this set of ideas have a long pedigree. Sexual difference and social role had been conflated at least since the sixteenth century with Luther's pronouncement that 'Women ought to stay at home; the way they were created indicates this, for they have broad hips and a wide fundament to sit upon, keep house and bear and raise children.'[47] The ideal housewife of the seventeenth century, 'of chaste thought, stout courage, patient, untired, watchful, diligent, witty, pleasant, constant in friendship . . . wise in discourse, but not frequent therein, sharp and quick of speech, but not bitter or talkative', bears close comparison with the paeans to the idealised wife and mother of two centuries later who exhibited 'industry, humility, neatness, gentleness, benevolence, and piety'.[48] Thus, it is widely accepted that discourses on femininity have continually been formulated and reformulated, but historians are generally agreed that the early nineteenth century sees the maturation of a set of beliefs on woman's role and a heightening of their importance. A series of enmeshing ideas came together at this time to produce a stereotype of a certain type of woman who was pious and chaste, respectable and reserved, a good wife and mother, a woman whose appropriately feminine qualities were equally important in the home and the 'public sphere'. A composite image of this women was produced in the Scottish *Free Church Magazine* in 1844. The ideal woman was:

> benevolent from natural sensibility, active from constitutional inclination, amiable from temper . . . Zeal and activity are, in their own places, excellent and essential qualities; but Christian women require to be very cautious, lest, even in the midst of praiseworthy exertions, they sacrifice those meek and lowly tempers which are so calculated to adorn and promote the cause they love and advocate. Female influence should shed its rays on every circle, but these ought to be felt, rather in their softening effects, than seen by their brilliancy.[49]

This powerful set of discourses on femininity was all-pervasive, emanating from the clergyman's sermon, the governess' lesson, the pages of women's magazines, even the mouths of working men. Femininity was as much about character and the way a woman presented herself as it was about her actions. Women were exhorted not to display an 'unhappy disposition' such as that continually on the countenance of Ann Williams, a fictional character whose story was presented to readers of one British religious journal in 1854, *The Day Star*, under the title 'Little Faults'. Ann, although priding herself on being a 'notable and saving housekeeper' was 'pale and thin, her face furrowed with deep lines, and her brow as usual gloomy'. Her sullenness was contrasted with the good temper of a visitor whose countenance reflected the 'genuine warmth of her true and loving heart'. Ann's little fault was her temper. It was not sufficient to be industrious, neat and respectable; Ann was rebuked for her disposition which 'destroys the happiness of your family; your husband confesses he has no peace at home; he cannot read or talk in comfort where there is constant scolding and strife; and your little ones have not half the spirit of other children . . . part of a mother's duty is to practice forbearance.'[50] Such injunctions seem bleak for a nineteenth-century woman, providing her with little more than a template for pleasing vacuity and the proper duties of motherhood. But there were others offering women an alternative, more active femininity incorporating the pursuit of education and the life of the mind as well as a woman's 'natural' duties to the home and family.

Amidst the plethora of novels, periodicals and pamphlets produced at the end of the eighteenth century there were many, not infrequently authored by women, that offered a more assertive and individualistic feminine ideal. Mary Wollstonecraft (1759–97) is the most famous female writer of the Enlightenment period. Her book *A Vindication of the Rights of Woman* (1792) is the most well-known feminist text of the period. It presents an empowering vision of female opportunity in which she explicitly denounces Rousseau's restrictive ideas on a woman's role. Wollstonecraft was not as widely read as Rousseau. Her lifestyle was probably regarded as too avante-garde for her potential middle-class audience. She disavowed the respectability through marriage that would have guaranteed her a more stable existence and instead was determined to become a self-supporting writer. She earned a living by teaching and journalism, travelled alone, lived in France during the Revolution, bore an illegitimate child to Gilbert Imlay, one of her several lovers, and attempted to end her own life by jumping from Putney Bridge in London on account of his infidelity. All of this was recounted by her husband William

Godwin in a candid biography of his wife after her death and which alienated her from her respectable female readership. It was only much later in the nineteenth century that the radicalism of Wollstonecraft's conception of woman was acknowledged as offering a realistic alternative model for more than just a rebellious few.

What Mary Wollstonecraft wrote was remarkable for 1792. She was offended by Rousseau's novel *Émile* and in particular the character of Sophie who acts as the foil for his hero. Sophie's role is contingent upon that of her husband; she does not possess an independent spirit or will, her very existence is dependent upon the public man, Émile, and his needs. This kind of femininity – weak to a man's strength, educated to please rather than for self-development or the social good, a femininity which valued beauty over duty – was of no benefit to women or to men or the social good according to Wollstonecraft. At the heart of the *Vindication* is the woman as autonomous and rational being; the woman capable of determining her own future, capable of using reason, and able to control her emotions. Wollstonecraft's woman was womanly rather than childlike, determined rather than sycophantic. She was contemptuous of the tendency to keep girls in ignorance and innocence, to teach them more of the art of pleasing men and feigning modesty than educating them for life.

> It would be an endless task to trace the variety of meannesses, cares, and sorrows, into which women are plunged by the prevailing opinion, that they were created rather to feel than reason, and that all the power they obtain must be obtained by their charms and weaknesses ... And made by this amiable weakness entirely dependent, excepting what they gain by illicit sway, on man, not only for protection, but advice, is it surprising that, neglecting the duties that reason alone points out, and shrinking from trials calculated to strengthen their minds, they only exert themselves to give their defects a graceful covering, which may serve to heighten their charms in the eye of the voluptuary, though it sink them below the scale of moral excellence.[51]

The key to transforming women from this infantile and demeaning state into autonomous beings was education, but not the kind of education advocated by Rousseau. Sophie was taught how to please a man, how 'to win his respect and love, to train him in childhood, to tend him in manhood, to counsel and console, to make his life pleasant and happy'.[52] Mary Wollstonecraft's vision of an education for girls, in contrast, encompassed the same elements as boys' education; indeed she believed the sexes should be taught together and that girls should be given the same freedoms as boys. She was 'fully persuaded that we should hear of none of these infantine airs, if girls were allowed to take sufficient exercise, and not confined in close rooms till their muscles are relaxed, and their powers of digestion are destroyed.'[53] This habit of restraint was debilitating for girls' minds and bodies. 'The pure animal spirits, which make both mind and body shoot out, and unfold the tender blossoms of hope, are turned sour, and vented in vain wishes or pert repinings, that contract the faculties and spoil the temper.'[54] Wollstonecraft was contemptuous of Rousseau's reasons for rejecting equal education. '"Educate women like men," says Rousseau, "and the more they resemble our sex the less power will they have over us" This is the very point I aim at. I do not wish them to have power over men; but over themselves.'[55]

Rousseau's vision of womanhood clashed with that of Wollstonecraft. The moral, home-loving and husband-obliging wife of Émile was mocked by Mary. For her woman had a responsibility to raise herself from a supine and ignorant state. This sense of duty extended to carrying out her role as mother and educator. The moral, virtuous woman was she who endeavoured to reach her potential in any sphere she chose, whether it be marriage and motherhood or employment in a trade or in commerce.

For most middle-class women, for this was the group for whom the feminine ideal espoused by both Rousseau and Wollstonecraft was most relevant, these two apparently contradictory messages were in fact complementary. By the early decades of the nineteenth century the ignorant, indolent woman at the centre of Wollstonecraft's critique was a rare creature. The headstone of Mrs C.M. Jones in a church in rural England epitomises the ways in which women were able to combine both the virtues of femininity espoused by Rousseau and the more independent and accomplished womanliness favoured by Mary Wollstonecraft. Mrs Jones was the wife of the local minister and master of the town's grammar school. She died in 1775 at the age of just 46, and was 'blest with a Pious and distinguished Education, the goodness of her Mind and the Accomplishments of Her Understanding were eminently conspicuous. Nothing was more Engaging than Her Manners, Her Heart was the Temple of Patience, all Virtues lie Buried in her Tomb.'[56] From these few words we can conjure up a picture of Mrs Jones as a virtuous woman who displayed all the appropriate characteristics of femininity at this time – she was polite and modest but at the same time she was educated, a woman who certainly never needed to use cunning wiles and false modesty in the company of men. She was also, though, a godly woman and, in the nineteenth century, female piety became the road to virtue.

PIETY AND SPIRITUALITY

Piety was the pivot of a woman's identity in nineteenth century Europe. 'To be a good wife is a high attainment in female excellence', wrote the Bishop of Birmingham in the 1860s; 'it is woman's brightest glory since the fall.'[57] Religious discourses on womanhood in the nineteenth century excel in their ability to idealise 'true femininity'. The Virgin Mary, of course, was the pinnacle of womanhood in the Catholic spiritual community; chaste, humble and gentle, she represented a sublime model to the wife and mother. Mary is a 'fixed, immutable absolute', 'feminine perfection', an archetype for wives and mothers, indeed women everywhere.[58] In the Russian Orthodox Church, obedience and silence were considered the virtues of the good wife. Within the Protestant religions, the Virgin Mary was replaced by the godly wife and mother as the sublime ideal; she who established an intimate, personal relationship with God, a guardian of the faith, a moral influence on her family but by extension wider society also. 'The Bible gives her her throne, for she is the queen of the domestic circle . . . it is the female supremacy in that interesting domain, where love and tenderness, and refinement, thought and feeling preside.'[59]

The place of religion, both the institutions of the churches and the role of religious discourses, in the lives of European women throughout the century must not be underestimated. It is easy from the perspective of the secular twenty-first century to either disregard the central importance of religion or to see it as a universal oppressor of women. The church was a patriarchal institution which not only excluded women from its structures of power, but also served to legitimise female oppression in society as a whole by means of ideological constraints such as the 'cult of true womanhood' which purportedly confined women to domesticity and submissiveness.[60] In the words of Barbara Taylor: 'once God had settled in the parlour, Mammon had free range in public life', an interpretation which sees the feminisation of religion as a legitimator of separate spheres.[61] Historians have tended to interpret Christian principles acting as a constraint on more progressive feminist goals. Recently, however, the study of women and religion has acknowledged both the profound importance of religion in all women's lives in the nineteenth century, and the ways in which women negotiated with the church and religious discourse. In Gail Malmgreen's words: 'If feminist historians ignore religion . . . we will have forfeited our understanding of the mental universe of the no doubt substantial majority of women who were believers.'[62] It is just as important for the modern historian to consider the role of religion in the world view of women as it is for historians of earlier periods.

In the nineteenth century there was a discernible change in the ways in which woman's relationship with religion was constructed. Since women had always been marginalised within the institutions of the Christian church, their spirituality was inevitably a more private, personal affair, practised within the 'holy household', informing women's everyday devotion to virtue. But piety in the early modern period was a male rather than a female virtue. When the sixteenth-century German poet Hans Sachs wrote of piety as 'obedient and humble, subservient, fair, true and gracious', he was talking about a set of ideal characteristics to be displayed not by the pious woman, but by the man.[63] But around the beginning of the nineteenth century piety was feminised and religion became woman's sphere. Not only was church-going and observance of religious ritual in Catholic and Protestant churches dominated by women – this was in any case not such a startling change – but the religious construction of the good or godly woman 'transcended the negative stereotypes of the weaker vessel'.[64] The privileging of women as the pious sex could be either confining or enabling for women; it could restrict opportunities but it could also give women the power to use their exalted role within the family and in the wider community. Piety was thus presented as a state of being for women, an attitude of mind which found expression in everyday matters.

Simultaneous with this more positive construction of female piety which gave women an elevated position in the hierarchy of spirituality, was the feminisation of church ritual and the rising popularity of religious orders and female activities organised around the church or informed by Christian principles. Women began to see the church and religion as a positive force in their lives. In turn, the church hierarchies were forced to negotiate with women to allow them greater power within the broader structures of the church. Feminine piety was enabling as well as constraining; it was an ideology that women took ownership of and used for the good of themselves and of others.

There is no disputing the feminisation of popular religion in nineteenth-century Europe whichever measure one uses. In France, Belgium and Spain the number of nuns increased dramatically in the nineteenth century; indeed, in France the numbers increased from 12,000 at the start of the century to 135,000 in 1878.[65] By the end of the century women's attendance at mass and at Easter Communion across France outnumbered that of men, sometimes massively. In some urban dioceses it was rare to encounter a man taking

Easter Communion at all.[66] Similarly, women formed around two-thirds of Protestant congregations in Berlin.[67] In west London in 1902–3 more than two-thirds of morning and evening worshippers at Church of England services were female.[68] Sunday was a special day for women when they proudly attended church wearing their 'Sunday best', displaying their femininity and their piety in their clothing. Girls went to church looking their most feminine with the young 'brides of Christ' at first Catholic communion exemplifying pious and virginal femininity in their white wedding dresses. Within the dissenting churches in Britain women also took a prominent role: Unitarianism, Methodism, the Quakers and the Salvation Army provided women with a spiritual space where they could develop a practical piety as female preachers or as lay evangelists and charity workers. Women were enthusiastic members of religious lay organisations everywhere, from Mothers' Meetings in London attended in the evenings or weekdays by working-class women who could not attend church on Sunday, to women's welfare organisations, many of which were semi-independent of the clergy.[69] In Scotland too, religion was something that women did – attending church services was but a small part of the round of meetings concerning temperance, motherhood, charitable work, moral crusades and more. In the Nordic countries where Lutheran Christianity dominated, women were prominent from the eighteenth century in the revivalist movement which permitted women a role in religious vocational work.[70]

After 1800 the churches became increasingly a women's domain. Furthermore, women played the key role in determining the religious habits of the family as a whole. They were responsible for children's prayers, Sunday School attendance and informal moral education. It was women who maintained the cycle of religious rituals in the family, observing the religious festivals and organising lifecycle events such as weddings, christenings, confirmation and first Communion. For some women, sacred rituals defined the contours of their lives. Jewish immigrant women became 'potent symbols of piety'; it was they who bore responsibility for the religious household through the ritual of festivals and preparation of kosher food. In London and Manchester, as the importance of the synagogue declined, especially for men, religious observance became the task of women in the home.[71] Amongst the Catholic middle classes of northern France, women's frequent attendance at mass, the taking of Holy Communion, regular ceremonies, retreats, pilgrimages and services, as well as daily domestic rituals such as saying grace at meals, adorning the household with statues of the Virgin and the wearing of crosses, endowed their lives with a sacred significance.[72] Religion became a female culture in the nineteenth century which, in many ways, increasingly excluded men. Visits to shrines and participation in pilgrimages in France were dominated by women, with one diocese in 1894 sending over 5000 women and only 400 men on a pilgrimage to Lourdes.[73] Women were also much more likely than men to experience miraculous cures at Lourdes and other holy sites. Women felt comfortable in petitioning the Virgin Mary for help with personal problems; indeed the new cult of the Virgin was pivotal to this female popular piety across Catholic Europe with numerous new shrines, religious orders and congregations dedicated to the Immaculate Conception, the pure Mary, at once a submissive and powerful figure.

In both Protestant and Catholic parts of Europe, women's historians have interpreted the feminisation of religion partly as an organic development whereby women increasingly stayed with the churches as men fell away or became passive believers, and partly as the result of the flourishing of discourses on morality, piety and femininity. Both involved women as active agents. In Catholic Europe, what is known as the Marian revival of the nineteenth century, contributed to an atmosphere in which women might lay claim to a certain degree of power within the church. Apparitions of the Virgin Mary seen by girls and women are a distinctive feature of the nineteenth century with the most celebrated, Bernadette Soubirous' vision of the Immaculate Conception at Lourdes in 1858, merely the tip of an iceberg. Indeed, hundreds of Marian apparitions were reported by women and children across Europe in this period, but the prominence of visions of the Virgin and the predominance of female visionaries contrasts the nineteenth century with earlier times. For these girls and women, most of whom were poor and often motherless, the Virgin offered 'emotional balm' and consolation in their troubles. But she also bestowed power on the visionaries who became the centre of attention, messengers of the Divine and conduits of miracle cures. The status of visionary, writes David Blackbourn in respect of the apparitions at Marpingen in Germany, 'was a resource of the weak, a means of escape'; but also 'the drama of the apparition' offered a 'veiled means of protest against real or imagined ill-treatment'.[74] Indeed, the ambivalent reaction of the local clergy to reports of apparitions in their diocese indicates their concern, not only to suppress 'superstition' but to maintain clerical control in the face of spontaneous mass devotion inspired by young women. The visionaries were using the church's construction of woman as the spiritual and pious sex for their own ends. Moreover, the association of femininity with piety provided these female visionaries with a platform from which to 'preach' Christian values to their communities. In the French Alpine village of La Salette in 1846, two young girls were entrusted with a warning from the Virgin that if the men of the village did not repent for their blasphemy, their failure to attend church and working on Sunday, the village would suffer catastrophe.[75] To critics of the Catholic Church and of those who sought to capitalise on the apparitions, the visionaries were the very antithesis of the Enlightenment project: madwomen, hysterics, mystics, the 'embodiment of superstition'.[76] But their visions might alternatively be interpreted as expressions of the girls' internalisation of the discourse on female piety.

In her study of the industrial bourgeoisie of northern France, Bonnie Smith interprets women's wholehearted embrace of mystical religion as a rejection of science and progress: 'The mathematical explanation of life proposed by modern science appeared as a patent fatuity to the visibly bleeding, swelling, pained women of the nineteenth century.'[77] For these women, as much as for the labouring women who reported Marian apparitions and the women who went on pilgrimages to shrines such as Lourdes to obtain cures, religion has been interpreted as a 'corrective to the excessive rationalism and individualism of the new industrial era' represented by those men who embraced industrialism and with it secularism.[78] But this interpretation of female spirituality as backward, as a protest against the new order which consigned them to the margins, or as a superstitious practice in the face of rationalism, fails to recognise the centrality of religion to women's identities. Women who found solace in the spiritual were more a sign of the times than a remnant of the past. Female visionaries such as Joanna Southcott and others like her who claimed to be the 'woman Clothed in the sun' spoken of in the Old Testament book of Revelations were millenarian prophets disillusioned with the prosaic religious practice of sermons and meetings and to some extent frustrated by the female domestic role. This was most clearly expressed in the case of British visionary Dorothy Gott who renounced housework for the work of the soul.[79] For industrial wives and for the poor visionaries, piety was not an old heirloom, it was a way of life. Religion provided the moral framework and the ritual for everyday occurrences. It remained vital precisely because it maintained and reinforced the virtues associated with femininity and it legitimised woman's domestic role.

In Protestant countries, then, as well as in Catholic and Orthodox ones, religion increasingly became something that women did and men often tried to avoid. Femininity and religiosity seemed, to some, to go hand in hand. The girls in one Berlin confirmation class were, according to their preacher, 'more faithful, more eager and warmer in the love of the Lord. With feminine tenderness they have used their talents and multiplied them a hundredfold.' In contrast to the boys' class, the girls were like 'a breath of fresh air', owing to the 'faithful application and the undiminished tenderness and receptivity with which the girls of all social classes listened to the word of grace and truth.'[80] Evangelical religions also placed a great deal of emphasis on the home and the importance of the pious mother who was to be relied upon to inculcate the next generation with moral values.[81] According to Jane Rendall, 'the dynamic evangelistic Christianity of the nineteenth century . . . exalted what were seen as [women's] essential qualities, defining their own sphere more clearly [and] offering a limited but positive role in the move-ment itself.'[82] Piety was a way of life which encompassed both personal devotion and public action. Indeed, the privileging of female piety meant that the latter was seen by women as a natural consequence of their individual spirituality. Increasingly, women who regarded their religious selves as their essential selves sought opportunities to demonstrate their piety outwith the home. Catholic women might enter a religious order as a means of combin-ing the two, although in France the more open *congréganiste* model of religious community which allowed religious women an active role in the community through teaching or nursing was more popular than the enclosed *religieuse* model.[83] The shift away from the contemplative orders clearly mirrors the trend within the church and society towards recognising women's superior role in imparting a moral message to others. Active Protestant women were always more likely to find a public outlet for their religious inspiration. Within the Protestant tradition, mythology was replaced by an idealised imaginary figure: she who established an intimate, personal relationship with God, a guardian of the faith, a moral influence on her family but by extension wider society also. 'The Bible gives her her throne, for she is the queen of the domestic circle . . . it is the female supremacy in that interesting domain, where love and tenderness, and refinement, thought and feeling preside', wrote John Angell James in his 'Female Piety' in 1852.[84] In Hamburg, Amalie Sieveking's establishment in 1832 of the Female Association for the Care of the Poor and the Sick was an attempt to combine spiritual and moral aid to the poor of that city.[85] Across Britain women found an outlet for their piety as teachers within the burgeoning Sunday School movement and women's temperance associations, devoted to the fight against alcohol and its pernicious consequences, can be seen as women exporting their Christian principles into the world. Only women could exemplify that combination of moral good and Christian endeavour. And women became prominent as home and overseas missionaries carrying Christian female virtue to the 'heathens' of the cities and the empire.[86] These women became exemplars of pious womanhood rather than exceptional, independent women carving out a space within the public sphere.

Religion, then, was central to women's lives in nineteenth-century Europe in ways that differed from previous eras. Women were given an exalted role, not within institutional religion but as everyday bearers of the faith and as moral icons. It was a difficult role to play, conferring on women responsibility for not just their own behaviour but also that of others. Undoubtedly there were many ways in which religious discourses on the pious woman or godly wife and mother constrained women's behaviour and opportunities. Nevertheless, what has been called the privileging of women's religiosity has been seen by some feminist historians as providing women with a sense of moral identity for themselves as well as a space and a language they could use to extend their moral influence beyond the personal, outside the home. Religion was not just a leisure activity for women, as some historians have suggested. Christian charitable endeavours were not just time-fillers for bored middle-class ladies. Religion was work requiring constant self-appraisal. In this sense the pious woman claimed for herself a privileged place in the family and in society. In the words of one German feminist and educator, Henriette Goldschmidt: 'Just as the moral strength of women is essential to the development of family life, in the same way, women must make a wider commitment to fulfil their mission to the national family.'[87]

CONCLUSIONS

Femininity was newly formulated at the end of the eighteenth century, firstly by the writers and scientists of the Enlightenment who redefined the natural as female and the cultural as male. By the dawn of the nineteenth century the body was the root of understandings of gender in European society. The scientific and medical discoveries of anatomy and bodily function began to displace earlier metaphysical thinking which disaggregated sex from gender. The body was the foundation for this new etymology, and physiological or sexual difference came to be used to legitimise an essentialist understanding of masculine and feminine character and roles. Biology was destiny and thus the female destiny was determined by her reproductive capacity. By the beginning of the nineteenth century this rather crude separate spheres model had been elaborated and disseminated through formal and informal channels: the sermon, the marriage manual, the novel and the broadside repeatedly told women that femininity was modesty, patience, self-sacrifice, piety, domesticity and motherhood.

'Woman's mission was by influence, tasteful economy, intelligent piety and faith to inspire and animate, soothe and resuscitate their men, so that the "mighty engine of masculine life may be aided in its action and its results".'[88] The Reverend Binney's reflections on gender roles in 1850 were acutely reminiscent of Jean-Jacques Rousseau's literary exposition on sex roles some hundred years earlier. For Rousseau and the minister, woman's role was imbued with responsibility; her subordination within marriage was compensated for by her powerful social role, supporting her husband and educating her children. What had been deemed natural roles for women became cultural. There was, though, an alternative route to respectable and virtuous femininity, active rather than passive, emphasising women's potential for self-development and personal autonomy rather than self-denigration. Mary Wollstonecraft's espousal of the 'improvement and emancipation of the whole sex' was ahead of its time, although her plea to 'make women rational creatures and free citizens' in order that they might 'quickly become good wives and mothers' was more in tune with the sympathies and preoccupations of the post-revolutionary era. Those women who attended church and who read Rousseau's novels and the mass of prescriptive literature telling them how to be good wives and mothers interpreted the message not necessarily as constraining but as empowering.

Chapter 2

◆

LEARNING TO BE A WOMAN

Nineteenth-century woman was not born with her femininity; she had to learn it. This was because codes of behaviour appropriate for a woman could differ between countries, cultures and classes. A peasant woman's language and demeanour might not be acceptable amongst the urban middle classes. In turn, the 'rough' language and physical violence displayed by some urban working-class women was considered unseemly in women from other communities. Yet, in a number of respects, the lessons in femininity taught to girls in the nineteenth century were surprisingly similar across the continent. Everywhere a girl learned to be a good wife and mother, a thrifty household manager, a willing worker, a chaste companion to her husband, and a dutiful mother to her children. A European woman of the nineteenth century was judged primarily by her role and deportment in her home.

This ideology of domesticity and the related notion of separate spheres is most strongly associated with the nineteenth century. But it was not new. Both the rhetoric and the reality of gendered public and private domains was well established at least two centuries prior to the industrial revolution. Men in the seventeenth and eighteenth centuries were associated with the world of work and commerce whilst women were associated primarily with the home and children. This organisation of gender roles was as much practical as ideological. In precarious agrarian societies, family survival was dependent upon complementary tasks assigned to each sex. Women's reproductive role located them primarily in the home, and thus a woman's work tasks tended to be focused on the household and nearby. Urban women may have experienced a greater variety of occupations and often participated in artisan manufacture, trade and commerce, but even in the towns women were more likely to spend much of their lives working in their own or someone else's household. Across Europe the guilds, which controlled artisan production, became increasingly restrictive from the seventeenth century onwards. Guild work was progressively seen as 'a learned art and given to men alone'.[1] The result was the marginalisation of women from some crafts and their consequent removal from this part of the worldly sphere. Even amongst the wealthier classes in the eighteenth century there was a degree of separation of spheres of activity in that women seldom engaged in the public world of political and commercial power. Yet, early modern society did not, on the whole, explicitly recognise the association of public and private spheres with gender difference. Rather, as historian Heide Wunder argues, before 1800 '"man" and "woman" were defined in relation to one another in terms of comparative differences as "stronger" and "weaker" . . . [This relationship] depended on the delicate balance of mutual obligations and reciprocity.'[2] So, while the sexual division of labour is generally assumed to be commonplace in all societies, the means by which this is manifested is chronologically and geographically specific to time or place, and not always determined by sexual stereotypes.[3]

However, there is little doubt that it was during the first decades of the nineteenth century that the notion of the woman's place in the home was most powerfully elaborated through discourses on femininity. These discourses were injunctions about ideal (and anti-ideal) behaviour for women, about what was appropriate and what not. It was in this century that such discourses became pervasive, distributed not only through the pens of intellectuals and the mouths of churchmen, but via popular tracts, romantic novels and a host of other media which were voraciously consumed by men and women. Hence, these discourses on femininity (and equivalent ones on masculinity) gradually found widespread acceptance amongst all classes of society owing to the rise of literacy and the spread of mass print culture, and the standards and norms of behaviour associated with concepts of womanliness began to be displayed in all sorts of social and cultural spaces. In this chapter we consider how European women both learned the lessons of femininity and experienced them in the home, the school and the community.

DOMESTICITY

The home was the prime location for the expression of femininity in the nineteenth century. In the domestic sphere, womanliness could flourish, a woman could express her true vocation. For the wives of the industrial entre-preneurs of northern France described by Bonnie Smith, 'home, cosmos and society constituted a tripartite axis of the domestic vision'.[4] Domesticity for these bourgeois women was a way of life entirely separate from the world of business and politics inhabited by their husbands. Reproduction rather than production was the focus of their world. The notion of separate spheres as it was lived in the early industrial period was a cultural form which expressed the *mentalité* of a distinct social group whose world view was focused on the domestic, on a private world whose rhythms were biological rather than commercial. The domestic culture fashioned by these women was a pro-duct of the increasing physical separation of home and work and the gradual decline of the overtly productive role of middle-class women. Whilst the ideology of separate spheres and its associated constructions of appropri-ate male and female roles were widely circulated well before this period of nascent industrial power, as British historian Anna Clark points out, 'the very meaning and function of domesticity were dramatically changed for the middling sort of people with commercialisation, professionalisation, urban-isation and the consumer revolution.'[5] Separate spheres was not an original concept but the new conditions of late eighteenth and nineteenth century western Europe facilitated the absorption and practice of the domestic ideal by the middle classes.

Where are we to find the roots of the ideology of domesticity? The late eighteenth century writings of the philosopher Jean-Jacques Rousseau played an important part in defining a popular form of femininity based on woman's 'natural' characteristics which fitted the conception of home as a moral haven and refuge from the disruption of industrial society. In his philosophical treatises and more especially in his two novels, Rousseau expounded a model of domesticity which rested upon the separation of the public and private spheres and which depended upon the 'natural' woman, personified by Sophie in the first novel, *Émile* (1762). Émile's future wife was to be brought up and educated to please her husband, to remain modest, chaste, respectable but also playful or coquettish in order to please him. For Rousseau, sexual difference was the key to harmonious domesticity:

What is most wanted in a woman is gentleness; formed to obey a creature so imper-fect as a man, a creature often vicious and always faulty, she should early learn to sub-mit to an injustice and to suffer the wrongs inflicted on her by her husband without complaint; she must be gentle for her own sake, not his. Bitterness and obstinacy only multiply the sufferings of the wife and the misdeeds of the husband; the man feels that these are not the weapons to be used against him. Heaven did not make women attractive and persuasive that that they might degenerate into bitterness, or meek that they should require the mastery; their soft voice was not meant for hard words, nor their delicate features for the frowns of anger. When they lose their temper they forget themselves; often enough they have just cause of complaint; but when they scold they always put themselves in the wrong. We should each adopt the tone which befits our sex; a soft-hearted husband may make an overbearing wife, but a man, unless he is a perfect monster, will sooner or later yield to his wife's gentleness and the victory will be hers.[6]

It is to Rousseau that we can ascribe the image of the 'angel in the house' – the idealised woman who personifies virtue, moral superiority and maternal sentiment. Although his view of woman's nature also incorporated a belief in woman's innate passion and sexual instinct, it was his portrayal of the true mother, the moral heart of the family unit, the educator of future citizens, which was to be taken up in the works of his admirers and by upper- and middle-class women who were searching for a meaningful role within the home.[7] Rousseau stands out amongst his peers as a populariser and even an evangelist for domestic ideology and separate spheres, but his was by no means an isolated voice. The belief in separate and distinctive male and female qualities was standard fare by 1800.

Amongst the new commercial and educated middle classes in Germany, France and Britain, domestic joy through the separation of men's and women's spheres was an aspirational and attainable ideal. A German merchant of the first decades of the century, David Lewald, attended to his business and other affairs whilst his wife bore, raised and educated eight children, directed the household, engaged in creative handicrafts and perfected the art of being the perfect housewife and hostess.[8] The German poet and philosopher Christoph Martin Wieland (1733–1813) compared the ideal wife to his own at the end of the eighteenth century: 'Without moods, even tempered, calm, agreeable, easy to amuse, used to an almost monastic way of life, content with everything as long as she can see an expression of contentment and affection in my face. She fits in effortlessly, and without being forced, with my taste, my mood, and my way of life.'[9] Dorothea Wieland's perspective on her marriage is, unfortunately, not known to us; it is her husband who speaks for her when he states that her 'very happiness is invested in and drawn from simply living for me and our family.'[10] A woman's fulfilment was to be achieved through domesticity, a belief reflected in obituaries and memorials erected to those women who lived the domestic life. In 1840, it was said of the late Mrs Frances Goodby, the wife of a vicar in the English Midlands:

what a demand must have been made on the piety, patience, frugality and industry of the mistress of a small family . . . But her ardent and unceasing flow of spirits, extreme activity and diligence, her punctuality, uprightness and remarkable frugality, combined with a firm reliance on providence carried her through the severest times of pressure, both with credit and respectability.[11]

Evangelical Protestantism offered women not a subordinate but an exalted role. The evangelicals' primary aim was the transformation of national morality, and it was via the home and family life that the struggle against sin and immorality was to be waged. The domestic woman was thus a key component of the evangelical vision which has been dubbed the 'religion of the household'.[12] Hannah More (1745–1833), an English evangelical philanthropist, rejected the radicalism of Mary Wollstonecraft, arguing that women should be content with their natural sphere: 'A woman sees the world, as it were, from a little elevation in her own garden, whence she makes an exact survey of home scenes, but takes not in that wider range of distant prospects which he who stands on a loftier eminence commands'.[13] By the 1830s and 1840s the evangelistic tone of More was replaced by more practical advice. Writers like Sarah Stickney Ellis (c.1800–72) argued that domestic management was as important as a man's profession:

it is but reasonable that man's personal comfort should be studiously attended to, and in this, the complacence and satisfaction which most men evince on finding themselves placed at a table before a favourite dish, situated beside a clean hearth, or accommodated with an empty sofa, is of itself a sufficient reward for any sacrifice such indulgence may have cost . . . and he will sit down to eat, or compose himself to rest, with more hearty goodwill towards the wife who has been thoughtful about these things, than if she had been all day busily employed in writing a treatise on morals for his especial benefit . . .[14]

Harriet Martineau (1802–76) believed in the value of domesticity for women's individual fulfilment – although in her 'On Female Education' (1822) she showed herself as a conservative disciple of Wollstonecraft in arguing that education would develop women's potential and create a 'race of enlightened mothers'.[15]

The ideology of domesticity which located the transmission of moral values in women was common across Europe, amongst both Catholics and Protestants. Amongst the Lutheran Nordic countries, the cult of domesticity, the belief in the moral regenerative power of the woman's vocation in the household, was taken up by religious revivalists.[16] In the restoration years following the Revolution in France, Catholics and conservatives regarded the household as the key to the country's moral regeneration after the excesses of the revolutionary years. According to the Vicomte de Bonald, a French aristocrat émigré and former civil servant who returned to France to work for the restoration of the monarchy, the patriarchal family was the key to stability and morality in public life. In his treatise on women's education in 1802 he began with the observation: 'Women belong to the family and not to political society, and nature created them for domestic cares and not for public functions.' Girls and boys

> have not received the same destiny from nature. Everything in [girls'] instruction should be directed towards domestic utility, just as everything in the education of boys should be directed toward public utility. It is a false education that gives one's inclinations a direction that goes contrary to nature, that makes the sexes want to exchange occupations just as they would clothing, that women would voluntarily take a hand in the government of the State, and that men would find a bit too much pleasure in private life and in domestic enjoyments.[17]

De Bonald's words are significant for they show that the language of separate spheres, and more important, the association of public and private with gender difference, was written and spoken by contemporaries. This was a new development but it was a trend that was to continue with a vengeance at all levels of society. In 1856 the women parishioners in one Dublin church were left in no doubt as to what was expected of them upon hearing the words of the Reverend John Gregg:

> *We* have features peculiar to us as men, and we also have our peculiar capabilities and responsibilities. The *great* and *weighty* business of life devolves on *men*, but important business belongs to *women* . . . The larger portion of the labours of life – of public life – fall almost exclusively to the lot of men; but a most important portion of the duties of life, especially of private life, falls to the share of women. God has adapted our sex to the peculiar duties to which we are especially called, and for which you are not so well fitted; and He has adapted your sex to the peculiar duties to which you are called, and for which we are not at all fitted. Society does best when each sex performs the duties for which it is especially ordained.[18]

Few middle-class women resented or resisted the strictures of domesticity. Some, like the German writer Sophie von La Roche (1731–1807), managed to combine what appeared to be an idealised domestic life as a wife and mother with a successful literary career. To the modern-day reader, Sophie's daily routine of supervising the servants, overseeing the affairs of the house and spending time with her son, may appear dull, but she expressed considerable contentment with her pivotal domestic role.

> I get up at 6 o'clock and get dressed, I write or read until half past seven, when La Roche [her husband] and Baron von Hohenfeld arrive for breakfast and stay until

9 o'clock. Then I go into the kitchen and give orders, because I know about the culinary arts, I inspect the housework, write my household accounts and then at around 12 o'clock [write] *Pomona* [her novel] and letters.

After lunch and an afternoon spent reading letters and sewing she returned to the kitchen to order the evening meal at 5 o'clock. In the evening she read with her son.[19]

The nineteenth-century middle-class woman embraced, celebrated and refined the cult of domesticity. It served what she perceived as her own interests. The wives of industrialists in the Nord region of France created homes that were a cultural expression of the female world, and not as a Rousseau-type haven to complement the world of industry. Their fashions, etiquette, domestic furnishings, social engagements, Catholic devotion and charitable activity all served to delineate a holistic, 'natural' universe within which women could demonstrate their power. To the last, the wives of German civil servants who struggled to keep up appearances and maintain respectability in an aspiring lower middle class milieu, practised elaborate deceptions in order to give the impression of a comfortable bourgeois lifestyle, and gained identity and satisfaction from this, notwithstanding the heavy toll exacted by the strain of domestic management.[20] The eighteenth-century image of the upper-class woman who spent her days idly exercising her creative talents, socialising with other women, and supervising the servants had, by the 1840s, been consigned to the realms of prescriptive literature. It had been superseded by the reality of the middle-class woman who worked hard to create her own domesticity, who fashioned her own private and public worlds.

The ideology of separate spheres was a central feature of middle-class culture in the nineteenth century. This applied equally to provincial England in the nascent industrial era, post-Napoleonic northern France, and Germany and Austria in the Restoration era following the 1848 revolutions. And yet the idea and the language of domesticity were adopted by elements of the working class too. Though separate spheres was an alien concept for the majority of plebeian men and women in Britain, Anna Clark notes that 'radicals stole the notion of domesticity from middle-class moralists and manipulated it to demand the privileges of separate spheres for working-class as well as middle and upper-class, men and women.'[21] Across industrialising Europe, working-men's calls for a 'family wage' implied the primacy of marriage and the exclusion of women from paid work outside the home. The language of respectability rested upon the notion that the domestic sphere was a woman's natural home. 'Everyone understands that her place is elsewhere than in the political arena', argued the French working men's newspaper *L'Atelier* in 1844; 'her place is at the domestic hearth. Public functions belong to the man; private functions belong to the woman.'[22] In place of egalitarianism in the workplace was protection in the home, and for many women this form of domesticity was far preferable to the position of a working woman.

It was not only working men who demanded the privileges of domesticity for their wives. Women were beginning to demand it for themselves in order to protect their status within the home. If separate spheres was to work then women had to be accorded their rightful status as wives, mothers and household managers. Such was the pervasiveness of the ideology throughout public life that German women engaged in divorce actions emphasised their 'womanly' qualities and their fulfilment of domestic duties in order to convince a judge of the validity of their claim. Women who bore their husbands' indiscretions with fortitude and patience, who devoted themselves to their children and their domestic duties, women who lived their faith, were held in the highest esteem. In 1860, Emilie Beil from Hamburg argued in court that she was never distracted from the 'dutiful care of the common household' despite the violent behaviour of her husband, whilst in the same year Henriette Bucke claimed that throughout her miserable, violent marriage she had always tried to be 'a faithful, active wife'.[23] So, domesticity, or at least its language, made sense for some lower-class women for whom security resided in marriage and home.

SERVICE AND SELF-SACRIFICE

The lessons of domesticity and womanhood were learned firstly at home, thereafter in the schoolroom, and then reaffirmed in the wider community. The daughters of rich and poor alike received lessons in femininity from their mothers, nannies or nurses and then their governesses, nuns or elementary school mistresses. Wherever it was learned, the lesson was the same: girls were to be good wives, household managers and mothers. To be an ideal woman of any social class in the nineteenth century meant neglecting one's personal needs – self-sacrifice – and devoting oneself to the service of others.

Girls first learned the lessons of womanhood at their mother's side. 'Your daughter, for some time, will be part of yourself', wrote one Russian mother to her own daughter in 1804 on the occasion of the birth of a granddaughter. 'Now she drinks your milk, soon she will begin to form herself according to your precepts, ideas and convictions. For a long time you will be her only soul, support, and finally her guide in the world . . . Your daughter is your property. She is the work of your hands.'[24] In northern France, the daughters of the bourgeoisie accompanied their mothers on charitable visits, they engaged in domestic tasks, they attended religious rituals and learned to 'mother' their younger siblings.[25] Within the British upper classes, daughters were often mothered by a host of female staff: wet nurses, nannies, nursery governesses and teachers. The nine Potter sisters (including Beatrice who was to marry Sidney Webb) were evidently close to Martha, the head servant, who was called Dada by the children. She was clearly more important than their mother according to Mary Potter:

> Dear, dear old Dada, what a good woman she has been all of her life and what a bless-ing to others! How much we owe her! . . . we could always depend on her sense and kindness. In our intimate child life she was our real mother on whom we could depend for daily comfort and discipline. Our own mother was never near to us, at least never to me, and never seemed quite natural.[26]

As they grew older, English girls were taught a series of elaborate and complex rituals consisting of afternoon calls, at-home days when visitors were received, the organisation of bazaars and charity events, and maybe the visiting of the poor. All of these activities were seen as social duties which women acted out in order both to confirm the social position of the family and the feminine role of the women of the family.[27] Early on in their lives, girls learned that the home was a female space. One popular German advice book taught that

> Nature creates the maiden for the home and family, all talents of the spirit and the heart point to that; if she is not allowed to be untrue to her vocation she will not fail in her purpose in life . . . whatever class she may belong to, she must early on learn to be busy about her tasks and to learn basic household management, then her education will be complete.[28]

It was a mother's obligation to provide her daughters with a good example of dutiful behaviour. Lily Braun (1865–1916), who later became a prominent German socialist and feminist, recalled: 'Everything that Mama did, when she had a really unhappy look on her face, she explained as the fulfilment of duty'.[29] By the end of the nineteenth century, homemaking had become a female role: 'a man can no more make a home than a drone can make a hive', remarked the English feminist Francis Power Cobbe (1822–1904).[30] With the disappearance of the patriarchal father-figure, at least amongst the middle classes, women became the focal point of home life. They were not only housekeepers but homemakers too; they became the symbol of homeliness. 'Whether she sits in her corner, smiling generally or walks from house to house spreading warmth, she is always at home, radiating cosiness', wrote one Swedish architect.[31]

For working-class daughters domesticity meant physical labour; cleaning, polishing, washing and looking after younger siblings were all learned at mother's side. Girls were described as mothers' apprentices.[32] They were generally permitted less freedom than boys, even in play. Whilst boys prowled far afield in gangs, taking part in daring escapades, girls were expected to stay closer to home, engaging in more modest and useful tasks.[33] Londoner Doris Frances, the eldest daughter, felt herself constantly labouring with housework:

> From the moment I was capable of wielding a duster I was given regular weekly jobs to do, such as polishing all the brass door handles throughout the flat with Bluebell Metal Polish, cleaning all the family's boots and shoes . . . I also had to shop for the groceries, do the washing-up, and peel all the vegetables (and for a family of five that was quite a lot of spud-bashing for one small girl). Worst of all, I was given all the family's mending to do – a most tedious and boring job.[34]

Anna Meier, recalling her childhood in Austria around 1900, wrote how, when other children were playing outside, 'I would watch them with envy from the window until my mother would slap me to remind me that I had to work to do.'[35] For Anna, school was a welcome respite from work at home. It was common to keep girls out of school more frequently than boys in order that they might help their mothers with laundry day or step in as a substitute when mother was sick. As a result, 'practical-minded, careworn, vigilant girls' were ubiquitous on the streets of urban centres.[36] These 'little mothers' faced only half-hearted attempts by education officials to enforce their school attendance, in the belief that girls were justifiably needed at home and that school was less useful for those whose future was domestic.

Daughters saw their mothers as paragons of self-denial, ensuring 'breadwinners' received a good meal at the expense of other family members, maintaining the semblance of a well-run and thrifty household by adopting secretive strategies – using pawnbrokers and money lenders for instance – known only to themselves and revealed only to husbands by accident.[37] The unequal distribution of resources in the home was frequently the woman's doing. 'Going without' was a common and often essential means to survival in the poorest households, and it was invariably the female members of the family who made the greatest sacrifices in terms of food and clothing, and space and time for enjoyment. At times of greatest hardship, mothers might make do with bread and tea, having served their working husbands with a hot meal separately. Daughters were initiated into these rituals early on.

'It seems only natural to a mother that a girl should help to clean or baby-mind', remarked one concerned commentator in London, who observed that boys were more likely to receive payment for any work they undertook.[38] In urban Scotland it has been noted that 'the allocation of domestic work to women was . . . part of a pervasive set of assumptions concerning appropriate behaviour for men and women', which was, in turn, reinforced by the structure of the labour market which saw women, first and foremost, as domestic workers. Girls were delegated indoor work by their mothers, a pattern that continued even when the daughter was in full-time employment. Mothers regarded it as their responsibility to turn out their daughters as good wives.[39]

In farming communities, children were similarly expected to help with the day-to-day tasks about the house and farm. On Scottish crofts, certain tasks were designated as children's work, such as stacking the peats, planting potatoes or helping in the dairy, jobs which were not especially gendered. However, as girls grew older their work tended to centre more on the household or was largely restricted to 'female' jobs such as berry-picking.[40] In the agricultural regions of lowland Scotland, girls were more explicitly confined to what was called 'inside work' which included housework and jobs in the dairy. Rural French girls soon learned how to manage a household while their brothers were out in the fields wielding heavy tools. Girls understood that certain tasks were defined as women's work, an observation that was brought home to them even more starkly in the urban setting. Although a significant proportion of married women did undertake paid work, a daughter would quickly learn that her mother's role was centred on the home and her duty was to serve her husband's needs. Employment outside the home did not, of course, grant married women the privileges enjoyed by their menfolk – a dinner waiting, leisure time, pocket money; these women bore a double burden of paid work and housework which meant they were continually toiling.

LESSONS IN FEMININITY

Lessons at mother's side were supplemented and reinforced by the teachings of formal education. As they grew older, privileged girls were either kept at home and educated by a governess or sent to a convent or private boarding school which offered 'a special indoctrination into the complexities of domestic life'.[41] The Catholic convent excelled in its task of instilling young women with a measure of superficial knowledge alongside the essential skills of the bourgeois woman: needlework, drawing, music, a smattering of foreign languages, as well as the more intangible lessons in posture, grace, virtue, purity and self-control. In Britain, amongst the wealthier classes, girls recall years of boredom and frustration at the hands of poorly educated governesses who equipped them for little more than ladylike behaviour and marriage. 'My mother's idea of the equipment required for her two daughters', recalled Molly Bell, the daughter of a millionaire industrialist, 'was that we should be turned out as good wives and mothers and be able to take our part in the social life of our kind.'[42] Adolescent girls were kept in state of limbo, what one mother termed a 'chrysalis state' which left them with little or no formal academic training, merely a few accomplishments for 'coming out'.

Mothers, it seems, were often responsible for repressing their daughters' desire for intellectual stimulation and knowledge. Amongst the Russian nobility during the upheaval of the 1860s, mothers tried to prevent their daughters reading radical literature which they believed would lead to them rejecting all they had been taught. 'Where did you get desires and thoughts so unlike mine', exclaimed one despairing mother. 'How can you express ideas without my permission?'[43] In Germany, Fanny Lewald was told by her mother, 'there is nothing more objectionable and useless than an educated and practical woman.'[44] Fanny recalled that, after leaving school at the age of 13, she spent her days 'pointlessly' so that by the evening she 'had the terrible feeling that I had done nothing worthwhile all day'. Fanny's daily schedule demonstrates why this intelligent child felt so frustrated. Piano practice filled her time between 8am and 9am, followed by three hours of knitting and sewing and an hour of reading over her old schoolbooks which bored her intensely. After lunch there was more handicrafts and piano practice and finally an hour of writing practice. Only once, and exceptionally twice, a week was Fanny permitted to go visiting.[45] Fanny Lewald's unfulfilling education was paralleled in England where the daughters of the new industrial bourgeoisie similarly lacked stimulation. 'For more than ten years I was bored to death all the time', recalled Molly Bell. Molly and her sister Elsa learned to speak French and German, and were taught to dance and play the piano by a governess, but 'the more serious side of education did not take any part in the plans my mother made for us. No girl that we knew was trained for any career or profession, nor did girls of our class go to school.'[46]

At the beginning of the nineteenth century these deficiencies in girls' education were widely recognised by conservatives and liberals alike. When the radical writer Mary Wollstonecraft adversely commented on women's 'natural cunning', their tendency to become 'coquettish slaves', she was criticising the kind of superficial learning and stress on amusing and ornamental accomplishments experienced by many young women of the middle classes. 'The woman who has only been taught to please will soon find that her charms are oblique sunbeams, and that they cannot have much effect on her husband's heart when they are seen every day, when the summer is passed and gone. Will she then have sufficient native energy to look into herself for comfort, and cultivate her dormant faculties?'[47] For Wollstonecraft, along with many who advocated improvements in girls' education, such superficial learning was not even appropriate for girls who were to become wives and mothers. Rather, she said that they should be educated to become 'better citizens': rounded, rational, independent beings who might then become 'more observant daughters, more affectionate sisters, more faithful wives, more reasonable mothers'. In short, education would provide women with a means of gaining some degree of independence of men and their self-respect.[48] At the same time, Wollstonecraft was alert to the importance of the maternal role, a concern echoed by conservative writers, for whom the upbringing of children was central to the maintenance of domestic ideology and separate spheres. As Louis Aimé-Martin (1786–1847), a French history professor, commented in his 1834 publication *The Education of Mothers*: 'On the maternal bosom the mind of nations reposes; their manners, prejudices and virtues – in a word, the civilisation of the human race all depend upon maternal influence.'[49] Education for motherhood was the common thread running through the majority of writings on girls' education – conservative, liberal, clerical, evangelical and republican – from Rousseau onwards. The concept of the mother-educator expounded by Wollstonecraft, Catherine Macaulay-Graham and many others, appealed to woman's natural role as bearer and nurturer of children. It assumed marriage and maternity were central to women's lives and offered women a moral role. Women, if educated properly, might extend their civilising influence into the wider world, primarily through their children. For educationalists such as the Scots essayist and novelist Elizabeth Hamilton (1758–1816), domesticity was a sphere in which women could exhibit their moral worth. 'If women were so educated as to qualify them for the proper performance of this momentous duty [the education of children], it would do more towards the progress-ive improvement of the species, than all the discoveries of science and the researches of philosophy', wrote Hamilton in 1803.[50]

But it was to be around a century before the progressive ideas of Wollstonecraft and her contemporaries were to infiltrate the European class-room. Napoleon Bonaparte (1769–1821) expressed a common attitude in

1807 on the occasion of the founding of a school for the daughters of officers and civil servants. For the French emperor, the new school should aim to produce not the pleasing coquettes imagined by Rousseau but good wives and household managers:

> In a public institution for demoiselles religion is a serious matter . . . it is the surest guarantee for mothers and for husbands. Make believers of them, not reasoners. The weakness of women's brains, the mobility of their ideas, their destination in the social order, the necessity for inspiring them with a constant and perpetual resignation and a mild and indulgent charity, all that cannot be obtained except by means of religion, a charitable and mild religion . . . I am desirous that they should leave not as pleasing women but as virtuous women, that their pleasing qualities be those of morals and of the heart, not of the mind and of amusement.[51]

'I am not raising vendors of style nor housemaids', he concluded, 'but wives for modest and poor households.'

The Napoleonic view, that women did not possess the ability to reason, and neither did they need to develop it, was not uncommon. 'The sphere in which the female sex is destined to work is certainly narrower than that which is assigned to the man,' wrote the pastor director of a newly opened girls' school in Göttingen in 1806; 'and only seldom can that sphere be enlarged beyond its natural limits without the loss of precious femininity.' Another remarked that he opposed 'that broad smattering of knowledge so insufferable in the second sex, which destroys delicate femininity'.[52] Early attempts to provide middle-class girls with some form of structured education sought to limit the amount of intellectual stimulation provided, since it was believed that over- or mis-education would invariably compromise girls' femininity. On the other hand, it was believed an appropriate education would be beneficial to counter the dangerous consequences of women's 'mania for reading', especially romantic novels which could ruin a woman's sensibility.[53] In the early years, knitting and sewing were deemed more important than reading and writing. Louise Otto-Peters (1819–95), later a feminist and outspoken advocate of an improved education for girls, recalled of the 1820s that 'knitting and the knitted stocking were already for the four year old girl the first serious work'.[54] Some three decades later it was still said that 'stocking knitting is essentially the steady companion of the young girl'.[55] In the Polish Kingdom, where access to and provision of education was expanded during the nineteenth century, usefulness was considered more appropriate than knowledge for noble girls. In Warsaw, the school authorities justified the rather small number of institutes of higher learning for girls on the grounds that a woman's 'destiny and duties, and consequently [her] skills and virtues, are to ensure the happiness of the family and its individual members . . . the education of this sex is domestic rather than public . . . the parents' home is the best and most useful school for them and their mothers are the proper teachers.'[56]

In middle-class single-sex schools for much of the century, education consisted of lessons for motherhood and domesticity in a tacit acceptance that women required preparation for their 'natural calling'. The daughters of the bourgeoisie were taught that their duty was to devote themselves to their children since, in the words of a character in a popular didactic text *Mathilde et Gabrielle*, 'the duties of a mother are sweet to fulfil'.[57] When the character in one French schoolbook asked her tutor why there were no female inventors, the reply was 'Women don't study science. They are important as mothers of future inventors.'[58] Even progressives, such as the Bremen schoolteacher and writer Betty Gleim (1781–1827), believed it was the purpose of girls' schools to develop the 'special qualities of women's nature' in order that they might fulfil the highest calling, that of wife and mother.[59] Hence, reading and schooling in intellectual subjects was subordinated to practical instruction in those tasks essential to girls' eventual duties in the home. For Caroline Rudolphi (1754–1811), teacher and writer on girls' education, schooling should help develop in girls not only practical skills in child nurture, but also the qualities they needed to survive in a male-dominated world: self-sacrifice and obedience.[60] In Bavaria, an 1804 decree barred the study of the sciences by women, but more common was the tailoring of the curriculum to suit the supposed nature of girls: conversational French for example, was preferred in Germany over the Latin taught to boys; history was boiled down to the stories of great men and women.[61] Girls of the English middle classes could expect a year or two of formal schooling. Some, it is true, received a liberal and broad education, often at the behest of their fathers, but even then it was likely their education would be interrupted by family obligations or business distractions. There were few boarding schools for girls until mid-century, and alternative educational institutes such as literary societies and the reading rooms of mechanics institutes usually excluded girls and women.[62] Such restrictions served to reinforce the messages received from didactic literature and learned at mother's side: that the home was the appropriate site for women's activities, enhanced by religion and separated from the world of business.

At elementary level the opportunities for instilling 'feminine' values and behaviour into young girls were multiplied with the expansion of compulsory and free schooling in much of western Europe. Primary schooling was made compulsory in Prussia (1812), Denmark (1814), Norway (1827), Sweden (1842), Switzerland (1848), Scotland (1873), England and Wales (1880) and France (1882). Alongside the mission to teach the basics of reading, writing and arithmetic, primary schooling was used for the dissemination of civic and moral values including dominant notions of femininity. This was made all the easier when boys and girls were educated separately, as was the case in France. Whilst few explicit distinctions were made for girls and boys in the official curriculum at elementary level, teachers were expected to emphasise the 'special duties', obligations and qualities of girls who were taught to be modest, patient and even-tempered, orderly and clean. One French teacher-training manual in 1832 advised its readers to 'make sure that [the girls] do not make with their hands, their feet or their heads any movement which could distract the others, or which would be improper . . . let all of them be arranged and directed in such a way so that the idea of order, of silence and of respect be joined to the class's spirit.'[63] 'Woman is the *guardian of the foyer*. Her place is at home . . . it is for the foyer that she must reserve all her grace and good humor . . . A woman who does not love her home, who has no taste for household duties . . . cannot remain a virtuous woman for long', instructed one widely used French textbook for the moral education of girls.[64]

Notions of service and self-sacrifice pervaded thinking on girls' education in France at the end of the century. Textbooks portrayed girls dutifully committing themselves to their families, thereby sublimating their own desires to the needs of the greater good. The popular heroine Suzette, who appeared in one French schoolbook, took over the running of a farm and the care of younger siblings when her mother died and her father was plunged into helpless despair. Such self-sacrifice, modesty, satisfaction with one's social status and acquiescence, narrowed girls' horizons to being a good housewife and mother. Irish elementary school textbooks designed for girls' schools both instructed girls in correct behaviour and gave practical advice on household management, cookery and child care. In 1846, the schoolgirl read that 'knowledge is not to elevate her above her station . . . It is to correct vanity and repress pretention. It is to teach her to know her place and her functions; to make her content with the one, and willing to fulfil the other. It is to render her more useful, more humble, and more happy.'[65]

In the English elementary school system, the message to girls was delivered in a more practical way. Schools were encouraged to provide domestic subjects to 'fit the girls for life'.[66] One consequence was the almost ubiquitous presence of needlework on the primary school curriculum, an activity which was admired as much for the desirable qualities it would impart to girls, such as neatness, patience, concentration and thrift, as for the skill itself.[67] By the 1870s the Department of Education had made domestic economy (cookery, laundry work and the 'household arts') a compulsory subject for girls in elementary schools, clearly demonstrating how the ideology of domesticity had come to determine girls' education. Certain class assumptions under-pinned these initiatives, one being that a practical education suited to their station would attenuate the poverty and poor living conditions endured by the working classes on account of poor budgeting and improvident household management by women. Hence the remark of one observer that working-class women would benefit more from learning to cook sheep's heads than cakes.[68] But whilst girls generally accepted that their fate was to follow in their mothers' footsteps, few enjoyed domestic subjects and many girls and their mothers believed the lessons learned at home to be sufficient. As Elizabeth Roberts discovered in northern England, girls regarded lessons on domestic management at school as no substitute or improvement on the real experience they undoubtedly had at home.[69] And, in France, surveys of female students' preferences consistently ranked domestic and practical subjects lower than academic.[70]

The last few decades of the nineteenth century saw a qualitative change in girls' experience of schooling. In Germany, France, Britain and Ireland, education for girls expanded at the elementary and the secondary levels, and a broader-based curriculum in middle-class schools taught girls that they might have career aspirations outside, or even instead of, the role of wife and mother. When, in 1870, Jules Ferry, a future French prime minister, spoke of 'equality for both sexes' in education, he was anticipating substantive changes in the provision and delivery of schooling to girls at the secondary level. Just six years later the Belfast resident Isabella Tod opened her Ladies' Institute for middle-class girls, a practical consequence of her campaign to educate girls for a productive life. 'Parents should remember', she wrote, 'that they cannot . . . obtain for their daughters exactly the situation in life which they suppose to be desirable. It is, then, short-sighted to fit them for no other; nay, it is even cruel.'[71] In Britain, some liberal headmistresses, whilst continuing to insist on ladylike behaviour, began to implement a broader-based curriculum for girls, consigning what were called aesthetic subjects to lesser importance and rejecting practical training in domestic duties which was assumed to occur at home. German secondary schools, though, made few curriculum changes in response to the concern about increasing num-bers of 'redundant' or 'surplus' women who required training for employ-ment, and there was constant opposition to academic training of women in

German secondary schools. As late as 1884 the Prussian minister of education commented that girls' minds should not be 'crammed with facts from all fields of knowledge'.[72] Instead, a number of private initiatives were set up for girls leaving school to provide technical training, from cookery and dressmaking to commercial skills and photography.[73] Such initiatives were paralleled elsewhere in Europe including France, Sweden, Russia, Poland and the Habsburg Empire.

The debate about the importance of teaching girls domestic subjects never really subsided. Indeed, in England those who campaigned to raise the status and prominence of domestic training tried to have it redesignated as an applied science taught in 'kitchen laboratories'. Thankfully, female science teachers resisted attempts to 'dumb-down' chemistry lessons to make them 'relevant' to girls' interests and needs. An initiative in 1908 by London's King's College to teach a three-year university-level course in Home Science was described by outraged feminists as a 'despicable prostitution of educational opportunities'.[74] Formal education always did more to reinforce dominant attitudes than to resist them and thus it should be no surprise that middle-class ideals of femininity pervaded schooling throughout the nineteenth century. On the other hand, the efforts of some liberal headmistresses, especially in secondary schools, did begin to shift the educational agenda towards a more positive and independent model for women, encompassing exercise and fresh air, fewer constraints on girls' freedoms and an academic as opposed to a practical or domestic training in recognition of the fact that many girls of the middle as well as the working classes would be forced to earn their own living.

READING ABOUT FEMININITY

There was nothing more influential than the example of one's mother and the reification of the domestic role in the schoolroom. But in the nineteenth century a new force came to exert a considerable influence over the construction of femininity within the domestic sphere. The explosion of popular literature in the form of advice books, religious pamphlets, magazines, periodicals and romantic novels meant that reading material became central to the discursive construction of womanhood. The growth of literacy, especially amongst the poor and women, supplied a massive new market for all manner of reading material. These publications, many of them explicitly designed for female readers – using a combination of the didactic and the entertaining – told women how to be feminine. They constructed the ideal domestic woman in a variety of guises and situations, but in each she was invariably gentle, pious, moral and self-sacrificing.

New family magazines of the 1840s idealised family life and promoted marriage as the only appropriate role for women. The first periodicals aimed explicitly at women readers appeared in the 1850s, exemplified by the most famous of the genre in Britain, *The Englishwoman's Domestic Magazine* (first published in 1852), and in Germany the long-running *Gartenlaube* (1853–1900).[75] Directed at the middle-class female market, these magazines constructed the woman reader as moral, maternal and feminine, expressed through a mixture of recipes, sewing patterns, advice on domestic management, fashion news, fiction and articles on subjects designed to appeal to women such as marriage, motherhood and child care. In Wales, *Y Gymraes* (*The Welshwoman*) aimed at the respectable middle class, set out to create and perpetuate the perfect Welshwoman: 'neat and tidy, modest, unassuming, thrifty, loyal, pure, religious.'[76] It was also the duty of the Welshwoman to uphold Welshness by wearing native dress and ensuring the use of the Welsh language in the family. The true Welshwoman saw her primary role within the home, venturing into the public sphere only via Sunday School and chapel.

Literature designed for girls, in the form either of school textbooks or of popular pamphlets and even religious tracts, tended to reinforce a view of the ideal feminine character. Indeed, girls' fiction was even more preoccupied with images of innocence, purity and the cult of domesticity than literature intended for the adult female market. The female heroines conformed to a moral, pious and self-sacrificing model of femininity which we can also see portrayed in school textbooks from the middle of the century. The heroine of *La Petite Jeanne* (1853), probably one of the most popular school-readers used in French primary schools, encapsulates the values deemed desirable in all classes of girl. When the motherless Jeanne is taken in by the wealthy Madame Dumont, we read that 'Mme. Dumont's daughters were very friendly with Jeanne because she was as modest in her language as in her behaviour. She loved them so much she would have gladly died for their sake.'[77] Jeanne, of course, was a good, pious and self-sacrificing child who always saw the best in others and regarded it as her duty to sublimate her desires to theirs. Similarly, the story of young Ethel May in *The Daisy Chain* by the popular British children's writer Charlotte Yonge, published in 1856, strongly parallels the trials and tribulations experienced by Suzette, the heroine of a series of volumes widely used in French primary schools from the 1880s.[78] Both Ethel and Suzette had lost their mothers and were forced, prematurely, to take on the maternal role enduring self-sacrifice in order to enable the survival of their families. Stories of 'household fairies in training' emphasised to young girls that their primary role was in the home and that such a role was a position of strength and honour as well as duty.[79] Ethel May is transformed from a tomboyish and studious child into the 'angel in the house', whilst Suzette, who had always known and understood her future role, became the idealised rural housewife. In the German *Backfischbücher*, novels featuring the trials and tribulations of adolescent girls, the female characters are portrayed learning to conform to expectations in order to achieve the ultimate goal, marriage. The story of Ilse, the heroine of one of the more enduring *Backfisch* novels, Emmy von Rhoden's *Stubborn Ilse*, first published in 1885, typifies the characteristic adolescent journey from stubborn and wilful teenager packed off to boarding school to teach her better behaviour, to her transformation into the perfect wife. The moral of such stories was clear: conformity brings happiness.[80] Those girls, on the other hand, who (selfishly) pursued their own wishes and desires predictably paid the price for their headstrong natures. One such character was Rachel Curtis, the heroine of Charlotte Yonge's *The Clever Woman of the Family*, whose determination to pursue knowledge instead of putting herself at the service of her family led to tragedy, albeit before she is redeemed by her marriage and her new-found happiness as a wife and mother.[81] Redemption is another key theme of both the religious and secular literature directed at women. The pious woman was repeatedly pitted against the heathen man, and the heroine, by exhibiting all the ideal feminine qualities, eventually wins over her man with marriage as the natural conclusion.[82]

The image of the daughter who sacrifices her own desires for the good of her family was, then, pervasive in secular and religious literature for girls throughout Europe until the end of the century. They were complemented by more practical works, clearly influenced by Rousseau, which instructed girls in how to be a good wife. In France the popular *Première année d'èconomie domestique* published in 1893, preached subservience to the husband and offered advice on how to please him, rejecting book-learning in favour of good grooming, a silent disposition and the ability to make a good omelette.[83] Sarah Stickney Ellis's training manuals for girls were packed with advice on how to fill the day productively, for a good middle-class wife could not be permitted to idle away her hours, a view promulgated by the author William Cowper (1731–1800), the creator of the term 'angel in the house'. 'Absence of occupation is not rest,/ A mind quite vacant is a mind distressed' were lines that influenced a wealth of didactic novels.[84]

By the end of the century a new kind of girls' literature began to appear which, to some degree, recognised the changing nature of opportunities for girls. Coupled with the extension of education and in the wake of the acknowledgement that marriage and domesticity was not certain for many women, the appearance of girls' magazines such as *Girl's Own Paper* in Britain, first published in 1883, offered new kinds of role models in a new kind of style whilst simultaneously sending the message that marriage and motherhood was still the ideal state. Containing fiction, fashion and home tips, practical advice and a readers' column, *Girl's Own Paper* continued to evoke the romantic feminine ideal with its stories on how to meet the right man and warnings of the perils of spinsterhood, and it was not until the 1920s that it spoke to girls in a language which recognised wider educational and employment opportunities. The readers of *Girl's Own Paper* were warned in no uncertain terms that marriage could not be every girl's destiny although it remained the ultimate aim.[85] The female heroines of popular literature began, gradually, to reflect the changes in women's opportunities and expectations. Such girls had resilient and resourceful characters, they had the capacity to cope with unexpected problems and stress. And yet, such mental and physical strength was not generally used to the heroine's personal advantage at the expense of home and domesticity; rather such women became 'home goddesses', professional, managerial women who had much to offer their future husbands or else they took on roles such as missionaries which allowed them to reinforce their femininity outside the home.[86]

The end of the century heralded a subtle shift in the messages conveyed to girls via reading matter and the education system. The demographic situation in much of western Europe had forced a reconsideration of the belief that women's only true role was marriage and motherhood. Structural changes in the agricultural and industrial economies resulted in new employment opportunities for women in teaching and the 'caring professions' such as nursing and missionary work overseas. Magazines began to prepare their readers for a scenario which included, even if it did not exactly celebrate, women's independence from men, motherhood and domesticity. Fictional literature began to feature a new type of heroine typified by Hilde and Daisy in the 1906 novel *Studierte Mädel*, who graduated from grammar school and went on to study medicine at university.[87] Schools did likewise, introducing vocational training for middle-class girls. This is not to say that the woman at the centre of the home, 'the household fairy', had disappeared, but rather she had been professionalised and constructed as a more realistic character who, with the relevant training, might be able to cope with life's challenges.

CONCLUSIONS

Learning to be a woman in nineteenth-century Europe was not a one-way process in which women uncritically absorbed the messages imparted in the home, the school and in their reading matter. However, the uniformity of the message and the sheer volume of literature in this period indicates that lessons in femininity were extraordinarily pervasive and mutually reinforcing. Although the prescriptive ideology of domesticity for women and the concept of separate spheres had been around for at least a century or so, it was undoubtedly in the course of the nineteenth century that this set of ideas was elaborated and deepened so that by mid-century the construction of femininity was taking place on several different levels and in many different places, but all were singing from the same hymn sheet. The similarities in the lessons taught to girls of all social classes and in different parts of Europe are remarkable, although the ways in which the messages were interpreted and acted upon were dependent on the constraints or opportunities determined by social class, relative stages of industrial growth and individual determination.

We should remain sceptical of the degree to which the ideology of domesticity was internalised. Passive acceptance of what may have been interpreted as bourgeois values seems unlikely, although it is clear that girls were receptive to the lessons in femininity incorporating cleanliness, piety, orderliness and so on, especially if they aimed for a better life than that of their parents. Interestingly, women who made their way in public life were often closer to their father than their mother. Fanny Lewald was devoted to her father who encouraged her to develop her intellectual interests, whilst her relationship with her mother, the archetypal middle-class Jewish woman in Fanny's eyes, was always difficult. Similarly, Helene Lange, who was to become one of Germany's leading feminists, regarded her father as her saviour in that he permitted her to defy conventional expectations of a middle-class girls' upbringing and education.[88] Formal schooling, especially at secondary level, reached few girls before the final decades of the century and in eastern and southern Europe girls had to wait even longer. Female literacy rates, though, were certainly improving and the reach of prescriptive literature and popular novels expanded rapidly. Those who did read women's periodicals or domestic novels could interpret their messages in a number of ways – admiring the tragic heroines of popular novels for instance, or finding in domestic advice books and even some literature a platform for women's power within the home and a recognition of women's skill. The authors of

French literature for middle-class women often portrayed maternity as a source of strength and inspiration which provided a spiritual foundation for self-discovery.[89] Neither should we assume that the seemingly uniform and pervasive lessons in femininity produced a shared notion of what it was to be feminine. The etiquette advice proffered in ladies' magazines served to distinguish a particular social class from other women; the domestic education provided in elementary girls' schools similarly identified the femininity of working-class girls as founded upon practical domesticity.

Self-sacrifice and service to others were the watchwords of nineteenth-century teachings on femininity but, at the same time, the identification of the woman with the home suggested that the domestic sphere could, and even should, be a centre of female power – a space where the special female qualities could be used to positive effect as the evangelicals had proposed in the 1780s. Women themselves began to realise that their role in the home was a springboard to participation in public life, that the qualities they exhibited in the domestic sphere might be transported outside. Women's moral superiority and religious vocation provided a platform for their public action beyond the family in ways that did not compromise their femininity.

Part II

◆

PRIVATE LIVES, PUBLIC WORLDS

Chapter 3

◆

MARRIAGE

The vast majority of European women in the nineteenth century married. For all the incantations to women that the married state was a duty, an honour and a joy, it was also an economic necessity. It was expected that girls would marry, and much of their girlhood was spent in preparation for this eventuality. Yet, a significant proportion of women in all European societies – up to around 20 per cent in some communities – were lifelong single women, or spinsters as they were known. Others separated or divorced their partners and most married women eventually became widows because of men's shorter life expectancy. Consequently marriage took up only part of a woman's adult life.

Transient though it was, marriage remained a woman's ideal. Within marriage, those lessons in femininity learned since childhood could be put into practice. To be a wife conferred certain virtues on a woman as well as some power. In law, marriage legitimised the subordination of the wife by defining her as the property of her husband. In most jurisdictions she had no independent existence. In reality things were much more complex. Relations between husbands and wives rarely conformed to the gender roles depicted in sermons, conduct books and romantic novels. Everyday reality for the majority of marriages was messy, characterised by negotiation, compromise and sometimes conflict. Marriage was about the distribution of power and authority, the use of resources, the division of labour and the expression of sentiment. However, during the nineteenth century the institution and conduct of marriage did undergo some changes. Sometimes this is explained as the transition from the patriarchal to the companionate form of marriage.

But it can also be regarded as a gradual accommodation of women's needs. By the end of the century a small group of women had rejected marriage altogether, preferring to live a life of single independence. The majority of European women still married, but their expectations were higher than those of their mothers and grandmothers. They were also more critical of their husbands for not fulfilling their expectations; and for a small but growing number of women, their greater economic independence allowed them ultimately to use the final sanction of the divorce court.

CHOOSING A SPOUSE

In a world in which marriage stood at the heart of social and economic life, both sentiment and economic interests governed the choice of a spouse. A woman's best chances of economic survival and moral standing depended in large part on her marital status. Women who did not marry were generally less well off, and in some communities were pitied or became figures of suspicion. Most people recognised that marriage was a partnership addressed to the tasks of bringing up children, economic survival and mutual support. Practical attributes such as strength, competence and, in a woman, fertility, were important amongst the rural lower classes and bear comparison with the mechanisms at work amongst the upper and middle classes for whom love and physical attraction had to be balanced with the ability of the future spouse to cement dynastic or business networks. It was rare, then, for love to conquer all, and this was less likely amongst the rich, since parents continued to have considerable influence over a daughter's marriage choice. When Gertrude Bell, the daughter of a wealthy industrialist, fell in love with a low-grade British diplomat in Persia and announced their engagement to her parents, she was informed of their disapproval and ordered to return home immediately to England. Her choice of husband was not acceptable on account of his being an 'impecunious diplomat'. The poor man died shortly after and Getrude never married.[1]

The case of German aristocrat Sophie von Hatzfeldt, who was matched with her cousin Edmund in 1822 at the age of 17, is a prime example of the failed arranged marriage. The union was designed to mend the rifts between two branches of this aristocratic Rhineland family and to produce a male heir. Edmund, at 24, was already experienced with women and, some might say, calculating and cynical in agreeing to marry his young cousin. It soon became clear that this dynastic marriage of convenience provided him with a veneer of respectability whilst he continued his extramarital affairs. The marriage was a disaster for Sophie who was subjected to cruel and callous behaviour at the hands of her husband and the Hatzfeldt family, who refused to allow her a means of escape for fear of damaging their reputation. When finally, after 25 years, the couple clashed in the divorce court, Sophie's case was seen to embody 'all the inequalities of the ancien regime', and the marriage was portrayed as a symbol of the abuses of aristocratic privilege.[2] The Hatzfeldt affair was a *cause célèbre* but mainly because the nature of the relationship was seen as an anachronism in the politically and economically turbulent 1840s. In court, Sophie was portrayed as the ideal wife and mother. She carried out her duty of bringing up her first son 'with an ardour which far exceeded the tenderness of a loving mother' and she 'was full of gentleness, goodness and kindness' towards her servants. In the end the Hatzfeldt affair came to represent more than just a warning that the arranged marriage was no longer appropriate; it also represented a turning point in the nature of the conjugal relationship in the nineteenth century. Edmund symbolised the patriarchal marriage model, outmoded and unworkable. Sophie came to stand for women's new expectations for a marriage that encompassed companionship, reciprocity and a recognition of a women's desire for autonomy within her domain.

Amongst the professional and commercial classes, marriages were central to successful business affairs; a good choice of partner could cement or even transform the fortunes of men who married into money, expertise and valuable networks. Sexual attraction was a secondary consideration. When Caroline Michaelis was married to a doctor ten years her senior in 1784 she commented, 'My fondness for him does not bear the mark of blazing emotions . . . It will last because it is not excessive.'[3] It was not uncommon for a young man to find a future wife in the family of his employer or business partner; such marriages, as well as those between close relations, served to keep things in the family. 'Marriage was the economic and social building block for the middle class.'[4] In Hamburg, the close ties between the great legal and commercial families were cemented by marriage. Within the powerful Amsinck family, for instance, marriages were conducted with lawyers, senators and merchants (or their daughters), thus maintaining the economic power and political influence of this family dynasty.[5] This is not to say that marriage was a purely economic relationship; many middle-class marriages could be characterised as sentimental, even passionate. But, most of the time, love was inspired by cool judgement rather than passion. The choice of marriage partner amongst the west European bourgeoisie was an altogether more pragmatic affair by the middle of the century. There was little chance that the daughters of the new middle classes would meet unsuitable matches in their round of balls and social gatherings, so class compatibility was rarely an issue. Thus, girls could be permitted an element of free choice governed by the emotions. Potential marriage partners were judged not only by their wealth and connections, but also by their character. 'He is just what a young man ought to be,' remarks Jane Bennet to her sister in Jane Austen's *Pride and Prejudice*. Mr Bingley was pronounced to be 'sensible, good-humoured, lively . . . so much at ease, with such perfect good breeding'. 'He is also handsome,' replied her sister, 'which a young man ought likewise to be, if he possibly can. His character is thereby complete.'[6] Amongst the industrial and merchant classes, although free choice appeared to reign, a degree of subtle family control remained. Richard Potter, father of nine daughters, exercised a shrewd control over their choice of marriage partners. Most of the girls married men of whom he approved – a barrister, a member of parliament and a merchant banker amongst them – but he was less enthusiastic when Blanche Potter became engaged to the surgeon William Cripps, who was described as 'at first sight repellent, almost unclean looking, with the manners and conversation of a clever cad'.[7] Nevertheless the marriage went ahead but Blanche, like her sisters, received a marriage settlement which allowed her some degree of financial security and protection of her family's assets if the marriage went bad.

By the 1840s the notion of the arranged marriage was increasingly coming under attack. Romantic fiction, exemplified by Friedrich Schlegel's *Lucinda*, published in 1799, proposed a new conception of marriage founded on the emotions and sexual intimacy. In 1817 the German *Brockhaus* encyclopaedia defined marriage as 'a life-long relationship between two persons of the opposite sex . . . which in its perfection is based on love.'[8] Women who had experience of a loveless union began to speak publicly of their unhappiness, influenced by the romantic emphasis on love as the only true foundation for an emotionally and sexually fulfilling marriage. The German writer Louise Aston (1814–71) married, when just 17, a man 'who was a stranger to my heart before the idea of love had been revived in me'. She questioned the conventional view that marriage was, first and foremost, a financial contract. Aston was the daughter of a countess and a pastor who themselves had married for love but whose relationship had been damaged by constant financial insecurity. Aston was urged to wed a man with solid economic credentials. She did just this, marrying the English industrialist Samuel Aston, but for her there existed an antithesis between love and marriage, inclination and duty, heart and conscience.[9] In her 1847 novel *Aus dem Leben einer Frau*, published two years after her separation from her husband, she presented a thinly veiled autobiographical portrait of her unhappy marriage. In Germany some of the most radical critiques of marriage were formulated by women writers of the period of the 1848 revolutions, most of whom belonged to religious dissenting groups. Although not rejecting marriage as an institution, they did reject the arranged marriage on the grounds that it could not fail to incorporate the subordination of the wife. Instead, love was regarded as the key to a successful and equal marriage. For the German Catholic dissenter Bertha Traun it was not enough that her 'entire family represented a picture of an honest, bourgeois and moral life and household', since 'the *heart* of the relationship of the married couple . . . was not satisfactory in that their characters no longer suited each other and the spiritual revival of [the] wife was a burden for the [husband].' 'Love cannot be construed as a duty', wrote Bertha to her husband of 15 years; 'love is the only ethical ground for marriage.'[10]

Some middle-class women simply refused to be married off to the most suitable match. Lily Braun, socialist feminist, passionate and strong willed, was critical from the outset of the social conventions of her upper-class upbringing, commenting in 1889: 'I will be allowed only a marriage of convenience, so I probably won't marry at all'. At the same time she was well aware of the pitfalls of passion: 'There was one man who talked to me of love, of eternal love indeed, and what became of it? It went away or passed on to every – pretty face!' In fact Lily was unable to marry the love of her life, a distant cousin some 20 years older, owing to his family's disapproval, but she went on to establish for herself an independent life of letters and radical politics before her first brief marriage to Georg von Gizycki, a socialist, atheist, wheelchair-bound professor – truly a marriage of heart and mind – and after his death to the socialist, Jewish, twice-divorced Heinrich Braun.[11] Neither of these men would have likely met with family acclamation.

Amongst the rural and urban working classes the choice of marriage partner was much the same: rational choice leavened by affection. Decisions had to be influenced by economic realities – an explanation for the relatively high age at marriage in most of north-west Europe. The 'European marriage pattern' identified by demographers for the early modern period, characterised by both a relatively late average age of marriage (around 23 years for women and 26 years for men) and a high proportion of people who never married (up to 20 per cent), has been linked to the belief common in north-western Europe that a couple should start their married life economically independent. By this age they had inherited property, served an apprenticeship or saved sufficient money and goods to start married life on a sound footing. In some German states, couples were not permitted to marry until they could prove they had the means to set up an independent household and would not be a drain on the poor rate; consequently few Germans married under the age of 20.[12] In Mediterranean Europe, on the other hand, marriage was almost universal, the proportion of singletons smaller, and age at marriage somewhat lower, especially for women, who tended to marry older men.[13]

Few made a commitment without a sense of being able to guarantee a reasonable standard of living. But physical attraction and mutual affection also played a part in determining spousal choice. In the Vendée region of France, a fairly free choice of marriage partner prevailed amongst rural inhabitants and premarital sexual relations were normal. Here pregnancy simply brought a marriage forward. Elsewhere, such as in Brittany, pre-marital pregnancy was not acceptable; it devalued a woman's 'currency'. Throughout peasant society, though, couples exchanged love tokens such as carved spoons, rings and scarves, and openly declared their love for one another in ways we might regard as less than flattering. 'I think you're so lovely, my great big darling', read the words on a card from the Vendée, 'that I can't do better than compare you to a field of young cabbages before the caterpillars have been through it.'[14] In Italy it was said that a girl with 'well kept hands' would not be an industrious worker and therefore a poor spouse.[15] In a society where strength and skill were important attributes in a potential farm wife, physical beauty was subordinated to good health and the ability to work. To state, as Borscheid does, that 'everywhere, love was in general nothing more than a thin whitewash covering the real material interests' is to simplify a complicated arrangement involving money and possessions but also future prospects, status and respectability as well as affection.[16]

Choice of spouse amongst the lower classes was not free from regulation but arguably women were subject to greater controls and less freedom of movement than men. To be a female singleton in the lower classes was to be either for ever in the service of others or to risk a life of economic hardship. John Gillis suggests that in southern England around the turn of the eighteenth century women were under particular pressure to marry early owing to limited employment opportunities and inadequate poor relief.[17] In these circumstances, marriage could bring a woman work through her husband, a practice especially common in parts of lowland Scotland where the bondage system prevailed (a system whereby male farm labourers were contracted to employ a wife).[18] By contrast, in industrial regions of Europe women stayed at home longer, saved their money and would not be rushed into an early marriage, especially in areas where young male immigrants outnumbered the local women.[19] As women's economic independence grew, they began to be more discriminating in their choice of spouse and timing of marriage.

By the second half of the century, marriage was being transformed from an economic institution to a romantic one, and the wedding came to symbolise a break with, rather than a continuation of, previous lives. Amongst the working classes, a wedding was the culmination of a close and often sexual relationship, and the ritual merely marked the creation of a new household and the assumption of new responsibilities by the husband and wife. The widespread practice of common-law marriage, cohabitation and prenuptial sexual relations, meant that marriage was merely the public recognition of a private arrangement. The couple wore their best clothes but otherwise preparations were limited and the wedding took place at any convenient time. This form of marriage continued for the working classes well into the twentieth century. However, in the Victorian period the middle classes made the wedding into a female rite of passage from childish innocence to adult maturity symbolised most potently by the bride's white dress and veil. By 1900 the wedding had become a special ritual; romantic love was a prerequisite for marriage rather than a consequence, and for women the wedding ceremony marked the beginning of a new life.[20]

THE PATRIARCHAL MARRIAGE

Man is the rugged lofty pine
That frowns on many a wavebeat shore;
Woman the graceful slender vine
Whose curling tendrils round it twine.
And deck its rough bark sweetly o'er . . .[21]

It was commonplace in the nineteenth century to portray the marriage partnership using the imagery of the sturdy tree and the slender vine; the tree was the husband – solid, strong and permanent; the vine was the wife, dependent on the tree to climb, otherwise in danger of being crushed underfoot.[22] The imagery is a crude but striking representation of the marriage relationship as it was depicted in the prescriptive literature and in the romantic fiction of mid-century. The young woman about to be married in Dinah Craik's novel *Agatha's Husband* published in 1853, was advised that her husband was a tree upon which she might lean, but: 'Always remember that it is a noble forest oak, and that you are only its dews or its sunshine, or its ivy garland. You never must attempt to come between it and the skies.'[23] The symbolism of the tree and the vine applies particularly aptly to the imagined domestic arrangements of the new middle classes. Yet, the central image of the independent husband and the dependent wife bears little relationship to reality for that group or for any other. In most marriages the dependence was mutual; neither spouse could carry out his or her role without the support of the other.

European law codes certainly upheld a model of marriage based upon male domination and female subordination. According to the Prussian Allgemeines Landrecht of 1794, 'The husband is by nature the head of his family . . . Hence it follows, judging by the sole light of reason, that the husband is master of his own household, and head of his family. And as the wife enters into it of her own accord, she is in some measure subject to his power.'[24] Some Enlightenment writers did reject automatic male authority within marriage on the grounds that the principle was contrary to natural law, but this more egalitarian view of marriage was never translated into law. The French Napoleonic Code of 1804, for instance, did define marriage as a civil contract, stating that 'Husband and wife owe each other fidelity, support and assistance', but Napoleonic prejudices overcame Enlightenment reason in the subsequent paragraph: 'A husband owes protection to his wife; a wife obedience to her husband.' Thereafter the Code legitimated male authority and female subordination by denying the wife independent legal rights: she could not purchase or sell property or take a case to court without the permission of her husband.[25] The legal view that upon marriage the wife became the property of the husband was most clearly articulated by the English legal scholar William Blackstone. His 1756 commentary on marriage law reinforced the notion of the *femme covert* (meaning a woman who was protected by her husband), a simple yet profound concept which was to have far-reaching consequences for married women all over Europe. In Blackstone's interpretation, a married woman did not possess an independent legal existence, she was deemed to be part of her husband's property, implying male protection of his wife but also permitting a husband to abuse his wife without fear of the law.[26] Yet the message from conduct books was more equivocal, reflecting the common-sense view that a relationship based on inequality was not a recipe for happiness. Thus, although the author of *The English Matron*, published in 1846, recognised that marriage should resemble a 'limited monarchy', this was tempered by the assertion that 'marriage was never intended to be a state of subserviency for women . . . the very word "union" implies a degree of equality.'[27] Most men were not tyrants and many wore their authority lightly.

It was often only when marriages broke down that the patriarchal foundation of marriage in a legal and economic sense came to the fore.

Judith Bennett has described marriage before 1800 as 'voluntary egalitarianism shadowed by inequality'.[28] James Hammerton has similarly suggested that in modern Britain married life for the majority of couples was neither starkly patriarchal nor entirely companionate. Most relationships operated flexibly and harmoniously within a framework – legal, economic and cultural – which rested upon patriarchal power.[29] Marriages characterised by mutual happiness and satisfaction – and they were probably the majority – were permitted by a patriarchal system that showed flexibility and modification.[30] Historians have argued that the companionate form increasingly found favour amongst the upper and middle classes during the nineteenth century. However, they have been slower to discard the patriarchal model for the working classes, partly since grossly unequal power relations do seem to pervade the stories of marriages amongst this group. The persistence of this view of working-class marriages as unequal and hierarchical is, in part, a consequence of the nature of the sources. Our picture of these marriages is drawn from the separation and divorce courts, civil and criminal disputes and from the representation of marriage in popular culture.[31] Conversely, our insight into the apparently more companionate middle-class marriage is based upon personal letters and diaries which provide an intimate view into marriage as it was lived in private rather than as it was fought in public. Marriage for all social classes was an emotional and economic partnership in the nineteenth century. Whilst it is undeniable that, for most of the period, men's greater material resources underpinned their power and authority, in practice most couples aimed for a complementary and companionate working relationship. For some unfortunate women, marriage was a tyranny, but for most it provided a power base in the home, a source of personal, emotional satisfaction, a source of economic support and security, and the guarantee of respectability.

Marriage was supposed to provide the ideal environment for the practice of an idealised femininity, or so the conduct books prescribed, whilst at the same time it was also a form of containment, a means of restricting women's independence. Women experienced a conflict between personal fulfilment through female autonomy in the home and the ideology of service and self-sacrifice learned since childhood. Many women did their best to fulfil the role expected of them but they expected something in return. Marriage was a contract – a financial contract certainly, but it also constituted an unspoken agreement that both spouses would respect each other's needs and do their best to support the common household. Increasingly for women of the middle classes, the patriarchal marriage was unworkable as the following case studies illustrate.

Wilhelmine Burmeister from Hamburg married her husband in 1849 when she was aged 24. When her marriage foundered a year later, Wilhelmine made it clear how she regarded the institution of marriage: 'The essence of man lies in his innermost soul, a marriage which has been founded upon Christianity, should be a happy one.'[32] Wilhelmine had married her Christian schoolteacher husband on the assumption that the couple would work together for the salvation of young people. She had great expectations for her marriage. Not only did she expect it to be a spiritual partnership, but she also regarded it as a springboard for her own ambitions as a schoolteacher. Her husband had promised that she would be permitted to open a school for girls alongside his own establishment. Yet, she was to be cruelly disappointed. Although she opened her school for girls she found the double burden of housework and schoolwork impossible to bear alone, especially when the couple moved to larger premises. Her husband criticised her housekeeping skills, prompting Wilhelmine to note that 'he had no concept of the position of the housewife in the household to say nothing of what one understood by an orderly bourgeois household.' Moreover, Herr Burmeister turned out to be parsimonious in the extreme, denying his wife sufficient housekeeping money so that she was forced to argue with him for every pfennig, and refusing to hire servants to help her in the house while she taught handicrafts in the school. 'Can a wife have respect for a husband', asked Wilhelmine Burmeister, 'whose meanness leads to blackmail?' She continued: 'Can she treat him with honour and affection when he, brazen-faced, declares to be a lie what she has seen with her own eyes? How can she not despise such a man, when she remembers that the same man in the school and outside preaches with devotion the observance of Christ?'

This woman was trapped by the conflict between her idea of a spiritual partnership and her husband's more conventional notion of a marriage characterised by rigid and unequal gender roles. Whilst her husband wanted an angel in the house, she saw her marriage as a means of achieving her own ambitions. He was unwilling to accept that responsibility for household management entitled his wife to a degree of power and authority in that domain. His criticism of her household skills and his refusal to provide her with the necessary means to run an extensive home indicated his unease at his wife's sense of self. His petty meanness suggests he was always unhappy with his wife's independence. Wilhelmine Burmeister was lucky in one respect: Hamburg civil law permitted divorce.

The Burmeister marriage was not unusual. For a woman, marriage signified that she had reached maturity and had attained a certain respectable status within her social group. Such women were unlikely to act in a docile and subordinate fashion. In the thirty-year marriage of Robert and Charlotte Bostock of London, a similar domestic drama unfolded which pivoted around Robert's recurrent business problems, his criticism of his wife's household expenditure, her desire for visitors to the house, and Charlotte's absence from home when he believed she should be available to assist him with the business, a chemist shop. Robert frequently became hysterical and violent towards his wife, his 'paroxysms of excitement' often being sparked off by seemingly trivial incidents which nevertheless signified to him the erosion of his marital authority.[33] Charlotte found herself torn between carrying out her wifely duty to soothe her husband and maintaining an autonomous existence as a lower-middle-class woman, which involved shopping, visiting, theatre-trips and receiving visitors.

It is the action of husbands like Robert Bostock, in what has been described as a 'persistent and desperate attempt to assert patriarchal supremacy', that provides the clearest indication of women's changing expectations by mid-century.[34] Men of all social classes increasingly saw their patriarchal privileges under attack but they felt it all the more keenly when men themselves were suffering an erosion of their authority. Men, whose dominance at home was undermined by economic insecurity, developed an obsession with their marital rights and 'a preoccupation with authority [which], when challenged, so often moved to the point of neurotic obsession'.[35] Thus, we can perhaps understand – although not condone – Herr Burmeister's petty attempts to control his wife's household expenditure and his refusal to allow her autonomy in the running of the household. Similarly, Robert Bostock's violent behaviour was not entirely unconnected to his business failures, although his financial problems neither fully explain nor excuse his aggression. Women, on the other hand, although not necessarily questioning their husbands' authority, saw an opportunity to negotiate a role within marriage that better suited their economic and social position in the household and the community.

Such contests for power and authority within marriage were not restricted to the middle classes. Marriages amongst the working classes were similarly having to adjust to changes affecting the household economy and the gendered division of labour within it, leading to a tension between the ideal of the domestic wife and the reality of the resourceful woman. In southern Germany at the beginning of the century, for example, the shifting nature of

rural production and the organisation of work as a consequence of the intensification of agriculture, resulted in greater female autonomy as men spent
more time away from home. Women began to take control of the purse-strings
since they had greater access to cash from their production of cash crops –
flax, hemp and yarn – which formed the raw materials for industry.[36] In these
circumstances, wives regarded it as their prerogative to allocate material
resources as they judged fit, but husbands saw this control of the income as
an abuse of female power in the household and an unwarranted incursion
into the husband's domain. Such changes in the household presented women
with an opportunity to negotiate a role in marriage which better reflected
their economic position. In the Rhineland, for instance, the 1840s witnessed
extensive impoverishment, especially amongst the artisanal sector and the
labouring classes. Men saw their claim to economic dominance disappear
whilst their wives strove to hold the household together by finding outside
employment or taking in lodgers. In an economic context that deprived men
of their ability to fulfil their side of the contractual marriage relationship,
husbands resorted to challenging their wives where they had most power,
in the household. Just as Robert Bostock had thrown his weight around –
literally and metaphorically – so the impoverished men of northern Germany
resorted to drinking, interfering in day-to-day household affairs and committing violence against their wives as a means of asserting their waning
authority.[37] For example, Gerhard Janssen, a cabinet maker by trade but with
a serious drink problem, lost his customers and was thus unable to fulfil the
breadwinner role. His wife Theodore endured years of abuse and violence
at his hands before divorcing him in 1842 on the grounds of almost daily
torture.[38] In cases such as this the husband forfeited his claim to authority
since he had lost his claim to be a household provider, but he translated his
frustration into the assertion of other forms of power. James Hammerton
argues that such conflicts around household management possessed a
'uniquely middle-class character'.[39] They did not. Husbands' confidence in
their domestic sovereignty and wives' demands for greater companionship in
marriage was not rooted in some middle-class gendered identity. Throughout the nineteenth century, women's struggle with the tension between the
ideal of domestic femininity and personal autonomy cut across class boundaries. Women of all social classes were demanding at the very least that their
marriage was founded upon reciprocity and mutual respect; many, through
their actions and words, showed that they demanded more than this. Moreover, across much of Protestant Europe by the end of the century divorce
was more accessible, women's rights in respect of married women's property

and child custody had been improved and women's position in the paid workforce provided some with greater economic independence. By 1900 the image of the male sturdy oak and the female slender vine was no longer applicable to most marriages.

THE LOVE-MATCH

In 1847 Elizabeth Barratt wrote of her marriage to the poet Robert Browning, 'He loves me more every day . . . If all married people lived as happily as we do how many good jokes it would spoil!' Staying in Pisa having been married just seven months, Elizabeth wrote exuberantly to her sisters of the joy, affection and passion of her marriage. 'Robert's goodness and tenderness are past speaking of . . . He reads to me, talks and jests to make me laugh, tells me stories, improvises verses in all sorts of languages . . . There has been a hundred times as much attention, tenderness, nay, *flattery* even, ever since [the marriage] . . . We never *do* quarrel!'[40] This letter provides a window on to the emotional and sexual intimacy within the private confines of marriage. Middle-class marriages, especially, have often been portrayed as lacking close physical and emotional intimacy, yet as Peter Gay has argued, 'The bourgeois experience was far richer than its expression . . . and it included a substantial measure of sensuality for both sexes'.[41] Amongst the British upper and middle classes it has been said that 'most Victorians liked to think that they married for love'.[42] Certainly, women expected their marriage to contain mutual affection and were cruelly disappointed when it did not.

The marriage based on a union of hearts and minds was a common model amongst the European middle classes. For women such as the German Henriette Schleiermacher, twice married, each time to a pastor, marriage was an emotional and an intellectual partnership. She saw her first marriage in 1804 as a joint vocation, in which both partners would experience intimacy and self-knowledge. Similarly, her second marriage she imagined as an intimate partnership: 'I could speak to you about anything and everything', she said of her husband Ernst. 'You are not to me as a man, but like a delicate maiden, so innocent, so like a child, and this to me is a delicious feeling.' Ernst, for his part, was besotted with his young wife, writing to her of his 'irresistible desire' to see her; 'I could never have loved any other woman as I love you.'[43] Henriette and Ernst's marriage was founded on a belief in equality: 'thus we shall ever be as one, and will not enquire if or why the one is superior or inferior to the other.' The pair were soulmates who regarded marriage as an institution within which each might grow and experience fulfilment. So-called political marriages had similar foundations. The union of Margaret Gladstone and Ramsey MacDonald at the opposite end of the century was based on mutual attraction and a shared commitment to socialism. Although the match was an unconventional one in terms of their quite different class backgrounds, Margaret was convinced they were well suited: 'the contrast between our upbringing is encouraging, not despairing: we have come by different paths to the same beliefs and aims.' Margaret was right; she described her marriage as 'blessed by a growing happiness as all true love ought to be'.[44]

Such unions of heart and mind could be regarded as exceptional. The typical bourgeois marriage was supposedly asymmetrical, in terms both of the respective age and experience of the partners and of their different gender roles. Both types are, to some extent, caricatures. Most marriages trod a middle course: couples aimed for a spiritual, emotional and intellectual relationship within a framework of separate spheres. Amongst the Hamburg bourgeoisie in the first half of the century, both spouses had high expectations of a 'union of the soul' but they did not reject fundamental gender inequalities as is demonstrated in the marriage of Ferdinand and Karoline Beneke. The couple resolved to pursue jointly the path of spiritual and intellectual growth – they studied literary and historical texts together every morning. Yet, Ferdinand remarked: 'Of incalculable value for my happiness in life is that Caroline has a degree of sympathy for these spiritual efforts, and is firmly convinced, apart from her obligations as mother and housewife, to accompany me down the road of spiritual development on this earth.'[45] Marriages such as this formed what Ann-Charlotte Trepp terms marriage work: 'understanding and intimacy on one side, subordination and inequality on the other.'[46] And it was these marriages which often grew and matured into intimate and long-lasting unions.

We know more about couples' intellectual relations than we do about their sexual relations. Middle-class women may have been ignorant about sexual intercourse when they married, but it would be wrong to assume that they for ever harboured feelings of shame and disgust about the sex act. In Britain it is the postwar publications of the sex-reformer and birth control advocate Marie Stopes that are frequently credited with improving the sex lives of thousands of married couples, but the belief that women were entitled to sexual fulfilment was already current in the nineteenth century, evidenced by the French bestseller *Monsieur, Madame et Bébé* which first appeared in 1866, advocating and encouraging sexual love within marriage.[47] Few women would admit in public to the enjoyment of sex for fear of being branded lewd or little more than a prostitute. One who did was Emma Inhoffen, the wife and soon to be divorcee of a Bonn industrialist. 'The most important thing in marriage is sexual satisfaction', she said in 1900; but with her husband, 'It's like making love with an old man.'[48] Happier couples, though, did express their sensuality and erotic passion for one another. 'I know on Thursday I shall be lying in your arms, close to your bosom, will press you to my heart, will be by you and in you, body and soul' were the unequivocal words written by Friedrich Perthes to his wife Caroline in 1799 during one of their separations.[49]

Love and sexual passion are harder to detect in the marriages of the lower classes, or at least in the romantic and sentimental form we discover in the letters of their social superiors. The relative scarcity of written sources detailing intimacy amongst men and women of the working classes has resulted in historians, like nineteenth-century commentators, representing working-class sexuality as brutal, immoral and divorced from sentiment. Emile Zola's description of the sexual relationships within a French mining community in his 1885 novel *Germinal* is typical of this tendency to portray sexual passion as animalistic. Moreover, historians' focus on premarital sex and illegitimacy amongst the working classes gives the impression that sex was instrumental (for instance, as a test of a woman's fertility prior to a marriage promise) or recreational but rarely an expression of love or passion. In industrial centres the combination of exhausted husbands and women's constant efforts to keep the family fed and clean in overcrowded housing and with insufficient resources may well have resulted in a 'deadening of emotion'.[50] There have been few attempts to present an alternative to the casual sex seemingly devoid of affection which has been described as 'hit and run'.[51] Alternatively, the expression of unbridled passion is interpreted as uncontrolled sexual permissiveness presaging a rise in illegitimacy rates. Yet, in the nineteenth century, partly as a consequence of the creation of a rural and urban propertyless class, affectionate relationships became the norm.[52] Letters that do survive suggest passion and intimacy no less than that presumed amongst the middle and upper classes. In the 1880s, in his frequent letters to his beloved girlfriend Bruce Barclay, Shetland cooper William Brack could not have been more categorical in his love for her.

Dear Bruce,
You should not vex yourself. You surely have seen enough of me to lead you to understand that I love you day and night. You are never out of my mind how I love you . . . Dear Bruce, O how I love you ever dear ever dear ever dear, your affectionate lover xxxxxxxxxxxxx.[53]

Marriage that was no longer determined by property considerations meant romantic encounters were more likely to result in matrimony. Couples separated, sometimes by thousands of miles, did often keep up a regular correspondence which included romantic poetry, frequent expressions of love, and promises of eventual marriage. When James Johnston left his home in Shetland in 1858 to seek his fortune on the seas, he wrote regularly to his fiancée Catherine in letters expressing his love and desire to marry her. In 1864 from Sydney he wrote, 'my dear it is a long time since we parted so I thought that you were got cold towards me but I hope that [it will] get a little warmer when we meet next.' A year later, from New Zealand, James was as eager as ever to express his affection for his wife to be: 'Dear Catherine there is one thing that I can say, that if you have not my body with you, you have my heart and where the heart is the body will be also some time, and I hope it will not be long before that time . . .'.[54] Unfortunately, when he finally returned home he refused to fulfil his marriage promise and Catherine, understandably after waiting nine years, took him to court for breach of promise. In this case perhaps James' liking for romantic language got the better of him, but his willingness to express his feelings indicates a ready use of romantic rhetoric to woo the opposite sex and that it was as familiar in working-class as in middle-class circles. It is rare, then, to hear plebeians speaking publicly of love for one another, but expressions of mutual support and affection indicate that marriage was perceived as an intimate partnership amongst the working classes. A Scottish cobbler and his wife were described as 'exemplary in conjugal felicity as they were in their habits of industry and sobriety'; kindness, warm affection, reciprocity, patience and mutual esteem seem to characterise the loving relationships recorded by the 'respectable' working classes.[55] Couples started out together with expectations of more than just a tolerable and viable relationship.

Women, especially, looked elsewhere for affection and passion when it was lacking in their marriage. Divorces involving adulterous wives illustrate women's unapologetic search for love and passion. When Hamburger Hans Berott discovered his wife Caroline in bed with her lover in 1846, she countered that her husband 'had not once fulfilled his marital duty and had continually neglected her'. Caroline thus justified her adultery on the grounds that her husband did not fulfil her sexual needs. Her adulterous affair appears to have been a passionate relationship as evidenced by the letters that she exchanged with her lover, containing promises of undying love and eventual marriage. 'O my darling girl', wrote Christian to his lover Caroline, 'don't forget what your true heart has promised me . . . Oh Caroline my love don't forget that I promise to be faithful to you until death.' And Caroline replied, 'it is my greatest heartfelt wish that in time I will marry you.'[56] Marriage, then, was still regarded by most as the most appropriate sign of one's love for another and the most fitting place for the passionate expression of that mutual affection.

MARRIAGE BREAKDOWN

Few marriages broke down irretrievably in the nineteenth century. Death of a spouse was more likely to bring about the end of a marriage than separation or divorce. It is not until after the First World War that Europeans began to divorce on a mass scale. Even in states where divorce was widely available, rates were low in comparison with modern times. In Scotland in the period 1770–1830 there were just 786 cases.[57] In Prussia, another state where access to divorce was relatively easy, the number of cases was considerably higher – an average of more than 5000 judgements a year by the 1900s, but this represented only 15 divorces per 100,000 population compared with a rate of 60 in the 1920s.[58] Even in England and Wales where the 1857 Divorce Act made divorce much more accessible, there was no significant increase in the rate until after the First World War.[59] Across Europe there existed a variety of religious, legal and financial impediments to formal marital dissolution. The Roman Catholic Church regarded marriage as indissoluble, with the exception of a few specific grounds for an annulment such as non-consummation of the marriage. Similarly, in the Orthodox Church a wife's adultery could precipitate a separation. In Protestant states, marriage was no longer considered a sacrament so that divorce and remarriage was permissible where civil law codes allowed. To summarise then, civil divorce was available in much of Protestant Europe in the nineteenth century including Scotland, Switzerland, Germany, the Netherlands, Belgium, Sweden and Norway. In France, divorce was not available until 1884, with the exception of the period 1792–1816 when first the revolutionary law permitted divorce equally for men and women for almost any reason, and thereafter the Napoleonic Code offered more restrictive grounds for dissolution. In England and Wales the notorious divorce by Act of Parliament was reformed in 1857. In the Catholic states of Ireland, Spain and Italy, however, marriage was still indissoluble.

From women's point of view, the existence of legal divorce was not necessarily advantageous. There were few states which treated women and men as equals in the divorce courts. The double-standard, whereby a woman's adultery was judged more harshly than that of a man's, was enshrined in divorce legislation in England, France, and in those states under the jurisdiction of the Napoleonic Code. Adultery by a wife was regarded as a greater threat to marriage because of the potential for pregnancy and the birth of a child with an uncertain paternity. Thus, female adultery struck at the heart of the aristocratic or bourgeois marriage on account of the importance of inheritance. By the nineteenth century a woman's adultery was also regarded as a crime against marriage and in turn, the social order. According to one speaker in the British Parliament in 1800:

> All other injuries, when put in the scale of . . . the crime of adultery . . . are as nothing. Is there any other private wrong which produces so many public consequences? The sanctity of marriage, of a contract which is the very foundation of the social world, is violated – religious and moral duties made a sport of – the peace and happiness of families utterly broken up – the protection of daughters destroyed, and their character, though innocent, disparaged in opinion by their mother's dishonour.[60]

The majority of divorce actions on the grounds of adultery were brought by men, but this is partly a reflection of an iniquitous law and partly an indication that men were less tolerant of their wives' infelicities than vice versa. The adulterous woman was a dangerous woman and, with the demise of the disciplinary powers of the church courts by the nineteenth century, the civil courts took on the function of controlling women's sexuality. In the divorce courts women's bodies were a battleground; women were represented as either good mothers or as possessing an unruly sexuality. Adulterous women were disciplined by the granting of a divorce to the husband, and the denial of permission to remarry. 'Innocent' women were revered as mothers or potential mothers, and freed from marriages so they might remarry.

When Anna Cords was divorced in 1835 by her husband Johann, a Hamburg ropemaker, on the grounds of adultery, she was condemned not only for the act of adultery with her husband's apprentice – who was also the lodger in the Cords' household – but also for her alleged failure to conform to bourgeois liberal definitions of ideal womanhood. In the suit filed by her husband, Anna was portrayed as being in possession of an unruly sexuality which the divorce court was called upon to regulate. Johann described in court how, early one morning after hearing his wife creep out of bed, he followed her to the lodger's room where he discovered the pair in bed together. Upon being confronted by her husband, Anna reportedly jumped out of the lodger's bed and cried: 'Ah, you gave me a fright, what are you doing here!' Johann, 'an extremely calm man', was so dismayed he did nothing except cry out in pain the words 'Mother! Mother!' Anna 'openly and unashamedly confessed that she and the apprentice loved one another and could not bear to be apart.' In an argument with the apprentice, Johann 'exercised his rights as head of the household' and ejected him from the living quarters. Some days later, after Anna had left home to live with her lover in neighbouring Altona, the three parties were summoned to police headquarters. The apprentice was requested to leave town for a year and Anna was 'reminded of her duty to return to her husband and to care for her children'. However, Anna and her lover disregarded these injunctions whereby Johann filed for a divorce which he duly received.[61] Johann's honour was restored; Anna was publicly chastised for her unruly sexuality.

Women were the main beneficiaries of the liberalisation of divorce laws across Europe from the 1850s, which not only extended the availability of divorce but also widened the grounds on which a divorce could be obtained. The woman was, more often than not, the weaker partner in a marriage in economic and physical terms. She was more likely to be the victim of domestic violence, more likely to be deserted, and women had fewer economic and cultural resources to survive alone. In London, for instance, a busy port and enlisting centre, the plight of the deserted wife was a common one, with a significant proportion of applications for poor relief at the end of the eighteenth century coming from women abandoned by husbands 'gone to sea' or 'gone abroad'.[62] The liberalisation of divorce was a response to the ideology of domesticity and the belief that women should be protected from male abuses such as drunkenness and sexual promiscuity. Divorce laws, comments Roderick Phillips, were 'part of a complex of paternalistic legislation that sought to protect women from the most harmful implications of their inferior status without attempting to change their status significantly.'[63] Whatever the intention, divorce provided a clean break, the possibility of custody and financial support for any children, and it permitted a woman to remarry. Separation, by contrast, left women in a state of limbo, unable to remarry. It comes as no surprise then, that women consistently formed the majority of plaintiffs – up to 70 per cent – in divorce actions.

Arguably it was the inclusion of cruelty as a legitimate ground for a divorce which was most advantageous for nineteenth-century women. Whether a woman married for love or for material reasons she did not anticipate ill-treatment. It is a fallacy that women fatalistically accepted the 'rule of thumb' which, in England at least, permitted a husband to physically chastise an 'unruly' wife with an instrument no thicker than that digit. Throughout the century, women who had been emotionally and physically abused by their husbands made it plain in the courts that such behaviour was not acceptable.

Antagonistic marriages were often the result of a conflict between a man's expectations of patriarchal dominance and a woman's desire for companionship and respect for her economic and domestic role. Changes in women's economic position could be seen as precipitating marital strife at the same time as some men were struggling to maintain their tenuous hold on their masculine identity. The motif of the 'struggle for the breeches' found in popular literature and songs, as well as political rhetoric, rather crudely represented plebeian marriage as a constant battle of wills, whereby men who were tormented by unruly and assertive wives were justified in using physical force to keep them in check. In the words of one popular song, 'A Fool's Advice to Henpeck'd Husbands':

> When your wife for scolding finds pretences, oh
> Take the handle of a broom,
> not much thicker than your thumb,
> and thwack her till you bring her to her senses, oh.[64]

Yet, ballads which condoned wife-torture were more a commentary on men's unease than a true representation of antagonistic marriage. Certainly, wife-beaters existed, if rarely as cruel and vicious as those depicted in popular songs – such as the husband who was advised to nail his wife's tongue to a growing tree.[65] Some did believe such physical chastisement was acceptable, but in many of the cases heard in the courts, physical abuse was used by men in their frustration at their own inability to fulfil the role expected of them. Domestic violence might also be interpreted as a sign that women were challenging male authority rather than as an indication of a decline of women's status within marriage. The overwhelming preponderance of women as plaintiffs in civil cases and divorce suits involving domestic violence suggests that it was women who were more anxious to question a form of marriage relationship which permitted men to abuse their authority.

Evidence from Britain, France and Germany suggests that men beat their wives when they felt their authority was being undermined. In Glasgow and the north-west of England as well as in parts of rural Germany, artisans in the traditional trades were more likely to beat their wives than other groups, a pattern that may be partially explained by the insecurity of this sector of employment especially in the first few decades of the century. Typical was the case of Agnes and Dominicus Mottmann whose divorce was granted in 1853 in the Rhineland. Dominicus was a master carpenter who had taken to drinking and mistreating his wife. Mottmann apparently felt himself under threat from all sides. His business was in tatters as a result of his drinking and at home he was outnumbered by his wife and her daughter from a former marriage. The couple argued about domestic issues, he rained insults on the women, especially when his wife 'remonstrated with him', destroyed household items and threw his dinner in the face of his wife.[66] The couple lived in a part of Germany undergoing economic crisis, particularly in the artisanal sector which was subject to overcrowding and competition as a result of the dismantling of the guilds. Industry was virtually non-existent.[67] Further south, in Göttingen, similar tensions focused on the decline of artisanal employment and the rise in work for women, predominantly in domestic service, which had a corrosive effect on married life.[68] Although miserable wages for women in most areas of work meant that women were forced to 'trade support for violence', those women who took their husbands to court were prepared to forgo a bad marriage in the knowledge that they would be able to manage alone, at least for a time.[69] In Basel, Switzerland, at the end of the century, women increasingly found work in textile factories and their wages played a significant role in the household finances, but women as wage-earners demanded more from their husbands and a more equal partnership. When the marriage became intolerable their economic independence allowed women to take the initiative and petition for divorce since they could at least envisage life without a husband.[70]

Plebeian marriages were regarded by the middle classes as an 'incomprehensible region', 'where many women were neither ladylike nor deferential, where men struggled to hold on to their authority over them, where "sexual antagonism" was openly acknowledged.'[71] If the middle classes had looked more closely, however, they may have seen more that was familiar to them than they liked to acknowledge. The violent and hysterical outbursts of men like Dominicus Mottmann bear a close relation to the 'paroxysms of excitement' of Robert Bostock; the difference was merely the public nature of lower-class conflict. Women of all social classes who found themselves trapped in a tyrannical marriage experienced similar problems, but by 1914 most European states had provided them with a means of escape.

SPINSTERS

The married state was certainly held up as the desirable norm for women, but for many it was unattainable or undesirable. From around 1850, evidence of a 'surplus' of women in the population fuelled discussion of the problem of the 'redundant' woman. In previous centuries there had always been a relatively high proportion of never-married adults in the population – up to

25 per cent. In the seventeenth and eighteenth centuries, northern Europe with its relatively high age at first marriage of around 26 had more single women than southern European states where women tended to marry younger, but by the end of the eighteenth century women in Italy, Spain and Portugal began to wait longer before marriage.[72] Lifelong single women were still more common in northern Europe, and in towns rather than rural areas, but local conditions such as the availability of work for both sexes, inheritance customs, real wages and the option of alternative ways of life, such as the convent, influenced the proportions of women never marrying in any one state, region or town. In the Haute Loire region of France, some parishes counted up to 25 per cent spinster or widow-headed households; similarly in fishing communities in the far north of Britain up to one-quarter of households were headed by women, the majority either unmarried or widowed.[73] Yet, despite the ubiquity of the spinster, her position has seemingly always been interpreted as marginal, 'a lifetime of peripheral existence . . . a functionless role played out at the margins of other people's lives without even that minimal raison d'être – the possibility of bearing children.'[74] It is no coincidence that accusations of witchcraft focused on the unmarried or masterless woman who was neither protected nor, apparently, sexually fulfilled by a man. In popular literature the spinster acquired negative connotations, she became, as Hufton describes her, a 'sempiternal spoilsport in the orgy of life.'[75] In Fanny Burney's popular novel *Camilla*, Mrs Mittin called herself 'Mrs' even though she was single, because to be thought of as a young widow was far preferable to the alternative: 'and if one is called Miss, people being so soon to think one an old maid, that it's disagreeable.'[76]

More recently, though, the single woman or spinster has been rehabilitated by historians who have insisted that not only was spinsterhood a state of choice for some, but it also permitted a woman to take advantage of opportunities unavailable to her married sisters. For some, spinsterhood has been interpreted as a form of resistance to the confinement of marriage and motherhood. Thus, the asexual, sad, unfulfilled singleton, unable to contract a marriage or kept at home by elderly parents, has been transformed into the independent career or businesswoman, the eternal aunt, if not at the centre then very close to family life, or the woman living in a female partnership.[77] In this process, the term 'spinster' itself has been given back its original meaning – a female spinner – casting off the negative associations of the nineteenth century implying a mean-spirited and bitter old maid.

Through the course of the nineteenth century the popular discourse on the desirability, if not the necessity, of marriage for a woman grew more

insistent as the ideology of domesticity took hold. This is not to underestimate the pressure on women to marry in earlier times, although a fair number
of eighteenth-century women seem to have gone to some lengths to avoid
it and some made positive choices in favour of the single life.[78] However,
by the early nineteenth century, marriage, not trade, came to be seen as a
middle-class woman's means of survival. Consequently, the plight of the
'redundant' woman symbolised to many middle-class commentators a wider
social disorder.[79] To counter the threat they supposedly posed, unmarried
women were urged to find a new respectable role, usually in a pseudo-
domestic context such as the girls' school, the hospital or religious community.
One English advice book of 1858 recommended unmarried women to 'find
some harmless mode of doing active service' on the grounds that in the
absence of such a role 'she inevitably becomes the prey of her own egotism'.[80]
Such admonitions were invariably directed at the middle-class spinster,
and significant numbers responded, although it is not entirely clear whether
institutionalisation was a positive choice for women who were disinclined
to marry or a necessary fall-back for middle-class girls who were in need of
a vocation and a place to live. Unmarried working-class women were perceived as less of a problem since they were more likely to be accommodated
within a household, most often as a domestic servant.

Changing patterns of employment meant that by the mid-nineteenth
century there were areas where women were in high demand as workers,
leading to a notable imbalance in the sex ratio – for example in textile towns
and other concentrations of female employment such as the lace industry in
Nottingham, jute in Dundee and herring-gutting in Shetland – and girls were
warned not to move to these places if they wished to find a mate. The *Girl's
Own Paper* of 1886 warned teenage girls that the chances of finding a husband
even in London were slim, citing the 1881 census figures of 1123 women to
every 1000 men.[81] In Shetland, where the fishing industry accounted for the
long-term absence and the high mortality of men, the average ratio of 131
women to 100 men between 1801 and 1891 resulted in a high proportion of
female-headed households on the islands and a large number of households
containing various combinations of unmarried female relatives: sisters, aunts
and daughters. In rural communities where work opportunities were scarce,
the unmarried needed to be part of a larger household. Survival alone was
very hard. In the more marginal agrarian economies of the Western Isles of
Scotland, many farms came to be run by women as men left to find work
in the towns. But in the more productive agricultural areas, the position of
single women was progressively marginalised. In Ireland at the end of the

century, female labour shifted into the home and women became increasingly dependent upon male heads of households. At the same time the number of women permitted access to the world of full-time housewifery via marriage was shrinking. The options for an unmarried woman in Ireland were limited: emigration was one of the most popular solutions; remaining as an unpaid familial servant was another.[82]

The single life was undoubtedly more difficult for a woman than a man in all kinds of ways. Economically, single women were worse off than their male counterparts. The limited employment opportunities for women and poor wage rates meant that many unmarried women of all social classes existed precariously. The gradual marginalisation of women from the artisan trades in the eighteenth century and the gendered division of labour which accompanied industrialisation, combined to exclude women from male earning privileges. The tendency for middle-class spinsters to find work as governesses and lower-class women to become domestic servants is unsurprising in an economy in which women's work and wages were based on their being wives within a wider household economy. In the absence of a male breadwinner a woman was obliged to find a substitute family to perform a similar function. 'Spinster clustering', whereby a number of unmarried women formed a household, was most likely an economic strategy although we should not rule out the importance of same-sex friendships or unions amongst women of all social classes.[83] Despite these survival strategies, single women were the largest group in receipt of poor relief, especially when they became aged and were unable to undertake paid employment. However, few poor and aged spinsters left their own homes for institutions. Women were keen to retain their independence – around 26 per cent of elderly women in England lived either alone or shared a household with unrelated residents in 1891 – and parishes in England often provided almshouses and cottages to keep them out of the poorhouse.[84] Amongst the middle classes there is some evidence to suggest the image of the desperate ageing spinster living in 'genteel poverty' may be an exaggeration. In the smart west end of Glasgow, by the end of the century spinsters headed 13 per cent of households and some of these women were financially quite well off, either from their own business success or as a result of inheritance.[85]

As definitions of femininity were increasingly predicated upon dependence, unlike in the early modern period, single middle-class women who engaged in trade or who acted as independent businesswomen were in some danger of compromising their femininity.[86] In the words of Sarah Stickney Ellis in 1839: 'if a lady but touch any article, no matter how delicate, in the way of trade, she loses caste, and ceases to be a lady.'[87] Yet, spinsters did continue to engage in business, both as major contributors to family enterprises and as independent women. They had little choice. In England, teaching, innkeeping and shopkeeping were the most popular activities for unmarried women. Moreover, by the end of the century single women, especially those who had benefited from improvements in girls' education, were the main beneficiaries of the new areas of 'respectable' white-collar employment. In one middle-class area of Glasgow, for instance, the census recorded single women in a wide range of occupations including governess, teacher, dressmaker (the most popular), shop assistant and clerical worker.[88] Single middle-class women in towns and cities who inherited property from the family business employed factors – middlemen – to appoint tenants, collect the rent and deal with the grubby, unladylike side of the property business on their behalf. In Imperial Berlin (1871–1918), numerous single and widowed women earned a respectable living by running boarding houses. Taking in lodgers could be seen as a natural extension of the role of housewife and it enabled middle-class women to maintain their status through erecting a façade of not working.[89] The landlady, though, always risked her reputation, working as she did at the interface of bourgeois respectability and urban prostitution since, undoubtedly, some boarding houses were fronts for brothels, at least in the popular imagination. Teaching remained one of the more respectable occupations for an educated single woman. In Glasgow by 1881, 84 per cent of female heads of households who were teachers were spinsters.[90] Teaching offered some degree of financial security and positioned the spinster within an acceptable occupational framework (working with children, often subject to a male head) which mirrored the home.

It would be a mistake to group spinsters under the umbrella of independent women, notwithstanding the fact that some from the middle class did forge an autonomous lifestyle outside marriage and free of family obligations. Indeed, the majority of unmarried women remained locked into familial relationships, whether their own or other people's. The family became either a 'refuge from the shame of spinsterhood', an arena of activity which provided an alternative identity, or a means of economic survival.[91] Consequently, single women typically worked as carers of young, sick and elderly family members, they were active in philanthropy, ministering to poor families, and they fulfilled similar roles for the state – as foster mothers, nannies, nurses and teachers. The story of Alice Jay, the eldest daughter of an Essex farm labourer, is a case in point. When still quite young she left the family home to keep house for her uncle and aunt, their daughter and her handicapped child in Durham. She stayed for a number of years until her uncle died, at which time she moved south to live in with another relative. She never married but was always part of a family.[92] The life of a single woman, then, was like her married sister's, defined by family responsibilities. It was this plight which roused feminists to demand improvements in education for girls in order that unmarried women might be given the means to pursue economic independence.

The First World War decisively shifted the sex ratio in Europe, creating a generation of young women for whom marriage must have appeared an unlikely prospect. Yet this harsh reality was not reflected in the popular discourse of the immediate postwar era. The so-called bachelor-girl was a temporary status to be enjoyed before marriage, a sentiment expressed in a British girls' magazine of the 1920s: 'But is there a single modern girl for all her modernity and, perhaps, her occasional scoffs at romance who doesn't deep down in her, look forward to a time when she will make a little home for herself and the boy she loves?'[93] In the nineteenth century the spinster had been marginalised by economic realities and the ideology of domesticity; after the war, a time when spinsterhood was a stark reality for many women, the legitimacy of the permanent unmarried state was still scarcely admitted.

WIDOWHOOD

At a time when divorce in most European states was unavailable or restricted, for most couples it was the death of a spouse which brought a partnership to an end. Most often it was the woman who was left to manage alone as a consequence of females marrying younger and living longer than men (and widows especially survived their bereavement far longer than widowers). In France at the end of the century, 43 per cent of all women over the age of 50 were widows. Of those who survived to the age of 70 in 1891, almost 70 per cent had lost a husband.[94] Moreover, a widower was more likely to remarry – and remarry quickly often to a younger, single woman – than a widow, partly on account of a man's dependence upon a woman's house-hold labour, but also owing to a widow's lack of physical capital in the marriage market. In the Auffay textile region of France, almost half of widowers remarried after an average of less than two years, whereas 81 per cent of widows never found another marriage partner and lived, on average, another 14 years.[95] However, there were some circumstances in which widows were desirable marriage partners. In male-dominated industrial communities where young immigrants outnumbered the available women, it was said that widows were spoilt for choice for a new husband even before the funeral was over. Their skill at household management was an appealing quality to a single working man who needed a woman (and her children) to assist him in his work.[96]

The widow occupies an ambiguous position in European society. She was notionally independent in a world where women were supposed to be dependent. She might have the means to continue her late husband's business in a society in which femininity and business activity were increasingly seen as mutually exclusive. And she may have chosen not to remarry in order to protect her legal status, hold on to her property and her moral authority.[97] Studies of widows in early modern Europe underpin this ambiguity: on the one hand they are economically active and engaged in public activity. They capitalised upon the independence gained from their former marital status. Some did manage to continue in the trades of their husbands, although operating as an independent artisan was difficult owing to guild restrictions. The story of the German-Jewish Glikl bas Judah Leib (Gluckel of Hameln) is a nice example of how a widow could build upon her husband's success in business.[98] When her husband died unexpectedly, Glikl assumed control of their business trading pearls and other luxury goods. Amongst Jewish and Christian women in seventeenth-century Germany, Glikl was not unusual, but we are accustomed to thinking that by the nineteenth century the independent, economically active widow had been consigned to the past. For England it has been argued that the middle-class widow experienced a deterioration in conditions on account of the law which passed the control of a married woman's property to her husband. Upon his death it was less likely at this time that the widow would gain her full inheritance. It was usual for a widow who remarried to forfeit any interest in her former husband's estate. Yet evidence from Glasgow suggests widows of wealthy businessmen in the city had inherited considerable property and possessions enabling them to lead very comfortable independent lives. Moreover, a widow had a right to her own earnings, unlike a wife before the 1882 Married Women's Property Act (1881 in Scotland). Some widows had benefited from ante-nuptial contracts drawn up to protect her interests should the marriage end. Widowhood, then, could bestow benefits on a woman desirous of independence if her husband had accumulated sufficient wealth. Thus, when Isabella Elder was left a widow in 1869 upon the death of her husband John, a Clyde shipbuilder, her lifestyle was not at all cramped. Not only did she take over the management of her husband's shipyard for a few months, but she became an active philanthropist and traveller. When she died in 1905 her legacy to

Scotland was considerable including the premises housing Glasgow University's Queen Margaret College for women.[99] Whatever her economic circumstances, it is worth noting that a widowed woman assumed a new status upon her husband's death. She did not revert to the singleton state but rather became identified as her husband's widow in the community.[100] She was never accorded the degree of anxiety or hostility directed at the spinster.

The legal status of the widow was more advantageous than that of a wife in respect of property ownership. But, the majority of older widows were likely to suffer a decline in status and income; indeed, widows formed a high proportion of those claiming poor relief and the prevailing characteristic of the widow was her relative poverty at a time when retirement from the labour market on the grounds of age was rare and pensions were even rarer. In 1901 in the manufacturing industries in France, 69 per cent of all women over 60 were still working.[101] In England and Wales just 28 per cent of women between the ages of 65 and 74 had retired from an occupation.[102] Indeed, a high proportion of widows were recorded in the census as economically active at the end of the century: 41 per cent in Germany, 39 per cent in France and 29 per cent in Britain – figures which almost certainly underestimate the numbers of widows earning their own living.[103] Only the German state introduced pensions before the end of the century and these were very limited in scope. State pensions were introduced for the over-70s in Britain in 1908. Since this benefit was means tested and targeted the very poor, the majority of recipients were female.[104] Elsewhere the use of widows' funds and other forms of insurance was patchy. A woman in old age was at the trough of her wage-earning potential and may have teetered on the brink between independent survival and reliance on charity, especially if she lacked children or extended family. A widow's difficulty in finding well-remunerated employment also affected the likelihood that she would remarry. In the rural proto-industrial economy of much of Europe, households were reliant on the complementary activities of each partner as the saying went: 'None but a fool will take a wife whose bread must be earned solely by his labour and who will contribute nothing towards it herself.' In the Auffay region of France, those widows who desperately needed to remarry found it hard to do so on account of their age (widows over the age of 30 had a low chance of remarriage) and their poor wage-earning capacity from agriculture or cottage industry once spinning had been mechanised and moved away from the villages.[105] In England, by the nineteenth century and especially in towns, a widow's moral claim to relief was diminishing. Widows were increasingly required to show that they were respectable, responsible and were willing to help themselves, and indeed were probably forced to fall back on kinship networks and mutual aid in order to survive in the early industrial economy which privileged young workers.[106]

Typical of the plight of the elderly widow was the case of 77-year-old Margaret Laurenson living with her two unmarried daughters aged in their thirties, in the north of Scotland. She had been a widow for 14 years, had been evicted from the tenancy of her croft and was dependent for a living upon the income from her knitting and the meagre earnings her daughters made from gutting fish. Although Margaret Laurenson housed a pauper lodger, it was said the five shillings a week she received barely paid for his board. In 1891 she applied to the sheriff court to force her married crofter-fisherman son to support her. According to the evidence of her daughter Helen:

> [my mother] is not able for outdoor work or for indoor work owing to her infirmities. . . . One cow is promised to a neighbour who advanced money for the rent . . . My mother could not subsist without help from me and my sister. I have been very ill for four years with chronic bronchitis . . . My sister Joan does most of the work on the croft. We have had to hire help for ploughing, cutting grass and peats and cutting and building the corn and hay and carting the peats. I have not worked at [fish] curing stations for five years. Sometimes I am too ill to knit and when I could knit I have to help my sister. I have not earned above two pounds a year recently. We have a pauper lunatic as boarder, 73 years old, for whom we get 5 shillings a week. He is of no assistance to us and we have no profit after paying for his keep. Last Martinmas rent is not paid and we are due a little for meal and groceries. We were able to sell nothing last year. The year before we sold a foal for seven pounds . . . We have had to buy meal and oilcake. Last year I paid twenty two shillings for cartage. What we all make together is not sufficient to support us. It would take almost all we have to pay our debts.[107]

Margaret Laurenson's plight was not unusual although few widows were as unlucky. Most would have been able to rely on their children to care for them in their infirmity. Few widows conformed to the stereotype of the rich, lustful woman – the 'merry widow' of the popular imagination. Poverty and loneliness were more likely to accompany the rest of her life.

CONCLUSIONS

Marriage for women in the nineteenth century became invested with far greater symbolic significance than it had been at any time in the past. By 1900, women's expectations of marriage had risen. As marriage became more of a unit of consumption than a unit of production, women assumed considerable autonomy within the home as domestic managers and 'angels in the house', whilst their husbands experienced a whittling away of their economic power and thus their claim to dominance. Women increasingly expected husbands to be not only providers but also companions in life. Women of all social classes were disillusioned with patriarchal marriage. Whilst wives got on with being household managers, wage-earners, homemakers and mothers, they demanded a form of marriage which took their needs into account. They desired husbands who encouraged their enterprise, who respected their work within and outside the home, and who, at the same time, would provide companionship, friendship, support and even love. The letter received by one young Birmingham man from his future mother-in-law just before the wedding sums up these expectations: 'I trust she will find a father, a brother, a friend all united in one of the tenderest and kindest of husbands.'[108] For a woman, entry into the married state involved a complex set of relationships and roles which cemented her position within the community. Marriage provided a woman with entry into another, mainly female, world which simultaneously gave her strength and purpose.

By the end of the century the institution of marriage had been subjected to decades of sustained criticism from women. In the divorce courts women told judges (and their husbands) how they were fed up with men who failed to fulfil their side of the contract, and they articulated their own preference for a marriage relationship based on mutual respect and reciprocity. Undoubtedly influenced by the stories told by countless women in the courts, a host of voices began to articulate a critical discourse on marriage. Liberal women writers objected to women's imprisonment in marriages of convenience and advocated spiritual partnerships. Feminist critics tackled married women's subordinate legal position and argued for improved property and child custody rights and the protection of women from domestic violence. Others from all sides of the political spectrum came to accept that women had legitimate grievances. Few of these critics wished to see the abolition of marriage as an institution – that argument would have to wait until the next century. What they wanted was an adjustment to the model in line with women's needs, a recognition that marriage was a partnership of (complementary) equals, an enabling institution providing the wife with the emotional and spiritual foundation for self-discovery rather than a constraint. The introduction of divorce in most European states by the end of the century with the exception of Ireland, Italy and Spain, did provide women with an escape route from a cruel or heartless marriage and a forum for the expression of a new kind of marriage. Indeed, the abuse of patriarchal power was explicitly named as a legitimate ground for divorce in the new liberal divorce laws so that husbands who failed to fulfil their marital duties were held up to public scrutiny.

By the last two decades of the nineteenth century, two large-scale changes – demographic and economic – began to influence marriage patterns. The excess of women in the population of marriageable age became especially marked by the 1880s. This meant that many women were unlikely to find a marriage partner. At the same time, women's increasing role as wage-earners may have influenced spousal relationships in favour of a more egalitarian or at least negotiated model. The marriage partnership was still an economic one – it always had been – but now the married state conferred on women a number of privileges not granted to their spinster and widowed sisters. It was possibly harder to survive as an unmarried or widowed woman now than at any time in the past. Both sets of unmarried women were constantly judged against the standards of their married counterparts. Marriage conferred the right to be a mother whereas single motherhood was increasingly vilified. Sexual relations were deemed appropriate for women only within marriage; the sexually active spinster or even widow could hardly be imagined. Finally, marriage conferred upon the wife the role of housekeeper not earner; it was an ideology that was to have far-reaching ramifications for the non-married female head of household trying to earn a living.

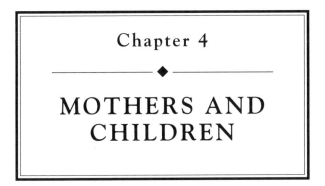

Chapter 4

◆

MOTHERS AND CHILDREN

I n nineteenth-century Europe, motherhood was the pinnacle of a woman's life. It confirmed her virtue and her fulfilment. Motherhood was expected of a married woman, and failure to conceive was almost always deemed a female problem. The childless woman was a figure to be pitied. Amongst the Russian peasantry it was noted that 'barrenness for the peasant woman is a most painful situation . . . it often constitutes a source of moral humiliation . . . deprives her finally of the joy of having children through whom alone a mother can firmly implant herself in the family of her husband and can be guaranteed consolation and comfort in her old age.'[1] Throughout Europe, childless women were encouraged to find work caring for children – as a governess or a nursery maid – in supposed compensation.[2] Motherhood ensured integration into female networks, it guaranteed status, and it was seen as security for the future.

Accompanying the increasing value attached to motherhood was a shift in the way the mothering role was conceived. Before 1800, motherhood was presented as natural, but already by the beginning of the nineteenth century the mothering role was being transformed from an instinctual or essential attribute of all women into something that had to be learned. In public discourse, if not in reality, motherhood was portrayed as a full-time job that could not be combined with paid work; it became a duty to the state and a social responsibility. 'As a biological condition as well as a set of social definitions, motherhood was all-encompassing.'[3] One of the consequences of this change was that woman's role as mother was used as the basis of republicans' and feminists' claims to female citizenship. The consequences of these shifts in conceptualising the mother were to be far-reaching for all mothers and indeed for all women.

At either end of the century stand a number of prominent women who, in their role as mothers, came to represent the good and the bad maternal figure. During the French Revolution, motherhood came to carry a great symbolic burden. Women argued that they had rights which flowed from their responsibilities as mothers. 'We would not be able to resolve to give birth to children destined to live in a country compliant with despotism' were the words of one group of women to the king Louis XVI, explicitly linking republican politics with their own rights and duties as mothers.[4] Queen Marie Antoinette was represented by revolutionary republicans as the antithesis of the republican mother, much as she tried hard to counter this perception by appearing in public with her two surviving children. In fact the queen was distraught at the death of her eldest son and her youngest daughter, and following the execution of her husband was desperate to prevent her remaining son, the dauphin, being taken from her.[5] Russia's Catherine the Great (1729–96) also came to symbolise the decadent and despotic past. Her very commitment to affairs of state and her lack of involvement in family life identified Catherine as a disinterested mother. By the 1850s, on the other hand, Britain's Queen Victoria (1819–1901) was affectionately portrayed as the ideal wife and mother. Depicted surrounded by her beloved Albert and her many children, Victoria was frequently described as the 'mother of the nation'.[6] Alongside Victoria were Queen Louise of Prussia and Louise's daughter Aleksandra Federovna, Empress of Russia, all of whom fulfilled the maternal role within the home, all of whom saw motherhood as just as important as, if not more important than, matters of court and state and in turn were regarded by their subjects as almost 'goddess-mothers'.[7] They epitomised the new model of virtuous womanhood.

THE IDEALISED MOTHER

Who fed me from her gentle breast
And hush'd me in her arms to rest
And on my cheek sweet kisses prest?
    My Mother.
When sleep forsook my open eye,
Who was it sung sweet hushaby
And rock'd me that I should not cry?
    My Mother.[8]

Ann Taylor Gilbert's paean to her mother in 1802 exemplified the new romantic attitude towards motherhood which Jean-Jacques Rousseau had promoted just a few decades earlier. In his 1762 novel *Émile*, Rousseau extolled 'natural' motherhood. Attacking the tradition that assigned child-rearing to fathers, he instructed his readers to trust the mother's natural instincts to lavish her child with affection:

> But when mothers deign to nurse their own children, then will be a reform in morals . . . Fix your eyes on nature, follow the path traced by her . . . When the child draws its first breath do not confine it in tight wrappings.[9]

Rousseau anticipated a massive shift in the way that motherhood was to be perceived. Within every mother lay a 'natural' instinct to care for her child though she might require some guidance in order to properly fulfil her duty. Rousseau's injunction to mothers to breast feed their children – on the grounds that wet-nursing went against the laws of nature – is credited with influencing a generation of literate women. Rousseau also insisted that the place of the mother was with her children, nurturing and educating them to become good citizens. It was a time-consuming regime, a system which could only be practised by women of the upper and middling classes who had the time and the wealth to pursue such a child-centred lifestyle. Emily Fitzgerald née Lennox, a member of the English aristocracy, was influenced by her reading of Rousseau. Although she continued to employ a wet nurse for all of her 22 children, she did endeavour to keep some of her younger children with her by establishing her own school on the coast south of Dublin where children could pursue a programme of exercise, games and learning in a free and natural environment along the lines advocated by Rousseau.[10] Middle-class women now succeeded in achieving true womanhood if they responded emotionally to their infants and bonded with them through breast-feeding and constant attendance. Yet, the ideal of true motherhood demanded that women be constantly there for their children; it implied a commitment to domesticity and was therefore incompatible with the demands of the labour market. The new motherhood was a full-time job.

By 1900, however, the 'natural' mother could no longer be trusted to care for her child without intervention. Her 'natural' maternal instinct was to be supplemented by education and instruction so that she might become the responsible mother. Maternity and motherhood – formerly two distinct concepts encompassing the act of giving birth and the nurturing role, respectively – had converged. 'There have always been mothers but motherhood was invented.'[11] This reconfiguration of the mothering role, from the biological to a public or social role, was formulated by pedagogues such as Pestalozzi and Froebel around 1800. For the Zurich-born Johann Heinrich Pestalozzi (1746–1827), the bond between mother and child was the basis of social morality. In his popular novel *Leonard and Gertrude* published in 1781, Pestalozzi portrayed the heroine as an active mother who bore moral responsibility in the family, primarily through her religious and educative role towards her children.[12] Unlike Rousseau's depiction of the rather passive Sophie, partner to Èmile, Getrude personified a maternal revolution which provided women writers with a model legitimising public participation. In 1810, the German schoolteacher and advocate of women's education, Betty Gleim, wrote: 'Truly, the saying that "Your child will become whatever you are" is of such immeasurable importance, that, if she really feels it and lives by it, every mother ought to tremble before the responsibility that she takes on as teacher and educator of the coming generation.'[13]

Rousseau had conceptualised a mother's role as duty determined by nature; the new pedagogues and their adherents went one step further. By conceptualising motherhood as a social and moral contribution to the state they allowed for the recognition of women's individual rights, an argument most forcefully articulated by Mary Wollstonecraft. She reconfigured the maternal role as a responsibility which first of all demanded that women be educated and thereafter conferred rights. Wollstonecraft envisaged the 'indispensable duty of a mother' as the route to citizenship. If it was a woman's task to raise and educate new citizens then she should be rewarded with the recognition of that most important responsibility: 'Make women rational creatures and free citizens, and they will quickly become good wives and mothers.'[14] For Wollstonecraft, then, motherhood was both individual fulfilment and social duty. It was a model which was appealing primarily to middle-class women from the beginning of the nineteenth century. Those women who practised the new maternalism were able to use their experience to transform both their own self-understanding and their world view.[15] Both the joys and the sorrows of motherhood in the lives of upper and middle class women 'could provide the basis for personal growth and social commitment'.[16] These women extended their role into charitable work, social reform and ultimately political discourse relating to women's education, employment and political rights. The power of this new maternal ethic was based in the fact that social motherhood was now separated from biological motherhood. All women could share in this new elevated maternal culture which was a source of strength in the public sphere.

Who was the responsible mother pictured in nineteenth-century discourse? She was the mother who breast-fed her children, who listened to and acted upon the advice provided by health professionals, who abandoned traditional practices and who no longer listened to the words of old wives. Across Europe, women were bombarded by doctors, health workers and philanthropists with advice and information. These professionals presumed that women wanted to do the best for their children but were hindered by their own ignorance. Nowhere was there more of a gap between the professionals and mothers than in rural Russia where infant mortality rates were higher than anywhere else in Europe, where children were dying 'like flies' from smallpox, malaria, diptheria, scarlatina and diarrhoea, and being crippled and blinded for life on account of ignorance and a reluctance to accept medical intervention. Physicians believed peasant women were the key to reform. If these women could be weaned away from their dependence on witch doctors, untrained midwives and village and religious elders, and if they could be educated to discard traditional beliefs and practices such as fear of the evil eye, the practice of swaddling and resort to dummies or rags dipped in milk or pre-chewed bread, then, it was argued, the battle against needless infant death would be won. To cause the death of a child by ignorance was regarded as 'the greatest sin a woman can commit against the law of God' according to one child care manual.[17]

Thus, the route to the child was through the mother. In the words of one contributor to a British National Conference on Infantile Mortality in 1908: 'it [is] assumed that the mother, as a mother, knows what is best for her child. But experience shows that the human mother, just because she is human, intelligent, and not instinctive, does not know.'[18] Infant welfare activists questioned the long-standing assumption that women possessed innate maternal expertise. Motherhood 'was proved to be a skilled job requiring a technique, which, like any other kind of technique, has to be acquired'.[19] Medical professionals did dispense a lot of valuable advice. They taught women the value of breast over cow's milk, how to sterilise feeding equipment, the danger of bacterial infection from dummies, and means of preventing the spread of tuberculosis. But of course most poor women simply did not have the time or the money to carry out all of these obligations in respect of hygiene and nutrition. Working-class mothers had limited control over their environments and yet the health visitors, sanitary inspectors and (mostly) female members of sundry philanthropic organisations 'had poor mothers coming and going, suggesting that they had powers that they actually lacked and holding them morally and sometimes legally responsible for deeds they could not do'.[20]

Moreover, few suggested that working-class mothers would gain any concrete public recognition for compliance. Indeed, attempts to teach mothers to ignore neighbourly advice and superstition in favour of medical or scientific diagnosis and treatment of infant illnesses inevitably resulted in a downgrading of women's own understanding of their children as well as the damage to women's confidence in their ability to care for their babies. For the working-class woman, motherhood would always be just one part of a complicated life during which she combined domestic and household management, paid work and child care.

The maternal revolution was an unequal process. Middle-class women embraced their new responsible maternal role in the private sphere of the family and, at the same time, negotiated for themselves a public voice and identity. But, a key element of this entailed advising working-class mothers of their duty to take on board the new mother–child intimacy and nurturing and hygiene standards. 'Social mothers overrode deficient biological mothers.'[21] In this way, the concept of responsible motherhood provided middle-class women with a power base. But as infant mortality rates rose across Europe during urban and industrial growth, the responsibility for infant survival was placed more heavily on working-class mothers who were treated, in the words of feminist social worker Anna Martin, as 'the unpaid nursemaid(s) of the state'.[22]

PREGNANCY

At the beginning of the nineteenth century women might typically have borne up to 12 children, although not all would have survived the first weeks or months of life. Amongst the English middle classes, women who married in their mid-twenties could expect to spend around 15 years either pregnant or nurturing young children.[23] Seventeen years of Queen Victoria's life were taken up by nine pregnancies and confinements. Across Europe, though, the average size of family was between 5 and 6.5 children for most of the century. Much of a woman's adult life would be spent mothering, but by 1900 most births were in the first years of marriage, leaving a woman freer of children by the time she reached 40. There were, however, significant variations around this mean influenced by social class and work opportunities. In London around 1850, one-third of couples had 8 children or more, with the larger families tending to cluster amongst the poorer classes. But by 1900 in England and Wales the average number of children had fallen to 4, accompanying a gradual fertility decline along with many other Protestant European

Table 4.1 Birth rates per 1000 population in selected European countries, 1800–1920

	England and Wales	France	Germany	Greece	Italy	Russia	Spain	Sweden
1800		33						29
1830		30	36					33
1850	33	27	37		34		36	32
1860	34	26	36	28	38	50	37	35
1870	35	26	39	28	37	49	37	29
1880	34	25	38	24	34	50	36	29
1890	30	22	36	35	36	50	34	28
1900	29	21	36		33	49	34	27
1910	25	20	30		33	45	33	25
1920	26	21	26	21	32	31	30	24

Source: Compiled from data in B.R. Mitchell, *European Historical Statistics, 1750–1970* (London, 1975), pp.114–30.

states, whilst in France (in contrast with other Catholic countries) fertility rates had declined significantly earlier owing to the general adoption of methods of birth control in the nineteenth century as Table 4.1 illustrates.[24] In Russia, on the other hand, rates remained significantly higher than anywhere else in Europe right through the century, not really falling until the 1930s.

Knowledge of how a woman became pregnant improved during the century. In 1800, medical knowledge of the reproductive process was still hazy. Ovulation was not understood, nor was the relationship between this and menstruation and conception. Nowadays there is a presumption that most people have a clear understanding of the biological processes around conception, and chemical pregnancy tests provide early confirmation of pregnancy. But before 1914 such knowledge and certainty were absent. Women knew they were pregnant by the sensation associated with quickening – the movement of the foetus in the womb – and of course there were external signs, some visible to observers and some only to the woman herself (such as swelling of the belly, hardening of the nipples and swelling of veins) which all indicated the possibility, but not the certainty, of pregnancy. 'She was larger in the body than usual but I did not know the cause', attested a neighbour of a Scottish woman, Margaret Johnston, accused of concealment of pregnancy as late as 1893. 'It did not occur to me that she was in child . . . She was not so big as I am when I am in child.' Another neighbour who observed Margaret's swelling belly agreed that 'any other thing might have caused the swelling'.[25] The cessation of menstruation was regarded as an unreliable sign which could have other explanations, although combined with other indicators some were confident in their own judgement. In 1862, Laura Scott's landlady was clear in her own mind about Laura's condition:

> I thought for the first time Laura came to my house . . . that she was with child. I noticed that she was *not* regular in her courses and she complained of being affected with headache and 'sleepiness' and she had an excessive desire for a particular kind of food. She was black about the eyes. She several times vomited in the mornings, particularly during the first three weeks.[26]

Ignorance about pregnancy and childbirth was surprisingly widespread amongst the working classes. Girls did not commonly learn the facts of life from their mothers. As one mother of five remarked, her own mother, 'a dear pious soul, thought ignorance was innocence'.[27] 'I might say', wrote another, 'that I was very ignorant when I was married; my mother did not consider it at all proper to talk about such things.'[28] Before the advent of higher standards of living and modern medical advances, pregnancy for women of all social classes could be a time of worry and discomfort, and not infrequently real sickness and ill-health. 'The first feeling of a young mother (to be) . . . is one of fear for herself', wrote one working-class mother of three who described the months of pregnancy as a time of trial.[29] It was widely believed that the mother's mental disturbance could affect the baby and in the worst cases induce a miscarriage. Georgiana, Duchess of Devonshire, although in a healthy physical state on the occasion of her second pregnancy in 1783, complained of what she called 'the feels' which prevented her from sleeping and caused her to break down in tears. Her mother, fearing she would lose the baby on account of her poor emotional state – she had already had several miscarriages – advised her to rest and to take laudanum. 'If you feel any violent [attacks] or agitation . . . be assured that whatever may happen *this time*, your health is much improved in the main, that if you can contrive by any means this winter, to keep your mind and body in a calm and quiet state, I have no doubt of your soon obtaining all you wish . . . do not make yourself unhappy.'[30] Most women of the rural and urban labouring classes had no choice but to continue working as normal through their pregnancies. As late as 1917 it was said that the women of Unst, the most northerly of the Shetland Islands, 'follow their ordinary occupation until pains of labour compel them to give in'.[31] Indeed, women who were accustomed to outdoor work were believed to experience easier labours than those who lived an indoor life although the strain of physical work also resulted in miscarriage and premature births. Amongst the urban poor, the necessity for a woman to continue working through pregnancy convinced reformers of the need for maternity pay. A British working-class mother said in 1915:

> I am the mother of three children. When the youngest was coming my husband was out of employment, so I had to go out to work myself, standing all day washing and ironing. This caused me much suffering from varicose veins, also caused the child to wedge in some way, which nearly cost both our lives. The doctor said it was the standing and the weight of the child. I have not been able to carry a child the full time since then . . . Once we can make men and women understand that a woman requires rest when bearing children, we shall not have so many of our sisters suffering and dying through operations, or, on the other hand, dragging out a miserable existence.[32]

The lack of money for extra food, items for the baby and doctors' bills meant that suffering was widespread amongst the poor. In 1915 the Women's Co-operative Guild in England invited women to write to them with their experiences of pregnancy and childbirth. The majority of the 400 respondents were wives of manual workers and they told tales of poverty, illness and pain, of miscarriages, stillbirths and abortion. 'I can speak from experience', wrote one woman who gave birth to four children but experienced ten miscarriages. 'For fifteen years I was in a very poor state of health owing to continual pregnancy. As soon as I came over one trouble, it was all started over again.'[33] 'I do not think I was very different in my pregnancies to others', wrote another who experienced four live births, three stillbirths and one miscarriage. 'I always prepared myself to die . . . and when bothered by several other children, and not knowing how to make ends meet, death in some cases would be welcome.'[34] Yet, the discourse of the natural joy of pregnancy and childbirth idealised by male writers such as Rousseau was still to be found in these women's experiences. 'Motherhood stirred the depths of my nature', wrote a mother of five. 'The rapture of a babe in arms drawing nourishment from me crowned me with glory and sanctity and honour.'[35] But the realities of poverty and ill-health meant that this romantic vision was a reality only for the lucky and wealthy few. Having given birth to a girl, 'Little G', Georgiana, Duchess of Devonshire, broke with aristocratic etiquette and breast-fed her baby, slept with the baby beside her, and was later rewarded by being described as a good mother by her daughter. 'One cannot know till one has separated from you how different you are from everyone else, how superior to all mothers, even good ones.'[36]

Women who wished to control their fertility did have access to a range of artificial birth control measures such as douches, pessaries, sponges and condoms, as well as the more common natural methods of coitus interruptus (withdrawal) and extended breast-feeding. Deliberate family limitation, that is the use of contraceptive measures, as well as abstinence, withdrawal and limiting intercourse to the so-called safe period, required male cooperation. In France, the birth rate had begun to decline after the Revolution as a result of the use of birth control well before the distribution of contraceptive technology in the second half of the century, and this trend continued amongst the French industrial working classes. In London around 1900 it was said that the richest 'systematically and largely practised' contraception whereas amongst the poorest contraception was practically non-existent.[37] But broad trends tell us little about individual experiences. By 1900, women were beginning to question the constant cycle of pregnancy and childbirth that left them worn out. Some actively reduced family size, either with or without their husband's consent. Others began to call for men to take more responsibility for such matters; conception was generally seen to be women's 'fault'. 'No amount of State help can help the suffering of mothers until men are taught many things in regard to the right use of the organs for reproduction and until he realises that the wife's body belongs to herself', wrote a mother of three in 1915. 'So it's men who need to be educated most. The sacred office of parenthood has not yet dawned on the majority.'[38]

Once a pregnancy was confirmed, abortion was the only option left to a woman determined not to have a child. 'Can we wonder that so many women take drugs, hoping to get rid of the expected child, when they know so little of their own bodies, and have to work so hard to keep or help to keep the children they have already got', remarked a mother of two.[39] Women had always taken drastic measures in an attempt to abort a foetus: they jumped from heights, swallowed concoctions, took very hot or very cold baths, lifted heavy weights and inserted sharp objects. Amongst rural women a wide variety of abortifacients were used to terminate a pregnancy; herbs such as pennyroyal and savin were commonly prescribed by wise-women, and roots and powders could be acquired from quack doctors and peddlars.[40] Urban women were more likely to use quinine or lead – drugs more readily available from pharmacists. 'I have resorted to drugs, trying to prevent or bring about a slip', wrote a working-class mother of eight desperate not to have any more children.[41] Abortion was a criminal offence in most countries, yet women seem increasingly to have resorted to poison and physical intervention to terminate a pregnancy in preference to abandonment or infanticide of a newly-born child.

By the end of the century, urban women and those of the wealthier classes were having fewer children; fertility rates were slower to decline in rural and less industrial parts of Europe. Overall, though, there was a general decline in the fertility of European women as they sought to take some control over both the number and the spacing of conceptions. In 1900, pregnancy and childbirth were still fearful times, not only on account of ignorance but also in the knowledge that this 'natural' condition brought with it illness, pain and anxiety. The next step was to deliver a healthy child.

GIVING BIRTH

A woman giving birth would be surrounded by women, a practice that continued until late in the nineteenth century. The early modern English birth room has been described as a 'gossip's parlour, busy with bustling women'.[42] We know that across much of Europe women typically gave birth at home, aided by a local midwife or wise-woman. Women probably assumed any position that was comfortable: standing or squatting or kneeling with the aid of others. Few would have been attended by a doctor; a physician was the dubious privilege of the aristocracy at the start if the century. The Duchess of Devonshire described the somewhat chaotic scene at the birth of her daughter in 1783:

> I was laid on a couch in the middle of the room. My mother and Dennis supported me. Canis was at the door, and the Duchess of Portland sometimes bending over me and screaming with me, and sometimes running to the end of the room and to him. I thought the pain I suffered was so great from being unusual to me, but I find since I had a very hard time. Towards the end, some symptoms made me think the child was dead. I said so, and Dr Denman only said there was no reason to think so but we must submit to providence.[43]

By the middle of the nineteenth century, general practitioners were more likely to be present at the birth in smaller non-manufacturing towns and amongst the more affluent classes in the towns and suburbs, whereas midwife deliveries predominated in working-class areas of large towns, in villages and remote parts of the country. Prior to the appointment of a doctor to serve the northerly Shetland islands of Yell and Fetlar in the 1890s, it was said that 'mothers reared families numbering ten to fourteen children, all assisted by local "skilful" women.' According to the testimony of one such 'wife' aged 87, 'I never had a doctor. The wife who came to me from Unst used to bring a [bible] and a razor with her. The razor she placed under my pillow for luck, and she used to read a chapter out of the testament now and then to keep up my spirits.'[44] By the 1880s in England and Wales it has been estimated that midwives and general practitioners each undertook around half of all deliveries.[45] Amongst the respondents to the Women's

Co-operative Guild survey a high proportion had consulted doctors during pregnancy; indeed, doctors were preferred to midwives in some cases. One woman, who was unable to afford a doctor, commented that, 'Had the midwife called in the doctor, as she should have done, I might have been saved a lot, for my back has never been right since.'[46]

However, much of northern Europe was arguably a safer place than Britain to have a baby for most of the century because of the reliance on home deliveries by trained midwives. Owing to the absence of a system of training and licensing in Britain, male surgeons or apothecaries were able to claim childbirth as one of their areas of expertise. By contrast, much of the rest of Europe had, early on, established a trained midwifery service, a development which almost certainly benefited mothers. Maternal mortality rates were lower where trained midwives were the norm. Death in childbed was the commonest cause of death amongst women of childbearing age as a result of complications during a difficult labour or infection leading to puerperal fever brought on by intervention in the birth or poor post-natal care. In the Netherlands, France, Norway, Sweden and Denmark for instance, training and the regulation of the midwifery service was seen as important in order to marginalise untrained midwives who, it was alleged, were often responsible for carrying infections that caused puerperal fever.[47] In Sweden, the decision to create a well-trained autonomous midwifery service at the beginning of the century, and the authorisation of their use of instruments such as forceps in 1829, effectively did away with unlicensed midwives or help-women (*hjälpkvinnor*), despite rural attachment to traditional birth attendants.[48] In rural Russia, where peasant women were attended only by a *povitukha*, equivalent to the wise-woman of western Europe, infant and maternal deaths were high. In 1900, Russia still had the highest infant mortality rate in Europe: 275 newborn babies died out of every 1000 compared with figures of 160 in France, 140 in England and only 80 in Norway.[49] The solution, according to reformers, was to create a corps of trained rural midwives, and by 1905 more the 10,000 were practising although the majority preferred to work in urban centres and the *povitukha* remained the choice of most peasant women.[50] 'Wherever a city, a county, a region or a nation, had developed a system of maternal care which was firmly based on a body of trained, licensed, regulated and respected midwives', argues Loudon, 'the standard of maternal care was at its highest and maternal mortality was at its lowest.'[51] Hospital births were still the exception. In Germany fewer than one per cent of all births occurred in hospital in the 1870s. At this time home birth was still safer for mother and child owing to the high likelihood of contracting an infection in an institution.[52]

Figure 4.1 Midwives and maternal mortality, 1860–1914

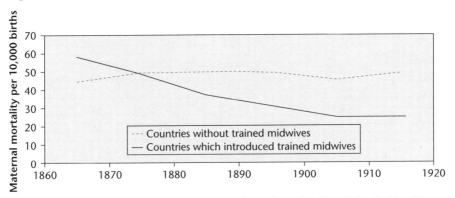

Note: This graph comprises the mean of available maternal mortality statistics in each decade. 'Countries without trained midwives' includes England and Wales (1867–1914) and Scotland (1867–1914). 'Countries which introduced trained midwives' includes the Netherlands (1878, 1883, 1888, 1893, 1898, 1903, 1905–14), Sweden (1867, 1872, 1877, 1882, 1887, 1892, 1902, 1907, 1911–14) and Denmark (1895, 1905, 1914).

Source: Figures calculated from data in I. Loudon, *Death in Childbirth* (Oxford, 1992), appendix 6.

Figure 4.1 illustrates the connection between maternal mortality rates and the existence of a trained and licensed midwifery service. In the Netherlands, for example, which achieved a notably low rate of maternal deaths in childbirth, particularly after the introduction of antisepsis in the 1880s, a long history of midwifery training dating back to the seventeenth century was enhanced by a regulatory system established in the first two decades of the nineteenth century. Midwives either followed an apprenticeship leading to official accreditation, or they attended a school for midwifery training. By 1900 the maternal mortality rate in the Netherlands was 24 deaths per 10,000 births whilst in England and Wales the rate was double that at 48 deaths.[53] The Dutch midwives were clearly dealing relatively successfully with sepsis (bacterial infection) and puerperal fever, whilst their general practitioner counterparts in England and Wales were shockingly cavalier in their use of forceps and anaesthesia without due attention to antiseptic techniques.[54] Similarly, in Denmark, following a scare which blamed midwives for carrying infections that caused puerperal fever, instructions were issued on cleanliness and hygiene, and midwives quickly learned antiseptic techniques, with the result that deaths from puerperal fever declined significantly.[55] The type of birth attendant was a key determinant of maternal mortality, more so than the social class of the mother.[56] The lesson of this story is that some training was better than none at a time when advances in medical understanding promised safer births.

Table 4.2 Infant mortality rates per 1000 live births in selected European countries, 1850–1910

	England and Wales	France	Germany	Ireland	Italy	Netherlands	Norway	Russia	Spain	Sweden
1850	162	146	297[a]	–	–	169	102	–	–	146
1860	148	150	260	–	–	192	102	–	174	124
1870	160	201	298	95	230	211	101	248	203	132
1880	153	179	240	112	225	218	95	286	190	121
1890	151	174	226	95	198	171	97	292	–	103
1900	154	160	229	109	174	155	91	252	204	99
1910	105	111	162	95	140	108	67	271	149	75

[a] Selected states only

Source: Compiled from data in B.R. Mitchell, *European Historical Statistics, 1750–1970* (London, 1975), pp.137–41.

Infant deaths, on the other hand, were rising for much of the nineteenth century as Table 4.2 illustrates. In England and Wales a peak was reached in 1846 when 164 infant deaths per 1000 live births were recorded. In rural Russia, mortality rates were almost double those in industrial western Europe, with 290 deaths per 1000 births in one province around the turn of the century, explained by the poor physical condition of the mothers, low literacy rates and the difficulties mothers had in combining child care with work, particularly in the summer.[57] More mothers were surviving childbirth by the end of the century, but the fate of babies was still uncertain. Yet, in contrast with the maternal mortality rate which was seen to be in the hands of the midwives or medical practitioners, the responsibility for the high infant mortality rate was roundly placed on the shoulders of mothers. Middle-class philanthropists, government inspectors and medical men united in their condemnation of the infant-care methods of poor women, conveniently ignoring the often appalling housing conditions of urban and rural working-class families characterised by overcrowding, poor sanitation and the pervasiveness of disease. Infant deaths, it was believed, could be prevented if 'ignorant' poor mothers breast-fed their babies and were taught baby care. This was an area of mothering where the state was to play a significant role.

MOTHERING

For some historians as well as contemporary observers, the 'natural mother' was also a selfish, irresponsible or uncaring mother. In a provocative analysis of the maternal instinct, the French sociologist Elizabeth Badinter argues that high levels of wet-nursing, child abandonment and infant death in the eighteenth century point to a time when a child was commonly viewed as 'a nuisance or even a misfortune' and when motherhood was not eulogised or sentimentalised. The French aristocrat who sent her children to be wet-nursed in the countryside, almost certainly consigning them to an early death, or the Parisian woman who abandoned her child to a foundling hospital, provide evidence of a widespread absence of a maternal instinct which was a nineteenth-century discursive and practical creation designed to subordinate women, restricting their opportunities and choices. Hence Badinter asks the question: 'What caused the apathetic mother of the eighteenth century to turn into the mother hen of the nineteenth and twentieth centuries?'[58] Few would disagree with the suggestion that a new ideal of motherhood was held up to women as an emotionally fulfilling duty, but the proposition that earlier child-care practices indicate of an absence of sentiment is misguided.

To argue that good mothering was an invention of modernisation indicates a wilful disregard for the social and economic context of child-rearing.[59] It is worth examining some of these alleged negligent practices in more detail. Wet-nursing was certainly fashionable amongst upper-class French women for a time in the eighteenth century. Madame Bovary, the heroine of Flaubert's novel of that name, is a prime example of the woman too concerned with appearance and her own amusements to nurse her child, and Rousseau, probably the most well-known promotor of breast-feeding, was contemptuous of mothers who 'got rid of their babies' to nurses to 'devote themselves gaily to the pleasures of the town'.[60] A number of reasons, some more plausible than others, have been put forward to explain this trend, including pressure from husbands to resume sex with their wives and the belief that intercourse when a woman was breast-feeding would make her milk curdle. Of course, some women had difficulty nursing their infants and, at a time when alternative methods of feeding were dangerous, recourse to a wet nurse was a practical solution. By the nineteenth century, though, there is evidence to show that even men were taking on board Rousseau's injunctions that mother's breast milk was best. Upon hearing that his daughter was unable to breast-feed, the Englishman Henry Alford wrote to her expressing his disappointment:

> Not being able to nurse it, is a physical relief to you; but on one account I rather regret it, that you lose the discipline in patience and long-suffering which makes the bloom of the maternal character. A mother who has borne with her infant's thousand wearing and worrying ways, who has given up her employ by day and her rest by night for it for months together, will be likely to bear with its moral faults and exercise

patience in disciplining it for Christ, better, perhaps, than one who has been spared all this.[61]

Working-class women were less likely to follow fashions; their actions were more likely to be in reaction to economic circumstances. Wet nurses were sometimes used by working-class mothers when employment was incompatible with full-time child care.[62] Their need was met by poor rural women who were content to breast-feed a stranger's child for modest wages. However, we also know that unscrupulous individuals known as baby-farmers preyed on unsuspecting poor mothers by offering to provide temporary child care. These women took out insurance on the infants, allowed them to die and then collected the payment. In Britain in the 1870s, the trial of two sisters in London and the subsequent hanging of one, provoked a public furore about the practice.[63] Newspapers were full of stories of infants being drugged with opium and starved to death by the baby-farmers, prompting legislation regulating child-care establishments. Only desperate mothers deposited their babies in this way and most were well aware of the potential dangers of wet-nurse care. They knew that a breast-fed child was healthier and less likely to succumb to the scourge of infants – diarrhoea. By 1900 around three-quarters of mothers breast-fed their babies for up to six months and often longer when times were hard, and it was cheaper to keep an infant at the breast than wean it on to solid foods.[64] Bottle-feeding, using dried or condensed milk or cereals mixed with water, was less hazardous by this time if utensils were sterilised but few working-class households had the facilities to keep bottles and teats scrupulously clean. During the cholera epidemic in Hamburg in 1892 mortality rates were highest among infants. In this city, breast-feeding, which conferred a degree of immunity, was not common, and poor mothers customarily diluted milk with tap-water, the main source of infection with the cholera bacillus during the epidemic.[65] In such circumstances, recourse to a wet nurse was a sure sign that a mother cared about her child and regarded breast milk, even from another woman, preferable to tainted bottle-milk. The decline of wet-nursing in France after the First World War had more to do with the provision of sterilised milk and the fall in female employment than with the modernisation of mothering.

Mothers in the past have been accused by historians of a range of neglectful and downright abusive behaviour towards their children with little basis in fact. Swaddling, the practice of wrapping newborn babies tightly in cloth, has been interpreted as a practice which inhibited the development of an affectionate and emotional relationship between mother and child. This interpretation of a common practice across Europe is plainly wrong. Swaddling, which survived in parts of Europe such as the Balkans, Russia, southern Italy and some areas of France into the twentieth century, was practical: it kept a baby warm and out of danger; and it was believed to aid hardening of the flesh and the strengthening of the limbs and back.[66] Similarly the use of comforters or dummies dipped in various narcotic substances has been cited as evidence of bad mothering, but we should be wary of such value judgements which pay little attention to the precise context in which mothers dealt with babies' crying, teething and sleeplessness. When one mother asked her doctor for help in soothing her teething son he recommended she use chloroform.[67]

The high infant mortality rates which, in some poor urban areas, meant that up to 30 per cent of infants died before the age of 5 years, have been both blamed on mothers' poor care and used to explain so-called tentative mothering, whereby mothers who recognised their child's provisional hold on life withheld emotional attachment until the child was relatively safe.[68] These mothers were not callous. Lawrence Stone's comment that the 'omnipresence of death coloured affective relations at all levels of society by reducing the amount of emotional capital available for prudent investment in any single individual, especially in such ephemeral creatures as infants' is broadly untenable.[69] The frequency of infant death might have encouraged a fatalistic attitude towards small babies – it was not uncommon to speak openly of 'letting them go to heaven to be with the angels' – but for some the ubiquity of infant death did not make it any easier to bear. In 1862, Melesina Trench recorded in her diary the death of two of her children: her newborn daughter and her 2-year-old son. The loss of her daughter was hard but 'she was merely a little bud; he was a lovely blossom which had safely passed all the earliest dangers, and gave clearest promise of delicious fruit . . . Oh, my child, my child! . . . when I saw you cold and motionless before me how came it my heart did not break at once.'[70] Indeed, contrary to argument that an infant life was worth little, we know that mothers' attachment to their infants was intense, perhaps even more so in the knowledge that a child's life was so precious. Lullabies sung to infants as they were rocked in their cradles reflect love, hope and concern for the child. In pre-revolutionary Russia, children were much hoped for and dearly treasured, reflected in the words of the lullaby 'Slumber, Vasen'ka, Slumber beloved, Go to sleep, precious. Sleep dear child, Precious, golden child'.[71] In London's poor East End, children were indulged and spoiled 'being commonly the pride of their mothers, who will sacrifice much to see them prettily dressed'.[72] A mother of four, who suffered terribly through each of her pregnancies and who often possessed little money, insufficient nourishment and inadequate housing, commented that she 'often wondered how the poor little mites managed to live, and perhaps they never would have done but for our adoration, because this constant admiration of our treasures did give them whiffs of fresh air very often'.[73]

THE UNWED MOTHER

Women who gave birth out of wedlock occupied an uneasy position in most communities. In nineteenth-century religious, moral and legal discourse, the single mother was represented as deviant, irresponsible and dangerous. Envisaged as either a fallen woman or a prostitute, the unmarried mother was held up as the archetype of the sexual woman; a woman who was not subject to a man within marriage.[74] And yet in popular portrayals and in material reality the single mother was not always so reviled. Rather, she was the object of sympathy and in some parts of Europe her existence (and that of her child) was accepted by a community which understood her plight even if it did not accept her morals. Attempts to marginalise and punish single mothers continued and even intensified in the nineteenth century, but the beginning of state provision for single mothers and their children is also in evidence. By the end of our period the impulse to castigate and punish had been leavened by some sympathy and the recognition of the possibility of redemption.

The vast majority of single women who became pregnant had not indulged in 'promiscuous' behaviour. In many parts of Europe, premarital sex was accepted as part of the courtship process prior to an agreed marriage if the woman conceived. In parts of France and Germany up to one-quarter of women were pregnant when they married. Illegitimacy rates appear extraordinarily high but the numbers conceal a reality of responsible and highly regulated sexual behaviour. In Bavaria, where the rate climbed to 25 per cent in some parishes in the middle of the century, children born to farm maids were easily incorporated into foster homes or cared for by grandparents.[75] In Protestant Aberdeenshire in Scotland, where the church commonly treated 'fornicators' in a punitive fashion by subjecting them to public condemnation, single mothers and their children were not only tolerated but actively incorporated into the community, with the children being brought up by grandparents whilst the mothers returned to service.[76] And in Iceland it has been argued that high illegitimacy rates were due to a liberal attitude towards premarital sex; children born out of wedlock were tolerated in this society which traditionally accorded women a high status.[77]

Premarital fertility testing was widespread in rural Europe, but it has been argued that this practice broke down as the looser community ties in towns allowed men to escape their responsibilities, leaving women to bear the consequences alone. In Glasgow it was noted that fathers simply assumed a new identity and disappeared into the streets, lanes and lodging houses where they could not be traced by the mothers of their illegitimate children or the parish upon which such women were forced to turn for financial support.[78] Certainly, contemporary observers believed that urbanisation was to blame for apparently rising illegitimacy rates. Big cities, according to the German feminist Marianne Weber (1870–1950) in 1907, brought about the 'disruption of traditional social communities' and the destabilisation of marriage and morals.[79] The fact that the majority of mothers were in their early twenties (similar to the average age of marriage) when they became pregnant suggests that these women had engaged in what they believed to be serious relationships.[80] These were not women of 'easy virtue'; the majority were employed in the typical occupations of working-class women – domestic service, garment work, seamstress – and had been expecting to marry their lovers. Indeed, there appears to be no real shift in attitudes towards sexuality associated with industrialisation. Illegitimacy rates were no higher in urban areas. Farm and factory workers alike engaged in premarital intercourse, but condemnation of the morals of the urban proletariat by critics fearful of the consequences of economic change was vociferous. What had changed, though, was the plight of the unmarried mother.

The single mother's most pressing problem was likely to be the practical and financial difficulties of looking after a child alone, rather than the implications of shame and lost virtue. The options facing the poor single mother were unenviable ones. The most extreme solution – and the rarest – was infanticide, usually by suffocation or exposure to the elements. The action of the infanticidal women must be seen in the context of mounting censure of extramarital sex, rural poverty and the relatively common occurrence of infant death from natural causes, although the fact that so few mothers took this drastic step should guard us against sweeping analyses. Infanticide in the early modern period is often interpreted as the unmarried mother's desperate measure to escape community reproach at a time when honour was integral to a woman's economic survival. By the nineteenth century though, it has been suggested that economic forces drove some to commit child murder. An unmarried woman presented a threat to the fragile stability of rural communities at times of economic hardship. Such women tended either to migrate to towns and give birth there or – and this was only a tiny minority of cases – they maintained a semblance of normality, denying or concealing their pregnancy until they gave birth and killed the child in secrecy.[81] The case of Mary Dempster is typical. Mary was employed as a servant in a hotel in Lerwick, Shetland, but she was not a native of the town. In 1895 Mary gave birth in her room having admitted to no one that she was pregnant, and the body of her child was discovered hidden in a hole in the water closet. She was sentenced to twelve months' imprisonment but the prosecutor demonstrated some sympathy for the girl:

> She was a young woman 25 years of age. She had neither father nor mother, nor a home. She was a domestic servant dependent on her own exertions for a livelihood. She came here a few months ago as a servant in the Royal Hotel here. She was a stranger among strangers and in all probability had she disclosed her condition she would have been turned off, so where was she to go? She had no home, she would have been out of a situation, and the distress of mind she must have passed through during this time, and all the circumstances . . . almost relieved her of moral responsibility for the crime.[82]

The sympathy shown to Mary Dempster is in marked contrast to attitudes earlier in the century. Across Europe, infanticidal women had been punished extremely harshly since the sixteenth century – the death penalty was widely applied and in Scotland hanging was the penalty until 1809. By 1900, though, the waning of strict church discipline and, perhaps more significant, the breakdown of kinship ties as a consequence of industrialisation and female labour mobility, resulted in greater understanding of the plight of these women. Even in Russia where harsh punishment had been the norm, infanticidal women were treated with a degree of understanding so that by the second half of the century psychologists were helping to acquit women on the grounds of psychological disturbance and diminished responsibility.[83]

Infanticide was extremely rare. Child abandonment, on the other hand, became a common, even popular, option in some countries, for single mothers unable to bring up a child alone. It has been estimated that as late as the 1850s as many as 100,000 babies were abandoned every year in Europe.[84] The majority of babies abandoned in foundling homes were illegitimate. In Paris, illegitimate infants accounted for never fewer than 85 per cent of foundlings throughout the nineteenth century. During the first three decades, around half of all illegitimate babies born in Paris and the department of the Seine were abandoned, although the increase in aid to unmarried mothers towards the end of the century and the phasing out of the turning cradle or *tour* which facilitated anonymous abandonment, resulted in a small abatement in these figures.[85] Elsewhere though, abandonment reached epidemic proportions. In Milan, for instance, some 50,000 babies were abandoned between 1860 and 1869, and in Russia and the Habsburg Empire, state-sponsored foundling homes were larger than any of those found in Catholic Europe. Protestant Europe, notably Britain, Scandinavia and much of Germany, was less hospitable in this respect, preferring to encourage an ethos of individual responsibility rather than collective provision.

A mother's decision to deposit her infant in a foundling home was influenced by a variety of factors including shame, financial restraints and the availability of an anonymous system whereby no one could trace the parent. In Brittany, for example, although illegitimacy rates were low, almost all illegitimate infants were abandoned on account of the strict moral climate. By contrast, in Russia it appears that the stigma of illegitimacy was less pronounced. According to one observer in Vologda province at the end of the nineteenth century, there were 'women and girls with families of illegitimate children who live on what is given in the name of "Christ." The people do not persecute them or chase out these women, but laugh at them and say: "Let them live as they wish".[86] Here, economic problems were possibly the deciding factor in a mother's decision to abandon her child, as the majority were peasant women from the countryside surrounding Moscow and St Petersburg. However, the act of abandonment does not necessarily imply indifference to the child and its future. Mothers frequently gave their babies identity tags or left them with trinkets suggesting either that they hoped to reclaim the child at a later date or that they wished to register their attachment to the infant. Few mothers would have been aware of the horrendous mortality rates in the foundling homes. In Moscow up to 90 per cent of babies abandoned to the foundling hospital there perished.

The position of the single mother in nineteenth century Europe was ambiguous. She was caught at the interstices of moral discourse and material reality, but ironically it was her religious detractors who provided a means of salvation through the provision of foundling homes or the local community which found ways of incorporating the child and its mother into economic life. However, the changes in attitudes towards motherhood and especially the creation of the 'responsible mother' had an impact upon unmarried mothers too. When the state began to attach value to motherhood (as a service to the state) and to children (as future citizens), unwed mothers became the objects of greater sympathy and understanding and, as a result, limited state aid. In France, aid to unmarried mothers was introduced in 1837 and increased after the 1860s in order to help the women keep their children. In Scotland, one local poor law officer remarked in 1873 that if such women were not granted some financial aid, 'the mothers would be compelled probably to leave their service to keep their children, depending on daily and precarious employment, a position of much greater peril than that which they now occupy.'[87] Survival as a single mother was difficult and the limited welfare payments may have made the difference between keeping a child and surrendering it to a charity. However, financial support did not come without strings attached. The incorporation of unmarried mothers into the agenda of respectability and responsibility was tinged with a punitive streak, especially in northern Europe. In the Magdalene homes of Scotland and Ireland, the refuge provided to unmarried mothers was complemented by training in domestic and nurturing skills in order that the 'fallen woman' might be rehabilitated and go on to assume a respectable lifestyle.[88] Unmarried mothers in Britain, Germany and Sweden received welfare at the cost of losing their children. In Germany, under the so-called Leipzig system, illegitimate children were farmed out to foster parents who were thought to provide a better upbringing than the 'depraved' mothers. Elsewhere, sympathy for the unmarried mother and her child was founded upon notions of maternal duty and service. Women were no longer persuaded to abandon their infants to the care of others; rather they were encouraged to take responsibility and thereby redeem themselves through work and self-sacrifice for the sake of their children. The single mother still had to be taught how to act responsibly.

By the 1890s the single mother attracted support amongst feminist activists who argued that the value being ascribed to married mothers should apply to single women too. The French feminist Louise Koppe founded the first maternity home in Paris for the children who otherwise would have been abandoned in 1891.[89] In Germany, Adele Schreiber, a member of the radical Bund für Mutterschutz (League for the Protection of Mothers), campaigned for homes for single mothers and argued in 1904 that unmarried mothers should no longer be marginalised: 'It is a disgrace to our culture that women are forced to conceal the maternity of which they should be proud', she wrote. 'No woman can "fall from virtue" through motherhood.'[90] The League's forthright views on illegitimacy and sexual morality – which included demanding equality of status for legitimate and illegitimate children and state support for motherhood – were not matched in other European states. The rehabilitation of the single mother still had some way to go.

MATERNITY AND THE STATE

Mothers were of little interest to the state until the end of the nineteenth century when national concerns about population decline fuelled a new political concern about maternal and child health. Population policy which addressed both the quantity of births as well as the quality was driven by international conflict within Europe and national self-aggrandisement. Fertility decline was evident across western Europe although it was most marked in France. Politicians and feminists – who described the falling birth rate amongst the middle and upper classes as a birth strike – focused attention on the absence of state support for women's most important social role, and on concern about the alleged poor quality of the offspring of the less well off. In the early 1900s many European governments had begun to assume the mantle of the so-called nurturing state, a term coined by the French feminist Hubertine Auclert (1848–1914) who, in 1885 challenged her own government to embrace its 'motherly' role, calling on it to be enabling and protective rather than merely siphoning resources away from the populace.[91]

The acceptance by European governments that motherhood was a political issue, even if for selfish national reasons, resulted in limited practical benefits for mothers before the First World War. Most west European states had introduced some form of maternity leave before 1914. As early as 1883 the German health insurance law provided maternity benefits to female factory workers for three weeks after the birth of a child. In 1900 a new labour protection law in Sweden made provision for four weeks of maternity leave for female industrial workers, but since no financial support was earmarked the law merely reinforced women's dependence on a male breadwinner during her four weeks' enforced leave.[92] Likewise the 1909 maternity protection law in France had good intentions, but no benefits were paid during the eight weeks' leave. Four years later the Strauss Act extended this law to six weeks' mandatory paid maternity leave for all working women.[93] In Italy, the Cassa Nazionale di Maternità (National Maternity Fund) was created in 1910 and came into force two years later. The insurance fund was intended to provide financial support for working women who, under the labour law, were prohibited from working for one month after childbirth, although problems in administering the financial contributions actually resulted in female workers going on strike against the scheme.[94] In Norway and in Britain, in 1909 and 1911 respectively, insured women and the wives of insured men were entitled to maternity payments. Similarly, in Denmark, Sweden and the Netherlands maternity benefit was incorporated into insurance schemes. Everywhere, such benefits to mothers were limited in scope and execution.

Women required practical help as well as financial support to enable them to combine child care with paid work. In Russia, the provision of summer nurseries which directly helped women working long hours in the fields, and which provided children with meals, health care and activities, were an unqualified success. They allowed women to work and they combated popular resistance to welfare at the same time as saving lives, although this success was achieved at the cost of weakening female child care culture and the bypassing of mothers themselves.[95] Elsewhere in Europe practical support took a less institutional approach. The provision of maternity leave and milk depots in France, without means testing, was a positive step towards real improvements in the condition of mothers and children, in contrast with the situation in Britain where a more disciplinary attitude was adopted. Here, mothers' entitlement to milk depended on their financial circumstances and in one London milk depot women were given detailed instructions regarding interval-feeding and disinfecting equipment.[96] Mothers everywhere resisted the patronising and judgemental maternity services provided by religious and middle-class philanthropists when alternative municipal services were available.[97]

In Britain in 1915, the Women's Co-operative Guild proposed an extension of state support for mothers in the form of weekly maternity payments, the establishment of maternity centres to dispense advice and nourishment, maternity homes, and an increase in the provision of maternity beds in hospitals.[98] Similar demands were being formulated across Europe by feminists critical of the piecemeal state benefits so far introduced and determined to capitalise on the growing understanding at the political level that motherhood was an important social role that deserved state support. In Britain, the concept of the mother's endowment, formulated and promoted by Eleanor Rathbone (well-known for her advocacy of family allowances) was predicated upon the belief that 'motherhood is a service which entitles a woman to economic independence'. This critique of women's dependence upon men and upon the myth of the breadwinner wage was also taken up by French feminists although, in both Britain and France, the legislation of the pre-war decade merely perpetuated women's dependence since women were identified, first and foremost, as wives and mothers rather than as workers.[99] In France and Italy though, some feminist campaigners recognised that there could be no fundamental change in the status of mothers until women were empowered as citizens. Women should be granted citizenship rights on the basis of their role as mothers: in the words of the French feminist Léonie Rouzade, 'If one gets rights for killing men, one should get more rights for having created humanity.'[100] Motherhood 'became a "political strategy" for feminist activism'.[101]

CONCLUSIONS

Motherhood could not be every woman's 'sweet vocation'. Full-time motherhood, as advocated by nineteenth-century romantics and evangelicals and then later by medical professionals and social workers, was only ever an option for a lucky few with the wealth and support that enabled them to give their children the time and the attention, as well as the medical care, they now required. For the majority, the rise in importance of the mother as moral force, educator and producer of the nation's future citizens, meant greater responsibility with few benefits.

Middle-class women had taken on board the notion that full-time motherhood could be both at the heart of one's identity as a woman and constitute one's public duty. The latter was seen in terms of bearing children, continuing the family enterprise, exporting middle-class maternal values to working-class women and more generally allowing maternalism to inform their public activity. Thus an ideology which was used by supporters of separate spheres to constrain women's participation in education and employment on the grounds that women were fitted for their natural duty and little else, was taken up by women themselves to elevate women's position in society. The main beneficiaries were those who used the halo of motherhood to extend their role into philanthropy, what was called woman's mission. Arguably, in the long term all mothers benefited, as those in positions of influence began to campaign for state support for the most important social duty: motherhood. However, in the short term, working-class mothers were forced to endure a great deal of criticism, patronising advice and condescension from health workers, social reformers and lady philanthropists who saw only ignorant women who required enlightenment so that they might become responsible mothers.

On the eve of the First World War most women still had little choice about whether they became mothers or not, and those who campaigned for women to be educated about birth control were criticised by those who expressed concern at fertility rate decline. Yet voices were beginning to be raised in support of family limitation on the grounds of maternal and infant health as well as on the grounds of family vitality and the national good. Couples who decided to practise birth control, according to the German welfare reformer Marie Baum, regarded 'every child . . . as a possession of high value, whose preservation justified every kind of exertion, because the new pregnancy was not simply willed by God but by the individual.'[102] But it was not until after the First World War that women experienced real change, when motherhood ceased to be a constant chore for all of a woman's fertile years, and when the state finally recognised its responsibility to mothers following the decimation of life in that conflict. The nineteenth century saw a shift from a focus on mothers and maternity to a focus on the child and infant health. By 1918 it was finally understood that the two were part of a whole, that the one depended on the other.

Chapter 5

◆

HOME, KINSHIP AND COMMUNITY

The home became the primary site of female identity in the nineteenth century. Women's lives became structured by their relationship with the home, and their economic value was defined in relation to their domestic role. Relations with kin, with servants, and other women beyond their own social realm encountered through their charitable activity, were all informed by this family-centred model. This also set a precedent for expectations of the working-class woman whose status and value in the labour market was affected. Paid work outside the home was given a value in accordance with the belief that a woman's place was within the home. Women were conceptualised as contained within and dependent on the family unit, in contrast with men who were regarded as self-sufficient and independent. Thus, the home assumed immense importance as a physical and symbolic space within which meaning and value was assigned to women's actions.

The home is usually seen as synonymous with the concept of the private sphere. It is undeniable that the concepts of the private and the public sphere had ideological significance amongst the middle classes in the nineteenth century and that the idea of separate spheres was a convenient framework used to understand gender roles in a rapidly changing society. Yet beyond this conceptual value, separate spheres should not be used as a determinist framework to organise our understanding of the place of women and men in society. Women had an enormous range of experiences. Historians of women have, for some time now, been wary of universal theories, and the public–private dichotomy has come in for considerable revision.[1] More useful, perhaps, is the position adopted by anthropologist Michelle Rosaldo who suggests that 'woman's place in human social life is not in any direct sense a product of the things she does (or even less a function of what, biologically, she is) but of the meanings her activities acquire through concrete social interactions.'[2] Rosaldo goes on to state that 'the significances women assign to the activities of their lives are the things we can only grasp through an analysis of the relationships that women forge, the social contexts they (along with men) create – and within which they are defined.' Thus we should examine women's social worlds and social relationships not just in terms of what they did, but also taking into account the ideologies by which they and others made sense of their position and lives. Separate spheres ideology was used in powerful ways to police boundaries, but notions of gender polarity were utilised by women as a means of negotiating civil and political society. In this chapter, the home is discussed both as a concrete place and as a concept which had tremendous power to influence women's experience in nineteenth-century urban Europe. The home could be a constraining idea for women but, at the same time, women made the home a female space. They recognised that their status as homemakers and household managers could provide them with a power base for collective action outside the home. The home defined a woman: it conferred femininity as well as influence in the economic and political spheres.

HOME SWEET HOME

Before the early industrial era there had been little or no discernible division between home and work. The idea of the household incorporated family life and working life. The boundary between the household interior and the work which was undertaken outside was permeable. In most rural areas before 1800 the household was a practical space, providing shelter for both people and animals and a functional workplace. Almost everywhere, woman's work in the home was valued on a par with farm labour; in the words of a Languedoc proverb, 'A dauntless woman in the house is worth more than farm and livestock.'[3] Early industrial growth in the eighteenth century in Britain (later elsewhere) initially reinforced the home as a unit of production and the woman as a worker in it. Indeed, the rise of domestic production based on women's low-paid work increasingly became associated with the household and women's industrial production became intertwined with housework.

Nineteenth-century industrialisation altered this situation. The home was gradually distinguished from the household. The functions – or at least those that were visible – which took place within the household gradually came to represent the opposite of work; the home became an ideological location for consumption rather than production. The decline of household production and the rise of large-scale capitalist agriculture presaged a shift in the relationships within the household. Increasingly, men left home to work. The male's position as primary wage-earner still supported his position as head of the household but it was predicated upon the dependency of the middle-class married woman and the wife's new role as homemaker incorporating manager of the household finances, juggler of resources and creator of domestic bliss. Housework was redefined as unproductive and the home increasingly became a female domain. It became the role of the woman of the house to maintain the separation between home and work, even if the separation was, in many respects, a fiction.

It is in this period that the household – a place of residence and work as well as a political term incorporating hierarchy and authority – was gradually transformed into the 'home' inhabited by the 'family'. The home became a place and an idea. It was a place of retreat, a sanctum, a symbol of family unity and peace, a source of social order. And it was women, and more especially the wife, who carried out this transformation, so that by 1881 the English feminist Frances Power Cobbe could state that 'It is a woman, and only a woman . . . who can turn a house into a home.'[4] Indeed, the wife or mother became so intimately associated with the home in the popular imagination that she came to embody the very concept. In the houses of the wealthy urban middle classes she even began to resemble the domestic interior, her voluminous dresses mirroring the heavy fabrics enveloping the cosy family space. Yet, of course, the very process of homemaking required more than a woman's smiling presence; it constituted physical and emotional work. The home nurtured femininity and was maintained by women's labour.

Home symbolised the separation between private functions and public activity, and thus delineated the boundary between the female private and the male public world. Of course, this boundary was never as rigid in practice as it seemed to be in theory, but the existence of a series of physical and ideological boundaries erected to separate the home from work, the street and the intrusion of the outside world, is testimony to the strength of an idea if not its success. The urban middle classes were the first to pioneer the idea of the private home which was both separated from the workplace and internally segregated in order to mask the physical labour of maintaining the house from the emotional work of creating the home. Across industrialising Europe the manufacturing and professional classes began to move away from the workplace, establishing genteel enclaves on the edge of cities such as Edinburgh's New Town and Hamburg's Harvestehude, or they moved to the suburbs like Edgbaston on the outskirts of Birmingham or even the countryside. Similarly, amongst the nobility in economically under-developed Russia and Poland, manor houses became centres of consumption for the display of fashion and taste often imported from France. It was in these homes that the bourgeoisie fashioned a culture which was decidedly domestic.

In 1864 the English writer John Ruskin put into words the sentiment that the home was a refuge, a sanctuary, from the outside world:

> it is a place of Peace; the shelter, not only from all injury, but from all terror, doubt, and division. In so far as it is not this, it is not home; so far as the anxieties of the outer life penetrate into it . . . and the hostile society of the outer world is allowed either by husband or wife to cross the threshold, it ceases to be a home; it is then only a part of that outer world which you have roofed over, and lighted fire in.[5]

With its heavy fabrics and furniture and decorated with family treasures and knick-knacks, the parlour became a retreat which contained the family in a cocoon-like state, but also allowed the family to represent itself to visitors and to its own members. The adornment of the home was not new. Wealthy families in the seventeenth and eighteenth centuries were addicted to interior décor. Parisian houses were full of pictures, tapestries, mirrors and collectables – snuffboxes, vases, clocks and porcelain which were indicators of status and wealth.[6] But nineteenth-century middle-class homes mirrored femininity; they were full of family photographs, embroidered footstools and antimacassers, fancy goods, sewing frames and china ornaments. All of these furnishings identified the home as a feminine space devoted to family and domestic activities such as needlework, music-making and taking tea. And it was the women of the house – mothers, daughters and servants – who were responsible for creating this cosy hideaway which purportedly served their interests. It was women who became the consumers of the new products for the home and the less wealthy swapped shopping expeditions for handiwork, turning all sorts of everyday items into fancy goods. The home was a focus for women's primary role: procreation and reproduction of the domestic private sphere.

This separation of home and work was manifested differently in working-class homes. Here space was at a premium. In working-class areas of towns, women worked hard to maintain the visible separation of home and work at the threshold. The practice of donkey-stoning or whitening the front step of English terraced houses – which involved considerable labour by the woman of the house – was deemed essential for the maintenance of a boundary between the street and the home, between the world of commerce and the domestic world. The practice served to identify women as proud and respectable custodians of the interior. In London, clean steps, pavements, hearths and so on 'were physical outlines of women's space in households and streets'. Men sullied these symbols of female power at their peril.[7] Inside, the maintenance of a front parlour or best room which was rarely used by family members served a similar purpose, signifying to visitors that the home was a familial space, unsullied by work. 'You lived in the kitchen and then you went in the parlour for your best room', recalled an inhabitant of a textile town in north-west England. 'It was dusted and kept nice and never sat on . . . It was just used on special occasions.'[8] Of course, behind the four walls many women were working, not only at housework and child care, but also undertaking paid work at home as home-workers.

One of the consequences of the sexual division of labour and the separation of the household from production was what Davidoff has termed the elaboration of domestic life.[9] Amongst the middle classes the transformation of the household into a home meant that the home became the symbol of their status as dependent women – albeit often at the expense of another woman's labour. As households became full of furniture and furnishings, as diets improved and new household technologies were introduced, there was simply more housework to be done. The maintenance of a household became woman's work; housework was feminised, domestic service became the major employer of women in the nineteenth century, and all women became symbolic as well as actual captives of their homes. In working-class homes, where few women could give up paid work altogether, the definition of housework narrowed. It became work done inside the house for no pay, a definition used by census-enumerators who identified women who had no outside employment as housewives.[10]

In rural and urban areas, amongst the middle and working classes, 'housework' was gradually distinguished from 'household tasks' and was consolidated as management of the domestic sphere. Even in agricultural regions, housework was slowly beginning to replace farm work for girls. In Italy, for example, the movement of men away from agriculture and into wage-earning left the women to carry on subsistence farming, but they were defined in official statistics as housewives rather than as farmers. This situation was particularly marked in Sicily. Here, the rise of cash-crop production in the 1880s – oranges, grapes, olives – provided many women with wage-earning opportunities, but the collapse of markets and the simultaneous decline of domestic cloth production meant women lost their public productive role. These newly 'domesticated' women – 44 per cent of the female active population – became defined as housewives.[11] In Ireland, by the end of the century women were undertaking unpaid domestic work in preference to paid farm work. In England, the 1833 Agriculture Select Committee reported that farmers' daughters were more likely to undertake housework than work in the dairy; and similarly in Denmark women's roles shifted from 'dairy wives to housekeepers'.[12] Now housework was associated with new standards of cleanliness and orderliness and it was women who were judged according to their ability to maintain these standards, either on their own or with the help of, usually female, servants. The interior of the home, then, was the woman's domain, and for women this alignment of responsibility implied both work and, in return, the expectation of a degree of autonomy within that sphere in the absence of a wage or recognition of the economic value of the role.[13]

It was in the middle-class home that housework reached its apotheosis. Bourgeois interiors were segregated so that the home would not be contaminated by the appearance of industry. The domestic area was physically separated from spaces used for preparing and cooking food, cleaning, washing and sleeping. Ideally, the Victorian wife was to allow 'no smell of washing and ironing [to] pervade the home, no talking of [the servants'] shortcomings; or of the baby's ailments – baby should be in bed when Mr Hall returns, and then be sure that no basket of stocking-mending or household needlework be introduced to his notice, under the idea that he may see how industrious you are.'[14] The employment of servants was the means by which women like Mrs Hall maintained a façade of non-work whilst at the same time consolidating their reputation as good housewives and household managers. The tasks carried out by servants were 'functional and metaphorical'; they did the cooking, cleaning and mending but they also 'helped focus attention on the central female figure in the domestic world'.[15] The lady of the house was judged on the appearance of her home, the 'domestic symbols' – furniture, décor, decorative handicrafts – and on her own appearance. One German housekeeping manual in 1845 advised women who wished to disguise the fact that they carried out household chores in the absence of sufficient help about the home, to rub their hands with bacon before they retired to bed 'to keep a soft hand like those fine ladies who have no heavier work to do than embroidering and sewing'.[16] The femininity of her home, adorned with numerous ornamentation, and the femininity of her dress which was so constricting and so fulsome as to preclude her from engaging in any domestic labour, expressed both the fragility and the power of the bourgeois woman.[17] She could only achieve this domestic femininity if domestic servants performed the coarse household chores unobtrusively in the background or if she could conceal their absence.

Household management became skilled work entailing considerable responsibility for the middle-class mistress. As the housewives' guru of her time, Isabella Beeton (1836–65) explained, in probably the most widely read British advice book of the century, her *Book of Household Management* published in 1861:

> As with the commander of an army, or the leader of an enterprise, so is it with the mistress of a house. Her spirit will be seen through the whole establishment; and just in proportion as she performs her duties intelligently and thoroughly, so will her domestics follow in her path. Of all those acquirements which more particularly belong to the female character there are none which take a higher rank, in our estimation, than such as enter into a knowledge of household duties; for on these are perpetually dependent the happiness, comfort and well-being of a family. In this opinion we are borne out by the author of 'The Vicar of Wakefield' who says: – 'the modest virgin, the prudent wife, and the careful matron, are much more serviceable in life than petticoated philosophers, blustering heroines, or virago queans [sic]. She who makes her husband and her children happy, who reclaims the one from vice and trains up the other to virtue, is a much greater character than ladies described in romances, whose whole occupation is to murder mankind with shafts from their quiver, or their eyes.'[18]

Household management was a full-time vocation requiring a combination of character, good temper, cheerfulness, firmness and moral conduct, as well as knowledge of how to manage servants, how to entertain, how to cook economically, how to manage children and so on. Mrs Beeton's book was written to help women achieve one of their most important roles in life: the creation of a welcoming and well-run household.

> Good Temper should be cultivated by every mistress, as upon it the welfare of the household maybe said to turn . . . Every head of a household should strive to be cheerful, and should never fail to show a deep interest in all that appertains to the well-being of those who claim the protection of her roof. Gentleness, not partial and temporary, but universal and regular, should pervade her conduct; for where such a spirit is habitually manifested, it not only delights her children, but makes her domestics attentive and respectful; her visitors are pleased by it, and their happiness is increased.[19]

Household manuals and women's magazines such as long-running *Die deutsche Hausfrauen-Zeitung*, the Norwegian *Manual of Household Arts* (1848) and the French *Guide des femmes de ménage, des cuisinières, et des bonnes d'enfants* (1862) were full of advice on how to maintain standards of cleanliness, neatness and thrift, but they also helped to create a common consciousness amongst middle-class women of themselves as good housekeepers. Some even formed housewives' associations which concerned themselves with domestic training for young women and the 'servant question'.[20] The message Isabella Beeton imparted to her readers was that household management was a fulfilling occupation in itself, but some of her contemporaries, not surprisingly, disagreed. The novelist Elizabeth Gaskell commented to a friend in 1850: 'One thing is pretty clear. *Women* must give up the artist's life, if home duties are to be paramount. It is different with men, whose home duties are so small a part of their life.' Elizabeth Gaskell was troubled by this tension between what she described as selfishness in wishing to pursue her art and the duty of home.

> I am sure it is healthy for [women] to have the refuge of the hidden world of Art to shelter themselves in when too much pressed upon by daily small Lilliputian arrows of peddling cares; it keeps them from being morbid . . . I have felt this in writing, you in painting, so assuredly a blending of the two is desirable (Home duties and the development of the Individual I mean) . . . but the difficulty is where and when to make one set of duties subserve and give place to the other.[21]

The exclusive association of women with housework in the nineteenth century might, alternatively, be interpreted as a positive choice on women's part. In rural Ireland, for example, where, by 1901, 81 per cent of women were recorded as unwaged full-time houseworkers, it has been suggested that housework provided women with an autonomy and status that could not be acquired from other occupations. The housewife controlled household expenditure, she was responsible for her family's well-being, and she could take pride in her skill. Housewifery was becoming 'a profession for which very careful training is required' for 'a woman wants something more than her sex to qualify her for her profession'.[22] In Britain, the working-class Victorian housewife carved out a powerful sphere for herself; the home was her space, and knowledge about housework gave her a degree of expertise that her husband was unable to reach. Domestic education classes organised by local authorities and private organisations were popular because domestic labour was raised above the menial to become something skilled and specialised.[23]

Housework was feminised but it was not always carried out by the mistress of the house. In earlier ages, young people of both sexes entered service. In Ancien Régime France, for instance, male servants in the houses of the rich were almost as numerous as female, and the work they undertook could not really be described as housework. Only the women at the bottom of the servant hierarchy – the *servantes* and *femme de charge* – spent their time cleaning.[24] In the industrialising states, domestic service soon became the largest employer of women. In Britain, around 45 per cent of the female labour force were employed in service by the 1870s, a figure never exceeded by other industrial states where urbanisation had been less extensive. In France, the equivalent figure was around 40 per cent, and in Germany 26 per cent. Around one-third of all employed females in Paris and Berlin as well as in London were classed as domestic servants by the 1880s. By 1871 more than 70 per cent of French servants were female; in England the figure was 92 per cent.[25] Domestic service had become overwhelmingly a female occupation.

The reasons for the feminisation of domestic service are manifold. Firstly, the redefinition of housework as the maintenance of domesticity favoured females. Many of the tasks required of a servant – attending to cleaning and personal hygiene, to clothing repairs and kitchen work – were already seen as woman's work. Secondly, male servants were not willing to undertake such work for the low wages offered to women. Thirdly, such employment was increasingly regarded as suitable for young women in contrast with industrial or even agricultural work. Domestic service confined a woman inside the home and helped to protect her from immoral influences. In 1843, the Royal Commission on Women and Children in Agriculture, reporting on conditions of work in England and Wales, noted that field labour 'is a bad school of morals for girls and that the mixing up with men on whom poverty and ignorance have encrusted coarse and vulgar habits, tends to greatly uncivilise and demoralise women'.[26] Similarly in France, concerns were expressed that female factory workers would be morally degraded by being exposed to the 'licentious discourses' consequent upon mixing with their male comrades.[27] Domestic service served a dual purpose then. It was the means by which middle-class women sought to maintain their femininity and it was the means by which they attempted to mould working-class girls into hard working, disciplined and above all moral women who would later go on to marry and run households of their own in the image of their superiors. Domestic service was regarded as a preparation for life evidenced by the efforts of philanthropists and welfare officials to train wayward or poor girls in housewifery.

The life of a domestic servant was hard. Most were young, single women and girls. The vast majority were under the age of 30; in England over 70 per cent were younger than 25. Many had migrated to towns from the countryside to take up their first job. In Paris and in London two-thirds of servants in the middle of the century had been born outside the city. In the case of France, agricultural decline and rural impoverishment was the spur for many young girls to move to the cities in search of work, and presumably their parents hoped they would be better off working in someone else's household than in a factory. The provision of room and board was certainly one of the attractions of an otherwise fairly unattractive job. However, although most lived in their employers' house they were not regarded as part of the family. Their living quarters were commonly squashed into the attic or, in some smaller French households, they were forced to sleep on a makeshift bed in the kitchen or share a bed with another servant. Only wet nurses, nannies and governesses had living quarters in the main part of the house. Servants generally worked a six- or even seven-day week with few holidays. The working day started at dawn and could continue until midnight and their day was spent carrying out a multitude of household chores, many involving hard physical labour such as carrying water, scrubbing floors and laundering clothing. Up until the 1880s, wages were good in comparison with the alternative forms of female employment, especially in the cities, but, on the other hand, female domestics earned far less than their male counterparts. By 1900, servants' wages began to level off and with no improvement in working conditions girls began to choose alternative employment which also guaranteed greater personal freedom. One woman from a small Scottish town began her working life in service for ten shillings a week. She stayed just one month commenting: 'About the back of seven in the morning you would be shouted to and you would be at their beck and call 'til about eight or nine at night . . . I didnae wait very long, I don't mind telling you.'[28] Many of her contemporaries had similar experiences and moved on to retail work or found a job in the local textile mills. It was not necessarily the hard work that women began to object to but the subordination.

The relationship between mistress and servant was complicated. The female servant was a status symbol; her very presence but also her neat and tidy appearance and her polite and submissive demeanour, reflected upon her household and more particularly her mistress. The home defined the identity of both mistress and servant but the separation of home and work, and the lesser value placed on housework in contrast with household management, highlighted the profoundly unequal relationship between these women. The mistress and the servant contrived to sustain a dangerous fiction: that women's work outside the home could only result in her neglect of her own home. 'The idea of women's work outside the home in industry became associated with squalor, fatigue, bad cooking and neglected children', wrote Winifred Holtby in a perceptive comment on the consequences of the definition of woman as housewife and homemaker.[29] The domestic servant thus helped to maintain the nineteenth-century notion of home as a serene and private place unsullied by physical labour, but her presence in such numbers in middle-class homes also helped to cast a spotlight on working-class women who could not afford hired help and who struggled to combine paid work with housework and child care.

WOMEN'S NETWORKS

No woman was an island, even when a lone, home-based domestic manager. Women cultivated networks amongst themselves based on their shared interest in issues of home and family. For the working-class woman the networks were usually economic in nature, focusing on assisting family survival, and they were often constructed around the public sphere of the street immediately outside the home. For the middle-class woman, networks were rarely economic in character (which would have conferred a loss of bourgeois status), but rather were based on kinship and good works.

Kinship is a set of socially recognised ties based on physical relatedness but also what are called affinal relationships, which might include relatives by marriage and even contractual relations such as godparents.[30] Women played an increasingly important role in constructing and maintaining kinship networks in the nineteenth century. 'If kinship relations are not seen as confined to the domestic unit alone', writes Jill Dubisch with reference to modern Greece, 'then the broader role of women in kinship structures becomes more clear.'[31] In south-west Germany, for example, the enhanced role of women in agricultural production by the 1840s encouraged women to manipulate kinship relations in order to maintain and enhance land, property and the enterprise. 'As women grew older', writes David Sabean, 'they became experienced in wielding authority, managing farm and trading enterprises, pursuing the interests of themselves and their families, and negotiating effectively with their kindreds.'[32] By the 1860s these women occupied a central position in the sale of land and they carefully used sisters and sisters' husbands as godparents, they arranged marriages within the kin group, building up credit or what may be called kinship capital for both their own prosperity and that of future generations. In Spain, where women had the right to inherit and pass on land, widows — free of husbands who managed property on their behalf — had some power to use their land for strategic means although the cultural traditions of Spain meant that it was much harder for women to translate their property into influence.[33]

Amongst the middle classes the reasons for women's central role in the maintenance of kinship ties were both functional and emotional. Bourgeois women were at the centre of kinship networks in the nineteenth century, creating and sustaining complex alliance systems by means of marriage negotiations, the choice of godparents, persistent letter-writing, frequent travel, the exchange of gifts, the care of children, visiting, organising social events and mediating in family disputes.[34] Women were also the active promoters of family and kinship relations: remembering birthdays and anniversaries, organising family events, creating a sense of family unity amongst members dispersed far and wide by frequent visiting, maintaining through correspondence and the display of photographs the family's constant presence even in its absence, and creating a family history through the collection of mementoes and the creation of albums.[35] These activities did not merely provide emotional sustenance for women confined within the home, rather they placed women at the core of business and family structures. As the German feminist Louise Otto-Peters explained in 1869:

> The family is . . . almost the only institution, in which not only the men but also the women, may develop characteristics and set in motion strengths which are dormant in them. Only in family affairs does the woman have the vote, and indeed not just in a consultative but in a decisive way, her influence here is by far the most powerful, so that she consciously or unconsciously as it were provides the tone, the keynote which rings through the whole house, and all members tuned to the same pitch sing together in a beautiful harmony.[36]

The example of Charlotte Kestner of Hannover, who assumed the role of 'emotional pole' for a wide circle of family, kin and friends, nicely illustrates how a woman might direct or even orchestrate family relations. It was said that, 'In friendly reciprocity her hospitable house was almost never empty of relatives and friends'. Moreover, 'In the large family network, however, and also way beyond it, Aunt Lottchen was Providence itself. Everyone turned to her in joy and sorrow, at any time of despair, in every difficulty and found even if not always material help then always wise and sober advice and heartfelt comfort.'[37] This was a woman who never married but who had brought up her widowed brother's family and helped the family of one of her nieces, thereafter actively keeping the dispersed family in contact and establishing herself as the focal point.

The attention paid to women's construction of kinship networks served a number of purposes. Women's personal contacts, their skill at providing hospitality, their matchmaking skills and assiduity in maintaining contact with distant relatives all contributed to the survival and success of the family enterprise.[38] Individuals found security in the network of interests and relationships formed in ever increasing circles around the nuclear core. The thousands of letters which passed between the four aristocratic Lennox sisters in Britain and Ireland between 1740 and 1832 demonstrate how contact between women did not merely centre upon the emotional or domestic sphere, although of course their shared concerns about health, marriage, pregnancy, children, home interiors and intimate relationships served to strengthen the ties between them. Rather, all four sisters corresponded with one another and with other male and female relations on the political issues of the day such as the Irish Question and the French Revolution, and thereby struggled to retain the position of the aristocratic Lennox family.[39]

Amongst the middle and working classes, neighbourhood groups and extended families had a similar structural function, 'providing a strict system for establishing and maintaining social mores'.[40] And it was primarily women who manipulated the networks, managed the relations amongst kin, and made judgements about whom could be relied upon and whom one might associate with.[41] Elizabeth Roberts suggests that working-class women who maintained kinship networks were not solely motivated by what Michael Anderson called calculative instrumentality whereby help was extended because one knew that a time would come when the tables were turned. The tradition of relatives taking in orphans – an arrangement which accrued few immediate measurable benefits to the adoptive parents – is illustrative of a more complicated conception of kin relations. In north-west England the extended family invariably took in orphaned children through a sense of obligation to kin, whereas in early modern France the legal adoption of children by members of extended kin – godparents, aunts, uncles – was a means by which the blood family could be maintained through the transmission of property to an adoptive child. And it was often widows who pursued what has been termed adoptive reproduction, suggesting the existence of female-headed households using kin for structural as well as affective or emotional reasons.[42] Women's maintenance and orchestration of kinship relations was not primarily a means to emotional fulfilment or even dominated by material considerations; rather, it had a functional role, facilitating women's participation in political and economic networks and maintaining a set of social and moral boundaries. Being integrated into a wider kinship network allowed women to interact with the world of business, politics and culture and for some it was a way of accruing a sense of power, yet it was done in a personal way, through friendships rather than through impersonal relations.

Amongst the rural and urban lower classes it was women's responsibility to manage; to distribute resources in order to ensure the well-being of household members. This task involved women in reciprocal exchange amongst neighbours and kin, the use of credit, the careful use of scarce resources and, at all times the maintenance of respectability when a woman was judged by the outward appearance of her home and its members. In the context of what has been called the family consumer economy, whereby wage-earning was often insufficient to meet consumer expectations, numerous historians have pointed to the need for working-class women to engage in a series of transactions in order to maintain the fiction that the male wage earner could keep his family. Resorting to the pawnshop, keeping on the right side of the local grocer, knowing who would lend a cup of sugar or a pinch of tea, taking in a lodger – all were female survival strategies based on women's control of family consumption and integration into a network of kin and neighbours.[43] Although the financial and practical support offered by family and neighbours should not be exaggerated, these wider networks beyond the immediate household were crucial: in-laws and neighbours were used as paid or unpaid childminders, sisters passed on outgrown baby clothes, grandparents helped to keep children out of the workhouse, neighbours rallied round in the case of illness.[44] All of these patterns of exchange bound together women and their households both materially and psychologically.

For working-class women the line separating the private from the public sphere, the home from the street, was permeable. It was simply not practical for such women to stay at home. Fetching water, disposing of waste products, doing the laundry and shopping, all required forays into the streets to public wells, sanitation facilities, wash-houses and corner shop and markets. Communal female activities – the twice or thrice yearly wash-day, waulking cloth in textile-producing areas, sewing and knitting circles – and the everyday realities of survival, helped to form and strengthen female networks outside the home. It was largely poverty and strategies for survival that forced working-class women to look beyond their immediate household although we should not forget the gaps in the working day when women might gossip, engage in public sociability on the street or at the wash-house. Not all relations between women were based on material need.

It is difficult to judge how far these material relationships translated into other forms of collective support or consciousness amongst working-class women. In the sphere of intimate relations there is some evidence to suggest that female networks functioned to support victims of domestic violence, with women more likely to intervene in disputes than men, who were reluctant to interfere in another man's sphere of authority. Women who fled the hands of a violent husband invariably sought refuge with female relatives or neighbours who provided shelter, financial support and presented themselves as witnesses if the case ended up in court. Such unselfish behaviour was more forthcoming in villages and small towns than in the larger urban centres where, by the end of the century, kinship networks were more thinly spread and informal regulation was giving way to police involvement.[45] However, there was one area where women's networks were less useful. Women's refusal to speak openly about sex meant there was no 'collective sense of where their "rights" lay and what their interests were'. Ellen Ross suggests that mothers deliberately kept their daughters in the dark about sex in order to keep them 'respectable', and that, added to the fatalism of women who felt they had no alternative but to submit to their husbands, meant that sexual relations were the one area where female networks were of little use until a pregnancy ensued, when neighbours and family once more came to the support of the expectant mother.[46]

In extreme circumstances, women's networks assumed a political function. In 1789, Parisian women marched on to the streets of the city to demand bread for their families. In Nottingham in 1812, women congregated and marched around the town in protest against rising bread prices. In 1871, French women again were out on the streets of Paris attacking bread stores. Spanish women engaged in a series of collective actions in the years 1910–18. During the First World War, strike action by women workers in German, Austrian and Italian cities on account of acute food shortages sent warnings to complacent governments, whilst, in Glasgow, female tenants spearheaded a rent strike in protest at rising rents at a time of extreme economic hardship. And in 1917 a women's protest against bread rationing in St Petersburg was a catalyst for revolution. Women's strikes and political protest had their origins in the neighbourhoods and women's immediate concerns associated with the struggle for survival. According to Temma Kaplan, working-class women developed a female consciousness which was drawn from a sense of female community in the shared work they undertook to sustain the lives of their families. 'When working-class women took collective action they were aroused by more immediate issues – social concerns of everyday life such as food, fuel and shelter. These women never created permanent associations based on female consciousness in the way that their male allies developed revolutionary organisations based on the principles of anarchism and socialism.'[47]

Women's collective action throughout the long nineteenth century has often been intimately connected with their relationship to household consumption.[48] Not only food riots, but also protests against enclosure of common land and grazing, against the recruitment of men for the militia and against the introduction of new machinery, all reflected women's concerns about family subsistence and were manifestations of female networks consolidated around everyday activities. During the defence of the Paris Commune in 1871, housewives were prominent amongst those on the streets. It was reported that 'the national guardsmen descended into the streets where groups of housewives were gathered, having left their homes to do their morning shopping. They learned of the retaking of the cannons, and they spread the news in all directions.'[49] Women also supported men during strikes, using existing female networks based on laundries, child care and soup kitchens. In the case of a textile strike in Barcelona in 1913, which involved thousands of male and female workers, women used their networks to mobilise support for the strike, sending representatives to the food markets to talk to female shoppers. They organised daily street demonstrations independent of the trade union. And women's private work – feeding their menfolk and patching up their wounds – became public work.[50] During these instances of collective protest, women demonstrated the permeability of the private and public spheres and showed how the household as a unit of economic and social organisation might be extended beyond four walls into the streets and into the realm of the political.

EXPORTING THE HOME

So powerful was the idea of the home in the lives of nineteenth-century European women that it moved wherever they went. The working-class woman took the home into the street when she networked with her neighbours. The middle-class woman took the home with her for a different function – to export it to the less fortunate.

To qualify as a lady of the middle classes, the bourgeois woman had an obligation to proselytise the home – to preach the virtues of the feminine domestic sphere to those amongst the lower working classes who were failing to fulfil the expectations of respectable society. The middle-class lady possessed a sensibility built upon her concern for women and children who required the guidance of her experience and knowledge. This was an act of evangelism which conferred on the middle-class woman access to the world. It took her out of the private sphere of the home, and gave her a legitimate role in the public sphere. Bringing the female world of home and family to the places of poverty, vice, drink and ignorance, the middle-class woman secured protection and privilege in a place which was otherwise considered dangerous. Indeed, many middle-class women undoubtedly regarded this as a source of excitement, and perhaps as a means of self-discovery. But walking in her fine clothes down the public thoroughfare of 'rough' areas, and even entering working-class homes in 'slum districts', she was effectively surrounded by a force-field which gave her protection from molestation and obstruction. In this way, the middle-class woman could go where others, including men, might fear to go.

Whether of a liberal persuasion like the female reformers of post-1848 Germany, Catholic conservative like the women of northern France or evangelical like those in England, female philanthropists or social activists shared a belief in their ability to bring about change. This so-called woman-centred approach to social reform was characterised by their faith in the value of the maternal role in 'the great social household'.[51] Moreover, these women's unshaking belief in their own domestic morality not only informed the kind of charity they chose to sponsor (mother and baby homes, kindergartens, temperance campaigns, health and hygiene reform), but also those persons deemed worthy of help and the conditions demanded for the receipt of charity. Members of the French Catholic maternal societies 'revealed a firm intention to mould members of their sex into their own image'. In sum:

> the working of the maternal societies corresponded to the workings of the microcosm of the home and the macrocosm of the universe. On the social level, it reflected the image of the women, demanded the mastery of reproduction in the maintenance of a chaste presence, ordered the relationship between rich and poor mothers, and connected them to the moral authority of God through the mechanism of *caritas*.[52]

It was this limited vision which determined the contradictory nature of their beneficence. These women could provide help to mothers and infants in the name of improving infant and maternal mortality rates, whilst barring illegitimate children from their crèches. They could lecture working-class women on cleanliness in homes resembling slums whilst they employed servants to maintain their own houses to the standards they required in others. To acknowledge the presence of unmarried mothers and their illegitimate children would have blemished the image of motherhood in whose name these 'lady bountifuls' were dispensing their goodwill. Philanthropy was seen as a natural extension of their domestic role, and there could be no compromise

Female charitable activity was informed by religious commitment, moral superiority and humane charity. In Britain, evangelism inspired the formation of an extensive range of female associations, from temperance, missionary and Sunday School societies to female benevolent institutions, societies for the care of widows, orphans, the sick and the infirm. The numbers involved were considerable. In Glasgow, for example, in 1895 two-thirds of the 10,766 Sunday School teachers were female.[53] In Germany the first such female associations developed under the aegis of the Catholic and Protestant Churches such as Amalie Sieveking's Women's Association for the Care of the Poor and the Sick, founded in Hamburg in 1832. Here the early female associations might also be described as patriotic in that they were established in response to the problems caused by the Napoleonic Wars; organisations such as the *Frauenverein von 1814* and the *Frauenverein für das Verschämte Arme von 1816* aimed to help needy families by lending them money to buy work tools, visiting, and ensuring the children attended school.[54] Jewish women also established their own philanthropic organisations. In Britain, in the context of the Jewish immigration in the late nineteenth century and the rise of fears about racial degeneration, Anglo-Jewish women worked to ensure respectability and good maternal standards in the new urban Jewish communities.[55] Women believed that the key to philanthropy was the personal touch: 'the primary goal for most women was the reestablishment of a network of friendships across class lines, between women of shared interests and concerns.'[56]

Personal charity, then, could be seen as an extension of the personal kinship networks so painstakingly established by middle-class women. Instead, though, of waiting for family and friends to approach her with their problems, the lady reformer ventured out to those in need. In London, however, it was found that one of the best ways of reaching the poorest families was by employing a 'Bible-woman' from the working classes who would more likely be welcomed inside as 'a motherly woman of their own class'.[57] Similarly, the English housing reformer Octavia Hill (1838–1912) also used women as sanitary visitors in an effort to exploit poor women's tacit acceptance of the dominant discourse on cleanliness and hygiene; male visitors, she found, were likely to be thrown out by the husband. All these organisations tended to use women on the front line as the first point of contact with the recipients of charity in their own homes, or at least on the doorstep. It was to this face-to-face task that women were believed to be most suited. Not only were they more likely to be admitted to a working man's home but it was also felt that female visitors shared a common set of moral and maybe also religious values with the working-class woman which transcended class difference. All of this activity rested upon the belief that all women shared common values about the importance of home and family.

The example of the founding of kindergartens in France and Germany illustrates how similar attempts to bestow charity were conceived quite differently. In northern France the kindergarten movement was conceived as a means of providing a basic education for working-class children. The nature of that educational experience was coloured by religious imagery and insistent catechising, reminding the children of the temptations of industrial society and the dangers of falling into sin. In northern Germany, by contrast, the Froebel kindergarten model which promoted creativity, healthy exercise and natural growth, was a more reformist philanthropic response to social problems. For activists such as Bertha von Marenholtz-Bülow, education was the key to reform, promoting social harmony and instilling in children the values of community and citizenship. Underlying this noble aim was the female mission to promote female values of nurture and community that the rest of male-dominated society neglected.[58] French and German women shared a common agenda which was to see maternal values influencing the 'great human household', but the difference between the two groups lies in their deeper objectives. In France, female charity was an end in itself, simply reflecting well upon the *dame patronnesse* and rarely evolving into a critique of society. In Germany, however, the philanthropic activities informed by 'spiritual motherhood' were to provide a springboard for a wider vision encompassing female emancipation, the concept of social work and, as in Britain, a challenge to the double-standard of morality.

Philanthropic work invariably carried with it a moral message involving an implicit criticism of working-class standards. Yet, the inevitable dissonance between the standards imposed by women philanthropists and the achievements of their working-class clients was sharper in some conditions than in others. Where infant care was concerned, it is clear that the first phase of involvement by voluntary associations prioritised the survival and health of the infant at the expense of the mother's interests, such was the eagerness to see infant mortality rates fall. We have already seen how middle-class mothers had embraced motherhood as central to their identity and had come to see child nurture as a key element in their duty to the nation. By the end of the century, in response to a number of external stimuli such as imperialist expansion, war and national aggrandisement, the stronger European nations were concerned not only for the quantity but also for the quality of their populations. In Britain, shock at the poor state of recruits to fight in the Anglo-Boer War (1899–1902) prompted massive official concern with the health of the population. Similar concerns were expressed in France following the Franco-Prussian war of 1870–1. The response was an army of health visitors, sanitary inspectors and sundry others who sought to educate working-class mothers on how to care for their infants, dispensing advice rather than financial aid and not infrequently casting a disapproving gaze over the homes of their struggling clients. Their belief was that 'bad' mothers could become 'good' mothers if placed under scrutiny and continual supervision.[59] Not surprisingly, mothers were often suspicious of the visitors' intentions, and sceptical about their chances of being able to put into practice the advice they had been given. In one London borough, though, there were some who understood the tensions implicit in the infant welfare movement. 'I do not think that my Hoxton mothers would let a lady in if she said: "I hear you have got a baby and I want to teach you about it"', commented one local worker in 1904.[60]

Two issues brought middle-class values into conflict with working-class life: temperance and sexual morality. Both of these social problems forced women reformers to address broader gender issues. Women active in the temperance movement regarded male drinking as a threat to women and children, to the very foundations of family life. Alcohol was seen as a corrosive substance which ate away at the foundations of domesticity. Female reformers, many of whom came to temperance from a religious background, regarded drink as an enemy of the family and domesticity, and women themselves could counter it if they adopted middle-class moral values. The temperance movement was, in part, an 'assertion of domestic priorities'.[61] Indeed, women were seen as the key not only to change in the family but also in the moral elevation of society as a whole. One of the most prominent temperance campaigners in Britain remarked in 1849 that women were the 'most influential moral teachers of society'; it was they who had the responsibility to reform those weaker than themselves.[62] The man who drank away his wages in the pub needed to be encouraged back into the home by a wife who created a peaceful domestic environment. But it was soon realised that the solution to the problem did not lie in the hands of women alone. The existence of a male drinking culture in pubs which excluded women, and the brutal consequences of excessive alcohol consumption in the form of domestic violence convinced many amongst the reformers that the provision of alternatives in the form of alcohol-free cafés and pubs, and the campaigning amongst women and children, did not reach the root of the problem. The solution to intemperance, like drink itself, had to be seen in the context of unequal power relations between men and women, in the home, in the workplace and in the social sphere.

Sexual morality forced women reformers to address broader gender issues in a more radical way. Prostitution, vice and moral purity took women activists into a whole new arena. Whilst they initially believed that the eradication of vice and commercial sex could be solved by encouraging working-class women to conform to the domestic ideal, they soon realised that change could only come about with a thoroughgoing alteration in the condition of women as a group. Chapter 6 considers this issue in more detail. This shift from criticism of the working classes, to self knowledge and a broader feminist consciousness on the part of the women philanthropists resulted in a realisation that female campaigning against the laws on vice (and drink) could never be successful as long as there was no equality before the law and as long as women were disenfranchised.

CONCLUSIONS

Women understood that the boundary between the home and the street was artificial. Middle- and working-class women recognised the constraints and the opportunities the idea of the home brought them. Working-class women used their female consciousness nurtured in the community to fight for better living standards for themselves and their families. Middle-class women, on the other hand, initially used the strength they gained from the home to preach to those less fortunate. However, they soon came to understand the contradictory nature of their position. They preached one thing but were doing another. The language of female moral superiority could only be taken so far; it had little meaning for the female victim of a drunken or violent husband or for the prostitute forced to work on the streets during economic downturns. Those involved in philanthropy and reform movements, most especially in Britain and Germany, began to see that the moral reform of the private sphere was not the solution to poverty, brutality and vice. Indeed, it was middle-class women's own colonisation of public space in the form of voluntary associations and charitable organisations which created a feminine public sphere from which a broader vision of social and gender relations would be formulated. Calls for improved education and employment opportunities for middle-class women, for better working conditions and wages for working-class women, and eventually for legislative change and suffrage reform, emerged from what might be termed a feminine public sphere – an arena which, nevertheless, had been shaped and informed by women's association with the home and which would continue to be informed by the language of domesticity and motherhood.

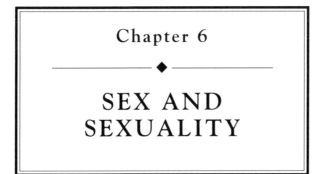

Chapter 6

◆

SEX AND
SEXUALITY

Sexual prudery and the nineteenth century are synonymous. Victorianism was a phenomenon which took its name from the prim and proper British queen in her advancing years, who symbolised the most puritan and apparently sexually abstemious period in history. Across Europe in general there was a sexually oppressive climate, and women were its primary victims. The perils and pleasures of the city came to be symbolised by discourses on sex. Women's sexuality especially represented all that was dangerous about modern society. The nineteenth century is sometimes described as the disciplinary century, when women were made to pay for what was regarded as their inherently unruly sexuality. Novels of the period are full of anti-heroines like Anna Karenina and Emma Bovary, women who pursued their sexual passions and were punished for their rejection of the respectable but passionless role of wife and mother. This was an era characterised by the sexual double-standard, whereby women were constrained and punished for public sexual activity, but men's less restrained (hetero-) sexual behaviour was tolerated. It was marked by a series of 'moral panics' centred on the fear of the spread of venereal diseases, the apparent rise in the number of prostitutes on city streets and the increase in illegitimate births. The passionless woman was held up as an ideal in middle-class circles whilst working-class adulterers, mothers of illegitimate children, women who lived 'in sin', prostitutes and even women who liked to enjoy themselves, were punished for allowing their sexuality to destabilise the fragile social equilibrium. Woman came to be regarded as 'the Sex'. She was defined first and foremost by her sexuality, whether she was 'sexually comatose or helplessly nymphomaniacal'.[1]

However, the stark distinction between the pure and passionless woman on the one hand, and the lustful deviant on the other, was not as sharply drawn in practice. The portrayal of nineteenth-century sexual mores as repressed pays too much heed to conduct books and prescriptive literature and to the legal repression of sexuality. Traditional modes of moral regulation were breaking down. By the 1880s, Victorianism was on the wane.[2] There was growing resistance to the disciplining of sexual behaviour and the beginning of a new sexual code which was more willing to acknowledge (if not entirely accept) the importance of pleasure. Urbanisation partially helps to explain the changes. It was harder to enforce strict moral codes in towns where men and women mixed freely and where a single woman could earn an independent wage. In the city the civil state was replacing the church as the moral regulator; morals' police took the place of ministers, doctors replaced midwives, and philanthropists stepped into what they saw as a moral vacuum but their control was much more diffuse in an anonymous society.

In 1861 the English doctor William Acton said: 'women (happily for them) are not very much troubled with any sexual feeling of any kind'. For Acton, the ideal woman 'seldom desires any sexual gratification for herself [but] she submits to her husband's embraces . . . only to please him.'[3] Views such as this, which propounded women's alleged passionlessness were, by 1900, overtaken by their critics who championed a woman's right to understand and control her body and to enjoy sex. The publication and wide distribution of works by the Swedish writer Ellen Key (1849–1926), the British scientist Marie Stopes (1880–1958) and the Austrian psychoanalyst Sigmund Freud (1856–1939), encouraged women – albeit mainly educated women in the first instance – to expect or even demand sexual satisfaction in marriage. Novelists began to create female characters who celebrated their sexuality, who pursued sensual pleasures without being labelled loose or sinful, or having to forgo personal autonomy. By 1900, fictitious sexual women had been joined by a rather strange alliance of sexologists (those who wrote about sexuality in a scientific way) and feminists who had begun to turn the debate on sex away from danger and towards pleasure.

This chapter discusses the ways in which female sexuality were constructed as problematic and disruptive to the social order, and considers how European states attempted to control women who displayed their sexuality in inappropriate ways. It goes on to examine feminist challenges to the double-standard and the formulation of a new kind of autonomous female sexuality by feminists and sex reformers.

SEX AND REPUTATION

Women have always been judged by their sexual behaviour. What has become known as the double-standard has informed our understanding of the ways in which, for women, sexuality was key to their position and experience in the community.[4] The double-standard connotes a complex system of honour and reputation founded upon the belief that in a patriarchal society women's impurity and immodesty was destabilising and therefore to be condemned, whereas men's sexual licentiousness might be tolerated. In early modern Europe, to call a woman whore was, with the exception of witch, the most powerful and damaging term of abuse since it called into question her moral behaviour, her chastity and her honour. There was no male equivalent. Gossip, idle talk and common insult were used to regulate women's behaviour and we know how powerful the tongue was from women's insistence on defending their good name against charges of sexual misconduct in church courts, indicating that a woman's standing in the community rested upon her sexual reputation as well as her social position. If London is representative, women brought as many as three-quarters of all defamation cases and defended up to one half of them.[5] The language of sexual insult was overwhelmingly female.

By the 1800s, although fewer defamation cases reached the courts, the power of sexual insult was as strong as ever. Anna Clark argues that 'the power of gossip derived from its ability to erase the boundaries between public and private life', hence women of the commercial classes were just as, if not more, vulnerable to sexual insult when their trade depended upon their (sexual) reputation.[6] To be accused of immoral behaviour in one's private life imputed one could not be trusted in a public role. Unmarried or widowed women were the most likely to defend their good name since they were most vulnerable to charges of dishonesty and immorality from competitors, male or female. 'Whore' along with 'slut' and 'dog' did not necessarily imply sexual impropriety on the part of a wife, but was more likely an attempt to cast aspersions on a wife's ability in her sphere – the household – thus imputing dissolute or slovenly behaviour.[7] In southern Germany the insult *Hur* (whore) suggested a dual threat, both to the legitimacy of any offspring and to the ordered household.[8] In the context of the divorce court it appears that men accused of using this word were attempting to control a wife who, in their eyes, had become too independent and perhaps had maintained their standing in the community whilst that of the husband had deteriorated owing to his dissolute lifestyle. In southern England too, 'sexual language was used by men to discipline women who challenged their supremacy', and it was increasingly used to control women who rejected traditional female roles.[9] Notions of respectability rested upon a woman's reputation within the private sphere, as a wife and mother. If her propriety within this sphere was questioned, then she was allegedly no better than a common prostitute whose place was on the streets, in public. So, the use of the insult 'whore' in early nineteenth century plebeian society was a potent way of disciplining female behaviour.

In a society where the language of defamation could be challenged, women were able to participate in the complex honour system to their advantage. Speaking in public about sexual reputation allowed women to restore their reputation. By the 1850s, however, sex moved out of the public sphere and became contained within the private sphere. Michel Foucault has argued that the nineteenth century was a period when discourses on sexuality were produced, multiplied and dispersed by a multiplicity of agencies including the churches, scientists, doctors, psychologists and feminists, resulting in the privileging of sexuality as the core of private identity.[10] Sexual activity became dangerous when revealed in public, thus legitimising the policing of society. This was a time when self-control was advocated in place of self-expression, and when the privileged site of sexuality became the family, rendering all other practices – including homosexuality and extramarital intercourse – dangerous or destabilising. As a result, language was moderated (few women now would have had the audacity to speak the word 'whore' in a public court), and sex became private. Modesty and secrecy became the watchwords. In the words of the leading British medical journal following a series of press exposés revealing the degradation of the London underworld: 'The publicity which has recently been given to the subject of sexual sin . . . is in itself an enormous evil . . . There are things "done in secret" which "should not be so much as named" in family circles or in newspapers which have an entrance into private houses.'[11] In public sex was moderated and sanitised.

REGULATING SEX

The urban environment was enticing and exciting to the young men and women who flocked to European towns and cities for work. London, Glasgow, Paris and Berlin and smaller urban centres were magnets, containing a range of amusements and leisure pursuits. To their critics, though, they threatened to undermine public morality. The London music halls, it was said, were inhabited by painted ladies revealing too much flesh – performers and audience alike. German *Tingel-Tangel's*, music-hall acts performed in ale-houses where 'provocatively dressed women sang risqué verses in an atmo-sphere impregnated with bad language and beer fumes', were singled out as a threat to decency, 'partly owing to the frivolous or suggestive content of what is performed and partly because of the suggestive nature of the perfor-mances themselves'.[12] The dance halls, the most popular form of cheap enter-tainment, aroused widespread criticism for their encouragement of intimacy. The atmosphere was summed up by a rather moralistic participant observer in the German industrial town of Chemnitz in 1895, where he witnessed 'un-bridled merriment, increasing tumult, sensual excitement which reached its climax . . . at the stroke of twelve . . . then couple after couple would silently withdraw for a midnight stroll to the fields . . . or straight to sweetheart's chamber and bed.' In this way, he concluded, 'our labouring youth is losing today not only its hard earned wages but its strength, its ideals, its chastity.'[13]

All of these forms of entertainment offered an escape from monotonous jobs in the factory, but single working girls were represented as both at risk themselves and a danger to society in general. Young girls, it was alleged, might easily become ensnared in vice and tempted to become commercial sellers of sex. Indeed, any girl who worked in the public sphere and who went about the city unescorted might be identified as a prostitute. In 1863, a visitor to the Glasgow Fair reported that he 'saw 94 prostitutes, also a large number of very young girls like mill-workers, scarcely distinguishable from prostitutes in their conduct'.[14] The practice known as treating – the exchange of treats, perhaps a meal or a night at the music hall, for sex – was not unknown amongst the urban working classes, but it was a system that was easily misinterpreted.[15] Women who worked as waitresses and in bars were often reliant on tips and, it was said, payment for sexual favours. These women were victims of the sex trade. It was so easy for a young girl, fresh from the countryside, to fall prey to procurers, or so the alarmists alleged. In England, the journalist W.T. Stead became famous for a series of articles published in the *Pall Mall Gazette* in 1885, under the title 'The Maiden Tribute of Modern Babylon', in which he recounted his own purchase of a young girl for five pounds. This was one of a number of attempts to dramatise the plight of girls seduced and corrupted 'in the nightmare world of London's inferno'.[16] Once she had 'fallen', the girl became a danger on the streets, an enticement to young men, and it was the single working girl who became the focus for numerous morality campaigns; it was she, rather than the male consumer of 'vice' who was in the front line in the fight against national decline in the European industrial states.

In the urban spaces of late nineteenth-century Europe, the prostitute was 'the central spectacle in a set of urban encounters and fantasies'.[17] The woman of the street, the working girl, the 'round-the-corner-Sallie', symbolised the opposite of domestic virtue and feminine piety. Prostitutes were portrayed as 'female grotesques, evocative of the chaos and illicit secrets of the labyrinthine city'.[18] Across Europe, from Dublin to St Petersburg, the disorderly, diseased, corrupt body of the prostitute was used as a metaphor for fears about urban decay, national decline, and transgressions across class, gender and racial borders.[19] She was a symbol of pleasure and danger, her body capable of satisfying her male clients and at the same time threatening the social fabric by spreading venereal disease. Offering sex for sale and accused of preying on men, she represented the obverse of the natural sexual hierarchy (the active male and passive female). By the end of the century a plethora of laws aiming to control female sexuality, and specifically to regulate prostitution, were in place in the industrialised states of Britain, France, Germany, Italy and Russia.[20]

A moral panic about commercial sex swept across Europe from the mid-nineteenth century. However, the supposed evil of prostitution was not a wholly new concern. In eighteenth-century cities, streetwalkers, as prostitutes were often known, were already confined to certain streets, and in London it was said that the freedom of prostitutes to ply their trade threatened decency, modesty and public order.[21] By the 1860s, though, prostitution became the currency for a range of concerns about the urban condition and the health of the nation. It also provided a field of experimentation for the new theories put forward by physicians, criminologists and anthropologists. Indeed, the similarities amongst different nation-states in their attitudes towards the issue are remarkable and it is important to note that virtually all industrialising European states adopted a range of similarly repressive measures designed to control 'vice'. The Contagious Diseases Acts were introduced in Britain and Ireland in 1864, 1866 and 1869 and applied only to ports and garrison towns. Police were given special powers to apprehend and formally identify women they believed to be guilty of procurement, and thereafter they were subjected to regular medical inspections. If found to be infected with venereal disease, a woman would be imprisoned in a special lock hospital or ward for treatment. These laws were only the most notorious. In parts of Germany, in addition to the registration system, prostitutes were confined to certain city streets and prohibited from frequenting areas such as parks, promenades and outside theatres where they might offend the (middle-class) residents and passers-by. The Parisian regulatory system confined prostitutes to brothels situated in designated areas although, towards the end of the century when fears of sexually transmitted diseases were at their height, a new surveillance system was introduced based on the *maisons de rendez-vous*, designated houses where prostitutes were free to come and go.[22] In Russia, a system similar to that of Britain was instituted in the 1840s, with the additional stigma whereby a registered woman was required to carry a ticket instead of the normal passport. The leeway given to the special police charged with identifying and registering prostitutes meant that no single working woman could feel safe; simply being a single independent woman in the city, divorced from a productive and reproductive household, without a male guardian, made her fair game for the morals' police. In all states, a system of surveillance and control of working-class women resulted in the disciplining of female sexuality.

The official justification for introducing regulations to control prostitution at this time was the fear of the spread of sexually transmitted diseases. Prostitutes were blamed for a decline in the nations' health and, more particularly, for the threat to the strength of the armed forces at a time of nation-state formation and imperial expansion (when there was no cure for syphilis). However, the regulations were more successful at controlling women than disease. It could hardly be otherwise when no efforts were made to apprehend the male customers. Registration, restrictions on movement, and medical intervention combined to stigmatise the prostitute but, at the same time, this raft of measures helped to define the prostitute as everything the ideal woman was not, and thus the control in effect extended to *all* women, working class and middle class, prostitute or otherwise. The prostitute was immodest, gauche, public and seemingly independent, and moreover she took sex on to the streets. No respectable woman would compromise her modesty in such a way, and by means of the control measures it was believed that no respectable women would encounter a prostitute, let alone be mistaken for one. The very existence of the prostitute helped to preserve the modesty of the respectable young woman. In his 1869 *History of European Morals*, William Lecky observed that the prostitute 'is ultimately the most efficient guardian of virtue. But for her the unchallenged purity of countless happy homes would be polluted.'[23]

Some professionals, particularly those in the new realms of forensic medicine and criminal anthropology, tried to explain prostitution in terms of sexual perversion and congenital abnormality. The views of the Italian forensic psychiatrist Cesare Lombroso were particularly influential not only in his home country but also abroad. Lombroso argued that the habitual prostitute was a congenitally depraved type, sexually assertive and criminally insane. In

Russia the country's expert on venereal disease, Veniamin Tarnovskii, tended to agree: 'A woman who willingly and consciously engages in the prostitution trade, is always a morally vicious and most often a physically abnormal being.'[24] However, societal explanations are more convincing. Prostitutes were drawn overwhelmingly from the ranks of single women in insecure and poorly paid occupations – they were 'the unskilled daughters of the unskilled classes' – formerly workers in the most common occupations of working-class women: service, laundering, char work and the needle trades.[25] All these jobs were precarious, seasonal and low-paid. Factory workers, on the other hand, were proportionately less likely to turn to prostitution on account of the relative security of the work and the higher wages. The majority of prostitutes were single, lived outside the family, and had turned to prostitution for economic reasons allied to personal circumstances. Rescue workers amongst prostitutes reported that they were characterised by their independence and assertiveness although they acknowledged the importance of a female subculture where prostitution was an acceptable solution to economic need.[26] There were complex reasons, then, for a woman's decision to take up prostitution; it was not premeditated and neither, as some critics suggested, was it hereditary.

The vice trade operated in ways which severed the link between the prostitute and her community. Prostitutes were harassed by the police and corralled into designated streets which were invariably in the poorest parts of cities. Local residents expressed their dismay at the proximity of the sex trade. No one wanted a brothel in their neighbourhood, both because of the inevitable heightened police activity it attracted and because the working classes were well aware of the fine line drawn by the middle classes between prostitutes and working-class women.[27] Moreover, attitudes towards prostitution spilled over to affect attitudes towards other women who fell foul of the 'chastity laws'. Unmarried pregnant women were the prime targets, although any working-class woman who was labelled as sexually precocious or promiscuous was equally in danger of being sent to an institution, to remove her from the perilous streets and incarcerate her in a substitute family. This was a means of making sex secret, by removing a woman who had transgressed so that she could no longer pollute the streets or her family, so that any woman's body that radiated sexuality, especially if pregnant with an illegitimate child, could be hidden away.

One of the institutions in which so-called immoral women were incarcerated was the Magdalene home. These establishments symbolised the dichotomy between the respectable working-class girl and the fallen woman.

Unlike the later lock hospitals which housed prostitutes against their will, the early nineteenth-century Magdalene homes took women defined as at risk but redeemable by magistrates, the police or even their families. Ireland had its first Magdalene Asylum as early as 1765 and established many more, most run by Catholic nuns, including eleven in Dublin by the 1830s. In Russia, the Russian Society for the Protection of Women founded in 1901, attempted to rescue young women before they succumbed to the clutches of brothel-keepers and established similar refuges for their rehabilitation.[28] The aim of the homes was to institute a regime of moral regulation whereby girls were remade into respectable working-class women. They were taught to be modest, silent, hard-working and subservient through religious indoctrination and training in domestic duties.[29] Laundry work was a favourite means of subduing and reforming the 'girl at risk'. As well as providing training for domestic service, it symbolised the cleansing of the girls' shame as well as the dirt of the urban environment and was a potent reminder of the girls' fall from grace. 'Through the Christian chain of command which paralleled the Victorian social class hierarchy and which sanctioned female inferiority, self-abnegation and duty, each inmate learned her appropriate gender-role and social class position.'[30] In some institutions the inmates were desexed – their heads were shaved and they were forced to wear rough and unattractive clothing. But not all inmates were as compliant as the reformers might have wished. In the Scottish asylums, girls rebelled against the strict regime of scripture-reading and laundry or sewing work whilst observing a 'becoming silence' at all times, by swearing, deliberate vandalism and running away. In one Russian lock hospital it was said that far from using decent and inoffensive language, 'disorders among women being treated for syphilis are frequent'.[31] Repeat offenders were numerous. Of course, women who defied the rules were regarded as merely acting true to type. Good girls were silent and submitted to the moral regulation designed to make them into model domestic women.

REFORMING SEX

The first generation of feminist campaigners in this field, often described as social purity feminists, were understandably concerned to challenge the dominant cultural construction of femininity and female sexuality. The dominant construction of the idealised woman in the nineteenth century was passionless, chaste and self-sacrificing. Her sexuality had to be suppressed and redeemed by taking on the roles of wife and mother. This redemption carried with it the role of moraliser; a women's denial of lust was the basis for her moral superiority, and it was this that spurred on many feminists to argue for a transformation of relations between the sexes based on the doctrine of sexual purity summed up by female passionlessness and male self-control. This strategy 'could empower women to attack the customary prerogatives of men; it could also validate a new social role for women outside the heterosexual family.'[32] It was only by questioning the cultural stereotype of the sexual woman that feminists could proceed to claim rights in the spheres of education, employment and politics. The second generation of feminists extended their analysis to the very cornerstone of middle-class respectability: marriage. It was not until the turn of the century, that these feminists – sometimes described as radicals – began to discuss in public the issue of women's control over their own bodies: birth control, abortion, sexual pleasure and sexual choice, all manifestations of a recognition of female sexual autonomy.

The first opportunity for feminists to articulate their opposition to the double-standard was in the campaigns against state-regulated prostitution. Although issues such as custody of children and married women's property had engaged early feminists with women's sexuality in an oblique way, it was the issue of prostitution which galvanised them into speaking out on a subject formerly regarded as taboo for respectable women. Why did this issue more than any other succeed in radicalising middle-class women around the question of female sexuality? Josephine Butler (1828–1906), the most prominent campaigner, not just in Britain but on the international stage, summed it up thus:

> [Prostitution was a question] which *directly strikes* at the physical and moral life of tens of thousands of women . . . which threatens the purity and stability of our homes, which stabs at the very heart of pure affection, which degrades all womanhood through foul associations of thought and feeling, and which murders chivalry and generosity towards women in the hearts of our sons and brothers.[33]

Prostitution degraded all women and poisoned the relations between the sexes. Moreover, argued Butler, by condoning prostitution, as was the case in all west European jurisdictions, those who supported its existence upheld a system which consigned 'respectable' women to ignorance in sexual matters. The campaign to repeal the Contagious Diseases Acts in England and Wales, spearheaded by the Ladies National Association for the Repeal of the Contagious Diseases Acts, and parallel feminist challenges to the state regulation of prostitution on the European continent, was a challenge to the notion that respectable women should have nothing to do with sex. Respectable, middle-class women found themselves speaking in public about women's bodies, the sex act and 'instrumental rape' as they described the forced medical examination by a man with a 'steel penis' or speculum. They surprised themselves in their boldness but also wrong-footed their male opponents who did not know how to deal with what one British Member of Parliament described as the 'revolt of the women'. Surprising as it may seem, social purity feminists allied themselves with prostitutes on the grounds that all women were the victims of men's unrestrained passions and were economically dependent on them. 'So long as men are vicious and women have no employment this evil will go on', concluded Butler in 1871.[34]

Prostitution was an issue that radicalised feminist campaigns elsewhere in western Europe, partly as a result of Josephine Butler's energetic proselytising on behalf of what became known as abolitionism – the total dismantling of state-regulated prostitution. In France, for instance, following Butler's visit in 1874, feminists came together with anti-clericals in opposition to state-regulated prostitution. They regarded the French laws as a repudiation of women's civil rights and they supported education for women in opposition to the church's influence over the schooling of girls which left girls sexually ignorant.[35] In Germany, Käthe Schirmacher, one of the most outspoken of the German abolitionists, argued that it was the duty of women to fight the regulation of prostitution and to address the issue of the double-standard head on by educating their sons to reject the notion that male virtue was synonymous with immorality.[36] Most abolitionists, though, continued to subscribe to a model of sexual morality that preached sexual restraint (for both sexes) rather than sexual emancipation, and protection rather than pleasure. In Britain, on the back of the successful campaign to abolish the Contagious Diseases Acts (suspended in 1883, repealed in 1886), social purity campaigners turned their attention to other sexual abuses, particularly affecting young girls. The raising of the age of consent for girls to 16 in 1885, following a scare about child prostitution, and the 1908 Act outlawing incest, were triumphs for the social purity movement.

Feminists who campaigned against the double-standard had taken the first step in challenging the view of female sexuality as inherently dangerous and unruly. Despite their appropriation of a model of female passivity and self-control they had made some progress towards women taking back control over their own bodies. It allowed women to speak out in public against the injustices – rape, incest and domestic violence – perpetrated against them. And it presaged the beginning of a recognition amongst feminists that reform of the private sphere was a prerequisite for reform in the public sphere. Women could not reform their position in society until they reformed their dominant notions of female sexuality. Sexual purity, although regarded today as a restrictive or disabling ideology, in fact provoked new 'possibilities of thought' amongst middle-class women, encouraging them to explore their own sexual identities.[37]

Sexual purity, as a feminist strategy, was not long-lived. It was superseded in the late 1880s and 1890s by a more libertine strategy: the inversion of the idealised 'pure' woman into the 'liberated' women who embraced sexual freedom. The pioneers were known as the 'new women'. They had benefited from the efforts of their feminist predecessors in opening up the debate about the double-standard, but at the same time they were also continuing a tradition of socialist-feminist thought on heterosexual relations which contrasted significantly with the rather conservative social purity stance preferred by moderate feminists. These women were stimulated to transform their critique of the double-standard into an agenda for sexual emancipation by the influence of science and the radical response to the new 'knowledges' about sex by the 'new feminists' of the 1880s and 1890s. Women like Eleanor Marx (1856–98) and Olive Schreiner (1855–1920) in Britain, Helene Stöcker (1869–1943) in Germany, Ellen Key in Sweden and Madeleine Pelletier (1874–1939) in France, shifted the terrain towards a more critical stance on heterosexual relations.

In 1880, Henrik Ibsen's play *The Doll's House* was premiered in Copenhagen and thereafter, in translation, was produced on stages around Europe. It caused uproar for its portrayal of a middle-class woman – Nora – leaving her husband and children and her home, or 'doll's house', within whose walls she had been stifled. A few years later, in 1883, Olive Schreiner's novel *The Story of an African Farm* paralleled Ibsen's portrayal of a frustrated and unfulfilled wife and mother by introducing its readers to the heroine Lyndall who, like Nora, refuses to accept the sanctioned mode of life of a woman of her social position. She turns her back on a conventional marriage to a local man by running away with a stranger who professes his love for her, but she refuses to marry him too, seeing marriage itself as imprisonment and akin to prostitution. In Lyndall's uncompromising words, 'a woman who has sold herself, even for a ring and a new home need hold her skirt aside for no creature in the street. They both earn their bread in one way.'[38] Like her heroine, Olive Schreiner also rejected convention, preferring to live by her principles. Following the publication of her book she received a letter from Havelock Ellis (1859–1939), the doctor and sexologist. The two became members of The Men and Women's Club, a London group of radicals, socialists and feminists who met to discuss, amongst other things, sexuality and morality, and Ibsen was an iconic figure for the group. For Olive Schreiner, the Nora character symbolised what she also had tried to represent in her novel and the way she tried to live her own life.[39]

Olive Schreiner and her contemporaries were less the daughters of the social purity feminists and more the inheritors of a much earlier school of thought known as utopian socialism. In France in the 1830s and 1840s, a group known as the Saint Simonians followed by the utopian socialists, espoused a new social order incorporating the emancipation of women and the individual's right to free love. At the heart of the vision was a belief in social harmony, an emphasis on the emotional or sexual basis of relationships, and an opposition to the exploitation of women, especially within marriage. The critique of marriage was at the heart of utopian socialist thought since it was this institution, according to the social visionary and communitarian Charles Fourier (1772–1837), that trapped women in dependence and militated against their liberation. For Fourier and his followers, the ideal society would be run on along communal lines, theoretically freeing women from housework and child care. Women interpreted these ideas rather differently. Female followers of Saint-Simon and Fourier were less concerned with free love and more with the reform of marriage and women's economic independence, which would allow women to pursue their own destiny. The lives and works of two of the most well known, the social critic and writer Flora Tristan (1803–44) and the novelist George Sand (1804–76), exemplified the utopian feminist agenda. For both women it was personal experience that led them to critique the position of women. Driven by her determination to regain what she thought to be her rightful inheritance, and by her experience of a violent marriage, Flora Tristan came to believe that the key to women's emancipation was education. 'It is imperative . . . that women of the lower classes be given a rational and solid education', she wrote in 1843, 'so that they may become skilful workers, good mothers . . . and so that they may act as moralising agents in the life of the men on whom they exert an influence.'[40] George Sand, in her novel *Indiana*, created a heroine loosely based on herself, a woman trapped in a loveless marriage. Less flamboyant but no less effective was Pauline Roland (1805–52), a French schoolteacher who refused to submit to the expectations of bourgeois society and who chose to be an unmarried mother. A campaigner for marriage reform and for divorce law she was a new woman before her time.[41]

It was to be another forty years or so before the disciples of those early trailblazers were able to put their principles into practice without having to endure quite the same degree of opprobrium heaped on the early pioneers of alternative lifestyles. By 1900, voices calling for the legal and moral reform of marriage were widespread amongst feminists. They built upon the critiques put forward by liberal feminists such as the German Louise Dittmar (1807–84), who, in the 1840s, had put the case for marriage founded upon love rather than material considerations. These later, more radical voices compared marriage to the institution of slavery incorporating the double-standard. In *The Sexual Emancipation of Women* published in 1911, the French feminist Madeleine Pelletier advanced her view that marriage should encompass sexual equality. Following a trenchant criticism of the 'conventional morality' of bourgeois marriage she commented: 'There is no equality in conjugal love. The man possesses and the woman is possessed; what is a right for him is a duty for her.'[42] For Pelletier, marriage was merely the institutional reflection of the sexual inequality which permitted men licence and confined 'respectable' women to their homes. In arguing that women should have the freedom to walk down the street, attend the theatre or go to a café alone, she was making a claim for women's right to inhabit public space without fear of character assassination.

Pelletier never married, but like most feminist critics she was not opposed to marriage in principle, only the form of conjugal union buttressed by patriarchal law codes. Yet there were others who went a step further. Eleanor Marx, daughter of Karl and Jenny Marx, was seemingly the quintessential new woman. She was clever, politically committed and for most of her adult life she lived in a 'free union' with the scientist, atheist and socialist Edward Aveling. The couple did not marry, but unlike her friend Olive Schreiner, it was not principle that made her eschew marriage. For Olive, marriage would have been an imprisonment: 'no-one will ever absorb me and make me lose myself utterly, and unless someone did I should never marry. In fact I am married now, to my books! I love them better every day, and find them more satisfying.'[43] Eleanor Marx, it seems, would have married but believed the couple were legally barred owing to the fact that Aveling was still married to his first wife. A similar situation pertained for the novelist George Eliot (1819–80) and her long-term partner. Certainly Marx was a critic of a sexual morality which degraded women, but she was above all a socialist for whom economic relations were the key to sexual equality. In the socialist state, she wrote, 'the contract between man and woman will be of a purely private nature . . . the woman will no longer be the man's slave, but his equal.'[44]

The key to understanding the tenor of these various critiques of marriage and of the double-standard enshrined within it, is to focus on women's demands for personal autonomy rather than sexual freedom. What united feminists, both those primarily concerned with sexual danger or male abuse and those who sought to liberate women to experience the pleasures of sex, was agreement about the importance of education and protection. As Madeleine Pelletier argued in *A Feminist Education for Girls* in 1914: 'the educator . . . must give her daughter a sex education so that she is capable of that self-protection.'[45] So-called new women, sex reformers, freethinkers, radicals and feminists did not so much espouse free love which had been so damaging to the utopian socialists some decades earlier, as a new morality which allowed women 'the right to be sexual'.[46]

A WOMAN'S RIGHT TO BE SEXUAL

In 1912 the Swedish writer on sex reform and motherhood, Ellen Key, commented on the nature of sexual relations in her publication *The Woman Movement*. 'The young girl of today, in spite of all intellectual development, is still won by powerful spiritual sensual love, which the woman move-ment has too long considered as a negligible quality.' Emphasising what she regarded as woman's most important role – motherhood – she went on to argue that it was precisely because of their understanding of their social role that girls 'no longer consider their erotic longing as impure and ugly but as pure and beautiful'.[47] Key was a controversial and influential figure. Her writings might well appear conservative and out of step with the new morality espoused by freethinkers – the main thrust of her argument was that women had a duty to reproduce and to fulfil their role as mothers – but she also had a radical edge. Her espousal of the pleasurable aspects of sex for women and her recognition that women possessed legitimate sexual desire, were in line with those who argued that women should claim their sexuality for themselves. And her proposal that motherhood outside marri-age should not be a subject of shame, reflected agitation on behalf of the rights of unmarried mothers by radical feminists.[48] In her important work *Love and Marriage*, first published in Sweden in 1904, Key shows herself to be a thoroughly modern woman in her espousal of individual choice: 'Our time has recognised the value to morality of personal choice. It admits as really ethical only such acts as result from personal examination and take place with the approval of the individual conscience.'[49]

In the decade or so before the outbreak of war, reformers across Europe successfully challenged the notion of the passionless woman by writing and talking about sex, by educating women about their bodies, and by demanding that women be permitted to own their sexuality and create their own sexual identity. In practical terms this meant sex education, campaigns centred on reproductive rights, demands for reform of the laws on illegitimacy, and advice and help to unmarried mothers. The diverse proponents of this 'new morality' broke with the earlier feminist concern with undesired sex and concerned themselves with women's freedom to have and enjoy sex, although their horizons were limited to heterosexual relationships.[50]

For much of the twentieth century the issue of reproductive rights has been seen as central to feminist concerns. Access to contraception and the right to abortion and thus the freedom of a woman to choose her reproductive destiny have acted as touchstones for the advancement of women. This should not be surprising in view of the lamentable situation which had prevailed in Europe in the previous century. Whilst it would be misleading to suggest that birth control was an invention of modernisation, since clearly couples had always used a variety of unreliable contraceptive measures, the more general and informed use of birth control with the potential to have a tremendous impact of women's lives, was an early twentieth century development.

It was not until the end of the nineteenth century that the relationship between sex and pregnancy began to disengage in popular understanding, with the widespread production and advertisement of contraceptive devices such as diaphragms, condoms and pessaries. Feminists were initially mistrustful and sometimes downright opposed to contraception. Even the advocacy of information about birth control was controversial. In Britain the tone was set by the 1877 trial on the grounds of obscenity of Annie Besant (1847–1933) and Charles Bradlaugh for distributing a birth control tract. Feminists were no more likely than any other group to support contraceptive advice which they regarded as likely to encourage promiscuity, brutalise the sex act and reinforce women's subservience to men. As late as 1912, contributors to *The Freewoman* journal maintained this stance: 'Common Malthusian practices', as contraception was termed, 'are a gross outrage on the aesthetic sensibilities of women, and the final mark of their sexual degradation.'[51] In Germany, similar arguments were presented by conservative feminists who supported the state's attempt to increase the birth rate in the service of the strength and vitality of the nation.[52] In Catholic Europe, the taboo against speaking about birth control on account of the church's teachings that contraception was sinful, silenced not only women's groups but also those willing to break free of the church such as anarchists. In Spain, it took outspoken individuals such as Hildegart Rodriguez, secretary of the Spanish League for Scientifically Based Sex Reform, to defend family limitation, not only on eugenic grounds but on the grounds of women's freedom to practice 'conscious maternity'.[53] In Russia where birth control, unlike abortion, was not illegal, there were nevertheless few supporters of deliberate family limitation. One of the few was Sofiya Zarechnaya, a socialist feminist who equated birth control with women's freedom and emancipation. Writing in the Russian feminist journal *Zhenskoe delo* in 1910, Zarechnaya argued that women should have the right to make choices about their own bodies and that birth control information would free both unmarried and married women from unwanted pregnancies.[54]

Feminists began to abandon their moralistic stance and proceeded to advocate sex education in order to help women to gain control within their marriages. 'I can conceive of nothing more profoundly "immoral" than the marriage of a young woman who is absolutely ignorant of the most elementary laws of physiology', exclaimed the French birth control campaigner Nelly Roussel (1878–1922) in 1904.[55] Women who married with no knowledge of their own bodies or the sex act placed themselves in a weak position according to Roussel and others of like mind, giving encouragement to men who consider her merely 'an object of pleasure'. For British feminist campaigner Elizabeth Wolstenholme-Elmy (1833–1913) the notion of conjugal rights which gave a husband the right to demand sexual relations with his wife even if she declined, constituted legalised rape. The next step was to give women control of their fertility.

Those who advocated what was known as the neo-Malthusian position on birth control began to stake women's claim to the terrain of knowledge concerned with fertility. Notably in Britain and Germany, feminist advocates of birth control focused their attention on the working classes amongst whom, it was believed, the effects of large families, poverty, poor housing and sanitation might be alleviated by family planning. In Britain, Alice Vickery (1844–1929), the first British woman pharmacist and one of the first female medical graduates, evangelised about the health benefits to working-class women of 'preventives', as contraceptive devices were called, and also campaigned to achieve reform of the illegitimacy laws, anticipating the later advocacy of this position by German radical feminists.[56] The issue of reproductive rights was first discussed on a public platform in Germany where one of the most outspoken and radical organisations to espouse the 'new morality', the Bund für Mutterschutz (League for the Protection of Motherhood), placed itself at the centre of the sexuality debate. Central to the League's agenda was the belief that women were as entitled to sexual fulfilment as men, that women had a right to contraception and abortion, and that unmarried mothers should be treated equally with their married counterparts. The League was interested not just in the lifestyle choices of the middle classes, but with the problems facing working-class women, especially single mothers. Hitherto, the reproductive rights agenda had been championed by campaigning individuals but not by feminist organisations. The League's agenda was undeniably radical, not only because it spoke out about sexuality, but also because its spokeswomen were prepared to defy the state which had been attempting to slow down the decline in the population growth rate by encouraging women to become mothers and by enforcing the abortion law more strictly. German feminists were blamed for encouraging women to make informed choices about their lives and turning their backs on motherhood for the sake of careers.[57]

But neither the League in Germany nor outspoken individual campaigners for birth control in Britain succeeded in persuading the mainstream women's movement to take up the issue of reproductive rights. Alice Vickery's enthusiasm for birth control had a limited impact upon British feminists who remained ambivalent about family limitation, despite her bona fide feminist credentials – she was a member of the Women's Social and Political Union and active suffrage campaigner. In Germany the Allgemeiner Deutscher Frauenverein (General German Women's Association) voted to reject a proposal to support abolition of the abortion statute, although they did support less stringent penalties on those, mainly working-class, women found guilty of aborting a foetus.[58] Interestingly, the abortion debate did not broaden out to encompass fertility control in general, and in 1913 the government of Prussia attempted to introduce legislation to restrict access to contraception and abortifacients, banning the advertising, manufacture and sale of such products. It was this blatant attempt by the government to restrict women's choice under the guise of population policy that stung one group of women into action – members of the socialist women's section of the German Social Democrats – who supported a proposed birth strike advocated by two socialist doctors active amongst the Berlin working class. When leading socialists Clara Zetkin (1857–1933) and Luise Zietz (1865–1922) sought to oppose the birth strike – on the grounds that birth control was 'imitation of the moral decadence of the bourgeoisie' – they immediately received the wrath of the working class for whom fertility control was a key aspect of self-improvement and better living conditions.[59] Similarly, in France, birth control and sexual liberation were taken up by a small group of radicals such as Roussel and Pelletier whilst the more conservative mainstream feminists focused their energies on the state recognition of motherhood, symbolised by the words of Hubertine Auclert: 'Maternity will cease to terrify French women when, instead of dishonouring or reducing them to dependency, it [France] honours them by payments for indispensable service to the state.'[60] Feminists did not make reproductive rights a priority issue until after the First World War.

Europe's first birth control clinic was opened by Aletta Jacobs (1851–1929) in the Netherlands in 1882. Elsewhere, women had to wait until after the war for access to inexpensive or free contraception and fertility advice. By 1914, Margaret Sanger (1883–1966) was advising working women in the United States to know their bodies and to practise family limitation: 'Learn the facts of pregnancy. The inevitable fact is that, unless you prevent the male sperm from entering the womb you are liable to become pregnant,' she exhorted in *Family Limitation* published in 1914.[61] But her solutions were still fairly crude if the suppository consisting of cocoa butter mixed with quinine, recommended as a 'simple recipe which anybody can easily make', is a typical example. A more holistic and romantic approach was taken by Marie Stopes (1880–1958), the most famous birth control advocate. In her books *Married Love* and *Wise Parenthood*, both published in 1918, Stopes acted as marriage counsellor and sex educator.[62] Her critique of male sexuality and her understanding of the female reproductive cycle were brought together in *Married Love*, a book which combined sex education with a commitment to female sexual autonomy. At its heart was her understanding of the rhythms of female desire. Once women and men understood that women did not always desire sex, men could adjust themselves to women's sexual rhythms. *Wise Parenthood*, as the title implies, was concerned more explicitly with birth control, and shortly after its publication she set up Britain's first birth control clinic in London in 1921.

The work of Marie Stopes marks the culmination of three decades of campaigning on sexuality. Today, Stopes is something of an ambiguous figure, hailed for her work on birth control and sex education, but at the same time pilloried for her apparent embrace of eugenics and her inability to form close personal relationships. Nevertheless, she does stand as an icon of progress for women. The daughter of a feminist, she was a beneficiary of feminist campaigns to open up the education system to women, attending the North London Collegiate School and afterwards University College London where she studied sciences. Her writings on marriage and sex were facilitated by the more open discussion of sexuality at the end of the century amongst feminists and sexologists. The result was a contradictory critique of sexuality which accepted the biological explanations for male dominance and female passivity advanced by sexologists such as Havelock Ellis, and advanced the argument for female sexual autonomy. At the same time her writings met a widespread desire, even desperation, for help and advice about the sex act and birth control. Her work was of its time, demonstrated by the thousands of letters she received from women and men thanking her for helping them and asking for advice.[63]

The birth control debate in a sense acted as a catalyst for a gradual shift away from the nineteenth-century preoccupation with the dangers of sex for women, and towards an acknowledgement of the pleasurable aspects. This shift had implications not only for women in heterosexual relationships but also those in what were euphemistically termed 'romantic friendships'.

LESBIAN IDENTITIES

Lesbianism was an unknown concept for most of the nineteenth century. It had always been known in European culture that women did engage in emotional and sexual relations with one another, but this female intimacy had no name. Across most of Europe, with the exception of Austria, female homosexuality was ignored by the law, unlike its male equivalent which was illegal. For most of our period, society either accepted close female friendships in the broadest sense as normal, or they were dismissed as being impossible. Such relationships were not perceived as disruptive or perverted, in part because prior to the late nineteenth century, romantic love was not automatically associated with sexual passion.[64] This changed with the writings of the sexologists in the 1880s. They called love between women 'sexual inversion'.

Lesbian love and female same-sex desire, as well as intimate friendship, are widely documented before 1800. Female intimacy was recognised as an acceptable expression of women's natural emotional sensibility. It was not unknown for women to marry and yet to conduct passionate relations with a woman too. By the eighteenth century it was accepted that women would develop immensely strong relationships with one another, perhaps to compensate for the absence of emotion within their marriages. These relationships were probably not sexual, but were culturally sanctioned intimacy amongst women providing an acceptable and desirable counterweight to arranged marriages. Such friendships may also have been in imitation of the male platonic homosocial relations which were so useful to men in their public lives. Women demonstrated their affections for one another by writing one another romantic poetry, sharing intimate secrets, exchanging love tokens such as locks of hair and miniature portraits, holding hands, and kissing and caressing. In a later period these could be manifestations of sexual love, but eighteenth-century culture regarded this behaviour as natural amongst women, and even to be encouraged.[65]

The rise of the ideology of domesticity in the early nineteenth century had a twofold impact on the expression and interpretation of female intimacy. The ideological containment of woman within the home and marriage, and the construction of ideal femininity as sexually passive, altered male perceptions of women's homosocial world. Female eroticism was now confined to prostitutes, because prostitutes were sexual deviants who inverted the normal rules of sexual relations by selling sex and rejecting motherhood. On the other hand, domesticity nurtured and reinforced women's friendships by allowing them to cultivate a separate and acceptable female world of sentiment and mutual support.[66] In 1778, Eleanor Butler (1739–1829) and Sarah Ponsonby (1755–1831), two upper-class Irish women, eloped with one another. When Sarah's family found out she had run away with a woman they were relieved rather than shocked. The Ladies of Llangollen, as they came to be known, settled down into comfortable domesticity in Wales and were admired for their enduring romantic friendship. In 1811, two Edinburgh boarding-school mistresses won a celebrated libel case in the House of Lords, against an accusation of improper and criminal conduct. It was alleged the pair had enjoyed vigorous sexual activity in the same bed as one of their pupils. Both cases demonstrate a common attitude towards female intimate relationships at this time. It was almost inconceivable that women of a certain social standing would or could engage in sexual relations. After all, in the words of one of the lawyers acting for the Edinburgh schoolteachers: 'If a woman embraces a woman it infers nothing.'[67] Indeed, one member of the House of Lords who brought judgement on the Edinburgh case, criticised the implication by the prosecution that 'wherever two young women form an intimacy together, and that intimacy ripens into friendship, if ever they venture to share the same bed, that becomes proof of guilt.' After all, women often shared beds; it was a necessary and standard practice, just as men shared beds. To sexualise the nature of same-sex cohabitation was to cast suspicion on domestic arrangements in all social classes. In these two cases it was beyond belief that respectable women, who were regarded as sexually passive, could engage in erotic relations. Furthermore, even those women who recognised the desire within themselves for another woman were inclined to attempt to suppress their feelings since there was no name for same-sex attraction. Alternatively they accepted female same-sex love but regarded it as primarily 'intellectual and spiritual, unprofaned by any mixture of lower instincts', which presumably meant untainted by the base or coarser physical aspects of heterosexual love.[68]

Improvements in women's access to education and employment from mid-century onwards allowed some women a degree of economic independence, and it has been suggested that these circumstances facilitated same-sex relationships between women who no longer needed to marry. Although there may be some truth in this, the focus on the material incentives behind the setting up of all-female households privileges middle-class educated women – those who 'live by their brains' – over working-class women who, it is assumed, could not engage in such relationships on account of their continued dependence. Surviving sources such as diaries and letters inevitably create a bias in our knowledge about such women and create the impression that only educated, literary women were able to live their passion. The correspondence of Bettina von Arnim (1785–1859) and Karoline von Günderode in 1805–6, illustrates this combination of intellect and emotion. When Bettina writes, 'Thou shinest on me with thy intellect, thou Muse' and 'If thou wert not, what would the whole world be to me?', we gain an insight into a relationship which thrived on the women's mutual passion for learning as well as love for one another.[69] There are many examples of similar partnerships, like those between the Irish writer Edith Somerville (1858–1949) and Violet Martin (1862–1915) who collaborated as writers and as feminists, and the French artist Rosa Bonheur (1822–99) and the inventor Nathalie Micas, whose relationship was not unlike that of a heterosexual marriage with Nathalie fulfilling the role of the supportive wife to Rosa the artist, so that she might be spared 'the material cares of the household, the daily worries of existence'.[70] Clearly such women benefited from their privileged position. They could afford not to marry (although one should not underestimate the moral and social pressures to succumb to the married state), they were literate and learned and therefore may have been able to resist the pressures to conform. Although we know that all-female households were common amongst the working classes it is generally assumed the reasons were economic and demographic, resorted to only because women had not found husbands.

What changed this relatively benign situation for women in same-sex relationships, whether romantic or sexual, was the invention of a new language to describe same-sex love. The science of sexology, pioneered and popularised by writers such as the lawyer Karl Heinrich Ulrichs (1825–95), the psychiatrist Richard von Krafft-Ebing (1840–1902) and, most influential, the sexologist Henry Havelock Ellis (1859–1939), applied a medico-scientific approach to what was formerly a religious or moral issue. The turn of the century was a time when sexuality and human relationships were being hotly debated in intellectual circles, and scientific knowledge bore considerable weight. What became known as sexual inversion – in Ellis' words 'sexual instinct turned by inborn constitutional abnormality towards persons of the same sex'[71] – both 'morbidified' and pathologised women's romantic friendships, and allowed women to identify themselves as lesbians.[72] For some women, their identification as an 'invert' was not necessarily a legitimation of sexual desire for another woman; indeed, the sexologists' continued resistance to a female active sexuality could be seen as limiting the identity of lesbians who did not regard themselves as 'mannish' (since, according to Ellis, only the masculine female invert would take the initiative). Ellis's case study, Miss H, now presumed to be based on his wife Edith Lees Ellis, is a singular example of such an invert-type whom he describes as engaging in physical, erotic sex: 'they used to touch and kiss each other tenderly (especially on the *mons veneris*) . . . they each experienced a strong, pleasurable feeling in doing this.'[73] Other women, perhaps benefiting from the feminist campaign to recognise sex as something women might own and even enjoy, were more willing to recognise the physical joys of sex, thus confounding those men for whom lesbian sex was merely kissing and cuddling.[74] Lesbians themselves, often uncomfortable with the language of the sexologists, developed their own slang vocabulary. In France a lesbian was called a *gougnottes* (dialect for girlfriend) or a garlic seller; a *gousse* or garlic clove referred to the active woman in a partnership (the passive was the *vrille* or vine tendril), and establishing a relationship was 'to get married at the garlic market'.[75]

The emergence of a lesbian subculture in the 1890s, primarily in the cosmopolitan cities, suggests that a confident group of women had benefited from the change in discourse. In liberal, and some would say risqué, Paris at the end of the century, lesbianism was something 'all the noteworthy women' were doing according to one salon hostess.[76] The novelist Collette (1873–1954) for a time lived with a cross-dressing woman in the Parisian lesbian quarter and described the ambience there in her 1932 fictionalised memoir *The Pure and the Unpure*. A lesbian bar in Montmartre was portrayed as a comforting space 'that welcomed these uneasy women, haunted by their own solitude'.[77] Similarly, in German cities it was said there was a lively lesbian community centring upon bars, cafés, dances and the aesthetic world. Lesbianism was also said to be fashionable in St Petersburg before the revolution. Yet, it was still illegal for a woman to dress as a man in France, and working-class lesbians were routinely identified as whores. Some were even imprisoned or treated for hysteria. The reality of the lesbian lifestyle was a far cry from the fantasies imagined by male writers and artists who tended to focus on the erotic and exotic at the expense of tenderness, companionship and love.

The women's movement in general did not explicitly take up the rights of lesbians. Even Madeleine Pelletier, who dressed like a man and who admitted she would have liked a girlfriend, was unable to speak publicly about female same-sex relations.[78] Only in Germany did the League for the Protection of Motherhood stand up for the rights of lesbians when the German government threatened to outlaw female sexual relations in 1911. Nevertheless, women in same-sex relationships were beneficiaries of more general feminist campaigning on sexual issues as well as the improved economic and employment prospects for middle-class women. The feminist challenge to the notion of female passionlessness gradually gave way to a recognition that women might be sexually autonomous, that is independent of a male partner. The scientific identification of the invert or lesbian gave some women greater confidence to publicly reject the stereotype of passive heterosexual femininity, and in the cities we can see some evidence of a thriving lesbian lifestyle. For twenty years or so, female same-sex relations encountered little direct hostility, perhaps 'because the fact of the New Woman and her revolutionary potential for forming a permanent bond with another woman had not yet been widely impressed on the public imagination.'[79] The publication and, more importantly, the banning in 1928 of Radclyffe Hall's coming-out novel, *The Well of Loneliness*, demonstrated how the freedoms gained at the end of the previous century could not be taken for granted despite Hall's depiction of her heroine Stephen as a congenital invert, to use the sexologists' terminology, and her suggestion that inversion was a burden, something to be pitied. It was only after the First World War, despite the renewed emphasis on motherhood, eugenics and repopulation, and the popularity of Freudian theories which saw lesbianism as a consequence of trauma in childhood, that women's same-sex relations found increasing acceptance, if still located within urban educated, middle-class circles. The story of the working-class lesbian remains to be told.

CONCLUSIONS

The story of women's sexuality in the nineteenth century is the story of women reclaiming their bodies for themselves. From sex being something assigned to women by others, and given meaning by others, sex became something that women owned. But the process was gradual and uneven, and it is easy to lose sight of the ordinary woman in the telling. The esoteric discussions about sex that took place in the rooms of middle-class intellectuals had little direct impact upon the majority of working women who, right up until the First World War, were given little in the way of practical information or choices as to how to accommodate childbirth, child care, paid and unpaid work. We would do well to remember that the issue of women's personal choice as a factor in fertility control is very much a twentieth-century phenomenon.

The impact of the sexuality debate on urban working-class women was ambiguous. The campaigns against the regulation of prostitution and more generally against the sexual abuse of women, brought the discussion of sex and morals into the open. It exposed the sexual dangers women were subject to and highlighted the predicament of working-class women forced to resort to prostitution for economic reasons. On the other hand, more harm than good may have been done in the short term by the social purity approach to the double-standard, the insistence on female respectability based upon a belief in women's innate moral superiority. This led to silence and ignorance about sex amongst women. To be ignorant was to be respectable, but it also left a woman vulnerable. Stories of women not knowing what would happen on their wedding night are legion.

However, this initial feminist foray into the hitherto unsavoury world of sex for sale helped middle-class women to begin to realise that women's sexuality was the key to all other feminist demands. Without female sexual autonomy, without freeing themselves from sexual objectification, all other political achievements would be worthless. Differences in approach were endemic within the women's movement, but most adhered to the belief that all women, of all social classes could progress only if the subjection of the female sex was eliminated. Thus a fragile consensus based on the rejection of woman as 'the sex' united feminist campaigners. Feminist activism, particularly on the issue of prostitution, brought many women to politics and to suffrage. The personal became political for many individual activists who were enraged at the double-standard that punished women for walking the streets and left men at their liberty. When the leading English suffrage campaigner Christabel Pankhust (1880–1958) coined the phrase 'Votes for Women, Chastity for Men' in 1913, she was making the connection between women's sexual objectification and their political powerlessness.

It was not until the twentieth century that we can see a glimpse of the sexual 'liberation' commonly associated with women's reproductive rights and sexual choice. Probably only a small minority of couples consciously cooperated to limit family size before the First World War. It was still more commonly the woman who took steps to prevent a birth by attempting to induce a miscarriage or obtaining an abortion, a far more frequent occurrence than most would admit. But it was not until after 1918 that a larger number of women could exert greater meaningful and informed control over their bodies and their sexual choices. It is even more difficult to assess the extent to which recognition of the pleasurable aspects of sex for women might have affected experiences, although the attempt by sex reformers to separate sex from reproduction offered a route to greater sexual freedom and to what Olive Schreiner called sex for 'aesthetic purposes'.[80] In the popular response to Marie Stopes' writings we can begin to identify a shift in thinking amongst ordinary women and men who wanted advice on how to enjoy sex as well as how to limit family size.

By the First World War, women in the industrialised states were beginning, if very slowly, to glimpse a liberation from the pure and passionless ideal and the unruly and dangerous stereotype. Elsewhere, notably in southern and eastern Europe, it was to be much longer before women's sexuality was to be divorced from the state of motherhood and for the politics of reproduction to be placed on the agenda. In Spain, for instance, 'for women to address the problem of voluntary motherhood or sexual conduct represented an inadmissible transgression of gender conventions and an implicit contestation to both modern and traditional cultural norms.'[81] The campaigns, debates and economic and social changes of the nineteenth century did not revolutionise the ways in which women's sexuality was perceived, or the ways in which women experienced sex. But the simple facts that more women had control over their fertility than ever before, that some women could conceive of alternatives to marriage, that women in same-sex relationships now had an identity they could call their own, did constitute progress.

Chapter 7

♦

WORKING FOR
A LIVING

Women have always worked, but the way historians look at this issue is starkly divided into two camps. The first emphasises the strong and enduring continuity in women's work histories. It focuses on how they have always participated in the labour of the household. Female labour has traditionally been clustered in certain occupations closely related to women's familial and reproductive responsibilities. And the work carried out by women has, on the whole, been less well rewarded than that done by men. These trends continued through the nineteenth century, despite the upheavals of industrialisation. At the end as at the beginning of the century, women's work was a synonym for unskilled, low-paid and under valued labour. According to Judith Bennett, 'women were as clustered in low skilled, low status, low paying occupations in 1200 as in 1900.'[1] This long-term view stresses continuity rather than change, and plays down the role of industrialisation in influencing both the sexual division of labour and the construction of women's work as low paid and low status. From this perspective, the nineteenth century does not represent a turning point in the history of women's work so much as a continuation of a very long story of female subordination in the workplace.

By contrast, the second approach stresses change in women's experience of work. It identifies the nineteenth century as time when the idea emerged of the economically unproductive woman. This perspective emphasises change with the emergence of industrial capitalism – from around 1750 in Britain, later elsewhere in Europe. Restrictions were placed on the types of work available to women, the sexual division of labour was reaffirmed with a vengeance, greater emphasis was placed on women's position within the family, and there was a reduction in women's status in the labour market.[2] The advocates of change see the nineteenth century as a moment when a particular confluence of conditions enlarged the significance of the pre-existing subordination of women in jobs. It was a time when 'the marital status of women took on a new significance as protective legislation, the cult of the family wage, and the ideology of domesticity interacted to emphasise gender inequality in the labour market and to establish a hierarchical structure of employment.[3]

Something did happen to women's position in the labour market from the eighteenth century onwards. There was an intensification of the gendering of work structures and practices, and different values placed on male and female labour across the whole range of occupations. Industrialisation intensified 'chronic sexual conflict, which was endemic to an economy where women's labour was necessary yet undervalued', according to Anna Clark.[4] The developing industrial labour market and the ideology of domesticity created new and different employment conditions for women, subordinating them to male breadwinners, downgrading their skill, and marginalising or 'proletarianising' female labour. So both continuity and change are vital to understanding women's diversity of work experiences between 1789 and 1918.

THE GEOGRAPHY OF WOMEN'S WORK

Europe's economic geography was especially diverse and complex in the nineteenth century, as industrial advance took hold at varying rates and in contrasting ways in different places. For this reason, women's opportunities 'were shaped by overlapping geographical and chronological changes'.[5] As Hudson and Lee argue, 'regionally divergent gender-specific labour markets' determined women's employment position probably more than overarching ideological or economic trends.[6] So, in the less developed parts of Europe – the rural peripheral regions of the British Isles, the Mediterranean, much of eastern Europe and Russia – women continued to be employed predominantly in agriculture and in small-scale manufacture. Elsewhere, where extractive and manufacturing industry had taken hold, such as in the Ruhr region in Germany and the mining and steel towns of England, the job opportunities for women were more restricted. And there were pockets of concentrated textile manufacture such as Lancashire, northern France and Belgium, where the factory or 'mill girl' was born.

It is important to remember that most of Europe was not industrialised for most of the century. Across much of eastern and southern Europe, agriculture remained the most important employer of women well into the 1920s. In Bulgaria, Poland and Romania, around 90 per cent of the female workforce remained on the land in 1910. Elsewhere, including Austria, Hungary and Italy, agriculture accounted for the employment of well over half of all economically active women. Even in Germany, probably the most advanced industrial state by 1914, more than 50 per cent of the female labour force was still employed in agriculture in 1890. In Russia, the female factory labour force amounted to just 3 million or barely 2 per cent of the population in 1914.[7] Only in Britain was the proportion of women employed on the land significantly smaller than the numbers in manufacturing and service, with less than 5 per cent of recorded working women in this sector from the 1860s in contrast with more than 40 per cent in manufacturing.

Precise data on women's participation in the labour force is hard to come by. Census enumerators are renowned for their under-recording of women workers, by failing to register female household servants, women who were assistants in family enterprises, and seasonal and casual workers. In Germany, for example, it is important to know that the employment statistics for the years 1882, 1895 and 1907 seriously under-record the number of 'assisting relatives', many of whom were wives and daughters working on farms. Similarly, in Britain in the 1881 census, women who assisted in family businesses were returned as unoccupied if they did not receive a wage. In general, the number of women categorised as unoccupied vastly underestimates the nature of seasonal employment for women. It is unlikely that so many women – 68 per cent of females in the 1901 census for England and Wales – were really economically inactive. The data on women workers underestimates the numbers involved in production by defining as productive activity only work that could be measured, which was visible and which was rewarded by the payment of cash wages. Unremunerated work was not counted. Women were presumed to be dependants, were not counted, and were classified as wives.[8] However, with these caveats in mind, it is possible to detect some broad trends from the statistics.

For most of the nineteenth century there was no major increase in the proportion of women in the paid workforce. The absence of figures for the first half of the century makes it difficult to assess long-term change but, from the 1850s to the 1900s, most countries recorded between 25 and 40 per cent of the labour force as female. It is only in the industrialising states of Britain, Germany, Russia, the Netherlands, Denmark and Sweden that some increase is evident in the last decades of the century. There was little or only moderate increase in the proportion of the workforce who were female in the southern countries of Portugal, Spain, Italy and Greece, where industrialisation was not to take off until the twentieth century, and in some states the figures show a decline. In Belgium, for example, women formed 35 per cent of the workforce in 1866 but only 29 per cent in 1900. However, there was a shift in the types of work undertaken by women, and again it is in the northern industrialising states that this is most marked. As Figure 7.1 shows, in the most industrialised states of Britain, Belgium, France and Germany, female employment in manufacturing rose as female employment in agriculture declined. The other marked development is the importance of domestic service for the female workforce, although again the figures may deceive the unwary. It is likely that in those states where domestic service was recorded as a significant employment sector for women – Britain, Ireland, the Netherlands and Norway – the category was interpreted extremely liberally to include not only women who were employed in personal household service but also live-in farm servants and general servants in rural areas.

The female labour market was marked by distinctive features of age and marital status. Unmarried and widowed women were far more likely to be recorded as waged workers than married women. It was mostly young unmarried women who took up the jobs in the industrial and service sectors. As women got older and married they often gave up recorded work in industry. Percentages of married women in formal employment vary enormously from one country to another. In Norway they accounted for just 4.6 per cent of women employed in full-time work in 1900, whilst in Britain the figure was 9.6 per cent in 1911, in France it was 38 per cent in 1896 and in the province of Moscow 53 per cent in 1908.[9] In factory work, young single women predominated. In Prussia in 1875 more then three-quarters of workers were single and 68 per cent were under the age of 25.[10] The disparity in the labour force between single and married women reminds us of the place of work in a woman's lifecycle. From a working-class girl's teenage years to her early twenties she was likely to be in paid work. In Germany in 1882, 46 per cent of women aged between 15 and 19 were in employment as were 31 per cent of those in their twenties. But this figure dropped to 18 per cent for women in their thirties. In Britain in 1911 the age structure is even more stark with 29 per cent of those aged between 25 and 44 in employment compared with more than 60 per cent of the 15 to 24 age group.[11] Marriage and, more especially, childbearing amongst this class influenced a woman's workforce participation. It was during a woman's prime child-rearing years that she was

Figure 7.1 Women at work c.1900

Note: The chart shows the distribution of women workers between the three main sectors of female employment. The data are derived from censuses taken between 1895 and 1911. Countries classified women's jobs differently, reducing somewhat the reliability of international comparison. See text.

Source: P. Bairoch, T. Deldycke, H. Gelders and J.-M. Limbor, The Working Population and its Structure (Brussels, 1968).

likely to adopt a mixture of paid work, casual labour and home-work with periods of unpaid 'housework' and child care.

The statistics can also alert us to the diverse range of jobs undertaken by women in this century. The pioneering English historian of women's work, Ivy Pinchbeck, listed almost 300 different occupations undertaken by women in 1841. Here we find actors (381 women recorded), anchor smith and chainmakers (103), bankers (7), boot- and shoemakers (10,564), cattle and sheep dealers and 'salesmen' (13), furriers (798), leech bleeders and dealers (52), millers (457), opticians (17) pawnbrokers (256), publicans and victuallers (5625), scissor-makers (148), toll collectors (446), undertakers (72) and whip-makers (49), to name just a few.[12] Indeed, there were few occupations that did not employ women, although it is true to say that the vast majority were clustered in four main areas of work: textile manufacture, the needle trades, laundry and domestic service. In Britain in 1891, 80 per cent of all women workers were concentrated in textiles, the clothing trades and domestic service. In France the distribution of women across the range of jobs appears to have been wider, but still in 1896 one-third of working women were employed in those three sectors with another 43 per cent in agriculture.[13]

Two types of female worker characterise the world of women's work in industrialising Europe: the domestic servant and the mill girl. For the majority of European women at the start of the nineteenth century, their first experience of paid work was as a servant in somebody else's home. Farm service was the most common destination of most young girls in rural parts of Europe. Female farm servants were both tied to another household enterprise and, in the case of lowland Scotland, north-east England and parts of Scandinavia, defined by their relationship to a man. The bondagers, as they were known, were female farmworkers provided by a male worker as a condition of the bond he made with a farmer.[14] Although this form of almost feudal service was not a widespread phenomenon, the treatment of female labour as a supplement to male wage-earning emerged as a common feature of women's work experience. By the nineteenth century, women were seen as dependants rather than independent wage-earners and thus the prominent place of service in all its forms in women's employment opportunities should not surprise us. Service was the ultimate dependant status. A job in service contradicted the desire of a man for independence; conversely it was seen as ideal work for a woman in the gap between dependence on her father and dependence on a husband. Although the period of peak demand for female domestic servants covers the middle decades of the nineteenth century, in some respects this form of employment may be seen as an integral feature of long-term continuity in women's work. As Bonnie Smith points out, service 'carried forward the old moral economy into a world of new values'.[15] In the towns and cities of industrialising states, domestic service accounted for up to 50 per cent of all female paid labour. In Madrid more than 60 per cent of women in the labour force were in this sector in 1900 compared with just 19 per cent in industry.[16] Domestic service epitomises the tendency to locate female labour in the domestic sphere. Domestic service was certainly hard work, but at the same time it could be seen as a training for a woman's future role as housewife. The tendency to address servants by their first name, thereby infantilising and subordinating them, the pitiful wages and the unrestricted hours they worked, all combined to deny the female servant a sense of economic independence.

Conversely, whilst the domestic servant merged into the background of urban life, the independent female worker in manufacture was highly visible. The 'mill girl' – most employees were below the age of 30 – came to represent the stereotypical non-domestic female worker. She was single, independent and liberated from the restraints imposed by home and family. Across Europe the sheer numbers of women employed by the textile trades fuelled this image of the woman worker whose identity was no longer located in the domestic sphere. In the Rhineland, the new mechanised woollen, flax, linen and silk mills depended on female labour.[17] Similarly, in Russia on the eve of the First World War, women constituted more than 60 per cent of the textile workforce, in northern France workers in the cotton spinning mills were overwhelmingly female, and in Lancashire more the half of textile workers were women.[18] The mill girl was held up as a spectre of family and societal dislocation. 'This mass of girls', as one horror-struck German observer described them, 'detached from their families and homes and thrust from rural isolation into the midst of strangers in the city' came to represent 'complete social and economic decay'.[19] It was the mill girls' apparent rejection of the traditional female role that lay at the heart of this fear. In northern Germany, it was noted in 1855 that the rise of factory employment and the emergence of young workers who gained early independence owing to relatively high wages, was playing havoc with gender roles. Young working women were said to 'no longer learn the job of housewife, and when they marry they have no pleasure in it and instead of taking care of the house they are becoming accustomed to pursue other amusements.'[20] Clearly the mill girl had a lot to be responsible for, representing both the transition to the industrial state and, at the same time, the perceived loss of a world in which home and work existed in a symbiotic relationship.

The rise of the visible woman factory worker in the nineteenth century coincided with public antagonism to the very idea of women engaging in waged labour. The outburst of historian and moralist Jules Michelet – 'The woman worker, what a blasphemous word!' – was a rather extreme expression of disgust at the phenomenon of the female factory labour force, but his sentiments were echoed by many others who believed the social fabric was at risk from the apparent increase in women's paid work outside the home.[21] The mill girl was, of course, a chimera, a fantasy in the minds of contemporary critics whose shock at the sight of hoards of young women on the streets with money to spend on clothes and amusements, blinded them to the more enduring continuity between home and work in the lives of most labouring women. And, were it not for the labours of thousands of working women, the industrial revolution would not have occurred in the way it did. As Maxine Berg has argued for England, 'those industries at the forefront of technological and organisational innovation were also mainly industries employing women's labour.'[22] This was not only because employers regarded women (and children) as cheap labour. Rather, manufacturers believed that women's 'natural' dexterity, their ability to adapt to new techniques and their 'female' working patterns were advantageous, whilst male protective practices were seen as problematic and more likely to develop into resistance to the new production regimes.[23] However, the demand of employers for female labour and women's need to earn a living collided with the notion of woman as primarily a mother and housewife. 'The ideology of virtue sealed working women's poverty and allowed the Industrial Revolution to succeed.'[24]

THE FAMILY ECONOMY

Woman's position in the labour market and her experience of work cannot be understood without a recognition of the relationship between home and work in women's lives. Employers and male workers used the rhetoric of separate spheres and the ideology of domesticity to justify their subordination of female workers as dependants or supplementary earners. In their important study, *Women, Work and Family*, Joan Scott and Louise Tilly emphasised the central place of the family economy in analyses of women's work and argued for continuity in women's experience as opposed to the sharp discontinuity favoured by those whose focus is the impact of industrial capitalism.[25] The absence of a linear movement from domestic to factory production, from the family or household economy to the separation of home and work, implies a considerable grey area, moments and places when home-based production coexisted with machine-based factories, when agriculture and domestic industry coexisted, where home-work complemented factory production, where housewives lived side-by-side with factory labourers, and when women were housewives and factory workers simultaneously. However, whilst acknowledging that women's relationship to the family economy is a continuous element of women's work experience, we should not exaggerate the extent to which women themselves conflated home and work or had aspirations to establish work identities separate from the identity of wife, mother and homemaker.

The concept of the family economy originally belonged to discussions of the pre-industrial, rural household, encompassing production and reproduction, the interdependence of all family members and the codependence of work and domestic life. As Deborah Simonton neatly summarises, the family economy ideal incorporated the interrelationship between economic survival strategies and what might be regarded today as the emotional needs of individuals. It is within this context that woman's work is seen as having value; her role in production – agricultural or proto-industrial – and in reproduction and household management, positioned the woman as pivotal, if not equal, within the household unit.

The family economy incorporated a sexual division of labour but it did not necessarily incorporate notions of sexual difference or hierarchy. The sexual division of labour in farming saw women commonly employed in activities closer to the farmhouse, in the dairy, the farmyard, the kitchen garden and in the kitchen, and engaged in tasks believed suitable such as weeding, hoeing and helping at harvest. There were certain tasks which were almost always carried out by one sex or the other – for instance, fishing, tree-felling and hunting are almost universally male tasks, whereas carrying water, cooking, collecting wood and preserving meats were female.[26] In Russia, although farms were organised along patriarchal lines, woman's work complemented that carried out by men and was essential to the survival of the peasant household. Not only did she carry out all the work in and around the home, she also worked to produce and sell goods for the market, and she worked to reproduce the family. Women gained in authority by performing their household tasks but also by ensuring the family's future.[27] The division of labour was practical and, indeed, women probably undertook a wider range of tasks than men, and were more likely to substitute for male workers than vice versa. But these divisions were culturally and economically specific and did not necessarily have anything to do with the physical differences between the sexes. In Shetland, for example, where most households were tied to their landlord in a neo-feudal tenure relationship, the household economy was sustained by fishing undertaken by men and crofting (small-scale subsistence farming), which fell to women for much of the year. In addition, women engaged in domestic production – mainly knitting – which was bartered for goods rather than cash. Here, it was often said that households were egalitarian, acknowledging the value placed on women's productive role. And yet this alleged egalitarianism was based on a fairly strict division of labour: fishing was men's work, whilst crofting and knitting were women's work.[28] In Scandinavia, on the other hand, although it was generally believed that women were more suited to handicrafts on account of their dextrous fingers, the knitting of woollen goods for cash sale was undertaken by both women and men.[29]

However, during periods of change on the land, for example during a shift to more specialised or commercial crop production, gendered power relations were likely to shift as the collective family or household unit lost its internal cohesiveness. Changes in the nature and extent of women's participation in agricultural labour were caused by many things: peasant emancipation and the ensuing migration from the land in Russia, enclosure in England, the Clearances in Scotland, the move to cash-crop production in Prussia and regional specialisation, mechanisation and the shift to large-scale agriculture in many parts of Europe, accompanied by the emergence of alternative employment in nearby industrialising towns. In the Scottish Lowlands the introduction of new crops, especially potatoes and soft fruit, resulted in a demand for seasonal female labour and the emergence of the female gang who moved from one farm to another, taking their children with them and sleeping in barns.[30] In eastern England, female field gangs were employed for turnip-singling, and in southern Spain, female gangs were hired to carry out the worst and most poorly paid jobs on the large olive- and grape-producing estates.[31] In areas which specialised in dairy and livestock farming, opportunities for women expanded. For the most part, though, the commercialisation of farming promoted men's opportunities and marginalised women's roles on account of increasing division of labour into specialist and non-specialist tasks. For example, in cereal-growing areas in Scotland and Scandinavia, the introduction of mowing with the long, double-handed scythe in place of reaping with the more easily managed short, one-handed sickle, meant women ceased their role in cutting the corn, but they continued to take part in other aspects of the harvest such as binding the corn in sheaves and threshing.[32] In fact threshing with a flail was extremely hard work, yet it was generally regarded as unmanly.[33]

Technical advances tended to oust women from some kinds of farm work. In grain-growing regions of England the use of heavy agricultural machinery in intensive cereal production resulted in women and girls being reduced to the seasonal work of weeding corn and haymaking.[34] In Norway, the milling of the corn in watermills was always men's work, whereas hand-milling remained the preserve of women.[35] In Sweden and Denmark the mechanisation of the dairy industry and the training of men to become scientific managers of dairies, edged out women from what had traditionally been a female-dominated skill.[36] Milk and butter production, which had previously taken place on small farms, shifted to large cooperative dairies in the 1880s, and women were displaced on the grounds that they lacked physical strength and technical knowledge, along with the belief that it would be unnatural for women to manage such an enterprise.[37]

Alongside these structural changes on the land, attitudes towards female agricultural workers shifted. It seems clear that, at least in England, women's work was increasingly being structured according to gendered notions of what constituted appropriate or suitable work for women. Already by 1843 a Royal Commission in England commented that cheesemaking was unsuitable work for women on account of 'the patience, skill and strength needed'. Moreover, field work was not only deemed to be too heavy for women, it was also regarded as unfeminine and a threat to male workers. 'There is an evil prevailing in this district . . . that of women going into the fields', remarked an agricultural union representative in Essex in 1879: 'Surely employment could be found for the women more congenial to their tastes and more in accord with modern civilisation?'[38] The net result of these changes was to move women off the land except in a seasonal or temporary capacity. This was especially true of England where, in 1843 it was noted that 'Now you never see a girl about in the fields' – almost certainly an exaggeration but notable nonetheless.[39] Instead, women worked in agriculture and horticulture more often as waged labour in a situation more akin to their town cousins.

The transition to industrial capitalism has been seen by some to herald the emergence of a different kind of economic and family unit characterised by the separation of home and work – what might be termed the family-wage or family-provider economy. Within this model, home and work are usually separately located, wage labour predominates over domestic production, and the position of women and the value of their labour is subordinated to that of the male breadwinner. However, there is no direct relationship between the functioning of a family economy and the value ascribed to women's labour. A number of case studies taken from quite different economic regions demonstrate the weakness of the ideal/typical model. In the Loire region of France, where domestic handloom weaving survived throughout the century despite mechanisation elsewhere, the family economy was infused with gender inequality. The male handloom weavers' struggle to maintain their skills in the face of declining piece rates forced their wives and daughters into waged work in order to ensure the family's survival. Here, the family economy, far from encompassing some degree of gender equality, instead reinforced inequality at the expense of the proletarianisation of women.[40] Elsewhere, where home- or cottage-based production not only survived but adapted and expanded (a stage often described as proto-industrialisation), work for women often expanded too. In the Caux region of northern France, the expansion of cottage weaving and a rise in agricultural production did lead to an increase in work opportunities for women, although the price to be paid was the intensification of female labour. As technical changes shifted cottage spinning into small factories, hand spinners – the majority of whom had been female – were forced to find work in the mills.[41] Women thus moved into the traditionally male job of weaving, but did not accrue any of the advantages of male employment. These women were paid less than men, they experienced problems in combining work with child care, and they lost the sense of female cameraderie which had characterised female spinners. Similarly, in the northern Italian silk-producing district of Como, where the silk industry existed side by side with agriculture, it was the women who worked in the silk factories, becoming proletarianised, whilst the men continued to farm. Thus women were exploited not only by factory owners, but by their husbands too.[42] The family economy was a flexible system that could as easily subordinate women as place value on their labour.

For another group of women, the emergence of wage-earning opportunities for men had some benefits. In Russia, in the years following peasant emancipation in 1861, the migration of more than 20 per cent of adult males to the industrial centres left villages dominated by women, children and the elderly. Migrants remained attached to their villages through marriage to local women, but they returned infrequently, and when they did so it was said they lived there 'like guests', neither able nor willing to work. In these circumstances, the family economy was maintained by women's work around the farm and in cottage industry, and the men's injection of cash. 'When a woman married a man who worked elsewhere, it tied her still more closely to the soil and increased her burden of physical labour', writes Engel. 'In "the woman's kingdom" even heavy agricultural labour . . . was conducted primarily, sometimes exclusively, by women.'[43] In men's absence, it was said that 'women worked harder, but breathed more freely'.[44] In the fishing-farming communities of Norway, the importance of the woman's role was so important that she was often described as a female farmer rather than a farmer's wife.[45]

The family economy did undergo shifts as women's responsibilities adapted to structural transformations, but, in the main, woman's work remained tied to the home in a number of ways. She carried out her work within the home or near it, and her earnings contributed to the household pot. And increasingly her labour was judged in terms of notions of appropriate womanly work defined by her domestic responsibilities. Ironically, whilst toiling in muddy fields was regarded as incompatible with a woman's homemaking qualities, working as a sweated labourer under one's own roof was acceptable. Home work, outwork, domestic industry or sweating, as such employment came to be called, was seen by women and by critics of women's paid work outside the home as one way of squaring the circle, of contributing to the family economy whilst not visibly engaging in waged labour.

WORKING AT HOME

Artificial flowers, umbrellas, Christmas crackers, sweets, bonnets and gloves, tassels and feather adornments, corsets, lacework, embroidery, knitted goods, shoes, clothing and all manner of tailored items. These products were commonly manufactured by women in their own homes for very poor wages. These were the new home industries of the industrial revolution, dominated by married women making the new consumer or luxury goods for the middle classes for very little money. The flowers and feathers worn in extravagant hats to the opera, the pretty umbrellas, the dainty gloves, the embroidered handkerchiefs, as well as the cigars and cigarettes smoked by a lady's male escort, were manufactured in working-class homes, especially in the metropolitan cities – Paris, London, Berlin, Milan – and ended up for sale in the new department stores.[46]

For so long a hidden area of women's employment, ignored by the census-takers and literally concealed in back kitchens, attics and basements, home work is acknowledged as representing women's archetypal position in the labour market. Its chief characteristics – casual or seasonal, unskilled, repetitive, poorly paid and unregulated – are features replicated in the wider picture of women's work in nineteenth-century Europe. In rural parts of Europe, women had traditionally turned to home work in the winter months, undertaking straw-plaiting, ribbon-weaving and even chainmaking when farm work was slack. But home work did not represent a transitional stage between the agrarian and industrial economy. It was not a remnant of a pre-industrial economy. It was central to industrial society. As production moved into mechanised factories and as manufacture was subdivided into a number of separate processes, much of the more labour-intensive, manual and unskilled work was farmed out to home-workers. An apocryphal example is that of needlemaking in Worcestershire which, it was said, involved more than 100 people in their homes to complete the finished product.[47] In Britain, Germany and Italy, as certain industries became increasingly feminised, there was a simultaneous expansion of home work too. In the clothing industry in particular, the association of sewing and the handicraft trades with women, the limited outlay required, and the flexible nature of this kind of work meant that thousands of women formed what were known as the 'sweated' trades. In Berlin, more than 100,000 in 1906 were employed at home in the clothing industry alone.[48] In Milan there were more than 30,000 garment workers in the city in 1881. Most of these women worked at home; others were employed in small workshops making dresses and suits, hats, gloves, furs and lace goods; all supplied for the new department stores run by the Bocconi brothers' garment company.[49] Home production allowed the coexistence of industrialisation and separate spheres ideology. It reinforced the idea of woman as homemaker and nurturer, and man as breadwinner, whilst at the same time allowing employers to keep capital and wage costs low. There is merit in what Maxine Berg says, that women (and children) working at home contributed significantly to industrial expansion and to the productivity gain associated with the technologically advanced sectors. At the same time they lifted their families out of destitution, hence fuelling demand for consumer goods.[50]

Domestic industry suited employers. Home-workers were used because they were cheap and flexible. They were paid piece rates, there were no overheads for the employers – workers commonly had to provide their own tools and other necessary items such as thread or glue – and workers could be called upon at any time to complete an order or be laid off when demand was slack. Employers' responsibilities towards their workforce were few, limited to 'his frequently doling out work as people dole out indiscriminate charity, and in his desire to have a reserve army of labour, which costs nothing for upkeep, and which he can count on for a few hours, a few days, or weeks as it suits his convenience.'[51] One Glasgow industrialist commented that home-workers 'do not add to capital expenditure . . . and do not make inroads on space'.[52] The vagaries of the fashion market in Paris meant that employers were reluctant to invest in machinery; it was cheaper to shift the costs and the insecurity on to the workers.[53] And with the introduction of the small, hand-operated sewing machine by the Singer Company in the 1850s, clothing manufacturers saw an opportunity to produce machine-worked goods faster and more cheaply. The Singer machines were explicitly marketed to women and designed as a decorative piece of furniture in order to help deflect criticism away from the association of women with technology. Around 20,000 of these machines were sold in France every year during the 1870s and 1880s, many of them to individual workers on a payment by instalment basis, since few working-class women could have afforded to buy one outright. Thus, women home-workers were easily locked into a system of credit, low wages and long hours to pay off the debt. However, for some women the purchase of a machine gave them greater freedom to work for whomever they wished, including wealthy private clients, liberating them from the crushing production line of the major clothing manufacturers.[54]

For the home-worker, though, there were few obvious advantages of such employment. The proposition that home work fitted in with a married woman's family and household responsibilities can hardly be supported. Home-workers frequently worked such long hours, sometimes late into the night, in order to complete an order or earn sufficient to make a small profit, that the work dominated home life, making a mockery of those who argued that home work complemented a woman's domestic role. On the contrary, home-workers had to manage their child care and housework to fit in with wage earning, not the other way around. The nature of the work meant that homes became workshops, dominated by the atmosphere, the smell and the accoutrements of work. And the fact that many women were forced to make use of the labour of their own children within the home made a nonsense of the argument that home work fitted in with child care. As Sonya Rose points out, for England, 'domestic responsibilities were given short shrift when they competed with activities that could put food on the table.'[55] Paper-bag making seemed particularly suited to child labour, with one German autobiographer recalling rising at six, 'then we would glue until five or six minutes before eight o'clock, in order to be able to get to school by eight . . . In the evening we had to work until our assigned quota [which might be several thousand bags] was finished.'[56] Similarly, in London, one investigator described 'case after case of little match-box makers working habitually from the time that school closes till eleven, or even midnight; of little artificial flower makers beginning to twist green paper round the wire stems at five a.m., and toiling through the long weary day in a small, filthy attic.'[57]

Home work was accepted when there was no feasible alternative. It was work to keep body and soul together, not a lifestyle choice. Some examples will serve to illustrate the unenviable position of the nineteenth-century home-worker. Henry Mayhew, on his travels around London in 1850, came upon a woman living over a coal shed who made shirts for between 2d and 3d each whilst having to provide her own thread, working from six in the morning until nine at night and living on little more than dry bread and weak coffee. On the Shetland Islands women engaged in hand-knitting, just about the only form of home work available in that part of the world, in order to stave off destitution. They were paid not in cash but in kind – the hated barter-truck system by which they received fish, corn or hardware goods at a poor rate of exchange for their knitwear. This kind of system exploited women's traditional skills whilst denying them an independent existence. As one hand-knitter remarked in 1872: 'Knitting does very well in Lerwick for those that have friends to live with and keep them, but not for me when I had to look after myself.'[58] Berlin garment workers, many of whom either purchased or rented sewing machines, still had to work up to twelve hours a day and sometimes more, in order to make a living.[59] Employers invariably assumed women home-workers were earning a subsidiary wage – 'pin money'. Home work was little more than 'the best alternative to destitution'.[60]

Home work was the logical consequence of the ideological embrace by employers, trade unions and workers, of the breadwinner wage. Bread-winning was a male occupation in the eyes of employers and the state; mothering was self-evidently female. Yet few working families could sustain this division of labour. Only a minority of men earned enough to be considered the sole provider in their families, hence women's home work was a crucial element of the early industrial household economy. It was resorted to most often by widows, and by married women who were prevented from finding a job outside the home because of their child care responsibilities or the absence of suitable work for women. In Nottingham, a city dominated by the lace and hosiery trades, where home work was relatively easy to come by, it was the wives of casual workers, mothers with large numbers of young children, and widowed mothers who resorted to working from home, often lace-finishing or seaming.[61] Nevertheless, home work was often preferred to work outside the home for good economic reasons. There were savings to be made from working at home. According to one home worker, women who worked in a factory had to 'pay for washing to be done and must buy tinned meats. If they stay at home they can do their own housework and their own shopping; and can better care for their children.'[62]

By the end of the century, home work became a symbolic battlefield precisely because of its status as neither housework nor factory labour. Although conservatives often saw the home as the preferred production locale, since it allowed women to stay within their 'natural place' and care for their children, this romantic vision of *industrie de famille*, harking back to a mythical family economy, was regarded by others as a regrettable development. For one British critic, the very future of the race depended on the removal of women from waged work, and especially the displacement of this work from the sanctity of the home. 'The value of maintaining a high standard in the home life of our people can hardly be averted, for upon it depends not only the present, but also the future of our race,' argued the trade unionist Clementina Black (1853–1922) in 1907. 'But these poor creatures have no time to attend to the pure, tender delight of motherhood, or the many little duties which cluster around that word so sweet to the English ears – "home".'[63] The home-workers themselves were trapped. When the National Home Workers League was formed in England, not to protest against the deplorable conditions under which home-workers laboured, but to campaign against proposed legislation which threatened to place restrictions on home work, many women joined in the knowledge that limits on hours would prevent them from earning a living.

Industrial home work was not a continuation of women's domestic labour; it was something qualitatively different. It was work specially created and defined by employers for women. From the outset, most types of home work were defined as unskilled, earnings were low as befitted a subsidiary wage, and as long as employers, trade unionists, male workers and the state told married women that waged work and work outside the home were incompatible, women were forced to work at home. Moreover, the continued association of woman with home had broader implications for women's position within the labour market as a whole, influencing what kinds of work they did, how much they earned and how their work was valued.

THE SEXUAL DIVISION OF LABOUR

One of the key features of the European industrial economies was the sexual division of labour that characterised waged work. It is also one of the hardest to explain. Some scholars blame industrial capitalism, whilst others blame men, or rather, patriarchy based on gender. Industrialisation did not create discriminatory labour markets. The employment of thousands of women in the textile industry, one of the most mechanised and technologically advanced of all industrial processes, demonstrates how a highly industrial, factory-based mode of production could successfully function using predominantly female labour. In this industry at least, there was no impediment to the employment of women in new jobs using machinery. Neither was it solely the hegemony of domestic ideology and the new construction of femininity that caused industrial labour to be divided into men's work and women's work. Women worked in mines until the 1840s in Britain, as hauliers pulling coal trucks through the underground shafts and in Cornwall's metalliferous mining industry, breaking lumps of rock with a sledgehammer. The tradition of employing family groups and the low wages paid to women miners offers a more convincing explanation for women undertaking such an 'unwomanly' job.[64]

It is in fact misleading to try to explain the sexual division of labour by adopting an either/or perspective: either capitalism was to blame, or patriarchy. Rather, it was a combination of the new tensions and insecurities of the industrial labour market and the appropriation of the middle-class ideology of separate spheres which resulted in an exacerbation of sexual conflict and a hardening of gender hierarchies (not just divisions), both within the workforce and within working-class culture. The late nineteenth century saw the culmination of a process of struggle during which working-class men had reacted to the new insecurities of the industrial economy by excluding other workers, including women, and by adopting a defensive consciousness based on the appropriation of skill and the breadwinner wage. In this context, Anna Clark writes, 'working-class culture was characterised by . . . a leisure culture of music-halls, betting, and drinking; moderate trade union activity; and a strict sexual division of labour both in the workplace and at home.'[65] Men had become the new 'aristocracy of labour', whose work opportunities, earnings, status and lifestyle separated them from women workers.

In her influential book *Working Life of Women in the Seventeenth Century*, published in 1919, Alice Clark argued that the rise of capitalism in Britain in the late seventeenth century resulted in a diminution of the woman's economic role: 'it seems probable that the wife of the prosperous capitalist tended to become idle, the wife of the skilled journeyman lost her economic independence and became his unpaid domestic servant, while the wives of the wage-earners were drawn into the sweated industries of that period.'[66] Clark's analysis implies that work opportunities for men and women were equal before the rise of industrial capitalism. Notwithstanding the relative freedom of women to engage in independent trade and a range of crafts, women's work has, for centuries, been bunched in particular occupations and their wage rates were generally lower than men's. For example, in London around 1700, the majority of women worked for a living but their working relationship with their menfolk was characterised more by competition than by harmony, with the majority engaged in occupations closely related to domestic tasks: charring, laundry, clothes-mending and making, and domestic service.[67] So, there was continuity in the status of women's work but changes in the economy, and the resultant undermining of traditional male work practices and bonds led some male workers to experience insecurity, both on account of a perceived loss of skill and control of the work process, and because of employers' strategies to replace them with cheaper female labour. This was especially true of the early feminised textile industry where, in Germany as elsewhere, male workers 'fought vigorously to define a place for themselves' and struggled to hold on to jobs against the attempts of employers to create a permanent core female workforce.[68] The response was that 'working men identified skill with manhood and sought to keep women out of the workplace.'[69] In other words, the failure of the (male) working class to defend the interests of women workers was a result of a 'construction of class that equated productivity and masculinity.'[70] Women were seen as competitors, as auxiliary and subordinate workers, and defined primarily by the domestic sphere as expressed by one of the French workers' newspapers, *L'Atelier*, in 1842: 'If the salary of the male worker were generally sufficient for the keep of his family – as it should be – his wife would not be obliged to frequent the workshops.'[71]

It is this attempt by male workers to exclude women as competitors that appears to be a key feature of the industrial economy. The overt exclusion of women from certain trades before the mid-eighteenth century was on the grounds that the work was not appropriate for women: it was too physical or would promote immorality, although men's desire to protect their privileged labour market status should not be forgotten either.[72] In the industrial economy, although physical difference was still used as a means of sex-typing jobs, or at least as a way of legitimating the practice, employers were just as likely to allocate tasks according to the perceived level of skill required and the degree of responsibility attached to a job. In Italian textile factories, sex was a factor in assigning tasks, but other factors such as the necessary or desirable qualities in a worker also determined who did what job. Hence the sorting and grading of wool in the Sella company of Piemonte was given to 'clever' women, whilst the beating and washing of wool was a job for 'robust' men. Carding, twisting and weaving was done by women in the daytime and men at night, whilst young men were required for finishing. However, across the industry as a whole, women were more likely to be employed in the preparatory stages of production and in weaving, whilst men were almost universally to be found in the central stages of the production and as supervisors.[73]

Neither was mechanisation necessarily central to sex-typing, although it is probably true to say that men dominated machine work in all industries with the exception of textiles where predominantly female labour was employed to work power looms. So women did work with machines, not just in textiles but in a range of manufacturing industries, yet in general this did not result in a raising of their status and pay. Female machine operatives were normally supervised by men who, it was said, were more technically minded and, in Italy it was said, more efficient at surveillance than 'humane' women.[74] Machinery was gendered, thus women were often restricted to machinery deemed suitable for female capabilities whilst men operated the larger, more powerful or more complex machinery. In the French hosiery industry, the sexual division of labour practised by artisans whereby men appropriated the knitting frame and women were employed in the more marginal preparatory tasks 'evolved out of custom, craft and convention.' 'In the transition from an artisan mode of production to an industrial one, the male knitter maintained his privileged position at the knitting frame, the most valorized and productive machine'. Women were set to work on labour-intensive, fragmented tasks which required those ubiquitous nimble fingers, good eyesight, patience and care.[75] As factory production came to predominate, male workers benefited from extended training and apprenticeships whilst women were given only on-the-job training. And the mechanisation of women's tasks – the seaming of knitted goods for example – resulted in a dilution of skill and the concomitant increasing productivity demands. In the paper industry, boys were preferred over girls, despite girls' 'nimble fingers', because, it was said, 'boys had more aptitude to manage machines and are better worth teaching, as they may grow up to be competent mechanics.'[76] In the Edinburgh printing industry, mechanisation resulted in a downgrading of women's work. There was no craft tradition behind some of the new mechanised jobs, thus they could be defined as unskilled with a wage rate to match – female work in other words. However, one new machine – the Linotype – was soon appropriated by 'skilled workers'. 'There was never any question of women working on the Linotype', despite the fact that 'the work required by the compositor is very little different from that required by a typewriter'. This machine was hot, noisy and a threat to hand typesetting whereas the Monotype could be operated by female compositors sitting at keyboards in a room adjacent to the noise and heat produced by the casting of type.[77]

Skill was gendered. It was widely believed that men and women possessed different natural skills: women were dextrous, dainty, sharp-eyed and careful. They were also, it was said, docile, better equipped to endure monotonous tasks, and willing to work hard. Men's skill, on the other hand, was defined by the type of work they undertook and the amount of training the job entailed. So, for women, definitions of their natural abilities circumscribed their work opportunities and ascribed a lesser value to the work they did, whereas for men the opposite was true. A nimble-fingered silk worker was expected to deploy her natural skills in her task, but work that came naturally was, perversely, ascribed a lower status. Male workers achieved skill through hard work and training or apprenticeships. Referring to female-dominated assembly work, de Groot and Schrover summarise the situation for women workers: '[assembly work] was perceived as light, clean, monotonous, and unskilled because women did it, and conversely women were perceived as the appropriate gender for the job because it was light, clean, monotonous and unskilled.'[78] If the relationship between sex-typing and mechanisation is complex, then the division of labour according to attributions of skill is no less so. Feminist historians have long recognised that definitions of skill are 'saturated with sexual bias . . . Far from being an objective economic fact, skill is often an ideological category imposed on certain types of work by virtue of the sex and power of the workers who perform it.'[79] The construction of skill and the definition of certain tasks as skilled or unskilled is contingent upon a range of variables including: the pre-existence of craft traditions, the technology employed, notions of appropriate work for men and women, ideas about natural competence, competition within the labour market, the level of unionisation, and women's work and lifecycle.

Whilst supervision is not conventionally defined as a skill, responsibility did increasingly become categorised as skilled work in mechanised sectors. Supervisory roles are seen as crucial to the efficient and cost-effective production process where mistakes or inferior work may compromise output and production quality, and where speed is crucial. Conversely, labour-intensive jobs were often assigned to female workers and involved little control or responsibility. In such situations the supervisory positions invariably are assigned to male workers. In Dundee's jute industry, in which the workforce was three-quarters female, positions of authority were assumed by men.[80] Similarly, in the German linen industry, also feminised with female workers comprising 76 per cent of the labour force by 1900, the remaining quarter comprising the supervisors, mechanics and office workers, were male. One of the consequences of this gender hierarchy of skill was the emergence of tensions between male and female workers in labour disputes. Male workers, who regarded themselves as skilled and therefore deserving of a higher status and wages than female operatives, not infrequently went on strike against the employment of women. The silk and velvet weavers of the lower Rhine region, desperate to preserve their identity as skilled workers in the face of mechanisation and the increasing employment of women, went on strike arguing, rather disingenuously, for higher wages and a ban on women's factory employment altogether.[81]

Another explanation for the subordination of women within the industrial hierarchy was the appropriation of the ideology of separate spheres and domesticity by male workers and trade unions defending their jobs, employers justifying their hiring and employment practices, and also the state in support of protective legislation. Yet, if the ideal construction of femininity had influenced the sex-typing of jobs, then women would not have been permitted to work in the dirtiest, dangerous and most unfeminine of employments such as fish-gutting, mining, smelting and chainmaking. Rather, the exclusion of women from certain sectors of the industrial labour force suited the interests of workers and trade unionists who sought to maintain wage rates and, as a result, cultivate an aura of respectability which encompassed a wife at home, thus creating a reservoir of cheap and readily available female labour to be utilised by employers. The combination of an ideology that positioned women in the domestic sphere, and practices which excluded women from the acquisition of skill, resulted in women becoming a 'glut on the urban labour market', a 'reserve army of labour'. Women were not excluded from the labour force but they were marginalised. Changing labour organisation then, was not the cause of these gender hierarchies; rather it was a combination of shifting ideas about masculinity and femininity and a changing occupational structure which reaffirmed rather than created the hierarchical economic order.

The introduction of protective legislation was both a contributor to and a consequence of the sexual division of labour in industry. Restrictions on the number of hours worked by women, the banning of female night work, and the imposition of health and safety standards, were all introduced on the principle that women were a different category of workers from men. By 1900, most European states had enacted legislation that raised the minimum age of a worker to around 13, and had imposed a maximum length of the working day of up to 12 hours. There were also laws restricting women's employment in jobs defined as dangerous. The 1892 Labour Law in France stated that 'Work of a hazardous nature, beyond the strength, or dangerous to morality, . . . will be forbidden to women, girls and children.'[82] As a result women were banned from a large number of trades, mainly those which used dangerous chemicals such as lead and mercury or which produced unstable substances, owing to the likelihood of 'deleterious vapours, noxious emanations or possible poisoning'.[83] The result was the restriction of women's work in what came to be seen as male occupations and the facilitation of it in occupations identified as feminine. Thus, protective legislation acted as a bulwark to labour market segmentation. As Stewart argues, 'Notions about women's reproductive role provided ideological support for this distribution of occupations as well as for sex-specific labour legislation. In turn such legislation raised expectations about women's domestic responsibilities and reinforced the assignment of occupations by gender.'[84]

The arguments of protective legislation campaigners were informed more by accounts of immorality in the workplace and the damage done to women's fitness for domesticity and reproduction, than by a humanitarian concern for working women's health and welfare. The example of mining is the most illuminating in this regard. When a British government commission investigated the plight of women in the mines they were not overly concerned about the physical demands of the work. Rather, they focused on the potential for immoral behaviour underground, the indecent clothing of the male and female workers, and the unfeminine appearance of female miners. In 1881, a visitor to a Cornish copper mine was shocked at the sight of a 'bal maiden' (female mineworker), shovelling ore into a cart working 'with the vigour of a young man'. 'Her petticoats were stained with the hue of the copper ore; her shapeless legs . . . muffled up in woollen wraps' so that he was unsure of her sex.[85] 'Legislators' increasing fascination with working women's sexuality and their fears about gender role reversal were provoked more by the growing social crisis . . . than by the actual conditions under which women laboured in the mines and factories.'[86] Nevertheless, almost all west European states, with the exception of Belgium, banned female minework. By 1900 in Britain, France, Germany and Russia, the social question was defined by concerns about the family, about infant mortality and thus women's reproductive and maternal role.[87] In Germany the bodies of female textile workers were made analogous with the body of the family and the body of the nation. Factory work destroyed the family by destroying women who were the lynchpin of the domestic unit. Thus the 1891 German labour code extended lunch breaks and reduced women's working hours on Saturdays 'to give the gainfully employed woman more time in the day to learn and perform her crucial household tasks.'[88] Similarly, in France, fears of depopulation and degeneration of the race were centred on working women. Women were identified, first and foremost, as mothers and house-keepers, not as workers, and thus legislation restricting women's working hours helped to create a dichotomy between the dependant mother and the working woman.

Protective legislation served to amplify and solidify a pre-existing sexual division of labour. In singling out women as in need of special treatment, reformers, employers and the state bolstered the ideal of the patriarchal family. The restrictive labour laws also had negative side-effects. Many women were forced to find work in the unregulated sectors where they would invariably work longer hours for less pay. The failure to compensate women for the wages or work lost by paying their husbands higher wages meant that the rhetoric about women's valued role as housewives and mothers was empty. There was never any serious proposal to prohibit women from working outside the home – although in Germany some did campaign for the banning of married women from factory work. Instead, as Stewart remarks, 'legislators limited women's working hours outside the home to facilitate a dual role as nearly full-time wage-earners *and* part-time housewives.'[89]

WOMEN'S WORK IDENTITIES

Almost all women of the working classes engaged in some form of employment outside the home for some or most of their lives, but still they were identified in discourse as primarily wives, housewives and mothers. In such circumstances, how did working women regard themselves? How did they develop and express their identities as workers when they were expected to be at home? For women, work offered an alternative identity, a sense of pride and achievement, and it promoted the development of a common female consciousness. Just because women were low paid and regarded as dependent on male breadwinners, argues Eleanor Gordon in her study of Dundee's jute workers, 'did not mean that women workers defined themselves solely in relation to their domestic role or that their responses to their work roles were conditioned only by their domestic responsibilities. Nor did it preclude resistance and struggle to either patriarchal authority or exploitation at the point of production.'[90] By the end of the century, particularly in those sectors with a high proportion of female employees, a 'collective culture of working-class women' was in evidence.[91]

It is easy to interpret women as victims of the twin forces of patriarchy and capitalism in the workplace, and it is easily assumed that they were unlikely to develop a workplace consciousness or a work identity. Early factory employers commonly employed paternalistic strategies whereby the factory was envisaged as a family incorporating gender and status inequalities. Within this hierarchy women workers were subjected to disciplining and were the recipients of welfare measures. The Courtaulds silk mill in Essex, England, combined both carrot and stick tactics: 'immoral behaviour' could lose a women her job; women with illegitimate children were discriminated against in the allocation of company housing; at all times Courtauld's female employees were expected to conduct themselves in a respectable manner. If they conformed they would benefit from the range of welfare measures, from on-site kitchen and wash-house facilities to a sick club.[92] In the textile mills of northern France, women workers were subjected to what Patricia Hilden terms 'a programme of clerical industrial surveillance'.[93]

Work identity and pride is more often associated with skilled occupations, only attained through a period of lengthy training or apprenticeship. Since most women worked in jobs defined as unskilled, and owing to women's interrupted working lives and the fact that much of women's work took place at home, it may be assumed that the kinds of work identities demonstrated by men were not present amongst the female workforce. As Canning argues, 'an ethic of work had no place in the popular image of the female worker'.[94] Yet, it is time to abandon the assumption that women's work identities were constituted solely or primarily by their domestic role. In her study of German textile workers, Kathleen Canning argues that: 'pivotal in imagining how women formed work identities is the development of *Berufsethos* (work ethic), a process by which they came to identify with their jobs, feeling pride in the products of their labour and forming bonds or "shared dispositions" with fellow workers based on common fears, aspirations, interests and loyalties.'[95]

There is plenty of evidence to support this assertion. According to the observations of Minna Wettstein-Adelt, a German social reformer who disguised herself as a worker in a weaving mill: 'Many of these girls work enthusiastically, especially those who follow the completion of a whole piece, like those who weave smaller rugs or single fitted curtains. They love their machines, as one loves a loyal dog. They clean them until they shine and decorate them with colourful ribbons, holy cards, and other trinkets.'[96] Similarly, women in the mills and factories of central Scotland had a pride in their machinery. As one worker recollected: 'And the girls . . . they thought they *owned* a machine; they were in charge of a machine but they thought they owned the machine. A Saturday morning was given to cleaning. And these machines were brass, and they were beautiful.'[97] Women workers also developed a sense of pride in their labour, whether or not it was categorised as skilled. Edinburgh's female compositors, whilst not defined as skilled in that they possessed no craft tradition and had not been initiated into the rituals of the craftsmen, still expressed a pride in and enjoyment of their work: 'I loved my work', said one. 'I would have worked weekends if they'd let me', recalled another.[98] Few were as articulate and idealistic as Jenny Heynrichs, the coeditor of *Neue Bahnen*, the journal of the General German Women's Association, who, in an article entitled 'What is work?' replied: 'Work, be it intellectual or physical, is always the lively and vigorous union of our intellectual and physical powers ... Work is creativity accompanied by the comforting realisation that one is bringing forth something really good and necessary.'[99]

Women's attachment to their jobs also developed out of the sociability that characterised female-dominated workplaces. In some factory towns the level of friendship amongst workers was already high as the women all started work together after leaving school, and this continued as they learned the job, got married, had children and returned to work for the money and the desire for sociable contact. Social life on the job took the form of singing, dancing, joking and gossiping; and these bonding activities helped to create a sense of collective identity amongst women as workers which did spill over into collective action. These 'fluid boundaries between factory and family' were reflected in women's work conflicts with employers and with male workers.[100]

The tobacco industry in Spain and France provides a good example of how a female-dominated workplace could lead to strong female work identities and to collective action. In Spain, especially, there were very few men employed in this sector – just 112 among the more than 15,000 workers in factories across the country in 1914.[101] The female world of tobacco production was advantageous to women in a number of ways. The absence of men from female workshops created a set of occupational categories within the factory restricted to women. This gave women a sense of work identity and it also established a clear career structure whereby women could rise to supervisory levels. A girl who entered the factory as a sweeper at the age of 14, could progress according to ability, aptitude and motivation, to an operator and then to an overseer or forewoman. Moreover, pay levels were established without reference to those attained by male workers, resulting in relatively high wages and a stronger bargaining position. In France, a strong collective identity developed amongst the female tobacco workers who were skilled and relatively well paid. They were often heads of households, they provided for their families, and they demanded the rights accorded male workers. 'No matter what her physical characteristics, a woman must not be considered a slave or a servant', exclaimed Marie Jay, the tobacco union delegate at the 1892 congress of the Confédération Générale du Travail; 'she must achieve her independence by her own efforts.'[102] Spanish *cigarreras* were frequently represented as mature, assertive and possessing a powerful sexuality; the character of Carmen in Mérimée's novel and Bizet's opera embodied the popular stereotype.[103] In reality, however, these were women with a singular status amongst female workers which gave them a sense of collective consciousness and a willingness to strike and take to the streets unusual amongst proletarian women at the time.[104]

Early industrial action by women workers was often characterised as spontaneous, impulsive and disorganised, the implication being that women lacked effective organisation and were liable to damage the more rational, male union-led disputes. Women did often down tools in what looked like spontaneous fashion, but male observers misunderstood the nature of female collective action. Amalie Seidl, an activist in an Austrian textile factory in the 1890s, described the means by which her fellow workers protested wage rates and her own dismissal for incitement.

> I addressed them from a stump, telling them that . . . if they really wanted to go on strike, they should demand more than just my reinstatement. What we should demand, we didn't really know, but strike we would . . . [The] demands for a reduction of working hours from 12 to 10 and my reinstatement were rejected [by the factory owners]. Because of the great heat in the work rooms, the women stood about half dressed and went barefoot, but at a moment's notice, they all left the factory . . . The first meeting was promptly held in the afternoon on the Meidling meadowlands. The work force of three other factories also joined us, and after a few days about 700 women were on strike. It caused sensation, this being the first women's strike [in Vienna], and the bourgeois press took notice of it, complaining that now women workers also were being 'incited'. [105]

The manifestation of women's protest may have differed from the models chosen by men, yet female action was similarly shaped by their experience of work and their understanding of the relationship between production and reproduction, workplace and family. The majority of disputes involving female workers, as for male, concerned wages. In the Milan textile factories, women's wages were around only one-third of male rates, a situation accounting for women strikers outnumbering men in textile strikes in the 1890s.[106] But it is in disputes over hours and conditions that we see the blurring of the boundary between public and private. In 1880 in St Petersburg, women workers demanded that nursing mothers be allowed to nurse their babies at work twice a day for nine months instead of six and, in 1895 in the same city, women workers in a cigarette factory walked out complaining about the bosses' behaviour as well as new rates of pay.[107] During the industrial unrest of 1905 in Russia, women made numerous demands including the right to a half-day off so that they could do their laundry.[108] In Milan in 1894, seamstresses went on strike complaining about the abusive behaviour of the foremen.[109] In the Saxon town of Crimmitschau, female textile workers mobilised to demand improvements in facilities such as separate toilet and changing rooms for women. Also in this textile town in 1903, the struggle by male and female workers to achieve the ten-hour day incorporated the needs of female employees by demanding a wage rise to compensate for the shorter working day. The slogan adopted by the strikers – 'One more hour for our families!' – highlighted the situation of married women workers. Trade unionists, middle-class social reformers and the women workers themselves agreed that a shorter working day would enable women to be better wives and mothers.[110] In Dundee, a strike in 1871 by jute workers brought women into conflict with organised male workers, demonstrating how female workers in full-time employment were still constructed in terms of their domestic role. When the men, led by higher-paid supervisory workers, initiated their demands for longer mealtimes, the women went on strike for a wage rise. The men were angry, regarding this as unjustified and spontaneous action, typical of rash and irresponsible women, that jeopardised the men's negotiations. Yet, as Gordon suggests, for the lower-paid women the wage demand was rational in view of the key role of women's earnings in the household economy of Dundee, a city where the proportion of women householders and the number of households dependent on women's earnings was higher than anywhere else in Scotland.[111]

Finally, the manner in which women conducted disputes in this period of low female trade union membership contrasted with the more sober strategies adopted by male-dominated labour unions. Women's disputes were often conducted in a carnival-like atmosphere. In Dundee the women refused to confine their negotiations to within the factory gates and took their campaign to the streets. 'Those on strike today paraded the streets in grotesque processions, bearing emblems of their trade, suspended from poles, such as mats, jugs etc', reported one newspaper. 'They also indulged in shouting and singing . . . Besides this they held threatening demonstrations in front of the works where nobody had turned out.'[112] On other occasions they marched through the streets bearing mocking effigies of employers. In French pit villages the wives of striking miners confronted scabs and humiliated them by removing their trousers and spanking them. And they disarmed police and troops dispatched to control their protests by handing them flowers and even lifting their skirts. [113] German women strikers often took to the streets, 'parading' past the windows of mill owners' homes, 'shopping basket in arm and knitting in hand'. For this they were described as 'impertinent' and 'worse than the men'.[114] In London and the Black Country in the early 1900s, women strikers produced leaflets, badges and ribbons reminiscent of the contemporaneous suffrage campaign, to draw attention to their struggle.

Perhaps women were drawn to this form of protest by the hierarchical and antagonistic nature of gender relations on the shopfloor between male supervisors and female workers. Ridiculing their bosses and celebrating a female work culture was a sign of strength. In Russian factories, female workers were subjected to degrading treatment at the hands of foremen and male workers. 'Flirting, pinching, innuendo, abuse and bad language are in abundance', complained one factory worker in 1905. Others complained of sexual abuse which occurred under the pretence of searches to prevent theft.[115] The behaviour of women strikers in public, their possession of the streets, their attempts to humiliate their bosses by the use of jokes and insults, suggests not only an expression of female sociability but also that they were taking the opportunity to turn the world upside-down, to overturn the gender hierarchy that ruled their working lives. As Gordon says, 'by using ridicule, embarrassment and sexual impropriety, they turned sexual divisions into an effective weapon which left the victims of their *badinage* emasculated and without redress.'[116] Like most appropriations of the symbolism of carnival, however, it was not a route to fundamental change. The gender hierarchy was firmly entrenched in industry through a widespread acceptance of the discursive construction of women as wives and mothers. It was left to women to negotiate the boundaries between factory work and home work in ways that accepted and celebrated work identity whilst building upon shared experiences as women.

Women's grievances at work were more likely to be expressed in these informal ways than through trade unions for most of the century. It is hard to know precisely what proportion of women did join a trade union but we can say that only a minority embraced collective bargaining by the First World War. Probably less than 10 per cent of the European female workforce was unionised by 1914, but in some states the proportion is likely to have been much lower.[117] In Germany the figure of more than 255,000 unionised women in 1912 sounds impressive but this accounted for just 7 per cent of women in the non-agricultural labour force.[118] The 90,000 French women who belonged to a trade union at this time were in an even smaller minority of 1.2 per cent although they accounted for around 10 per cent of all unionised workers. Russian women were no more eager to embrace the union movement, with just 4.4 per cent of Moscow women workers unionised in 1907.[119] In the female-dominated textile industry, membership was stronger. In Germany, women constituted 36 per cent of members of the Social Democratic Textile Union in 1907.[120] In Britain there were 154,000 female trade union members in 1900 – just 3.2 per cent of the workforce – but this figure did increase quite significantly in the decade before the war so that by 1914 around 8 per cent of women workers were unionised.[121] By the beginning of the twentieth century, though, working women were beginning to realise the disadvantages of their labour market status and the benefits of collective bargaining, the English union organiser Mary MacArthur commenting: 'Women are badly paid and badly treated because they are not organised, and they are not organised because they are badly paid and badly treated.'[122]

There was little incentive for most women to join a trade union. Few had either the time to attend meetings or the money to pay union dues. A few unions discriminated in favour of women members by offering them lower membership rates, but these paid out lower strike benefits to women than their male co-workers.[123] The majority of female workers, many of them domestic servants and home-workers, worked in sectors where there were no unions. Nineteenth-century unions were factory-based, geared primarily to men's employment patterns and concerned with job security and advancement, training and apprenticeships and, of course, the maintenance of the family or breadwinner wage. Moreover, many of the early trade unions were overtly hostile to women workers, regarding them as competitors rather than comrades. They were suspicious, too, of women's apparent indiscipline. Many male trade unions simply did not trust women to act in the interests of all workers, women and men. Male-dominated unions experienced difficulty penetrating women's work culture and in turn, female textile workers, unimpressed by the unions' failure to represent their needs, resorted to strategies which challenged the factory system and male bargaining traditions. Women were not underrepresented in unions because they had been socialised to be submissive, as one English female union organiser argued; rather, they frequently regarded the unions as part of the structure of industry which could not acknowledge women's identity as workers. 'Comrades! When will you understand that you are working not with a woman but with a person just like yourself?' exclaimed a Russian typesetter in 1914. 'Only when you learn to see that the woman is the same kind of worker as yourself will you really be able to organise.'[124]

Towards the end of the century, however, male unions began to recognise women as workers and some even began to support the principle of equal rights. In Russia, a number of unions, including the St Petersburg Textile Union, supported equal pay – presumably on the basis that cheap female labour undercut men doing the same jobs – and some, recognising women's double burden, even established child-care facilities.[125] At the same time, women began to organise themselves in unions modelled on those of their male comrades, and in Leagues and other cooperative organisations. In Italy, for example, in response to state legislation limiting the hours women could work, women in the clothing trades, 'being touched to the heart by the enchanting words "brotherhood" and "solidarity"', organised themselves into a union in 1903 and wrote to their unionised sisters in England for support and information. 'Our union will base its aspirations on the evidence of your conditions; it will know how to fight and win.'[126] Unfortunately, women workers would have to wait until the end of the twentieth century before governments enacted equal pay and equal opportunities legislation. Women's struggle to be recognised as workers was long and hard.

NEW JOBS FOR WOMEN

Towards the end of the century, new job opportunities arose in new sectors of employment. These were mainly in the service sector, incorporating white-collar (or blouse) occupations in insurance companies, in book-keeping and government service, the post office, telegraph and telephone exchanges, in retail sales and, most publicly, in department stores. There were also some professions opening up for the middle-class woman, notably teaching and nursing. From the outset, most new jobs in services were taken by women – they became 'feminised'. In France, 40 per cent of workers in banking, insurance and retail were women by 1911. In Germany, the percentage of female employees in the white-collar sector rose from 21 to 30 per cent between 1882 and 1907, and by 1914 up to 80 per cent of retail employees were female, as were 22 per cent of office workers.[127] In Britain, similarly, the percentage of civil service employees who were female rose from 13 per cent in 1881 to 27 per cent in 1911. They also constituted over half of telegraph workers and a quarter of commercial clerks. Nursing and teaching were feminised on a far greater scale. In Britain, almost all of the more than

80,000 nurses and midwives were female in 1911, as were almost three-quarters of teachers.[128] The vast majority of these employees were young – 68 per cent of British telegraph employees were under 25. This kind of work became especially attractive to young women of the middle classes for whom there had been few respectable opportunities on offer. But the expansion of the tertiary sector did not challenge the traditional gender hierarchy embedded in the labour market. In fact, although there existed the potential to do away with sex-typing, the sexual division of labour was just as pervasive in the offices and stores as in the factories, and for many of the same reasons. Women's supposed 'natural' skills, male 'craft' traditions, and the struggle for control of new workplaces and processes, all contributed to a segregated labour force. Men became managers and supervisors, women were recruited to clerking; women became typists and switchboard operators – work that was regarded as light, clean and ideally suited to those nimble fingers. In retail sales, women dominated the sale of light consumer goods on the shopfloor, whilst the managerial positions and jobs as buyers and in travelling sales – jobs with career prospects – were reserved for men. And whilst apprenticeships operated for men in this sector, few women benefited from this form of structured training programme because they were expected to leave when they married. There were some office occupations that did not open up to women until after the First World War, most notably banking and stockbroking, the most prestigious and highly paid white-collar work. In Britain, women's share of employment in the banking sector was pitiful, there being just 476 female bank officials and clerks in 1911, a mere 1.2 per cent, compared with the 20,337 employed in the less prestigious post office.[129] In Spain women were barred from competing for civil service posts until 1918. The idea of a female employment career was for the future.

How can this sex segregation be explained? In her study of the German postal service, Ursula Nienhaus shows how a sex-specific employment policy which resulted in rigid sex segregation was based upon the traditional notion of male employees as breadwinners and women as mothers and housewives. The expansion of telephone communications, albeit based on male-dominated military technology, saw women flood into the postal service, especially as telephonists. Yet, the old ideas about fit work for women were employed: women were suited to telephony, not only because it required a good speaking voice and nimble fingers (albeit that these fingers regularly received electric shocks) but also because women were cheap and flexible labour.[130] In Britain it was said that women were ideal telegraph operators because:

In the first place, they have in an eminent degree the quickness of eye and ear, and the delicacy of touch, which are essential qualifications of a good operator. In the second place, they take more kindly than men or boys do to sedentary employment, and are more patient during long confinement to one place. In the third place, the wages, which will draw male operators from but an inferior class of the community, will draw female operators from a superior class ... They are also less disposed than men to combine for the purpose of extorting higher wages, and this is by no means an unimportant matter.[131]

Male civil servants, it was noted, expected their salary to increase year on year, whether or not their performance had improved. Women, on the other hand, 'will solve these difficulties for the Department by retiring for the purpose of getting married as soon as they get the chance.' Male employees were protected at the expense of women, receiving insurance and pension benefits as 'breadwinners', whilst the female workers were never accorded full civil servant status and thus were denied those same benefits. The German female postal workers were treated little better than their factory cousins; they were a reserve army of labour, an army called upon during the First World War when the number of female employees increased more than threefold, but then dispensed with when the postal service rationalised its operations in the postwar years. In the large retail establishments and department stores, similar perceptions of the working woman determined the shop assistant's status and conditions, albeit youth and good looks replacing dexterity as the desirable attributes.

The expansion of the service sector did not, at least in the pre-war years, challenge entrenched industrial notions of skill. In fact women experienced a form of deskilling in these occupations. Whereas the specialist retailers and small offices employed men and women who learned a trade and developed a specific set of skills, the department stores, large offices and typing pools relied upon a larger number of employees who were trained for a specific job rather than a career. At the same time, jobs in these sectors too became segregated according to gender: men remained associated with heavy goods whereas the sale of cloth, ladies' fashions, lingerie, cosmetics and confectionery became girls' work. The female sales assistant was associated with the goods she sold, she was part of the presentation, her physical attractiveness used to stimulate the purchaser's desire. And, behind the scenes, department stores relied upon hundreds of women in the offices dealing with the mail-order business, and seamstresses whose status and pay was more akin to that of their sweatshop predecessors.[132] The Parisian flagship department store, the Bon Marché, was typical in this respect. Its 2500 sales assistants worked long hours for low pay. They were housed in nearby supervised dormitories and ate their meals in communal dining halls where a watch was kept on the girls' social behaviour. Far from being a beacon of modernity, the department store operated along paternalistic lines. Gender hierarchies not only remained but were accentuated in some new employment situations. Moreover, this workforce was mostly new with no history of workplace culture or agitation. Shopworkers and clerks were regarded as docile, far less likely to strike for higher wages than their factory counterparts. Thus their position in the labour market was tenuous and in any case they were not expected to stay. The notorious marriage bar, which permitted a business to terminate a woman's employment, operated everywhere except in France and thus it was impossible for women to combine a white-collar career with family life.

Yet it is undeniable that white-collar work was often more attractive to women workers for very good reasons. A job as a shop assistant was often preferable to domestic service or factory work. Retail was often perceived by women themselves as skilled work. The skills of personal service and technical accomplishments such as in the grocery, florist or drapery trades, were transferable and better rewarded than domestic service. And even a job as a shop assistant in one of the new department stores such as Woolworth's where the pay was better, the work cleaner, the status higher, and women could dress more attractively, was often preferable to factory work. 'A lot of them at work in the brewery did that,' commented a former bottler in a Scottish factory. 'We must have thought we were toffs for leaving the brewery and going to work in Woolworth's.'[133] Office work similarly had a higher status than many other occupations and, as Simonton argues, 'For women workers anxious about respectability, strict discipline and sexually segregated employment were positive features.'[134] It would be wrong to portray white-collar work as glorified domestic service, notwithstanding the fact that by the turn of the century its workforce was drawn from a similar social group and the similarities in terms of working conditions and employment prospects. At this time, white-collar work was usually a positive choice for women of the working and middle classes.

CONCLUSIONS

A number of conclusions may be drawn about the nature of women's work in nineteenth-century Europe. Firstly, there was a change in what constituted work for women. At the beginning of our period, across most of Europe, women's work was unspecialised and not as clearly demarcated as it was to become by 1900. Notions of appropriate work for women became sharper as the century progressed, which meant that although the range of jobs expanded, the opportunities for women were increasingly delineated and the work they did was rewarded accordingly. Secondly, a continuous feature of women's work was women's flexibility. Whilst men's identities became more fixed by occupational role and status, women moved in and out of a variety of jobs influenced by the availability of work, the demands of employers and women's own life stage.[135] This flexibility met women's own needs, but at the same time it was a feature of the female worker exploited by employers who could readily call upon a cheap labour force. Thirdly, the persistence of the association of women with the household and the fuzzy line between housework and paid work has been a continuous theme running through this chapter. It would be difficult to exaggerate the degree to which what we call 'domestic ideology' determined women's place in the labour market from the types of job women were admitted to, to the wages they earned, the status they were accorded and the recognition given to women's skills. Women's right to work, to earn an independent living wage, was something that had to be fought for by feminists and labour activists, so entrenched was the notion of the woman as secondary earner and primary care-giver.

On the eve of the First World War the range of occupations undertaken by women, especially in the industrialised states, was wider than in 1800. The emergence of the service sector around the turn of the century did open up new kinds of work deemed appropriate for women. But what good is choice if the rewards are no better than before? Women remained concentrated in low-paid, low-status employment with few prospects. Very few had made it into the better-paid and high-status jobs by 1914. The expansion of white-collar and professional work really took place after the war. If anything, what constituted fit work for women became more restricted, so that by 1900, ideas about gender roles and women's place meant that women were assumed to be temporary workers, with wages reflecting this second-class status.

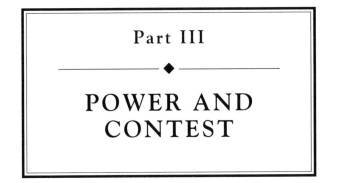

Part III

POWER AND CONTEST

Chapter 8

◆

POLITICS, NATION AND IDENTITY

On 5 October 1789, several thousand Parisian women marched on the royal palace at Versailles to demand bread and the king. This was an important episode in the French Revolution. But it had a significance of its own. To the English philosopher Edmund Burke, the women's march overturned the 'natural' gender order. In his influential pamphlet opposing the Revolution, he wrote disparagingly of 'the horrid yells, and shrilling screams, and frantic dances, and infamous contumelies, and all the unutterable abominations of the furies of hell, in the abused shape of the vilest of women.'[1] The man was not there. Yet, in his imagination he conjured a picture that equated women's engagement in politics with the undermining of civilisation. Women contributed significantly to the great national and political revolutions of the nineteenth century, but they gained little in return. From the French Revolution of 1789 to the Russian Revolution of 1917, Europe witnessed the age of revolutions, the rise of nationalism and the heyday of the empire-building nation-state. There is no period in the historian's calendar more crowded with momentous events. But, in all this drama, women have been customarily allotted only walk-on parts – as bread-rioters, mothers, writers and salon hostesses.

Yet, this was the time when concepts of citizenship, civic virtue and sovereignty entered their modern forms, and when these concepts were 'gendered in ways that signified sharp, deeply embedded cultural distinctions and differential valuations of human endeavour in both the public and private spheres.'[2] Revolutionaries and reformers who sought to overturn the ancien régime and pursue political democracy and national sovereignty, did not, in the main, discard existing notions of male and female gender roles. On the contrary, male-dominated movements for democratic change incorporated gender difference and inequality in their reconstruction of citizenship. It was increasingly difficult for politicised women to express themselves in the public domain because the very notion of the public woman was becoming incompatible with respectability. For separate spheres silenced the 'respectable' woman. If a woman expressed grievance in public, she was liable to be ridiculed by conservatives and radicals alike as 'unnatural'. For women to speak of politics, let alone to mount the barricades, was to turn the world upside-down. To claim rights as political citizens, women had to speak in a language and with a sentiment resonant with duty, responsibility, family and respectability.

Revolutions and nationalist uprisings litter the course of the nineteenth century and women played a prominent role in these events. Those who forsook their 'natural' sphere for the unnatural realm of politics were cast as symbols of the end of the old order and of civilisation. Women's political activity is always regarded as exceptional because their actions are taken to represent the violation of the natural order, and yet, simultaneously, women are also called upon both to represent the 'inviolate centre' of the nation and to be responsible for its maintenance.[3] At a crucial moment in the formation and consolidation of nation-states, women were identified as bearers of culture and custom and as essential components in the generation of the nation as mothers and educators. Women's involvement in national and political movements, then, is paradoxical. As has been pointed out in respect of Ireland but might be more generally applied: 'women came onto the public stage in large numbers through the great nationalist movements . . . However, their involvement in the revolutionary movements was not matched by their place in the newly created states.'[4]

For some women the overthrow of tyranny or of absolutism was enough in itself. Others saw democratic reform and the formation of the nation-state as an opportunity to stake a claim to equal citizenship. Not surprisingly, the rhetoric of universal rights and national sovereignty raised expectations amongst women; when these expectations were not fulfilled after the French Revolution, the 1848 revolutions, the unification of Italy and Germany and the creation of an Irish state, women realised they would have to continue the struggle themselves. For some, then, the national struggle became a feminist struggle.

CITIZENS WITHOUT CITIZENSHIP

For most of the long nineteenth century, European women did not possess citizenship rights. Despite waves of democratic revolution and political reform – in the 1780s and 1790s, in 1848 and again in the 1860s and 1870s – women remained excluded from the formal sites of political power and representation until the end of the century. The earliest in Europe to gain the franchise for national parliamentary elections were the women of Finland in 1906, the last were the women of France in 1944. Yet, the history of women's participation in movements for democratic change indicates that they were acting as de facto citizens long before they were granted equal citizenship.

In the pre-revolutionary world, citizenship – the possession of civic and political rights – was restricted to property-owning, tax-paying heads of households. Since women could not own property in their own right in most European countries, women could not be citizens. Citizenship was male, and it was restricted to a certain kind of man. But the French Revolution of 1789 changed the way citizenship was conceived virtually overnight when the representatives of the Third Estate ('commoners', in reality the male professions) announced themselves to be the representatives of popular sovereignty. Having constituted themselves as the National Assembly, they derived their authority not from God or the king, but from the people. In revolutionary France, though, citizenship was still restricted – to independent males over the age of 25 who could meet a minimum property requirement. Women were defined as 'passive citizens' and to all intents and purposes they were non-citizens. When this distinction between active and passive citizens was abolished in 1792 and all men over 21 were given the right to vote and to bear arms, women were explicitly excluded.

Yet, Thomas Paine's *Rights of Man* published in 1791 had offered a new conception of citizenship based upon the idea of inherent human rights. If all human beings were born equal and all possessed 'reason', then political rights should be extended to all. Paine's notion of citizenship was a radical departure from previous definitions. In theory, Paine's formulation, based on natural rights, meant citizenship and political participation could also apply to women and there were some who immediately contested the gendered definition of citizenship of the revolutionary government. The Marquis de Condorcet, in his 1790 *Essay on the Admission of Women to the Rights of Citizenship*, took Paine at his word, arguing that all human beings possessed natural rights, and thus the political and civil rights enshrined in the *Declaration* should be applied to all, with no distinction of sex, race or religion. Condorcet argued that men acquired rights on the grounds that 'men are beings with sensibility, capable of acquiring moral ideas, and of reasoning on these ideas'. 'So women, having these same qualities, have necessarily equal rights. Either no individual of the human race has genuine rights, or else all have the same; and he who votes against the right of another, whatever the religion, colour, or sex of that other, has henceforth abjured his own.'[5] Similarly, although perhaps with more theatricality, the actor and women's rights activist Olympe de Gouge (1748–93), prompted by the inherent unfairness and irrationality of the *Declaration*, produced her own *Declaration of the Rights of Women* in 1791 in which she baldly stated that the principle of equality before the law implied that women – 'the sex that is superior in beauty as well as in courage of maternal suffering' – should possess full rights of citizenship. 'Men, are you capable of being just?' she exclaimed. 'Who has given you sovereign authority to oppress my sex?' 'Woman is born free and remains equal in rights to man.'[6]

These seem, on the surface, to be feminist challenges to the revolutionary conception of citizenship. But these were abstract appeals to natural rights and had a limited impact on legislators and on the populace in France and elsewhere. However, there were other attempts to appeal to the revolutionaries and a wider audience, by women who developed notions of an inclusive citizenship based on women's distinctive contribution to society. Mary Wollstonecraft, who was in Paris during the Revolution, argued in her *Vindication of the Rights of Woman* (1792), that women's claim to citizenship rested upon their role as mothers and educators. Other female writers took up the baton to demand the extension of rights to women on the grounds that women were essential for the continuation of the revolution. 'Our revolution . . . requires from all citizens of the republic a tribute of work, wealth or knowledge', argued Madame Demoulin, president of a revolutionary woman's club. 'It is time for a revolution in the morals of women; it is time to re-establish them in their natural dignity. What virtue can one expect from a slave! . . . Wherever women are slaves, men are subject to despotism.'[7] What is important here is not just the de facto exclusion of women from definitions of citizenship, but the very existence of a language of popular sovereignty and political rights which provided a framework within which women writers and political reformers could contribute to the debate. As a result, women themselves increasingly engaged in what has been called proto-citizenship without the formal political rights of citizens. Over time, the idea of citizenship was gradually being redefined.[8]

Let us begin in revolutionary Paris. Few women demanded full citizenship rights during the Revolution but large numbers participated in the political process. They behaved as citizens.[9] The key events in which women played a central role are well known: the march of 6000 Parisian women to Versailles in October 1789 to protest to the king, Louis XVI, and the National Assembly about the shortage of bread, and their accompaniment of the king and his wife, Marie Antoinette, back to Paris; the involvement of armed women wearing liberty caps in processions in 1792 demanding a recognition of the legitimate power of the sovereign people which in turn induced a second revolution and the establishment of a republic; and in 1793 the conflict between militant women of the Society of Revolutionary Republican Women and the Jacobins, resulting in the silencing of women's political voice and the destruction of women's organisational infrastructure.[10] But women were also active in the political sphere as demonstrators and rioters, pamphleteers, journalists, speech-makers and as political activists on the streets, in the workplace, at home and in the revolutionary clubs. They addressed the National Assembly, incited their menfolk to defend the revolution, took up arms and regarded themselves as part of the sovereign people. According to Levy and Applewhite,

> [women] engaged in decisive collective demonstrations of force and acts of violence; they were the key actors in the co-optation of the armed force available to the authorities who supported the constitutional monarchy. These acts, in combination with women's discourse – everything from shouts and slogans denouncing tyrants, proclaiming liberty, and validating the *sans-culottes* to formal addresses before the Legislative Assembly demanding women's right to bear arms – contributed to the delegitimation of constitutional monarchy, a reformulation of rights and responsibilities of citizenship, and a redefinition of sovereignty as the will and power of the people.[11]

These are bold claims for *citoyennes* who had no political legitimacy to their name. Not all of the thousands of women involved were conscious of their political role. Few explicitly claimed rights for themselves as women and only a minority demonstrated a sustained engagement with political concepts. But it is equally true to say that active women were not motivated primarily by their relationship to subsistence as some have claimed. As housekeepers responsible for eking out a meagre living, women were at the front line at times of economic hardship, but their actions must be seen in the context of broader social relations encompassing tensions between producers and consumers, householders and the authorities. Remembering that plebeian women were likely to be breadwinners in a proto-industrial household economy and not housewives responsible merely for consumption, women who had no other means of access to political dialogue engaged in the food riot as 'proto-citizens'.[12] In revolutionary Paris, not all women put food before politics: 'Bread, but not at the price of liberty' was the call of women at Versailles in 1789.[13] Women's relationship to consumption was not confined to the domestic hearth; the availability and price of goods was a matter very much a part of the political sphere.

But what of those women who can be identified as militant or politically conscious? What did they do to allow us to see them as active citizens? Apart from engaging in food riots, women found spaces in which to demonstrate their political will: they attended executions, they observed the revolutionary tribunals, they spectated at political clubs, they gathered in groups on the streets, they wore revolutionary symbols such as the liberty cap, and they incited their menfolk to defend the revolution. Women, it was said, were 'firebrands'. All of this developed women's political consciousness and 'attests to the women's understanding of their entitlement to the rights and responsibilities of citizenship.'[14] French women found alternative ways of expressing their political will, sometimes independent of, and at other times alongside, their menfolk, but always in the knowledge of their place as members of the popular sovereignty. 'By identifying with the Rights of Man and the Constitution of 1793', writes James McMillan, 'and by publicly advertising their commitment to the Revolution by word, deed and even dress . . . women effectively made themselves into active citizens, whatever the law might say.'[15]

Women who engaged in political action during the Revolution contributed to the democratisation process, but their participation did not break through gendered restrictions on what political democracy meant.[16] In France, the bourgeois republican sphere of political debate and the formation of public opinion was structurally and ideologically masculine.[17] The banning of all women's political clubs and associations in 1793 by the Jacobin authorities, set in the context of the policy of terror pursued by the Committee of Public Safety, was a warning shot across the bows of women's claims to equal rights. It foreshadowed further attempts to restrict women to the private sphere, whilst women's political clubs were seen as a threat to republican order.

Perhaps we should not be surprised at this outcome to the gender issue in the French Revolution. Male revolutionary leaders had never indicated that they would make concessions despite women's political commitment. On the contrary, women's political participation was tolerated just as long as it was instrumental to the revolutionaries' cause. Women could be useful on the barricades as firebrands, but also because the militia were less likely to fire upon women. Underlying this toleration was a deeply held belief that a woman's place was not on the barricades or in the revolutionary clubs, it was in the home, in the private sphere. By 1793, the female revolutionary was considered potentially dangerous and out of control. According to the Jacobins, woman's nature predisposed her to emotional outbursts and incitements to disorder; as such women could not be allowed the responsibility of political duties – they were a liability. 'Since when is it permitted to give up one's sex?' expostulated the male Jacobin Chaumette, in reply to those who were angered by the suppression of women's political clubs:

> Since when is it decent to see women abandoning the pious cares of their households, the cribs of their children, to come to public places, to harangue in the galleries, at the bar of the senate? Is it to men that nature confided domestic cares? No, she has said to man: 'Be a man: hunting, farming, political concerns, toils of every kind, that is your appanage'. She has said to woman: 'Be a woman. The tender cares owing to infancy, the details of the household, the sweet anxiety of maternity, these are your labours: but your attentive cares deserve a reward. Fine! You will have it, and you will be the divinity of the domestic sanctuary; you will reign over everything that surrounds you by the invincible charm of the graces and of virtue.'[18]

Revolutionary leaders thus appropriated the language of Rousseau to redefine citizenship on the basis of separate spheres when they became fearful of women's subversion of traditional gender roles. Active citizenship remained a male preserve, not just in France but also in the Netherlands where women's participation in the Batavian Revolution of 1795 had mirrored some of the forms of French women's activity: the forming of clubs, the planting of liberty trees and the writing on women's issues in political journals. But women's actions were in the sphere of popular politics, and when the revolutionaries consolidated the system of government such expressions of popular sovereignty were no longer desirable, hence limiting the space within which women could act.[19] Male revolutionaries sought to solidify the division between the public and private spheres which women revolutionaries thought they had dissolved. In France the reversal of the truly revolutionary Constitution of 1791, which had defined marriage as a civil contract, which limited the powers of the male head of household over women and children, and which introduced divorce, was finally accomplished with the Civil (or Napoleonic) Code of 1804. Incorporating a combination of liberal theory and republican virtue, the code consigned women to a subordinate status which was to some degree worse than the situation under the pre-Revolutionary regime. 'Virtue applied to women', writes Bonnie Smith, 'whereas rights belonged to men.'[20]

In France and the Netherlands the definition of citizenship came to be embodied by the public or active man. In Britain, where democratisation was a more gradual and peaceful process, public discourse on citizenship was carried on in radical clubs and reform societies, rather than on the streets. This is significant for the form that the citizenship debate took in Britain. In contrast with France, where the Revolution had so disrupted social life that women had been able to mark out for themselves a political space, in Britain radical reformers more quickly discredited female crowd violence as undisciplined and unhelpful. The power of the people was not harnessed in the name of popular sovereignty. Instead, male reformers preferred formal, rational debate in smoke-filled rooms to the confusion of the crowd. As Anna Clark points out, the retreat 'into respectability and constitutional politics' shut out women from political debate and pushed them into the corresponding respectable sphere for women – the home.[21] In Britain as in France, women who advocated female citizenship in public were accused of overturning the gender order, of acting contrary to their nature, of 'wearing the breeches'. This was to continue to be a common refrain.

In the immediate aftermath of the revolution in France, the contest over popular sovereignty and citizenship abated, whilst in Britain radical politics was only just beginning to rethink notions of citizenship to encompass wider sections of the population. In the north of England and in Scotland, both the nature and extent of women's work and the importance of radical religion provided women with a platform from which to speak about the reform of parliament. In the industrial towns, women formed female friendly societies and reform societies such as the Blackburn Female Reform Society, founded in 1819 'to assist the male populations of this country to obtain their rights and liberties'.[22] In Glasgow, women participated in reform marches wearing liberty caps and carrying banners although they refrained from demanding women's political rights outright. Women's involvement in reform campaigning gradually forced a widening of the discourse on citizenship to encompass the language of the home, of domestic life, of children and of female virtue. The Queen Caroline Affair of 1820 seemed to encapsulate this shift away from the masculine citizen and towards a broader-based concept of political participation. Caroline of Brunswick was the estranged wife of the newly proclaimed King George IV. When she returned to claim her crown upon the King's ascendancy to the throne, her corrupt and profligate husband took steps to divorce her. Caroline became a popular sympathetic symbol for republicans, for advocates of political reform and for supporters of women's rights. The affair brought domestic issues – marriage, wife abuse, child custody – into the political realm, and provided an arena for respectable women to enter the political fray. Caroline was represented as a courageous and rational woman, allowing other women to see themselves as rather more than weak or passive wives and mothers. This was a womanhood that 'encompassed the virtues of courage as well as purity'.[23]

In France and in Britain, women's attempts to appropriate the language of the abstract rights-bearing citizen had few concrete results. The messages of writers like Condorcet, Olympe de Gouge and Mary Wollstonecraft were lost as formal political institutions were constructed which excluded women. But women's involvement in revolutionary and radical politics did prompt a change in the discursive landscape. Women certainly acted as if they were citizens, but it is clear that their definition of citizenship was not necessarily the same as that of the men they supported. In France this disjuncture resulted in the repression of politicised women. In Britain, radicals were more accommodating, understanding that the politics of reform had to encompass the politics of the hearth. By the 1830s and 1840s, male and female reformers and revolutionaries in both countries were using the ideology of separate spheres, domesticity and the notion of women as moral agents to bolster their demands for political change. The images of rioting women, of 'the furies at the guillotine', the 'revolutionary termagents', were replaced by the image of the virtuous, modest woman who was at once an example to her sex and no threat to the other. The noisy, theatrical Olympe de Gouge thus no longer stood as a role model, 'having forgotten the virtues fitting for her sex' – apparently she had not even the grace to go to the scaffold in an appropriate manner according to one commentator; instead she falsely claimed to be pregnant in order to postpone her execution. By contrast, Charlotte Corday, murderer of the demagogue Jean-Paul Marat, was represented in the post-revolutionary years as the ideal revolutionary woman – youthful, modest, innocent – who approached the guillotine serenely and heroically.[24] Corday embodied the acceptable virtues of woman; virtues which were to be used later to reshape the language of citizenship so that women could find a place in the political sphere.

By the 1830s and 1840s there were a few of both sexes who expounded the view that women were entitled to be politically active in their own right. In Britain, individuals drawn for the ranks of the Owenites, Unitarians, Chartists and anti-slavery campaigners put forward the argument for the extension of the franchise to include some or all women.[25] However, the majority of those who advocated universal manhood suffrage in Britain and in France were more inclined to emphasise women's indirect political influence within the family. In Britain, Chartism – a movement of working men and women for parliamentary reform established following the disappointing limitations of the 1832 Reform Act – encompassed large numbers of women, most of whom supported the aims of the People's Charter which demanded universal adult male suffrage amongst other political reforms. However, although the majority of Chartist women did not claim political rights for themselves, nor did they accept that politics was an exclusively masculine sphere. 'We have been told that the province of woman is her home, and that the field of politics should be left to men,' commented the Female Political Union of Newcastle-Upon-Tyne. 'This we deny . . . is it not true that the interests of our fathers, husbands and brothers, ought to be ours?'[26] The belief amongst most Chartists, that 'the proper sphere of woman is home', was not deemed antithetical to women's politicisation. According to the author of an 1841 Chartist circular, the notion that 'women should not meddle with politics' was unsustainable since politics meddled with them, thus 'ought not the woman who values her home – that human nest – to be sensitive of everything that threatens its welfare?'[27] For Chartists like Thomas Wheeler, questions of employment and wages, welfare and consumption all impinged upon a woman's sphere and necessitated her interest in politics and her duty to support her menfolk in their struggle, if not her right to the vote.

The Chartists' appeal to women contributed to the redefinition of the political. True, male Chartists and their counterparts in France, constructed a vision of the future which rested upon the practice of domesticity in working-class homes. 'Public functions belong to the man; private functions belong to woman', opined the journal *L'Atelier*, a mouthpiece of French skilled workers. 'If you remove woman from the function for which she is destined, lead her to the political theatre and give her the right to speak there, you will have all the inconveniences of the babbling of infants and the influence of sensuality.'[28] But, the ideology of separate spheres was helpful to political radicals. It demonstrated to the middle classes that political radicalism was not to be equated with drunken, violent masculinity. The advantage of this appeal to the domestic meant that women had to be included in the political struggle as active participants, and this caused most Chartists problems as their desire to protect women came into conflict with the realities of everyday life for the majority of women who required not protection but rights.

So, women were citizens without citizenship. As in France during the 1789 Revolution, British women, in the 1830s and 1840s, found a space and a language in Chartism and political radicalism more generally in which to articulate their political demands. And the excitement surrounding political reform – in 1832 and 1867 in Britain, in 1789, 1848 and 1871 in France – encouraged women of all social classes to engage in political dialogue, to think of themselves as political subjects. Margaret Mylne, an inhabitant of Edinburgh at the time of the 1832 Reform Bill, commented on how, hitherto, politics had not been considered a polite talking-point for ladies, but the prospect of a more democratic and public politics 'drove [Edinburgh's] inhabitants, both male and female, half frantic with delight'.[29] Although few women claimed the vote, in their public speaking, their collective protest and their petitioning and canvassing, working women developed an understanding of themselves as a conscious group just as their middle-class sisters were doing in relation to the contemporaneous anti-slavery movement. But whereas in Britain the political struggle continued, if in abated form, in the 1850s and 1860s, across the rest of continental Europe it intensified culminating in the revolutions of 1848 and the national struggles of 1860–71.

DISAPPOINTED REVOLUTIONARIES

'Be patient, women's rights are not important now. The most important problem is the success of the revolution.'[30] In the midst of the 1848 revolution in the German lands, Kathinka Zitz-Halein (b. 1801), writer, democratic activist and president of the Humania Association for Patriotic Interests in Mainz, wrote these words to Sophie von Hatzfeldt, aristocrat and liberal supporter of the revolution in Düsseldorf. By contrast, Louise Dittmar (1807–84), radical liberal and 'feminist' was more outspoken in her advocacy of women's rights and regarded the German revolution as an opportunity for women to claim equality. Both women were to be disappointed. Neither the gradualist optimism of Zitz-Halein or the more impatient stance of Dittmar was rewarded. The liberal revolution in the German lands failed; the liberals were defeated. And when the German lands were unified in 1871, it was under a constitutional monarchy which, although embodying some liberal and democratic principles, excluded women. Across revolutionary Europe it looked as if the French revolutionary experience was being repeated. Women's participation in revolutionary movements was accepted, even welcomed in some quarters, but this did not signify a shift in attitudes towards the place of women in the political and civil spheres. In France the declaration of universal suffrage in 1848 explicitly excluded women. Moreover, the repression of women's public political activity was even harsher than in 1793.

Not only were women's clubs closed, but in France and Prussia their freedom of association and of speech was restricted. By 1851 the victory of the forces of counter-revolution appeared to be complete.

Yet, despite the disappointing outcome of the 1848 revolutions for liberal women, this period of political upheaval is seen by many as the starting point of the women's movement in Europe. In Italy and France, Germany and the lands of the Habsburg Empire, the combination of women's political awakening and their participation in the public sphere culminated in a realisation that only women themselves could articulate changes in society since liberal, democratic men were unlikely to do it on their behalf. As Joan Scott has argued, 'feminists dramatized their conviction that their place was in the public sphere by entering it.'[31] Once more, women were acting like citizens without citizenship, but this time they were more politically adept and ideologically informed.

The tactics and the positions adopted by women revolutionaries in 1848 were determined by the specific political and economic circumstances that had fuelled the revolutions in each state. In Italy and in the Habsburg Empire, a combination of foreign domination and conservative rule meant that nationalist sentiment influenced political debate. In the German lands, liberals and radicals combined a commitment to democratic government with a desire for national unification. For women, the struggle for national self-determination and liberal reform presented opportunities for both engagement with political debate and participation in a patriotic resurgence. Domestic tasks harnessed to the national struggle, such as knitting clothing for the revolutionary soldiers, became as important as writing political pamphlets and demonstrating on the streets. During 1848, women could become 'patriotic mothers', political activists or feminist writers. The opportunities for consciousness-raising were great. For women activists like Louise Otto-Peters in Germany and Jeanne Deroin (1805–94) in France, who later described herself as an 'impulsive and reckless' pioneer, the establishment of a new, representative political system was a chance not to be missed.

The 1848 revolutions were precipitated by urban unrest in response to harvest failure and food shortages, but the popular energy released by poverty and unemployment was soon harnessed by those demanding political reform. In many respects, 1848 resembles a rerun of 1789, only on a wider European canvass. Women were prominent amongst the street protesters during the early days of political and economic unrest. In Stuttgart in 1847 the uprising started out as a protest against the city's bakers who, it was alleged, were profiting from speculating on the rising price of bread. What started out as an attack with sticks and stones on the bakers' houses, ended as a full-blown political uprising as barricades were erected in response to the authorities' intervention on behalf of those under siege. Echoing women's stridency in France some decades earlier, the women of Stuttgart are said to have urged on their menfolk and harangued the soldiers, calling them cowards and *Hosenscheißer*.[32] In Italy, hunger brought women on to the streets, but food protests soon turned into attacks on the representatives of the old regime and the foreign oppressors, with women unabashed about engaging in physical attacks on soldiers and joining the barricades. Women assumed they had a public, political role to play in the revolutionary uprisings. They attended political meetings, they formed their own political clubs and they began to reconceptualise their own position in the context of the new political conditions, establishing associations to promote women's education for instance and calling for women to be admitted to appropriate fields of employment. In France, a group of former Saint-Simonian women (followers of the social thinker Henri de Saint-Simon) formed the Club de l'Emancipation des Femmes (Club for the Emancipation of Women) in 1848 and published the first women's newspaper, *La Voix des Femmes* (*Women's Voice*). In Germany, women in sympathy with the liberal revolutionaries such as Louise Otto-Peters, Malwida von Meysenburg (1816–1903) and Mathilde Franziska Anneke, began to use the *Frauenzeitung* (*Women's Journal*) to discuss the relationship between the political events of the time and the position of women. After the defeat of the revolutionaries in Germany, women formed associations to support those in prison and in exile. These, like the Humania Association in Mainz, were not merely philanthropic welfare organisations. Whilst Kathinka Zitz-Halein, its founder, acknowledged this was an appropriate sphere for women's activity, at the same time she emphasised that, 'We must cease being just women and become entirely citizens and patriots.'[33]

What was different about women's participation in the 1848 revolutions in contrast to France in 1789 was the nature of their demands and the maturity of their thought following several decades of political activity. In Italy, women had been involved in secret societies and salons; in the German states, religious organisations attached to the dissenting churches had given lay women a voice, along with newspapers and journals which published articles on the woman question. In France, alongside a revolutionary tradition which to some extent legitimised or at least familiarised women's public political action, there now existed a language of feminism which had emerged from the utopian socialist movement of the 1830s, the Saint-Simonians. The women associated with this movement including Pauline Roland (1805–52),

Jeanne Deroin and Eugénie Niboyet (1800–83) and, to a lesser extent, Flora Tristan, published their own newspaper, *La Femme Libre* (*The Free Woman*), and went on to develop theories of women's emancipation which saw women's rights as part of a wider struggle for the rights of workers in general. Thus the woman question became part of the social question, instead of being bound to men's struggle for political rights. Women were not slow to realise that political upheaval and, specifically, the new republican and democratic impulses, offered them an opportunity to stake a claim to participation in political affairs. Whilst some, notably in France, demanded immediate enfranchisement, others adopted a more gradualist approach which built upon the identification of women as citizen-mothers.[34]

Supporters of women's rights adopted different strategies. The direct and impulsive tactics of Deroin contrasted with the more evolutionary approach of the novelist George Sand. Sand (a pseudonym for Aurore Dupin, Baroness Dudevant) was the most famous female writer of her day, a controversial figure known as much for her unconventional personal life (a separation from her husband, a series of affairs and a preference for male dress) as for her passionate and radical novels. As a republican and a socialist, she was a stalwart supporter of the Second French Republic, but the stability of the regime and its ability to deliver a new social order was, to Sand, the best guarantee of civil rights for women in the long term. 'Should women participate in politics some day?' she asked, answering, 'Yes, some day . . . but is this day near? No, I think not, and in order for women's condition to be transformed, society must be radically transformed.'[35] In her opinion the new republic's priorities were the condition of working women, jobs and wages, education and marriage rather than political rights. For Sand, political equality was the culmination of women's progress, not the starting point. Intervening in what she called 'male politics' was not the way ahead according to the French writer Marie d'Agoult (1805–76) who, like Sand, took a male pen name (Daniel Stern):

> Instead of . . . addressing simply and modestly the questions regarding the education of women of all classes, the careers that could be opened to women, the wages of working-class women, the authority of the mother in the family, the dignity of the wife . . . instead of progressing step by step with prudence as public opinion becomes more favourable, [feminists] acted very impoliticly; they noisily started political clubs that quickly became laughable.[36]

The year 1848, then, marks something of a turning point in the history of women's struggle for political and civil rights. More than fifty years after the first emancipatory claims made by Olympe de Gouge and Mary

Wollstonecraft, the woman question had been reconfigured. The majority of revolutionary women based their arguments for women's political rights on the belief in difference. In France in 1848, legislators made duty the prerequisite for citizenship and within this discourse women fulfilled their duty to the state as workers and as mothers. Maternity was considered by Jeanne Deroin and others as productive work, social labour. By moving away from the notion of the citizen as an abstract individual, legislators allowed the concept of the citizen to become socially differentiated to include proletarians and even women. In the words of Jeanne Deroin, 'It is especially the holy function of motherhood, said to be incompatible with the rights of the citizen, that imposes on the woman the duty to watch over the future of her children and gives her the right to intervene, not only in all acts of civil life, but also in all acts of political life.'[37] Deroin's position was that 'childbearers were rights-bearers'.[38] Hereafter, the idea that fulfilment of duties to the state entitled the individual to citizenship rights, informed the campaigns of those who argued for women's rights.

The broadening of the discourse on citizenship in revolutionary Europe, prompted those who addressed the woman question to consider more than just political representation. Women's emancipation encompassed wider issues, such as the right to work, the value of women's reproductive and productive labour, women's economic independence, the condition of marriage. For the privileged Malwide von Meysenbug, the German revolution made her realise 'the necessity for a woman to win economic independence through her own force'. Education was the key to providing an alternative to the 'almost inevitable marriage'.[39] In France the republican writer Marie d'Agoult proposed changes in women's legal status: 'I want competent mothers, assiduous and thrifty homemakers – in short, *strong women* capable of policing the small state that they rule.' Legal equality, in d'Agoult's view, would result in marriages based on equality and harmony and better education would form better wives, mothers and housekeepers and better selves. 'The time has come', she wrote, 'for all those authorities in the life of a woman (father, husband, confessor, lover) who pass from one to the other their despotic sceptre, to be replaced by the only legitimate authority – that of reason.'[40] Thus we see women beginning to argue for improvements in women's condition using the liberal republican discourse of duty. This involved a rejection of separate spheres in the Rousseauian mould, and later articulated by the French socialist Pierre-Joseph Proudhon (1809–65) who equated sexual difference with different public functions, and ludicrously compared a female legislator with a male wet nurse. Feminists like Jeanne Deroin,

Louise Otto-Peters, Louise Dittmar, and later, Hedwig Dohm (1831–1919), did not deny that men and women were different, but they argued that difference was a consequence of social conditioning and organisation. Separate spheres implied a hierarchy of the sexes and their social functions; the alternative was predicated upon equal value and women's functions and duties were pre-requisites for citizenship just as men's were. In a riposte to Proudhon's comment on male wet nurses, Hedwig Dohm rejected biological difference as the basis for discrimination in her typically forthright style: 'Because women bear children they are to have no political rights, and if I say, because men do *not* bear children they shall have no political rights, I see no reason why the one remark should not be considered as profound as the other.'[41]

From a conventional political perspective of left versus right, the 1848 revolutions failed – conservative governments reasserted themselves – and it would seem at first sight that the revolutions failed women too. In France and in Germany, women's political activities were suppressed and in several German states new laws of association prohibited women from forming or even joining political organisations. Yet, from the perspective of women's history it is clear that the revolutionary circumstances presented women with a space in which to articulate their conviction that they should be included in the new democracies. Even in the dark days of the reaction, feminists maintained their commitment. In 1851, Jeanne Deroin and Pauline Roland appealed to the women of America from their Paris prison, where they were detained following their arrest for contravening the law banning women's political association. Their tone is defiant, their message unchanged:

> Sisters of America! your socialist sisters of France are united with you in the vindication of the right of woman to civil and political equality. We have, moreover, the profound conviction that only by the power of association based on solidarity – by the union of the working classes of both sexes to organise labour – can be acquired, completely and pacifically, the civil and political equality of woman, and the social right for all.[42]

THE NATION AS WOMAN

'As a woman, I have no country. As a woman I want no country. As a woman my country is the whole world.'[43] The English feminist and writer Virginia Woolf (1882–1941) uttered her appeal to universal sisterhood in 1938, at a moment in European history when the fragile peace following the First World War was under threat as a consequence of the rise of fascism in Germany, Italy and Spain. For Woolf, the issue of the oppression of women was global. She equated the 'tyranny of the patriarchal state' with that of the fascist nation-state. From the perspective of the nineteenth century, Woolf's appeal to the universal woman stands in contrast to more than a century of entreaties to women to embrace their patriotic duty, and historians have recognised that women are central to the 'biological, social, cultural and symbolic reproduction of nations'.[44] In France and in Germany, the images of Marianne and Germania respectively have been used to symbolise the nation. In Prussia, Queen Luise, and in Norway, Queen Maud, became icons of the nation and of idealised femininity; in Spain, Isabel II (r. 1833–68) was represented as the good Catholic mother figure, the hope of the nation following several decades of political turmoil.[45] And, as mothers, women have been charged with the responsibility of reproducing the race; as educators they were responsible for shaping responsible citizens; as sexual and moral beings women's virtue has been placed at the centre of the defence of the nation against 'degeneracy'; and as bearers of 'traditional' culture women have been given a central role in defining and maintaining national cultural identity. During the nineteenth century, when liberal, emancipatory impulses across Europe found an outlet in campaigns for national unification and self-determination, this association of woman with the nation could be both empowering and constraining. Whilst, on the one hand, women were regarded as 'guardians of the traditional order' or, in Anne McLintock's words, 'as the atavistic and "authentic" body of national tradition (inert, backward-looking, and natural), at the same time women have been given (and have sometimes embraced) an active role in the reproduction and maintenance of the nation and national identity.'[46] Like it or not, women are implicated in the flowering of cultural nationalism, resistance to foreign domination and the emergence of nation-states. This means they are also implicated in struggles for national supremacy.

Feminist historians have recently begun to think about the ways in which nationalism is gendered and, for the most part, have concluded that despite incorporating women into the liberationist struggle, nationalist movements are sites of masculine domination. Writing about European nationalism Pierson argues that

> the formation of national identities was predicated on an imagined community of shared sameness (sameness of language, culture, blood, soil, economic interest), but the achievement of that unity entailed the violent suppression, exclusion or denial of difference and conflict . . . in their strategies to preserve dominance over women in general . . . lay the seeds of 'scientific' racism and a socio-biology based gender ideology.[47]

In the context of later nineteenth century nationalism in its encounter with colonialism, Pierson's analysis carries some weight (see in Chapter 9), but this description of the heavy hand of nationalism as a universal oppressor of women does not ring entirely true for earlier in the century. It fails to take account of women's own perception of their contribution to the national project. Women did share in the resurgence of national identity, although they often expressed their national consciousness using different symbols and rituals. Indeed, for most women, national identity began at home.

The Revolutionary and Napoleonic Wars (1793–1815) offered many women an opportunity to exhibit their patriotism. The events of the Revolution and especially the representation of women's involvement, had already produced a debate in Britain and in Prussia about the potential threat to the social and gender order if women there were allowed to emulate their French sisters. Prussian and British women were thus urged to act in ways that demonstrated the qualities and virtues associated with Germanness or Britishness. Modesty, timidity and dignity were feminine virtues to be cherished and counterposed to the Frenchwomen's unnatural desire for power and their immodesty on the streets.[48] The invasion, or threat of invasion, by the Napoleonic forces, however, gave women a new role: that of patriot. British women, hearing of the alleged brutality of the French soldiers, cheered the militia men sent to fight and jeered those who refused. They also collected subscriptions towards the raising and equipping of volunteer forces, they gathered clothing, they made banners and flags, and collected money for wounded soldiers. These women were fulfilling an acceptable patriotic role but, as Linda Colley argues, 'by extending their solicitude to the nation's armed forces . . . women demonstrated their domestic virtues possessed a public as well as a private relevance. Consciously or not, these female patriots were staking out a civic role for themselves.'[49] The experience of war in Britain (the American Revolutionary Wars and the Napoleonic Wars), in Prussia (the Napoleonic Wars and the Wars of German Unification) and in national uprisings such as the 1861 Polish Insurrection, helped to forge a patriotic identity that encompassed women's participation. In Spain, on the other hand, which was occupied by the French, the patriotic woman took part in the resistance. Women were active in riots and uprisings constituting the urban revolutions of 1808; some, such as those in Zaragoza, engaged in combat, but more commonly they provided back-up in the form of intelligence and supplies. Their role in the defeat of France contributed to the formation of women's national identity as Spaniards and as citizens.[50]

Elsewhere in Europe, the emergence of new nation-states was double-edged for women. On the one hand, nation-states did institutionalise gender difference via what has been termed civic nationalism, that is national law codes, constitutions and the formal structures of power. On the other hand, in the realm of 'cultural nationalism', women's contribution was often valued and women themselves began to use their leverage in this sphere to demand improvements and ultimately greater civic rights within the nation-state. The spirit of liberalism and democracy which had swept across much of continental Europe in the middle of the century was both a consequence of and a contributor to a heightened sense of national identity, notably in Italy, Germany and the member nations of the Habsburg and Ottoman Empires, all of which were keen to emulate the national unity and power of France. Here, the old regime had been replaced by the nation-state founded upon the principles of liberty, equality and fraternity; her male subjects had become citizens and she established a popular army to defend the nation against reactionary enemies. Czechs, Hungarians, Bulgarians, Poles and Greeks as well as Germans, Italians and Irish, nurtured their language, culture and customs in the service of the national idea. Women participated in these national movements as patriots, contributing to the cultural creation of national identity in their writing and music-making. At the same time, the ways in which nations were conceived of and imagined contributed to the definition of the feminine and to the ways in which feminists constructed their arguments for equal inclusion in the nation-state.

Nationalism took many forms in this period. In some places it was a liberal or revolutionary ideology with the aim of resisting domination, and in others it was a dominating ideology concerned with upholding the interests of those who were deemed to belong to the nation at the expense of others. It is clear that women might be implicated in a number of different ways. In Germany, for instance, women played a prominent role as writers in the liberal romantic nationalist movement of the early nineteenth century, but following the unification of Germany around economic and political imperatives in 1871, this spirit gave way to a more aggressive nationalism focused around right-wing associations like the Colonial Society and the Pan-German League wherein women played a rather different role. In German-speaking Austria, where bourgeois Germans were determined to defend their position against the rising power of Slavic groups from the 1880s, women were given the responsibility of maintaining German ethnic purity and of German culture. Schoolteachers in particular were at the forefront of these efforts to strengthen German cultural unity at the expense of other ethnic groups.[51]

Nineteenth-century nationalism was neither a coherent movement nor a coherent ideology, and perhaps it is precisely on account of its inchoate and shifting nature that women could find in the national idea a place to nurture their own aspirations. As writers, women contributed to national literature; as recognised carriers of language and custom they could be incorporated into the discourse of national liberation, especially in those states dominated by foreign rule. But women's role in promoting cultural nationalism was permitted within quite narrowly defined limits. The nation was conceived of as a family incorporating the gender roles already familiar to us, and in turn the family was regarded as the 'nursery of the nation'.[52] Thus, in nationalist discourse women were symbolised as mothers, housewives and educators, as bearers of national tradition, and as guardians of culture. Women were given significance then, as custodians of the past in a project spearheaded by men to create a new future.

THE NATIONAL FAMILY

In the search for appropriate and permissible patriotic roles for women, one of the first was that of woman as the heart of the national family. Wearing her national dress, singing traditional folk songs, speaking her 'mother tongue' and cooking traditional recipes, woman embodied the idea of the unity and authenticity of the nation. National costume, usually based upon some notion of traditional peasant dress, came to symbolise national identity in concrete form, but more importantly the dress worn by women, as in Iceland and Norway, identified women as members of the national project, but in their role as mothers and keepers of custom. In both of these Nordic countries, women's national costume, which was invented in the early nineteenth century in the context of the struggle for national self-determination, consisted of a heavily embroidered dress overlaid with a sparkling white apron. In Iceland, the full skirt, the corset and the apron, all served to symbolise the nation as mother.[53] Women who wore national costume, on feast days, weddings, Sundays and later as workers in the fledgling tourist industry, were walking examples of womanly virtues, exhibiting their skill at handicrafts and their pride as mothers, housewives and patriots. Similarly in the Netherlands, Brittany, Wales and the Austrian Tyrol, national dress for women emerged as a complement to movements of national or regional awakening. In contrast, nations such as England and France which were more comfortable with their national identity and which possessed large empires, felt less need to conspicuously display their women as national mascots.

The wearing of dress which harked back to an imagined rural culture, served to locate women within a gender order which identified them with the domestic or the private but which also linked the home with the nation. In Germany after unification the bourgeoisie increasingly anchored its national identity in virtues such as cleanliness, thrift and hygiene and it was housewives who expressed these virtues every day in running a home. Pride in maintaining the high standards of German domesticity – in contrast with French housewives' alleged obsession with fashion and Englishwomen's ignorance of the basic rules of cleanliness on account of their habit of employing servants – was one way in which women of the middle classes could identify with a nation that placed so much value on the home as the heartland of Germanness.[54] Elsewhere, women linked the home with the nation through the collection and performance of 'traditional' folk songs and dances. In mid-nineteenth-century Latvia, for example, an agrarian Baltic state belonging to the Russian Empire and dominated by Germans, women who collected Latvian folk songs and who then performed them at special festivals became important bearers of a national history. According to Irina Novikova, 'The politically instrumentalised ritual of the festival was central to Latvian peasant women's individual and collective participation in the emancipatory vision of the national family, their consciousness of womanhood and motherhood confirming unity with nationhood.'[55] Interestingly, the Norwegian national anthem, first performed in 1864, incorporated the relationship between the home and the nation and the gender relations therein. With the words, 'all that the fathers have fought for, the mothers have wept for', Norwegians affirmed their belief in the gendering of public and private spheres.[56]

But it was in their role as mother-educators, as preservers of the mother tongue as well as the national culture, that women were most valued by national movements. At a time when a common language and culture was used as the key legitimator of movements of national self-determination, influenced to some extent by the successful monolinguistic nation-states of Britain and France, the perpetuation of linguistic tradition and memory within the domestic and the national family was central to the national project. This was especially important for national liberation movements struggling against foreign domination. The language spoken at home – Czech, Croat, Polish – was in the trust of women who, in the role of mother-educators, were in the front line of the attempt to counter the imposition of a foreign culture and language in schools and public life. In Italy, Guiseppe Mazzini's version of republican nationalism placed the family at the centre of the struggle for national unity and freedom from French and Austrian oppression, and hence women's maternal role was privileged just as it had been in America where, during the Revolution and the War of Independence, women who possessed no independent political rights were nevertheless valued as patriots whose role as educators was crucial to the success of the republic.[57] Amongst Czechs, women's role in educating their children to become patriots in the Czech language was regarded as essential to combat Germanisation of the Czech lands within the Habsburg Empire.[58] In the Kingdom of Croatia (until 1919 part of the Habsburg Empire), women of the nobility and upper middle classes were active in the Illyrianist movement of the 1830s and 1840s, a cultural reaction to the fear of Germanisation and Magyarisation. In the following decades, prominent women Croat writers such as the author of fairytales, Ivana Brlić Mažuranić (1874–1938) worked hard to promote Croat language and history.[59] Similarly, in Poland following partition in the eighteenth century, nationalists understood that the forging of a Polish identity was dependent on the cultivation of the Polish language. In schools, boys and girls of the noble classes were taught in French following a French curriculum and using French or Latin texts. In the Russian part of Poland, following the intensive Russification of the elementary education system in the 1880s and 1890s, a group of women educationalists established the Secret Teaching Society with the aim of teaching the Polish language, history, religion and geography to working-class girls and boys in Warsaw and the smaller towns, meeting a demand from Polish working-class families – especially mothers – that their children should receive instruction in their mother tongue.[60] Following the 1905 Revolution in Russia and the consequent flowering of Polish national consciousness, the Polish School Promotion Society established numerous classes taught in Polish, many of which were popular with working women. Patriotic themes were also prominent in the works of Polish women writers of popular novels and books for children.[61] One woman who recognised the importance of women's role in reviving Polish culture was the writer Klementyna Tanska Hoffmanowa whose *Memoir of a Good Mother, Her Last Advice to her Daughter* was published in 1819. 'We have so few who are writing [in Polish]; I suspect that among women in particular those writing in Polish exceed those who read it,' she commented in her diary. 'Our sex seems to think it was born on the Seine instead of the Vistula. But since almost everyone follows the example of the beautiful sex, it is safe to assume that until women declare themselves in favour of the Polish language, it will not spread.'[62] Hoffmanowa combined in her writings a commitment to separate spheres with a zeal to promote Polish identity. *Memoir of a Good Mother* thus nicely articulated the acceptable role of the female nationalist or *Matka Polka* (patriot mother). The editor of the conservative Polish women's periodical *Bluszcz* (*Ivy*), Maria Ilnicka (1825–97) promoted the role of the Polish woman as homemaker in her belief that the Polish family was a bastion against foreign domination.[63]

Hoffmanowa was not an advocate of female emancipation through education, although she noted that her intention in writing books for schools in Polish was to 'familiarise [children] with everything Polish and to instil in growing girls the realisation that although God created them female they could still be useful.'[64] But there were women who expected more of the mother-educator role within the nation state. In contrast to *Bluszcz*, the Polish liberal women's journal *Świt* (*Dawn*), promoted women's education and work as the route to women's emancipation and the building of a healthy national community.[65] The German writer and women's rights activist Louise Otto-Peters made one of the earliest calls for women's education so that they might be of service to the German fatherland. Criticising the tendency for wealthy girls to be taught French, English and Latin as she had been, she argued that girls' schools should employ 'true German women who find their highest calling in educating German maidens.' Moreover, she advocated education to enable women to become independent so that 'they will be capable of doing their duty on behalf of the State in a proper manner.'[66] In the wake of the nationalist movement and the 1848 Revolution in the Habsburg lands, Czech women began to campaign for female education to produce the teachers of the new generation of Czech nationalists. In Bulgaria, following independence in 1878 and the establishment of the first national university in Sofia, women who had participated in the struggle for liberation began to demand improvements in girls education at all levels.[67] And in Greece at the end of the century, women were regarded as not only 'the potential producers of soldiers' but also 'the untarnishable source of the true national language'.[68] Their central role in the teaching of Greek was used by feminists to demand equal education and ultimately was used to bolster demands for political rights on the grounds that Greek national renewal was dependent on gender equality.

It is easy to be rather critical of those nineteenth-century nationalist or patriotic women who expressed their national identity through the wearing of national costume and taking their duty as mother-educators seriously, since they appear to have been merely fulfilling the stereotypical roles expected of them. Some took their engagement with national ideas further than tokenistic display and literary endeavour by adopting a more chauvinistic and xenophobic form of nationalism. However, at a time when the discourse on citizenship was being redefined as the reward for fulfilling one's duty to the state, most women looked for ways in which they could contribute which would correspond to male military service.

DISAPPOINTED PATRIOTS

It has often been observed that whilst women participated in movements of national liberation on a roughly equal basis, being incorporated as members of the oppressed race or culture, once the struggle was over and the nation-state established their sex once more became the crucial marker of their identity. The dichotomies of race, ethnicity or culture were replaced by the dichotomy of gender which was institutionalised in the civic sphere, notably in national constitutions and law codes but also in the day-to-day practice of politics. In the nineteenth century the new political sphere was created as a masculine arena. Equality on the streets or at the barricades was replaced by inequality in the parliaments, in the workplace and in the home. In France, Germany and elsewhere, citizenship rights rested upon the individual's duty to the state. For men this was interpreted as the ability to bear arms and defend the nation-state (and implicitly defenceless, weak women). Women's duty was reproduction, ostensibly carried out in the private realm. The consequence of gendered conceptions of citizenship was the subordination of women in the new structures of the state. Thus, the subordination of women was written into the Napoleonic Code after the French Revolution which placed women in legal servitude to men. The same was true in Italy and Germany where new legal codes were introduced in 1865 (Codice Pisanelli) and 1900 (Bügerliches Gesetzbuch), respectively, ostensibly to consolidate the new nation-states which had hitherto been governed by a complex patchwork of law codes, some of which had been distinctly female-friendly. In both newly unified states and in new nation-states such as Bulgaria and Ireland, women had expectations that their civic position would be improved, not so much as a reward for their support of the nationalist struggle but in recognition of the principles of self-determination and democracy. In Italy, Anna Maria Mozzoni (1837–1920) was one of the first women to claim rights for women in the new Italian state, both as natural justice and in the name of civilisation and national survival. She was to be disappointed.

In the new nation-states, those women who saw national unity as an opportunity to stake a claim for women's political and civic rights did not use the equal rights language of the French Revolution. Rather they perceived their position within and against the state as different from and yet as legitimate as men's. There were numerous opportunities and forums for women – feminists, patriots, conservatives and socialists – to demonstrate ways in which they saw themselves as full members of the nation. In Germany, those who belonged to women's organisations and patriotic activists found ways of participating in nation-building outside formal political structures. Following the tradition of one of the earliest women's organisations in Germany, the Frauenverein zum Wohle des Vaterlandes (Women's Association for the Good of the Fatherland) founded during the Napoleonic occupation of Prussia, and in a similar vein the Vaterländische Frauenverein (Patriotic Women's Association) established by Queen Augusta of Prussia in 1866 at the end of the Austro-Prussian war, German women enthusiastically joined what might be described as patriotic charitable and cultural nationalist associations. Patriotic Women's Societies had mushroomed during the early years of the new nation-state so that by 1891 there were almost 800 branches.[69] These groups initially envisaged their role as complementary to that of men. They embodied acceptable female domestic virtues and did not envisage their role as extending beyond the bounds of patriotic charity. But, from around 1900, patriotic women began to look further than charitable works influenced by an aggressive nationalist political discourse in German political life. Encapsulating this shift was the stated aim of one branch association in Posen in 1911: its mission was 'to encourage women here to become involved in civic problems, so that we might cast their gaze more broadly – beyond the narrow confines of personal calling and family responsibilities – out on to the whole picture, on to the responsibilities which we women too, as citizens, owe to our nation and country.'[70]

By 1900, the range of women's organisations, most of which were affiliated to the umbrella Bund Deutscher Frauenvereine (BDF), was huge, permitting thousands of women to participate in cultural nationalism. In an atmosphere of heightened nationalism during Germany's imperial and naval expansion, these organisations began to conceive of ways in which women might contribute to the nation comparable to male military service. The idea of a 'female service year' put forward by the BDF in 1912 seemed to fit the bill, envisaged as instruction in home economics for those with a basic education and a year spent in a female social-work school for those of higher social classes. On the outbreak of war in 1914 the female service year became National Women's Service. 'The invocation of the nation proved an ideal catchphrase for expanding women's sphere of influence without appearing to be too radical.'[71] Nationalism was thus used by some feminists as a means to an end. They hoped by demonstrating their allegiance to the nationalist agenda they would be granted greater access to the political sphere, although as Gertrud Bäumer (1873–1954), chair of the BDF, warned, it would be dangerous to pin too many hopes on what could be 'a Trojan horse of the worst kind'.[72]

German unification was not the outcome of a popular nationalist uprising but was accomplished through war and economic domination. Women's participation had been limited, restricted to their traditional role as supporters at home of the men carrying out their patriotic duty. In this context it was not surprising that women gained so little from the new nation-state. When feminists campaigned to influence the codification of the new civil code they were denied equality even in the realm assigned to them – the family.[73] In Ireland though, the national liberation struggle against the British had fully involved Irish Catholic women and yet even here women were marginalised from public political life in the new Irish Free State established in 1922. Women's militant activity within the 500 branches of the Ladies Land League, which adopted a policy of active resistance to landlord power in the 1880s, was first and foremost in the service of Irish nationalism, but its leader, Anna Parnell, saw the organisation as a means of developing female autonomy. Subsequent activity by nationalist-feminists in Inghinidhe na hEireann (Daughters of Erin), founded in 1900, focused upon the promotion of Gaelic culture and the education of the young, but its cultural slant belied its uncompromising stance as expressed in its paper *Women of Ireland*: 'Freedom for our Nation and the complete removal of all disabilities to our sex.'[74] The Daughters of Erin believed that women's strong and active presence within existing nationalist groups such as Sinn Fein would result in female enfranchisement in an independent Ireland. As their critics pointed out, they were impervious to the obvious retort that rural, Catholic Irish society in which women were subordinated in virtually all spheres, was unlikely to jettison its cultural baggage just as soon as Ireland was free. Women members of Cumann na mBan (Irishwomen's Council) engaged directly in the military action of the 1919–22 war of independence, servicing the Irish Republican Army Volunteers, carrying out intelligence work, gun-running and scouting. Indeed, it was precisely nationalist women's fervour, and their rejection of the cultural stereotype of the Irish woman, that allowed male nationalists to reassert their power in the political sphere 'in order to create an independent state based on masculine authority and feminine domesticity'.[75]

Moreover, in the 1920s, the consolidation of the Irish state and the construction of an Irish national identity based on supposed shared cultural traits, placed the family at the centre of national life so that 'the nation came to be symbolised more and more by Irish motherhood and the sanctity of the Irish Catholic family.'[76] There was little space within this discourse for feminist alternatives.

By the end of the century even those women who had been content in their role as cultural nationalists were beginning to feel frustrated. Governments remained intransigent in their unwillingness to include women in the nation-state as citizens, despite their encouragement of women to fulfil their role as mother-educators and as transmitters of culture. Women took on board the entreaties to rear and educate future citizens, they tried to be good patriots, they grasped at opportunities to serve the nation in comparable ways to their menfolk but, as Ida Blom makes clear, women's service to the nation was judged according to prevailing constructions of gender roles. 'To create life [and presumably to sustain and nurture it] resulted in a need for protection, whereas to be prepared to take life resulted in independence and rights in the nation.'[77] The continuation of this gendered notion of duty and rights was to continue to plague feminists throughout the First World War. However much campaigners for women's rights sought to demonstrate their loyalty and patriotism to the nation – for example in the German National Women's Service or in the emphasis placed by British suffragists on women's wartime work – they did not see that service to the nation would never guarantee them equal participation in the state. Women had far more freedom of movement within campaigning nationalist organisations when the idea of the nation was still in flux, than within nation-states concerned to wield power and consolidate political and legal structures. Thus in Germany, Italy, Ireland, and amongst the peoples of the Habsburg and Ottoman Empires, we find the optimism of women engaged in a liberation struggle which offered the possibility of fundamental political and cultural change, including changes in gender relations. Within the new nation-states women found themselves hemmed in by power structures which did not acknowledge any possible reordering of social relations in the name of social stability. Women remained defined by their familial role; the nation was conceived of as a family and hence, in Geoff Eley's words, 'the pioneers of nation-making found familial metaphors excellently suited for a modernising vocabulary of reform that simultaneously upheld the gender regimes of men.'[78]

CONCLUSIONS

At the outbreak of war in 1914 the active citizen in the nation-state was still male in all European countries, apart from Finland and Norway which granted female suffrage in national elections in 1906 and 1913, respectively. Yet women had been actively engaged in political life as de facto citizens and as patriots throughout the century. Everywhere, politically conscious women bypassed the limitations put upon their engagement in the public sphere, but nowhere were they granted political rights. Why was this? The most persuasive explanation concerns the continued adherence to ideas about difference amongst men and women. Men's claim to citizenship was founded upon their difference from women; their ability to bear arms was predicated upon their defence of the nation, including women and children. Women's duty was different, encompassing reproduction, nurture and the education of future citizens. Legislators could not or would not see past this ingrained conception of gender roles. So women who sought to engage with national politics on the same terms as men seemed to justify the portrayal of them as female incendiaries, militants and political radicals. Attitudes had changed little since Burke's description of female revolutionaries in 1789 as 'the vilest of women'. As Gay Gullickson has vividly described in the context of the 1871 Paris Commune, 'the *pétroleuse* [female incendiary] became the negative embodiment of the publicly active woman and cast a long shadow over debates about women's rights and proper roles.'[79] Women, like the *pétroleuses* and the Irish nationalists during the war of independence, were seen as having violated their nature.

In an attempt to speak to those who held power, women revolutionary and nationalist activists began to talk the language of difference too. They embraced their role, they found ways of carrying out their duty to the nation that were comparable with, but not the same as, men's activities, and they attempted to build on the work assigned to them to make gains in the fields of education, employment and civic and political rights. More comforting to men in power was the image of the domestic woman teaching folk songs to the child at her knee (and probably wearing her national costume).

It is clearly misguided to interpret women's activism in revolutionary and nationalist movements as always informed by feminism or a desire for women's emancipation. But the very fact of their engagement did eventually force some women to begin to campaign for women's rights *per se*, since it was recognised that no matter how hard women actively demonstrated their loyalties to the nation they would never be regarded as equal citizens of the state. Meanwhile, in the more mature, economically strong and self-confident nations of France, Britain and the Netherlands, women who had less need (or maybe less opportunity) to demonstrate their own patriotism began to participate in the imperial project. This not only cemented white women's national identity in states from which they were still politically excluded, but it also provided them with another space in which to articulate the language of duty and rights.

Chapter 9

◆

WOMEN'S MISSION TO EMPIRE

The scramble of European nations in the nineteenth century to create empires around the world, had a major impact upon women's experiences, their social movements, and upon women's identity. Historians of gender and imperialism have demonstrated that the colonial experience is a site where we can observe the interactions between cultures centring on gender, race and class. From the perspective of women's history, the imperial possessions of the dominant European powers present us with spaces where women found opportunities as members of a race considered to be superior, but where they also experienced constraints as members of a supposed inferior sex. The experiences of the British in the Caribbean, India and Africa, the French in North and West Africa and South Asia, the Dutch in the East Indies and the Germans in South-West Africa, provide a rich canvas for an examination of the ways in which ideas about gender and race at home were played out in a foreign setting. Women, as McLintock makes plain, were not 'the hapless onlookers of empire', marginal characters in a landscape populated by real men; rather they were 'ambiguously complicit both as colonisers and colonised, privileged and restricted, acted upon and acting.'[1] Whether as wives of colonial administrators, independent missionaries, campaigners for indigenous women's rights or as consumers of imperial products, white European women rarely questioned the imperial project and thus were complicit in it.

Overseas, white women grasped the new opportunities open to them as missionaries, wives of colonial administrators, and as teachers and nurses. Just as they had stepped out of the home and into the urban slums of European cities as philanthropists, the overseas colonies offered mainly middle-class women to step beyond the realms formerly deemed appropriate to their sex to engage with the race tensions thrown up by the imperial contest. The two domains were intimately linked by the middle-class 'cult of domesticity' and the 'invention of race'. At home, the so-called dangerous classes of the new urban slums were being defined as a different and even degenerate, heathen race. In the colonies, the cult of domesticity was used to demarcate racial boundaries and to impose order on the colonised peoples. Women were active in both of these domains. 'The Victorian middle-class home became a space for the display of imperial spectacle and the reinvention of race,' argues Ann McLintock, 'while the colonies . . . became a theatre for exhibiting the Victorian cult of domesticity and the reinvention of gender.'[2]

Middle-class philanthropic activity, at home and in the colonies, was informed by gendered notions of appropriate roles for men and women, and by ideas about racial hierarchy. Charles Darwin's *Origin of Species* (1859) introduced evolutionary theory and the idea of racial struggle. The writings of the French diplomat Arthur de Gobineau focused on race and civilisation. And the sociologist Herbert Spencer wrote on social Darwinism. Each provided intellectual and scientific justification for an engagement with the 'other', whether the poor of the urban slums or the native peoples of the colonies, and they shaped responses to what was discovered. Critiques of the intemperate, 'degenerate' working-class family at home rested upon the idealised bourgeois domestic model incorporating a breadwinner husband and a non-working wife. But they were also informed by racial ideas which placed the working classes at the bottom of the evolutionary ladder. At the same time, women's excursions into streets inhabited by 'degenerate' types – the working classes, immigrants, prostitutes and so on – helped them to formulate a model of society ordered by race. In 1839, one British report commented upon 'the outcast thousands of the people whom we have culpably suffered to grow up in the heart of our country, [who are] more profligate and more perverted than the Hindoos.'[3] Imperial adventure imported the language and the conceptions of race to domestic European society. Conversely, conceptions of the civilised and the uncivilised which had been formulated in the cities were exported to the imperial project. The disciplining of the 'dangerous' classes at home, whilst at the same time building imperial strength by means of encouraging reproduction amongst the desirable classes, provided a language and a system for regulating gender, race and class boundaries in the colonies.[4] The resulting effects for women in the colonies – both the colonisers and indigenous women – were ambiguous and often unsettling.

MISSIONS AND SLAVES

The first 'colonial encounter' between European white women and black women of the colonies was in the context of two parallel endeavours. The first was the foreign missionary movement, the second was the anti-slavery campaign. Britain had an especially large arena in which to advocate and practise missionary and reforming principles. The British West Indies and Imperial India surpassed in scale the interests of the other west European powers. France did have extensive overseas interests in the Caribbean, but the French Revolution declared the emancipation of slavery in the French colonies, and thereafter French anti-slavery activism was never such a popular cause as it was to become in Britain. In the 1790s the British churches established foreign missionary societies, whose aim was to spread Christianity and to improve the welfare of indigenous peoples. By the middle of the nineteenth century, foreign missions became the most important vehicle by which the British middle classes experienced colonised peoples, mostly indirectly through subscriptions, meetings addressed by foreign missionaries and missionary publications. From the 1810s 'Female Societies' were established as auxiliaries to the main evangelical missionary societies. At first, women were engaged as little more than back-room helpers. However, it was soon recognised that women's special qualities might have particular value where men had failed on account of their special difficulties in gaining access to women and children. As one male missionary said in 1890, only female missionaries could 'find their way into the zenanas [women's domestic apartments] and rescue the unhappy section of humanity they found there'.[5] Women's natural piety also was regarded as a positive advantage. Christianity, it was argued, had elevated women to their rightful respected place. It was thus Christian women's duty to liberate women in the colonies from the 'hard bondage of heathenism'.[6]

The anti-slavery movement was a product of a similar agenda and sensibility. The early female anti-slavery campaign is important since Britain's later colonial expansion was often justified on the grounds that slavery had been abolished in their Caribbean colonies, giving rise to the view of Britain as a civilising imperial power. Moreover, the female anti-slavery campaign of the first half of the century provides a rough template for later attempts to reform the status and position of women in the colonies. By the 1860s, what has been called imperial feminism maintained a concern for women's oppression overseas, though using a language which prioritised racial inequality.[7] These reforming endeavours had three things in common. Firstly, there was a belief in the superiority of western civilisation; secondly, there was an understanding that a civilised society did not tolerate 'barbaric' practices such as slavery which were antipathetic to the 'natural equality of man'; and thirdly there was a belief that female emancipation was the endpoint of western progress. According to the Scottish writer Marion Kirkland Reid in 1843:

> It is well known that, among savage nations, she is the menial slave of her lord; in barbarous states, she is alternately his slave and his plaything; while in lands like our own, which have made considerable progress in civilisation, though she has won herself many privileges, she is still very far from being allowed legal and social equality.[8]

In this context, black slavery in Britain's Caribbean colonies was an anachronism since it did not sit well with Britain's claim to be a civilised power. More profoundly, the advance of 'civilisation', the abolition of slavery and the emancipation of women became linked in the bourgeois liberal thought of much of Europe.

The first stage in the anti-slavery movement was the abolition of the British slave trade, which was achieved in 1806 with the notable participation of women. But slavery itself remained legal in the British Empire. So, a movement to free the slaves of the Empire developed strongly in the 1810s, 1820s and early 1830s, engaging mainly middle-class women in ladies' auxiliaries and pressure groups. Ladies were staking a claim to the spiritual and moral high ground in the rescue of women and children. They applied separate spheres ideology from women's issues at home to women's issues within slavery. So, there was a distinctively female anti-slavery agenda, comprising compassion for the female slave, for the indignities and suffering she was forced to endure, and a sympathy for black women who were prohibited from enjoying freely what any white woman regarded as her right – family life and motherhood. Women abolitionists adapted the language of the male anti-slavery movement to their own agenda. For example, they took one key image of kneeling male slaves, with the caption 'Am I not a man and a brother?', and redrew it as a kneeling woman with the caption 'Am I not a woman and a sister?'[9] Slavery was being attacked not just because it was evil in a general way, but because of its distinctive humiliation and cruelty to women. The anti-slavery movement brought into being the notion that any woman would identify with any other woman in a position of vulnerability. To be torn from a child, forced into manual labour, or flogged in public was unacceptable to any woman, be she slave or free, black or white. So strong was this thrust of the women's anti-slavery movement that it created tension with those who upheld the institution of slavery – not some 'half-wild, benighted native Race', but middle-class women's own white Christian fathers and brothers. Women were prioritising their own enlightened Christianity as a moral evangelism superior to any that men might construct.[10] The women's movement was putting forward in the early nineteenth century what was the first widely accepted argument in white society against racism: that it denied the right of every woman to be free to experience womanhood and thus God.

The anti-slavery argument put forward by women sat firmly within the bounds of appropriate gender roles. Slavery destroyed the family and the proper gender roles of men and women within that unit. Slavery separated wives from husbands and mothers from children. The proper place for a woman was in the home and not working on a sugar or cotton plantation. The strategy of female campaigners 'brought home' the slavery issue. Less able to campaign in the political public domain, they made slavery into a domestic issue and targeted the housewife and her consumption of slave-produced products. The campaign to persuade British housewives to abstain from slave-grown sugar was part of a broader attempt to pressure the government to equalise the import duties on slave-grown and free-grown sugar in order that slave-sugar no longer enjoyed an unfair price advantage. Parliamentary campaigning was taken on by male anti-slavery activists but it was women who took the abstention campaign into the home – using pamphlets and door-to-door canvassing – public activity which merged into political campaigning as the abolitionist women progressed to petitioning and public meetings.[11] The anti-slavery campaign was a crucial first step in the creation of a female collective consciousness in Britain, albeit limited to the middle classes. It provided these women with practice in public speaking and political skills which their husbands had gained by means of the 1832 Reform Act which enfranchised property-owning males. It also raised questions about the comparative position of enslaved and free women in society, prompting anti-slavery activists to challenge the power of men in the colonies and at home. Slavery and patriarchy were challenged simultaneously with the same argument from the same women.

British women, it has been argued, 'played an important part in harnessing evangelical ideas about feminine sensitivity to the fashionable cult of sentimentalism – a sentimentalism that romanticized Africans as pathetic creatures incapable of resisting slavery themselves and promoted English women as their helpmeets and saviours.'[12] Another arena in which British women sought to draw on their belief in the special ability of women to empathise with their poor sisters in the colonies was in British India and especially in respect of sati or widow-burning. Recalling the spectre of the enslaved woman subject to flogging at the hands of her white master, campaigners against sati used the horrific image of the widow burning on her husband's funeral pyre and the fate of her orphaned children to appeal to British women's sympathy and maternal concern to improve the position of Indian women.[13] But unlike the position of female slaves which was due to the white institution of slavery, the fate of Hindu women was seen as part and parcel of an uncivilised, idolatrous culture, contrasted with Christian domesticity which privileged the role of women in the family. In the case of sati, female campaigners saw their role as one of moral reform. Indeed, the very existence of the empire bestowed upon these women the power to rescue female victims of ignorance and superstition. The solution was female education. According to the Reverend William Ward, an early Baptist missionary in India, the existence of sati was directly linked to the ignorance of Indian women, and British imperialism was the means by which the 'long degraded state' of India might be reformed.[14] Under the guidance of the Christian missionary teacher Mary Anne Cooke, who established a number of girls' schools around Calcutta in the 1820s, the objective of the reformers was brought closer: the transformation of ignorant and powerless women into good Christian wives and mothers.

Widow-burning was outlawed in British India in 1830. Three years later slavery was abolished in the British West Indies with the passing of the 1833 Emancipation Act. It would be misleading to claim too much credit for women's campaigning on these issues since they were already in the public political domain. What is interesting here is the approach adopted by both anti-slavery campaigners and those who wished to see the end of sati, most of whom had never set foot in the British colonies, let alone spoken to an African or Indian woman. The moral maternalist position adopted by female campaigners drew upon an evangelical tradition which was starting to inform women's philanthropic activity at home amongst the urban poor. Middle-class campaigners and later missionaries, based their ideas 'both on notions of cultural superiority and on a sense of identification and empathy with non-Western women on the grounds of women's common experiences as wives, as mothers, and as widows.'[15] It was not deemed necessary to listen to the voices of these oppressed women; after all, shared experience and previous work in the domestic philanthropic arena were regarded as sufficient to inform their imperial reform agenda and, as Burton points out, black voices were inconvenient and unnecessary when there were white women prepared to speak on their behalf.[16] When the former British West Indies slave Mary Prince (1788–1833), attempted to tell her story in her own words in 1831 in her autobiographical *The History of Mary Prince, a West Indian Slave*, she was not initially believed, even by anti-slavery campaigners who required proof of the floggings she endured before they would welcome her into their fold. Moreover, it undoubtedly helped that Prince was described by her sponsor as respectable, industrious and holding 'sincere Christian beliefs', the archetypal victim so beloved of anti-slavery campaigners.[17]

By portraying the native woman as a helpless victim, the white woman was able to justify her engagement with the plight of black females. One of the consequences of this unequal engagement was the perpetuation of the belief that imperialism was a moral necessity, giving the state's attempts to intervene in hitherto private aspects of the indigenous culture greater legitimacy. Women campaigners were making imperialism a moral issue as they saw it. In India the attempt by the British state in 1891 to raise the age of consent for girls from 10 years to 12 years aroused intense opposition from the male population of the Indian community, yet the state's allusion to the sympathy for its position from British women suggested the anti-sati campaign a few decades earlier had had some effect.[18] Middle-class women's actions on behalf of female slaves and the 'culturally oppressed' were no doubt well-intentioned. Many were truly shocked at the condition of enslaved women and children and indigenous women who appeared to have no rights. Yet, these early reform missions were informed by white women's conception of the Christian family and of separate spheres. They exported their idea of home and women's elevated place within it, thereby privileging their own conception of the gender order over that of other cultures. And in doing so, of course, these early reformers helped to legitimate the colonial project.

DOMESTICATING THE EMPIRE

In the nineteenth-century imagination, the empire was an extension of home rather than a foreign place. By 1900, when the major west European powers had consolidated their imperial holdings, the human and commercial intercourse between home and the colonies was of such significance that the two formed a continuum. Men and women were travelling continually between home and the colonies. For Britain, at least, empire was 'not just a phenomenon "out there", but a fundamental part of domestic culture and national identity'.[19] Solutions to domestic problems could be found in the colonies – witness the emigration of thousands of homeless British children to the

British Dominions of Canada, South Africa and Australia – and the domestic market could benefit from the commercial advantages to be accrued from overseas possessions. From the perspective of European women, the empire was to become part of the domestic interior whilst, at the same time, those women who went to live and work in the colonies were exporting a set of gender roles and ideologies designed to remake colonial culture into the image of home, what McLintock describes as 'imperial commodity racism'.[20]

West Europeans, at least those living in the metropolitan and provincial cities, were familiar with empire. They collected money for foreign missions, they had relatives who had gone there, they campaigned on behalf of imperial subjects and they consumed its products. The presence of empire in the domestic imagination was ubiquitous by 1900. Imports of cotton provided work for thousands of working-class women who then aspired to purchase imperial consumer goods such as tea, coffee, sugar, rice and spices. The luxury goods found in so many European homes – soap, toothpaste, biscuits, tobacco – and more prosaic commodities such as bootlaces, toffees and bleach, were packaged and advertised emblazoned with imperial imagery bringing the empire right into people's front rooms. Soap in particular – that ultimate symbol of civilisation, purity, social hygiene and domesticity – was the imperial product par excellence. The production of soft body soaps from oils sourced in imperial plantations made possible the mass production of a previously luxury item. Moreover, the manufacture of cotton clothing based on the raw material picked on slave plantations, coupled with a rising standard of living amongst the middle classes, fuelled a demand for cleansing products. Advertisements for Pear's soap in Britain featured images which reinforced gender and racial boundaries, appealing to the housewife's desire for cleanliness at home as well as her pride in the imperial project.[21]

Outside the European home one did not have to go far to be confronted with further reminders of empire. There were endless colonial exhibitions to visit: the 1886 Colonial and Indian Exhibition in London, the 1908 Franco-British Exhibition, and numerous other smaller-scale 'entertainments' serving as reminders of the educational and commercial value of the colonial encounter. Across Europe, what would now be described as freak shows were dressed up as scientific exhibits, appealing to the middle classes' hunger for pseudo-intellectual satisfaction and to popular desire for amusement. European cities were regularly visited by circuses, menageries and travelling exhibits featuring representations of 'exotic' races and 'savages' and, by the end of the century, museums featured native peoples plucked from their homelands and served up as anthropological exhibits which applauded the imperial adventure and reinforced racial and sexual stereotypes. The exhibition of the black South African woman, Sara Bartman, in England early in the century served both to bring the colonies to England and, at the same time, to reaffirm the distance and difference between the races. Sara, most probably a slave, was not exhibited as a freak but as an exemplar of her race, featuring what were regarded as abnormally large buttocks, and as such she came to represent the 'sexualised savage'.[22] The men and women who went to see Sara Bartman not only came to view the Empire and all it stood for but, as Yvette Abrams argues, reinforced the sexualised and racial stereotypes applied to black and to white women. The domestic, asexual angel was posited against the sexual savage.

European women were familiar with the idea of empire from encountering its images, even unconsciously, in their everyday lives. This familiarity helped to inform women's responses when the empire impinged upon their personal lives. The wives of colonial administrators regarded indigenous women as other, whilst single women eagerly responded to appeals for female missionaries, and professional women regarded work in the imperial possessions as an opportunity to pursue a career barred to them at home. Crucially, the empire was not regarded as an alien land of discovery, but as something already understood and an opportunity for altruism or self-advancement.

Female emigration to the colonies was encouraged by officially sponsored organisations such as the Society for the Emigration of Women to the Colonies established in France in 1897, the Women's Division of the Colonial Society in Germany and the Church Missionary Societies in Britain, as well as the British Women's Emigration Society. This was the start of a significant influx of mainly single women into the colonies and dominions to work as domestic servants, teachers, nurses, nannies and governesses. These societies sponsored around 20,000 British women between 1884 and 1914, most of whom went to South Africa and Canada. In a domestic atmosphere extolling the virtues of marriage and motherhood, the position of the single woman was problematic. By sending these so-called surplus women overseas they could become part of the national regeneration and reform project. 'Without marriages, without families, there will be no future colonies', remarked one French supporter of the programme.[23] 'Although French women may have been invested with a modernizing mission abroad,' comments Janet Horne, 'this mission remained rooted in the general cult of domesticity and motherhood long established as a nineteenth century archetype.'[24] In Germany, the patriotic and nationalist Colonial Society assisted the emigration of young women to South-West Africa to become domestic servants there in order to help prevent racial mixing between German settlers and Africans and to help ensure the maintenance of German values and customs.[25] It was accepted by one English emigration association that women who initially went to work as servants or lady's helps in rural areas of South Africa almost inevitably made their way to Johannesburg because that was where all the men were. This was not a problem 'from the imperial point of view', since one of the aims of the society was to 'provide English wives for them'.[26] At the same time it was hoped these women might contribute to the stability of colonial society, not only by marrying but also by spreading civilised values especially to native mothers.

Women who decided to become missionaries were given a rather different objective. British missionaries were sent to India with the express purpose of gaining access to 'secluded' Asian women whose degraded and oppressed condition was attributed to their confinement in the zenana. These women were then taught how to become good wives and mothers, thereby establishing 'the critical bulwark against heathenism'.[27] Thus, the characteristics ascribed to the 'good woman' at home – moral, spiritual, self-sacrificing and modernising (in the sense that she imbibed the lessons of education, social hygiene and infant welfare) – were transported to the colonies and held up as a model to native women who needed to be instructed in good practices. Women's position in the household was the key to the reform of society at large.[28] Ironically, these female missionaries were preaching a nineteenth-century model of marriage and domesticity that they themselves had forgone for independent employment. As Jane Haggis remarks, 'the lady missionary negotiates her way out of the garden along a path of convention rather than a path of rebellion'.[29]

These apparently unconventional missionary women – at least in the case of Britain – were not rejecting nineteenth-century female stereotypes, but rather carrying out their duty to God. This combination of unconventionality and commitment to the Christian cause overseas can be found in the figure of Mary Slessor (1848–1915), Scotland's most famous female missionary. Slessor grew up in a working-class, Presbyterian weaving family in Dundee where she regularly attended mission visits in the slums of the city. Inspired by another Scot, David Livingstone, she was accepted for foreign mission service in Calabar (today, part of Nigeria), West Africa, and at the age of 28 she arrived at her mission station ready to minister education, health care, Christianity and civilised values to the tribes which practised polygamy, slave ownership, ritual human sacrifice and twin murder. Mary

Slessor's commitment to the people of the Calabar was genuine, and she regularly interceded on behalf of women and children to their undoubted benefit, on one occasion rescuing two young girls, who had been caught visiting young men in their compound, from a punishment of 100 lashes, while criticising the village elders for the 'system of polygamy which is a disgrace to you and a cruel injustice to these helpless women'.[30] Slessor did not conform to the image of stereotypical lady missionary, she who saw her role as 'raising the tone' of life in the colonies with her 'imperious maternity'.[31] Slessor was known for her hands-on approach, her endeavours to learn and understand the native culture and language, her shabby clothing, her relative tolerance for non-Christian beliefs, and her eventual role as an emissary during the setting up of the British Protectorate in southern Nigeria, paving the way for further British imperial expansion. In 1898 she became a British vice-consul (probably the first woman magistrate in the British Empire) and later a judge in a native court.[32] Evangelical ideology, which had such a profound impact on middle-class conceptions of gender roles in Britain, 'offered women an active role in the saving of Hindu and Muslim souls and in the promise of civilization and uplift that followed from conversion.'[33] Missionaries like Mary Slessor took up the challenge of that role, but on being confronted with the realities of life among indigenous peoples, many like her realised that practical work amongst women and children had a higher priority than conversion.

NO PLACE FOR A WHITE WOMAN

Until recently, empire has been portrayed as a male adventure populated by explorers, diplomats and civil servants. Women, in this narrative, were regarded as out of place in a tough, man's world. They have walk-on parts as dependent wives or as nurses and missionaries, and they are invariably portrayed as obsessed with class and race status, and with maintaining rituals more appropriate to upper-class European society. But, women in the Empire were implicitly charged with preserving 'civilisation', and in order to fulfil this role they reverted to what they knew best.[34] Dressing for dinner, organising lavish cocktail parties, refusing to wear the more practical local clothing, all helped these women to preserve a veneer of 'civilised behaviour' in a society in which they felt uncomfortable. Moreover, all European families in the colonies had servants, something not all would have been able to afford at home, which not only meant that European women lived leisured lives but also reduced the necessity to engage with indigenous society.

Shopping in the bazaars and markets – often regarded as risky places for a white woman – could be avoided, as could any real understanding of native people's actual circumstances. As a result, these European women who isolated themselves within their white compounds and social circles only intensified the racial divide. Of course, unlike the missionaries, most colonial wives and daughters had not chosen to live overseas, but had dutifully followed their menfolk. In the absence of a mission to rescue and reform, these women were more concerned to protect themselves in an inhospitable country which presented all kinds of hazards. Creating a European-style home life overseas was, for many women, the only way they knew to cope with cultural disorientation and fear of the unknown.

It is for these reasons, or so it was said, that the arrival of white women caused a deterioration in race relations. Colonial white women were regarded as an unsettling, disturbing presence, unwilling to accept the fragile consensus between colonisers and colonised which could include a tacit acceptance of sexual relations between white men and native women. White men felt obliged to protect their womenfolk from 'predatory' native men. 'Women were not always welcomed by men in the bush,' commented Monica Cardew in A.C.G. Hastings' novel *Gone Native*, set in Nigeria. 'Women meant afternoon calls, ties and collars, a sense of social duties often out of keeping with the life of work and play which men lead in the wilds.'[35] In E.M. Forster's *A Passage to India* (1924), the character of Miss Quested fills the role of the destabilising female force who arrives in India to marry a white man, only to involve herself in Indian life to the disapproval and unease of the British community. Her accusation of assault against an Indian doctor who had accompanied her on a visit to the Mirabar Caves, and her subsequent withdrawal of the accusation at the trial, is a story indicative of the way in which white women were seen as potentially destabilising if they did not adhere to the unspoken rules of colonial society which promulgated the avoidance of racial mixing in a social context.

But we should be wary of accepting these assertions that white women's presence led to a worsening of race relations. In colonial Nigeria, women themselves appear not to have expressed a sexual fear of African men, and indeed were happy to go about their business freely and in safety. Rather, the notion that white women needed to be protected was a symbolic device used by colonial men, both to maintain control over the subordinate racial group and over white women themselves. The white woman who developed anything more than mistress–servant relations with a native male was supposedly endangering the safety of all white women who were now the prey of licentious native men. She threatened the hierarchies of race, class and gender established by male colonisers. Women who transgressed these boundaries found themselves in an impossible position. The case of Alice Hume, the wife of the British government prosecutor in India, is a prime example of how precarious a white woman's place was in the Raj. By 1883 Alice had endured ten years of stifling boredom, and had an affair with Giridhari Mehter, a young Indian servant. The response of her husband James was first to beat his wife and then to act on the advice of British lawyers which was to prosecute the servant with a series of offences, including attempted rape, in order to deflect the scandal that would inevitably ensue if the truth was known. In court, Alice betrayed her young lover, backing her husband and the white colonial community in the knowledge that her reputation and that of her husband was at stake. Mehter was found guilty and transported, and the fragile equilibrium resting upon racial, gender and class inequalities, was maintained.[36]

From around the 1890s, though, the role of European women in the colonies was beginning to be regarded differently. Darwinism and eugenic ideas of race science were accelerating the separation of races in colonial administration. British colonial officers were under new pressure to refrain from sexual relations with native women, on the grounds that such behaviour could result in a destabilisation of authority relations between administrators and native peoples. Racial mixing, or miscegenation, came to be feared by colonial governments. This focused attention on white women. Instead of being viewed as destabilising to good imperial government, women emerged from the 1880s onwards, as agents of the policing of racial and sexual boundaries. Women at home in Europe were being exalted as mothers, and as the solution to the deteriorating condition of army recruits (notably in Britain during the Anglo-Boer War of 1899–1902). It was women's duty to produce good quality babies for European powers to sustain political, economic and imperial power. It was at this moment that single women arrived in European colonies in ever greater numbers – as teachers, nurses and missionaries. It was these single women, rather than colonial wives, who were expected to patrol the 'boundary' between white and black races. As single women they were most definitely required in imperial culture to be sexually unavailable to native men. The symbolic role of the single white woman was to signal racial difference and ultimately contribute to the strengthening of the white race by marrying white men.

Other colonial powers were as concerned as Britain about racial degeneration by the turn of the century, as more and more women became resident in the colonies. In the German colonies of South-West Africa, East Africa and Samoa, mixed marriage was banned in the context of German fears of a threat to colonial rule, a situation that was, incidentally, supported by some German colonialist women who argued that only they could carry out the female cultural tasks in the colonies, thus staking their own claim for inclusion in the colonial project.[37] In the Dutch East Indies the popularity of eugenic ideas and fears about the decline of the white population there resulted in miscegenation being discouraged, in complete contrast with the earlier decades of colonial rule when interracial unions were condoned as facilitators of good colonial relations.[38] Similarly, in French Cambodia, where male administrators had traditionally kept Cambodian concubines, warnings about interracial liaisons between French officials and native women were issued from the 1890s against background fears about declining births amongst the French middle classes. In French West Africa too, fears about racial degeneration and about the potential for rebellion amongst the *métis* – the mixed-blood offspring of interracial unions – served to justify a stricter set of rules regarding morals and hygiene.[39] The colonies were henceforth regarded as alternative sites for the regeneration of France itself. Increasing numbers of single women were encouraged to emigrate, thus providing a potential pool of French wives for colonial officials and a means of transplanting European domesticity on foreign soil.[40] The export of women to the colonies thus served to drive a wedge between the European and indigenous communities; it was woman's duty to 'create France' overseas both by establishing a European domesticity and by reproducing.[41] Thus white women's bodies in the colonies, even more so than at home, carried the symbolism of racial and cultural identity. In Cambodia, for example, the role of the white Frenchwoman was strictly circumscribed. White women were there to keep the boundaries, by wearing European clothing and protecting themselves from the sun, by upholding French traditions and cuisine and by not straying from the European compounds into 'native spaces' such as the market.[42] In Dutch Indonesia, household servants in effect protected European women from the contamination of the indigenous culture so that the European household could be maintained as an oasis of cleanliness and hygiene.[43] At the same time, the bodies of indigenous women bore a negative value; their sexuality was increasingly defined as dangerous and polluting, thus helping to sustain the image of the asexual white woman.[44]

By 1900, European women increasingly came to be accepted as a desirable addition to colonial society. Wives, missionaries and single professional women were encouraged to go as a means of relieving the surplus of women at home and contributing to the regeneration of the white race abroad. Indeed, from being regarded in 1850 as 'no place for a white woman', the colonies came to be seen by 1900 as spaces where white woman could contribute to the maintenance of a stable society based on unequal racial and class hierarchies.[45] Initially seen as a destructive force, European women were eventually crucial to the continuity of empire.

CIVILISING INITIATIVES

The European imperial project was regarded as a civilising as well as a commercial process. The role of European women in the attempt to bring civilisation to colonial subjects was paramount, especially since the position and status of indigenous women was so often used as the yardstick for a more general assessment of social, economic and cultural progress in any particular colony. 'It seems to me that in all the countries of the world the condition of woman allows us to evaluate the social state of a people, their mores and level of civilisation', wrote a French military officer in Algeria in the 1840s.[46] It almost goes without saying that the model against which the indigenous woman's degraded status was judged was the white, European middle-class, Christian woman. And against the background of imperial discourse which privileged western ideals of family and domesticity over other cultural traditions, western women almost unquestioningly saw their role as one of rescue and reform of the female victim of native superstitions and practices. As Midgley explains in respect of the British campaign against sati in India: 'English women's campaigning on behalf of Indian women was made possible by the context of British imperial rule in India, and shaped by missionary beliefs about non-Western peoples: their innate capacity, regardless of biologically-defined "race", to become civilized; and their present cultural inferiority.'[47] Western women's 'equality' was set against the perceived oppression of women in societies where patriarchy was seen to be underpinned by (non-Christian) religious belief and custom.

Throughout the European empire and at home, female evangelicals, missionaries, philanthropists and feminists addressed a whole range of practices and belief systems they regarded as signifying the 'uncivilised' character of indigenous society. Sati, genital mutilation, child marriage, polygamy, female seclusion and the veil, were just some of the cultural practices in Hindu and Islamic societies deemed to necessitate urgent intervention by white women in the name of 'women's mission to women' and in the name of the civilising process. It was only later in the nineteenth century, when organised feminism was beginning to make inroads in European society, that western women began to seize on the condition of women in the colonies as a political cause under the umbrella of 'universal sisterhood'. However, at the heart of all reform efforts was the belief that women would only enjoy an improved status through education. This was the key to greater autonomy for women and, as western women saw it, the means of their escape from superstition, seclusion and oppression by their own menfolk.

The anti-slavery and anti-sati campaigns of the 1820s and 1830s did act as an impetus in Britain for women to travel to the colonies to make a difference on the ground rather than from afar. They initially went as missionaries and teachers and then as doctors and nurses, making careers for themselves, but in their encounters with native women they helped to shape and perpetuate an image of them as victims of 'bad (Indian/Asian/African) patriarchy' whilst European women were spreading the values of 'good (white) patriarchy'.[48] Although the image of the single female missionary suggests a degree of resistance to the dominant values of domesticity and separate spheres which so constricted middle-class women's horizons in the late nineteenth century, in fact the educational work carried out by these women in the colonies all too frequently sought to reproduce precisely the model of the good Christian wife and mother left behind, if not entirely rejected, by the missionaries themselves. Female missionaries were expressly preferred to male in some spheres since only they could penetrate the seclusion of the Asian woman. Missionary women portrayed themselves as answering a calling to help their sisters who were portrayed as helpless victims of an abusive system. Once they gained access to the female world, though, women missionaries refrained from offering to Asian women the opportunities and freedoms they themselves had grasped, preferring to transform them into good Christian wives and mothers. As Jane Haggis argues in her study of British missionaries to India, missionary work was emancipatory but not necessarily for Indian women; it was the missionaries themselves who experienced freedom from domesticity whilst consigning their Indian sisters to just such a model.[49] Even women doctors, who perhaps most personified the image of the newly emancipated, educated single woman, often regarded healing the souls just as important as healing the bodies of the women they treated.[50]

Cultural imperialism was not restricted to the British. Albeit well-intentioned, white female missionaries carried with them western prejudices about indigenous cultures and the place of women. In practice this meant that colonial encounters between Europeans and native women were characterised by misunderstandings, and an arrogance on the part of the former in assuming that improvements for women, or 'emancipation', could only come about through an acceptance of western social models of social progress. In Dutch Sumatra (what is now Indonesia), for instance, there was a clear mismatch between missionaries' aims and native peoples' own understandings of the position of women. Missionary work centring on education, health and infant welfare, and sewing was shaped by the belief that women's work was incompatible with marriage and motherhood whilst, amongst the Karo peoples, women traditionally carried out much of the work in the fields, prompting missionaries to regard the women as virtual slaves to their menfolk. With the practice of polygyny (the practice of men taking more than one wife) and bride payments, it is easy to see why the Dutch Christian missionaries saw female education as the key to women's 'emancipation' in Sumatra. However, the outcome was not what the missionaries expected or wanted. Karo women certainly took advantage of the educational and training opportunities but not in order to emulate the European missionary wife, but rather for their own needs.[51]

The status of women was used as a measure of civilisation, with western Europe used as the model of civilised society. The 'Asiatic' or 'Oriental' woman was invariably represented as oppressed by a religion and culture described as heathen or despotic. The widow on the funeral pyre, the veiled and secluded Muslim, the child bride and even the working woman, were all legitimate targets for rescue and reform in order that colonial society might progress towards an image of the paternal/maternal colonial power. In these colonial encounters on foreign soil, women's mission to women was double-edged. European women did draw attention to some of the worst discriminatory practices experienced by women and they did bring about some improvements. 'Fewer women were burned or had their genitals cut', in Strobel's words.[52] Also, more women received an education and more mothers and babies survived. On the other hand it is hard to escape the conclusion that white women gained more for themselves than they achieved in the name of their Asian or African sisters. Their commitment to Christian conversion and to the western model of middle-class domesticity informed their limited concept of emancipation and amounted to an extension and even a legitimation of colonial authority. Thus, far from criticising the imperial project, female missionaries, reformers and even teachers and health workers contributed to its continuation.

UNIVERSAL SISTERHOOD

Philanthropic or missionary work, whether at home or overseas, had the potential to transcend the differences between women of different classes and races, allowing women to identify with one another. Just as middle-class women drew on their identity as wives and mothers to reach out to working-class women at home, likewise the domestic maternal image was used by anti-slavery campaigners and missionaries concerned at the plight of Asian and African women in the European colonies. But, these women did little to dismantle class and race hierarchies. Indeed, it was not until the interwar years that white women, at home and overseas, began to examine their own complicity in the capitalist and colonial agendas which determined the fate of oppressed working-class and native women. Instead, white middle-class women used the image of the degraded, downtrodden and oppressed woman – whether she was the victim of a drunken husband, a 'backward' culture or a superstitious belief system – in order to stake a claim to their own emancipation. Their cause was dependent on the predicament of their working-class and black sisters.

White women who sought citizenship of the imperial nation-state used the image of the native woman as victim in order to bolster their claims. Antoinette Burton has argued, in the context of the British Empire in India, that feminists represented 'Indian women as a colonial clientele dependent on the goodwill and uplift of their British sisters, whose support of India's women in turn . . . guaranteed the future stability of the British empire itself.'[53] Similarly, claims to municipal and parliamentary representation on the part of female philanthropists on the domestic scene, especially those engaged in temperance work, were fashioned on the backs of working-class women and children – the victims of the demon drink – thereby contributing to the uplift of the working class and the maintenance of the imperial nation-state by means of a healthier labour force and a more stable working-class domesticity. In the colonies and in the urban slums, domesticity 'rooted in European gender and class roles was transformed into domesticity as controlling a colonised people.'[54] Domesticity had provided white middle-class women with the strength and the justification to traverse the ideological divide between the private and public spheres. Having done so they now used their new-found position to argue for their own civil and political rights.

Feminist historians have come to see the development of modern western feminism in the nineteenth and twentieth centuries as shaped by imperial culture. The links between feminism and imperialism were probably strongest in Britain, but it is also clear that in France and in Germany elements of the women's movement drew upon imperial discourses, both in their campaigns to improve the condition of women in the colonies but also to bolster arguments for women's rights at home. The beginnings of imperial feminism, as the phenomenon has been described, anticipated the main period of European colonial expansion in the second half of the century. Its antecedents can be traced to early writers on the woman question who had a tendency to characterise non-western societies as backward compared with the civilized culture of Europe. Catherine Macaulay (1731–91), Mary Wollstonecraft, Marion Kirkland Reid and Harriet Taylor Mill (1807–56) set up an opposition between Oriental or 'barbaric' societies on the one hand, in which women were little better than slaves, and on the other hand, the West, which was further along the road from savagery to civilisation. Female subordination was regarded as an anachronism in a civilised society; female emancipation was the culmination of western progress.[55] It was this mode of thinking that informed the anti-slavery and anti-sati campaigns in Britain, but these had another consequence: they engaged women in public, political activity analogous to women's involvement in temperance work and campaigns around sexuality later in the century. The writing of pamphlets and the petitioning and campaigning activities undertaken in the name of the suffering slaves and widows, not only provided women with organisational experience and networking skills, although this was important in itself, but also established a recognised and legitimate sphere of public activity for middle-class women – 'an appropriate area of female concern'.[56] Furthermore, it put women's opinions firmly in the political sphere at a time when women did not have the vote. And finally, these campaigns put women in touch with, like-minded women, encouraging a collective identity as they assembled a distinctively female approach to the method of campaigning and to the issues at hand. According to Clare Midgley:

> anti-slavery propelled women into independently organising together for political ends, into developing an approach to campaigning which was rooted in concern for other women, into emphasising their own responsibility for the perpetuation of slavery and thus viewing themselves as responsible adults, and into challenging men on policy matters and thus acknowledging that their views were not always adequately represented by their male colleagues.[57]

One could make similar remarks about women's involvement in the temperance campaigns in western Europe. Women concerned about the corrosive effects of alcohol on the working-class family and, driven by a sense of Christian moral mission, knocked on doors, canvassed support for the cause, wrote pamphlets and organised petitions – a decidedly female style of activism which translated, for some, into a political (feminist) consciousness. The links between anti-slavery and the campaign for female suffrage are not direct but they are present. For liberal feminists active on the domestic and the colonial fronts, the campaign for female suffrage was predicated upon a belief in the superiority of white, middle-class culture. Political representation would allow women to bring their superior morality to bear on the political stage. Thus a shift in thinking took place in the decades between the 1820s and the 1860s. By the time of the emergence of what we now call first-wave feminism, the empire was so much a constitutive element of west European identity that what had been framed as the duty of the privileged European woman (that is supporting enslaved and oppressed women in the colonies against their imperial masters) had become a claim to white woman's emancipation within the imperial nation. This was especially the case in Britain where men had already achieved a shift in identity from colonisers to imperial citizens by means of the 1867 Reform Act which enfranchised all ratepaying adult male occupiers.[58] Middle-class male identity had been constructed around men's 'assertion of their superiority over the decadent aristocracy, over dependent females, over children, servants and employees, over the peoples of the Empire, whether in Ireland, India or Jamaica, over all *others* who were not English, male and middle class.'[59] White, middle-class women were to travel a similar road somewhat later, staking a claim for their citizenship upon their superiority over colonised women. Alongside European women's acceptance of imperialism was their inherent racism so that colonised women became the 'white woman's burden', conveniently ignoring the fact that in some cultures women possessed greater freedoms and rights than the European women who promised to liberate them.[60]

Interestingly, few late nineteenth century feminists had first-hand experience of the empire. One of those who did was the French radical feminist Hubertine Auclert (1848–1914). Having been an outspoken advocate of women's suffrage since the 1870s, Auclert left France in 1888 to live in Algeria for four years, until the death of her husband precipitated her return home. On observing the degraded position of the Arab woman in Algeria and in particular condemning practices such as child marriage – or what Auclert called child rape – polygyny and the absence of female education, she became an audacious campaigner for improvements in the rights of Algerian women. In her *Les femmes arabes en Algérie* published in 1900, Auclert showed that whilst she shared the assumption of moral superiority of her European sisters, at the same time she was sensitive to the fact that French rule had degraded rather than improved the position of Arab women. French male colonisers, she argued, had colluded with Arab males in the subjection of Arab women under Islamic laws. A combination of race and gender prejudice on the part of European colonisers had left women 'little victims of Muslim debauchery.'[61] Her solution was borrowed from her experiences at home in France: the position of Arab women would be improved only if they were granted French citizenship rights. At the same time though, Auclert held to the belief that the enfranchisement of French women would lead to concrete changes in French colonial policy. 'If women in France were accorded their share of power, they would not permit in a French territory the existence of a law allowing the rape of children.'[62] Thus, although Auclert, like her British sisters, had great faith in women's civilising influence, holding little respect for indigenous customs and culture, she was not blind to the degenerative impact of the colonising power and in this respect her stance resembles that of the early British anti-slavery activists rather than her contemporary 'imperial feminists'. The writer and feminist Olive Schreiner, who was born in South Africa to missionary parents and lived there until the age of 26, was more critical of British policy in Africa. A supporter of the enfranchisement of all Africans, she resigned from the British Women's Enfranchisement League when it limited its campaign to white women.[63] However, it was not until the interwar years that feminists and reformers in France and Britain began to formulate a new vision of colonial womanhood, one which ascribed the agency for change to the colonised women themselves.[64]

Clearly, universal sisterhood as it was advocated by European feminists before the First World War was not built upon foundations of racial equality. White women adopted moral superiority in their dealings with women in the colonies and assumed that the trajectory of progress experienced at home, encompassing a steady acquisition of legal and political rights, was also relevant to non-white women from quite different religious cultures and social traditions. Women's mission to women in the imperial context was carried out in a spirit of empathy and good intentions but it was to be challenged by the 'beneficiaries' who went on to develop their own routes to emancipation.

CONCLUSIONS

Female philanthropy on the domestic and imperial stages may be interpreted critically, whilst not losing sight of the positive outcomes of middle-class women's engagement with the class and race dynamics of industrial society. Many women acted out of a genuine concern at the predicament of the oppressed. Perhaps naively, they moved into the realms where they believed their common interests as women, wives and mothers would overcome class and race differences. In some respects, and with regard to particular issues, they were successful. The anti-slavery campaign was one example of an early critical engagement with imperial policies which was lacking in the moral superiority characteristic of later campaigns. Yet, it is difficult to escape the conclusion that middle-class women gained more for themselves through their efforts than they did for those they aimed to help. The organisational practice and confidence in public speaking and campaigning gained through their involvement in philanthropic work at home and overseas certainly stood the activists in good stead when they moved on – as many did – to campaign for women's civil and political rights. Furthermore, it was their engagement with women's issues in foreign contexts that made campaigners realise not only that they could use their moral superiority as a lever against governments, but also that they themselves needed to be involved in political decision-making if they were to have any significant impact on the policies they criticised. The road from domestic and imperial philanthropy to the suffrage campaign was twisted and beset with diversions, but it is plain to see the linkages in terms of personnel, strategies and discourses on gender, class and race. The race and class tensions and hierarchies that gave feminists a platform were reinforced as the same women attempted to dismantle the gender hierarchies they perceived as a constraint on their own freedom.

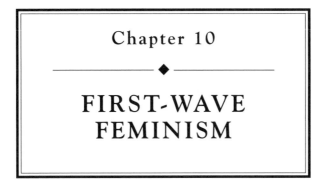

Chapter 10

◆

FIRST-WAVE
FEMINISM

In the 1850s and 1860s women began to organise on a significant scale to challenge their subordinate position in European society. By 1900 there were organised women's movements in most states, including all of western Europe, the Nordic countries, Russia and the Austro-Hungarian Empire. Between 1906 and 1919, women in most European countries obtained the vote. This women's struggle is known as first-wave feminism. It involved much more than merely suffrage. It initiated fundamental change to the way in which women perceived themselves and were perceived by men, and to the life destinies to which women aspired and were, by the beginning of the twentieth century, accomplishing. This was the beginning of women's liberation.

First-wave feminism was born out of 'the woman question' which had simmered since the third quarter of the eighteenth century. Ironically, it arose out of the attempts of Enlightenment writers like Rousseau to rationalise and legitimate women's subordinate status on the basis of their morally 'higher' domestic role. From this, women and men had been engaged in a dialogue about women's position. First set alight by the French Revolution, the European intellectual scene thereafter witnessed progressive waves of criticism about the condition of women. Anti-slavery campaigners, utopian socialists, evangelists, liberals, political radicals and revolutionaries – all with their different agendas – had addressed the status of women, often in the context of broader critiques of social and political organisation, and they proposed reforms to improve woman's position in the home, education, the workplace and the state. In this way, the Enlightenment had created 'the woman question' by questioning privilege and subjecting all social relations to analysis, and as a result made feminist thought and the feminist movement possible by inventing a language concerning the rights of the individual. By inventing separate spheres as an ideology, the Enlightenment also made possible feminism as an ideology.

Yet, organised feminism was not just an intellectual response to the contradictions of the Enlightenment. It was an active protest against the very real discrimination of women in diverse areas of public and private life: in marriage, in education, the workplace, the courts and in politics. In the new conditions created by industrial capitalism, women were being excluded from opportunities open to men on grounds of their sex. Men, and especially those of the new middle classes, were making advances at women's expense. The barring of women from admission to higher education and the professions, denying women economic independence, treating married women as possessions – it was such practical experiences of overt discrimination that stirred the first wave of feminists to action.

Feminism was, and is, a practice as well as a theory. It was about protesting and challenging injustice in the home, the workplace and on the streets, in words and in actions. The language used was important, but so were the things feminists did; their presence was as powerful as their words. Feminist campaigners adopted a variety of ideological and tactical positions, but for simplicity one might categorise their arguments as either individualist or relational.[1] The individualist approach was the more straightforward inheritor of the Enlightenment discourse on rights, adopting the position that theories of the rights-bearing individual should be applied equally to women as to men. Individualist feminism has sometimes been regarded as the more legitimate and certainly more radical form, perhaps because it equates more closely to the uncompromising equal rights position adopted by feminists of the second wave in the 1960s and 1970s. By contrast, relational feminism (sometimes called social or maternal feminism), emphasised woman's difference, relating women to men in terms of differences rather than similarities, echoing the Enlightenment construction of woman's natural moral superiority, and thus seemingly playing into the hands of those who advocated separate spheres. 'Equality in difference' was the leitmotif of relational feminism. Its advocates accepted, even valorised, women's different qualities and duties, and stressed the complementary roles of women and men, whilst arguing that female difference should not disbar women from access to the public sphere. Indeed, women's moral superiority was regarded as a positive reason for their inclusion. Though the 'equal but different' stance has been interpreted by some historians as conservative in its acceptance of women's special character, most nineteenth-century feminists recognised no contradiction between equal-rights arguments and an ethic of citizenship, valuing women's special qualities.

The words 'feminism' and 'feminist' did not enter widespread popular usage until the 1890s, some decades after women had begun to organise in a commitment to change. They were coined by Hubertine Auclert in France in the 1880s as terms to denote those who concerned themselves with the woman question. But *féminisme* and *féministe* soon became catch-all descriptions incorporating a diverse range of beliefs and standpoints, and yet flexible enough to include all those who agitated for the emancipation of women.[2] Despite the differences in theory and tactics between individualists and relationalists, radicals, moderates and socialists, working- and middle-class women, these women shared a number of characteristics which allow us to speak of feminism as a movement and an ideology which Karen Offen described thus:

> First, they consciously recognised the validity of female experience. Second, they analysed women's subordination as a problem of institutional injustice . . . Third, they sought the elimination of such injustices by attempting both to enhance the relative power of women and to curb the coercive power, whether political, economic or cultural, available to men.[3]

Although some scholars have traced elements of feminist consciousness and action to earlier in the century – notably in connection with the anti-slavery campaigns and radical politics in Britain and the utopian socialists in France – it is the phase of feminist activism that started in the 1850s that combined these three characteristics.[4]

THE ORIGINS OF FIRST-WAVE FEMINISM

What is so startling about the emergence of organised feminism in Europe is the fact that it developed in different countries at the same time and took on a similar character. The 1860s saw the growth of women's activism focused on gaining improvements in education and employment, and in the sphere of legal and moral reform, in the Protestant industrial states of Britain and Germany, in Catholic France and Italy, as well as in places where industrialisation had hardly gained a foothold such as rural Scandinavia and autocratic Orthodox Russia (as well as in North America and Australasia). In England in the 1850s, campaigns began to reform the married women's property laws and to gain women's admission to higher education. In Germany in 1865, Louise Otto-Peters formed the General German Women's Association to agitate for improvements to women's education and economic status. Russia in the 1860s saw the emergence of a plethora of feminist organisations such as a Women's Publishing Cooperative, a Society for Women's Work and, from 1868, a campaign for access to higher education.[5] In Scandinavia, the Danish Women's Association was founded in 1871, and by 1884 Finland, Norway and Sweden had their own organisations. In Italy the League for the Promotion of Women's Interests was born in 1881. The Belgian League for Women's Rights was established in 1892 followed by Austria's first women's association in 1893. In 1894 the Icelandic Women's Association was formed, followed in 1897 by the Central Association of Czech Women. By the end of the century there were women's organisations in almost every part of Europe, including Bohemia, Hungary, Serbia, Holland, Switzerland and Greece, and by 1918 Spain and Portugal had followed suit.

There were a number of common causes for the emergence of first-wave feminism across Europe.[6] These were intellectual, economic and political. Modern feminism had its origins in the intellectual debates spawned by the Enlightenment. As described in Chapter 1, the Enlightenment has traditionally been regarded by women's historians as a double-edged sword: on the one hand offering radical critiques of traditional institutions such as marriage and the church, but on the other asserting the polarisation of sex roles confining women to the private or domestic sphere. However, there is an alternative perspective which 'reclaims the Enlightenment for women'. It argues that the woman question was central to the Enlightenment project. Karen Offen sees this philosophical outpouring as a deep reservoir for discussion and debate, 'for asserting women's equality to men, for criticising male privilege and domination, for analysing historically the causes and constructions of women's subordination, and for devising eloquent arguments for the emancipation of women from male control.'[7] Feminist ideology had its origins in Enlightenment ideas generated by women intellectuals such as the French writers Madame de Graffigny who, in her 1747 *Lettres d'une Péruvienne* (*Letters from a Peruvian Woman*) criticised the institution of marriage; the Swedish poet Charlotta Nordenflycht who penned a delightful retort to Rousseau, the *salonnieres* of Paris, Berlin and Vienna, as well as the more famous Mary Wollstonecraft and Catherine Macaulay. Male and female writers in conversation with one another began to imagine a female role which encompassed authority and morality, justified by the appeal to natural rights and which separated the roles of the sexes.

The philosophical debates of the Enlightenment provide only the ideological foundations to the story of feminism since there were no attempts by women to organise a collective movement around a feminist platform at this time. Women who claimed their rights as citizens, who participated in food riots and who made public their plight as female workers, were shaping a female, but not an explicitly feminist, consciousness. This was not enough for a feminist movement. There was no collective movement of women's rights at the time of the French Revolution.

The real impetus to the formation of organised feminism came from political and economic change: it was when the 'crust of patriarchy' began to crack from 1848 onwards, as outspoken women and men seized the moment to stake a claim for female citizenship rights. As we saw in Chapter 8, during the 1848 liberal revolutions when demands were being made for democratisation and parliamentary politics, individual feminists appealed for complete equality in the realm of civil rights. Despite the post-revolutionary reassertion of conservatism in continental Europe, which included the suppression of women's activism, women did not keep quiet. In 1848 at Seneca Falls in the United States, a small group of mainly Quaker women had rewritten the American Declaration of Independence as a Declaration of Sentiments, which boldly stated all the injustices experienced by women and resolved to secure for women 'an equal participation with men in various trades, professions and commerce'.[8] Their outspoken sentiment encouraged European women to continue the struggle, and by the 1860s and 1870s political reform was back on the agenda providing feminists with renewed opportunities to engage in debate although in very different circumstances in each state. In Russia, the emancipation of the serfs in 1861 stimulated discussion about civil rights amongst the urban intelligentsia; in Poland, the land reform of 1864 and the ensuing economic crisis amongst the nobility forced women of this social class to address their changed circumstances, and to begin to consider education and means to an independent existence.[9] In Britain, the 1867 Reform Act extended the parliamentary franchise to wider sections of the male working classes; in Italy and in Germany, political unification in 1861 and 1871 respectively had been accompanied by universal manhood suffrage; and in France, the 1871 Paris Commune once more ignited discussion about women's public role. The modernisation and gradual democratisation of the political system across Europe created a space and a language for those advocating women's political rights and public participation in civic society. That is to say, women's rights became a political possibility. In Russia, as a response to defeat in the Crimean War and the more enlightened rule of Alexander II, ideas imported from France – including debates on the woman question – began to find fertile ground. The writings of M.L. Mikhailov (1829–65), who advocated equal education for both sexes and the admission of women to the professions as well as marriage reform, and of Nikolai Chernyshevsky (1828–89) whose 1863 novel *What is to be Done?* featured a heroine seeking economic independence and personal freedom, constitute a turning point in intellectual conceptions of woman's role in Russia, prompting those who wished to change women's circumstances rather than just debate them to initiate the road to reform.[10]

In 1867, the British Member of Parliament and liberal philosopher, John Stuart Mill (1806–73), inhabiting the most privileged space of all, the House of Commons, used his position to argue that the franchise should be extended to women by changing the word 'man' to 'person' throughout the Reform Bill. Two years later, Mill's treatise on *The Subjection of Women* was to emerge as a timely and truly influential explication of the case for women's rights, widely translated and debated. Mill's eloquent argument was important because it constituted a reformulation of Enlightenment writings on woman's nature. Personal liberty was Mill's watchword; without it, women could not fully develop their character, their true 'nature'. There was no need for society to force women to marry, to nurture children, to tend to the domestic, and indeed he argued that the very existence of such restrictions on women's opportunities was suggestive of a flawed logic. 'The anxiety of mankind to interfere in behalf of nature, for fear least nature should not succeed in effecting its purpose, is an altogether unnecessary solicitude.' Rather, the real reason for such constraints on women was men's fear, 'not lest women should be unwilling to marry, for I do not think that any one in reality has that apprehension; but lest they should insist that marriage should be on equal conditions.'[11] If the restraints on women were removed, Mill believed that women would go on to develop their full capacities in education, employment, indeed in all spheres in which they chose to act, and thereby contribute to the development of a civilised society. Mill did not believe that women and men were the same – rather that difference should not be a bar to equality in marriage or in politics; the family just as much as the political sphere was 'a school of the virtues of freedom'. After Mill, those who campaigned for women's rights could set aside their claims to education and civil rights based on 'woman's special nature'. The strength of Mill was his ability to unite arguments resting on 'equality in difference' with those based on personal liberty and freewill.

However, it was women's concrete experience of oppression at a moment of intense economic, social and political change in mid-nineteenth-century western Europe, that predisposed them to listen to and act upon the language of emancipation. For the majority of feminists, personal experience lay at the base of their engagement with the movement, either experience of oppression in their own lives or having observed it in others through their philanthropic work at home or in the empire. Middle-class women started to accept feminist arguments as a protest at domestic confinement. Men of their social class were benefiting from the expansion of the professions, the creation of wealth and freedom in the urban centres and from the influence they derived from political emancipation. But women were not. They, their daughters, sisters and friends saw gross inequalities in the opportunities and choices open – or closed – to women of their class. The 'surplus of women' problem is sometimes used to explain this concern amongst women themselves to find alternatives to the poorly paid and low-status occupations such as ladies' companion and governess for those who did not marry, and certainly the image of the destitute spinster was used by supporters of reform to garner support. But it was more likely the changes occurring within the middle classes which forced 'middle class women to redefine their role in society in terms of work and achievement'.[12]

It made sense, then, for these women to begin to look to legal reform and improvements in female access to education and the professions, especially since the limited number of acceptable and respectable female occupations – nurse, governess, teacher – were declining as those with higher educational attainment – men – sought to protect their occupational identity. Women began to demand a share of the new middle-class privileges: control over property, the right to divorce, the right to an academic education and an independent existence. Only later did they turn their attention to issues that sat less comfortably with their middle-class sensibilities, such as prostitution and the sex trade, and, of course, the right to vote. For socialist women it was the difficulties facing working women that concerned them: wages and conditions, the double burden of housework and paid work.

First-wave feminism was a multifaceted movement operating on many tracks, which diverged and came together at different moments and for different campaigns. It never spoke with a single voice and it is important to remember that organised feminism was, in effect, a host of small, local organisations run by women. In most countries there was never one feminist society or women's campaigning organisation. Germany is unusual in this respect, but even there the umbrella Federation of German Women's Associations incorporated hundreds of small, single-interest groups. In Hanover, for instance, the women's movement consisted of a large number of social, charitable and later professional clubs, including the Women's Association for the Care of the Indigent (founded in 1845), a Women's Educational Association (1877), a Magdalene Society (1877), Association of Christian Spinsters (1889), Association of Prussian Female Elementary School Teachers (1895) and an Association for the Reform of Female Clothing (1900).[13] This fragmented and devolved character of the movement is typical. In Edinburgh, women organised themselves into debating societies, anti-slavery organisations, educational associations and later, suffrage societies. In parts of eastern Europe, including Poland and the Ukraine, it has been argued that this form of 'community feminism' prevailed in contrast with a more ideological feminism of western Europe.[14] But in all European countries, women's self-help coexisted with feminist goals.

The women's movement was never unified but it is possible to identify particular strands of thought articulated by its spokeswomen, many of whom speak to us as representatives of this cultural and political phenomenon via women's journals such as the *Englishwoman's Review* (founded in the 1860s), *Neue Bahnen* (1865) in Germany, *La Donna* (1869) in Italy, and in France *Le Droit des Femmes* (1869). The movement was disjointed, the ideologies often conflicting, but feminism was international in its connections and scope. The women's movement was inchoate and fluid but it was sustained by self-perpetuating networks of mainly middle-class women who had cut their feminist teeth at the local political level dealing with temperance and sex reform, local politics, education, welfare provision and child care. Their philanthropic activity was a crucial training ground for their engagement with feminist objectives in practical and ideological terms. They gained experience in public speaking, political lobbying and popular campaigning methods. Feminists began to understand that their power to bring about change was hampered by their lack of political representation, but they could not wait for the vote. There were pressing issues to which the women's movement was drawn after 1860: legal reform, education and employment opportunities, and the feminist contribution to the socialist alternative.

LEGAL REFORM

'Marrying is like dying', wrote the English writer Margaret Oliphant (1827–97) in 1856, 'as distinct, as irrevocable, as complete.'[15] This is a pithy statement which still speaks across the generations to radical feminists. Oliphant's comparison between marriage and death was not intended as a criticism of the law; indeed, she believed that woman's legal subordination within marriage was necessary for the strength of society. However, Oliphant's turn of phrase encapsulates why women's legal and civil status was one of the first campaigning issues for European feminists and why it was central to both the perception of woman's role and the reality of her experience. Across Europe, women's legal position was lamentable.

In the 1850s, English middle-class women mounted a sustained critique of the law. In 1854, Barbara Leigh-Smith (1827–91), better known as Barbara Bodichon following her marriage, wrote a plain guide to the laws of England concerning women, spelling out the consequences of their subordinate legal status in respect of marriage, divorce, property and child custody.[16] Her plain speaking, her measured and unemotional statement of facts, drew support. In addition, the more sympathetic and stable political climate in England – in contrast with that in France and even Germany and Italy – helped Leigh Smith's Married Women's Property Committee, established to campaign for reform of the married women's property laws, to be taken seriously. In France, it was not until the establishment of the Third Republic in 1871 that appeals for legal reform could be seriously entertained. Decades of political turmoil in that country had retarded the women's rights movement. It was argued that any concessions to women would simply destabilise the hard-won republican regime. And even then, when the republican and feminist Léon Richer (1824–1911) published his critique of the Civil Code, *La Femme Libre* in 1877, in which he described the legal status of women as servitude, he still met with intransigence. In the newly unified states, moves to implement a unified law code offered women like Anna Maria Mozzoni (1837–c.1920) in Italy and Hedwig Dohm in Germany the opportunity to make a case for an improvement in women's civil rights. Both Mozzoni and Dohm adopted a similar stance: woman's role as wife and mother was no reason to preclude her from civil and political rights. Legal equality to these feminists was a fundamental right; in Mozzoni's words, '[natural] rights are not based on social roles', just as, in her view, they were not based on intelligence, or strength or good health or physical make-up.[17] Similarly, Hedwig Dohm rejected arguments based on difference and the protection of woman by man: 'Men, they say, represent women. When did women ever give men the right to represent them?'[18] The First International Congress on Women's Rights was held in Paris in 1878, organised by Léon Richer and Maria Deraismes (1828–94), and attracted both French and international participants.

The Congress restated the position of those who advocated women's equality on the basis of the Enlightenment concept of individual rights, resolving that 'in every country where woman is made inferior, the entire body of civil legislation be revised in the direction of the most absolute and complete equality between the two sexes.'[19] Amongst its demands were the legalisation of divorce, the recognition of equal inheritance rights, and the abolition of the morals police on the grounds that there was only one morality.

Feminist legal campaigns had mixed results. The lengthy list of reforms implemented across Europe points to some success. In England, women benefited from the Divorce Act of 1857 (despite its inbuilt inequality) and the Married Women's Property Acts of 1878 and 1882. In Italy the new Italian civil code of 1865 was more generous to married women in respect of property rights. In France, women were granted the right to open an independent bank account in 1881, in 1893 single and separated women were recognised as legal subjects in their own right, in 1884 divorce was reintroduced after its abolition in 1816, and in 1907 women were permitted to do what they wished with their own earnings. In Denmark and Sweden, single adult women were granted legal emancipation in 1857 and 1872, respectively. Conversely, in those states with no organised feminist movement such as Spain, there was no legal reform until after 1918. Moreover, we must recognise that reform did not mean equality. In terms of both civil rights and political rights, woman's alleged different nature continued to be used to justify their legal subordination.

'The stronger the emphasis on the difference between the sexes, the clearer the need for the specific representation of women', wrote the German feminist Hedwig Dohm in 1873.[20] Dohm and her intellectual 'sister', the young Frenchwoman Hubertine Auclert, argued that if women had political influence they would have the power to change the laws on issues that affected them such as child custody, marriage and divorce. For these radical feminists, political rights were the key to women's emancipation including legal emancipation. But there were others who disagreed with this position. In France, Auclert was pitted against those who believed the stability of the Republic to be more important than the rights of women. If women were given the vote, it was argued, they would invariably support the forces of conservatism on the grounds of their tendency to be influenced by the church, and thereby postpone further liberal reforms for many years to come. In Germany, Hedwig Dohm was on the margins of the organised women's movement which sought to raise the status of women within the family. The Allgemeine Deutsche Frauenvereine (General German Women's

Association) increasingly used difference as a bargaining counter with the government and especially in its campaign to influence the formation of the new civil code. However, feminists' efforts to ameliorate the status of women as wives and mothers were not necessarily at the expense of claims for more fundamental individual rights. Their claim to citizenship was based on the rights of mothers as moral guardians which permitted their entry into the public sphere. Thus maternalism (or relationalism) and individualism were not necessarily in conflict and were never entirely analytically distinct. In some respects, the disagreement between the two was more about strategy than about fundamental philosophy, as Jenny Hirsch (1829–1902), one of the first feminist activists in Germany, made clear in her criticism of Dohm's approach in 1873:

> she throws down the gauntlet to existing institutions, ridiculing the errors and prejudices that we also recognise, which have often hampered us and filled us with rage, but which cannot be abolished in this way [female enfranchisement]; rather it causes them to become ever more entrenched and obdurate. Meanwhile she looks down pityingly at those virtuous German women 'who are struggling to recommend a few improvements in girls' schools . . .' Indeed, honoured Madam, these are truly small and modest beginnings . . . Does it not also require some courage, some self-denial, and some endurance to work doggedly and quietly . . .'[21]

Dohm and Hirsch were working towards the same objectives but they approached their targets from different positions. Both strategies had their relative strengths. In respect of legal reforms in Germany, Dohm was proved right. The lawmakers ignored feminist campaigners whose arguments for civil equality had rested upon women's roles as wives and mothers. Although some concessions were made in the realm of women's ability to pursue a trade or a court case, these rights were severely restricted by those of the husband in respect of his wife's property and her person so that the legal status of the married woman was largely unaltered under the new German Civil Code of 1900.

By the end of the century it was recognised by most feminists across Europe that little further headway would be made in respect of legal reform without the vote. 'Is it to be wondered at that little respect is paid to women when the law classes them with regard to their political status . . . with criminals, paupers and lunatics?', exclaimed a supporter of the British suffrage campaign in 1913.[22] Feminists understood that the private sphere could not be distinguished from decisions made in the public sphere. In Britain and Germany in particular, issues such as domestic violence, incest, child custody and prostitution were all addressed head on by feminists who realised that the laws affecting women in these areas were man-made. Laws that permitted husbands to beat their wives, and that allowed men to exploit women for sexual gratification, were made by all-male parliaments. For many feminists, then, it was their engagement with legal issues that convinced them that female suffrage was the answer to the subordination of women.

EDUCATION AND EMPLOYMENT

Voices calling for the education of girls and women had been a constant feature of public debate on the woman question since the late eighteenth century, although the early advocates of women's education did not, on the whole, see access to knowledge as the route to female independence and freedom. Rather they believed that women's maternal responsibilities demanded that they receive help to raise their children according to the right moral principles. English evangelicals were firm in the belief that women should receive an education, but preferred to recommend training for marriage and motherhood rather than education for a woman's self-development. By contrast, Mary Wollstonecraft argued in the 1790s for education to enable women to 'become enlightened citizens' and to enable them 'to earn their own subsistence, independent of men'.[23] The pedagogues Pestalozzi and Froebel had advocated a mother-centred child-rearing as the key to a new relationship between the individual and the state. In the wake of these, a host of writers brought forth reasoned arguments in favour of improvements to female education. In justification they argued it was necessary to bolster the notion of the mother-educator, to encourage independent judgement in women and to broaden the opportunities and conditions of those who became governesses amongst whom there existed 'an abyss of ignorance so profound that qualifications had to be replaced by an attempt to provide the teachers with teaching'.[24] The views of the German feminist Louise Otto-Peters are instructive here. Education was necessary, she argued, in order that women 'be capable of doing their duty on behalf of the State in a proper manner', so that women might become economically independent and so that 'she will be able to develop her true womanliness more easily and much better when she is not endlessly led about on leading reins'.[25]

Otto-Peters' arguments are important as she attempted to straddle the gap between those who used the mother-educator argument and those who regarded education as a means of escape from female confinement. Of course Mary Wollstonecraft had already blazed this particular rhetorical trail, as we saw in Chapter 2, but by the second half of the century it was necessary for feminists to state the case again for education as a means to liberation and self-development, perhaps because the extended education received by most women in the intervening period was still what the French feminist writer Harlor (1871–1970) described as 'light nourishment'.[26] The insubstantial education served up to women, she argued, was mere decoration for marriage and a husband's amusement, hardly sufficient to encourage self-development and self-knowledge. 'Creatures of reason want to be the mistresses of their own destinies.'[27] Similarly, Madeleine Pelletier (1874–1939), French feminist, physician and ardent promoter of education for women, argued in 1914 that 'a woman must raise herself for her own sake and not for a man'.[28]

Some of the earliest women's rights organisations were established as pressure groups to improve female access to education such as the General German Women's Association (founded 1865), the Lette Society founded in Leipzig in 1865 and in Berlin in 1866, and the English National Union for Improving the Education of Women of all Classes established in 1871 whose predecessor had been the Langham Place group which had started meeting in London in the 1850s. In addition, women's groups across Europe were already actively engaged in providing, on a small scale, training for girls beyond elementary school level and more especially to equip them to be teachers. In Britain, Frances Buss and Dorothea Beale became educational trailblazers in their founding of girls' private schools, but also in the Netherlands, Germany, Spain and the Nordic countries activists founded training institutes and trade schools with the aim of equipping women for suitable employment. In Germany, activists played on bourgeois fears about the rising numbers of unmarried, uneducated middle-class women to argue for new education and employment opportunities. In Hanover, leaders of the women's movement did not seek to storm the bastions of male privilege but to create new professional openings for women which would be suited to women's special qualities: social work, nursing and teaching. In the first instance the aim was to train women to become secondary school teachers; 'women must be raised by women' was the cry of German women's educational associations. Helene Lange (1848–1930), educationalist and moderate feminist, typified this position which saw girls' education as a route not to equal rights but to prepare women for their roles in the community. However, once accepted as teachers in secondary schools, women went on to desire equal treatment and pay with their male colleagues, and to attain this they needed equal educational qualifications and a university education.[29]

The struggle to gain admission to higher education waged by feminists at the end of the century is somewhat curious in the light of the fact that some institutions had been willing to admit women to lectures as early as the end of the eighteenth century. In Italy, the University of Bologna could claim two female professors of distinction: Laura Bassi occupied the chair of physics and Maria Agnesi that of mathematics and moral philosophy. These were, of course, exceptional women. Yet elsewhere, notably in Glasgow and London, there were early attempts to open higher education institutions to a wider stratum of women from the middle classes. At Glasgow's Anderson's Institution, a new kind of university established in 1796 to offer vocational education for working men and women, courses of science-based lectures deliberately targeted women. Throughout the 1830s and 1840s the curriculum of the now Anderson's University expanded to include natural philosophy, geography, mathematics and logic, all of which attracted women students who were charged half of the normal course fee. In fact, men were admitted to these courses only if accompanied by a woman. In 1842, another establishment opened in the city, Queen's College for the Education of Ladies. Queen's opposed 'the unfortunate notion of the inferiority of the female mind' and countered its critics by suggesting that if they considered 'the natural capabilities of the female intellect . . . they surely would not discourage our attempts to communicate this hitherto forbidden knowledge, and to foster that intellectual strength, which may exercise an incalculable influence on generations yet unborn.'[30] In London, Queen's and Bedford Colleges (founded in 1848 and 1849, respectively) came to perform a similar purpose. In a tradition where tickets of university attendance were more important that getting degrees (for men as for women), these were not just tokenist developments. But as degrees became increasingly the male passport to the professions from the 1850s, women's exclusion from higher education increased. The middle decades of the century became a lean time for women with educational aspirations. Higher education increasingly became a bastion of male privilege, bolstered by the legitimating ideology of separate spheres, female difference, and the exclusively male 'paper chase' for degrees. The professionalisation of law and, especially, of medicine created exclusive clubs of those who had followed privileged routes to qualification, thus marginalising not only so-called quacks in the case of medicine but also untrained midwives.

Once institutions of higher learning had opened up to the men of the middle classes they began to find justifications for women's exclusion. In all seriousness, learned scholars argued that a woman's reproductive capacity would be damaged by too much intellectual stimulation; that her brain was too small to cope with the rigours of academic study; that the presence of women in lectures would be distracting to male students or that female students' modesty would be compromised by exposure to the realities of a medical education. Arguing fiercely against coeducation, the influential American physician Edward H. Clarke (1820–77) typified the stance of those who sought to provide scientific justification for unequal treatment of women. Clarke advocated 'an appropriate method of education for girls – one that should not ignore the mechanism of their bodies or blight any of their vital organs.' A girl who pursued the same education as a boy risked a future blighted by 'neuralgia, uterine disease, hysteria and other derangements of the nervous system'. She who studied 'every day of the month' risked diverting 'blood from the reproductive apparatus to the head'.[31] Every European state had its equivalent of Clarke. In Austria, for instance, anatomists, physicians, gynaecologists and psychiatrists lined up to explain why women were intellectually less able to benefit from higher education and why, in any case, such an education would be damaging to their health. 'It seems to us, that the seat of thought, the brain, is developed to a far lesser degree in women than in men', remarked one popular publication in 1872.[32] Another fear expressed by the English physician Henry Maudsley was that education would de-sex women and turn them into men or, at the very least, hermaphrodites. Excessive mental stimulation would create 'a monstrosity – something which having ceased to be a woman is yet not a man'.[33]

Feminists were easily able to counter these arguments and the criticisms of those who feared 'bluestockings' (originally referring to women who frequented the early salons but by the middle of the century becoming a derogatory term for a woman who aspired to an education). Elizabeth Garrett Anderson (1836–1917), the second woman licensed to practise medicine in Britain in 1866 and an ally of Emily Davies (1830–1921), founder of Girton College, Cambridge, argued that both women and men were taxed by intellectual demands at university but

from the purely physiological point of view, it is difficult to believe that study much more serious than that usually pursued by young men would do a girl's health as much harm as a life directly calculated to over-stimulate the emotional and sexual instincts . . . the stimulus found in novel-reading, in the theatre and ball-room, the excitement which attends a premature entry into society, the competition of vanity and frivolity, these involve far more real dangers to the health of young women than the competition for knowledge.[34]

Women's supposed predisposition to nervousness, to fainting and languidness was directly attributable, according to Garrett Anderson, not merely to the wearing of corsets and the lack of fresh air and exercise but also to the absence of intellectual stimulation and interest. Others used separate spheres arguments to justify the need for trained female doctors when some considered it unseemly for a woman to be examined by a male physician, especially for 'woman's diseases'.

By the later decades of the century, admission to higher education on an equal basis and the question of equal access to the university curriculum had become a pressing issue for feminists for a number of reasons. It was important for women seeking professional careers not merely to attend university courses, but also to graduate with degrees, and it was arguably the threat posed to men in the professional marketplace that really fuelled opposition to female access to higher education on equal terms. It was no coincidence that the propagation of fears surrounding the notion of the atrophy of women's reproductive systems if they received too much education surfaced just as women began to argue for access to the medical schools in the 1860s and 1870s.

The first challenge was preparing girls to reach the standard required for university entry in order to counter the argument that girls were not qualified. In Germany, prospective students needed to pass the school-leaving examination, the *Abitur*, but since it was possible to sit the examination only if a girl had attended a *Gymnasium* (grammar school), and because there were no girls' *Gymnasien*, women activists had to set about establishing girls' schools. In France a similar situation prevailed in respect of the *baccalauréat* so that girls who aspired to university were forced to study privately, the route taken by Madeleine Pelletier who gained admission to medical school, one of the first women to do so. Yet, here in France, those who argued in favour of a secondary education for girls had some powerful supporters, notably those who wished to reduce the power of the church over educational provision. In 1870 the lawyer Jules Ferry, later minister of education and prime minister, presented a cogent argument in favour of equal education as in his view, 'in their present state of education, it is impossible to say that [women] could not be something else if they were raised differently.' Ferry, influenced by John Stuart Mill, believed that there was nothing natural about the subjection of women; that given equal opportunities women would find their own level.[35] In 1880, then, girls' secondary schools and colleges were established across France by the Sée Law and a year later the Ferry Law introduced free and secular education for girls and boys, but more as an attempt to counter clerical influence and bolster the Republic than in response to feminist campaigning. The deputy, Camille Sée, had explicitly denied suggestions that his law would facilitate women's access to university, believing that the professions were the preserve of men. His aim was 'not to tear [women] away from their natural vocation but to render them more capable of fulfilling their obligations as wives, mothers, and mistresses of households.'[36] Some thirty years later, though, even the Sée Law was being criticised on the grounds that girls' secondary education was not geared to preparing students for their future destination. In her radical reform agenda for secondary education in 1911, the French teacher and writer Jeanne Crouzet-Benaben (c.1870–1961) argued that, 'women's secondary education as currently organised is too feminine, and not secondary enough. It is not secondary enough because it does not lead anywhere and because it is not scientific enough, not prolonged enough . . . Women nowadays have need of diplomas that will open up careers.'[37] Nevertheless, the French state's commitment to public schooling for girls had a positive spin-off: thousands of new female teachers were required to teach the girls and two new teacher training institutions in Paris were founded for the purpose.[38] It was to be some time, though, before girls were educated to the same level as boys, and by 1914 just over 2500 girls had gained entry to the French higher education system by passing the *baccalauréat* exam.[39]

By the 1860s, then, the focus of the education debate had shifted; there was little opposition to the view that women should receive some kind of education; it was the content and level of that education which were still at stake. Feminists were united in their aim to gain women access to a university education but they were divided over how to achieve it. Their ideological and strategic differences mirrored tensions within feminism as a whole, between those who pursued an equal rights agenda, making no allowance for any special or different qualities of women, and those who sought recognition of women's difference. Women were gaining a university education across Europe from the 1860s, though the numbers were tiny. The founding of women-only colleges such as Girton (1869) and Newnham (1874) at Cambridge signified a major step forward (separate colleges were required on account of residence requirements of the traditional universities) but also the two founders, Emily Davies and Anne Jemima Clough (1820–92), symbolised the different approaches adopted by those who sought to create a space for women within a male-dominated university system. Clough was the more pragmatic of the two. She argued for a continuation of the special lectures system as a stepping-stone to women's full and equal integration into the university system once women had caught up with their male peers. Davies, on the other hand, was not willing to make allowances for women's special needs; indeed she argued that the route advocated by Clough would only allow detractors to call attention to women's inability to perform at the same level as men. 'Is the improved education . . . to be identical with that of men, or is it to be as good as possible, but in some way or other specifically feminine?' asked Davies in 1868.[40] Women students should take the same university entrance examinations as men, according to Davies, despite the fact that girls' secondary education was of an inferior quality, for no one would respect the achievements of a woman judged according to a separate standard. 'No one is the better for being told, on mere arbitrary authority, that he belongs to a weak and incapable class', she wrote; but 'this, whatever may be the intention, is said in effect by the offer of any test of exclusively female character.' Women had to show they were as capable as men in order to prove they were worthy of emancipation. Many did just this. One of them Grace Chisholm Young (1868–1944), entered Girton in 1889 and gained the highest marks in the final examinations in mathematics, although of course she did not graduate with a degree, only an informal certificate. She was one of the first three women to be admitted to doctoral study at Göttingen University in Germany, and thereafter, although she never held an academic position she continued to practise and publish in pure mathematics.[41]

Equal access to medical school was a key campaigning issue for feminists of both equal rights and relationalist persuasions. Whether one believed that women should train to be doctors in order to meet the demand for female physicians from woman patients on account of concerns about modesty and propriety, or whether one regarded the ability to earn a medical degree a basic right, the obstacles were the same. The all-male medical profession was united in opposition to women entering the profession and they erected a number of spurious arguments to protect their privileged domain. Elizabeth Garrett Anderson had to study privately to gain her medical qualification – the first licensed woman doctor in Britain, Elizabeth Blackwell (1821–1910) had trained in the United States – but such was the outrage amongst doctors that no more women were permitted to enter the profession by this means. Until 1877, when London University became the first British university to award medical degrees to women, all that was on offer were special courses for female students leading to a Licentiate qualification, less prestigious than a university degree. In Scotland, Sophia Jex Blake (1840–1912) had struggled to receive a medical training in Edinburgh, enrolling in separate ladies' classes in 1869, but after three years of study she and three others were refused permission to take the examinations. Queen Margaret College in Glasgow was the first Scottish institution to prepare female students for medical degrees in 1890, although Edinburgh had permitted women to study for the Licentiate since 1886. However, separate teaching was still the norm in many medical courses and this disadvantaged female students when they came to sit their examinations. Meanwhile, Zurich University admitted women to its medical faculty for a short time between 1863 and 1874, attracting more than 100 Russian women who sought both a scientific education and an immersion in radical ideas. In the 1870s, women who wished to receive a medical training were accepted in Ireland from 1877, London (1878) and Edinburgh (1886). France had permitted women to study in its medical faculties since the 1860s, but in Germany and Austria physicians remained intransigent in their opposition to female medical students until the end of the century. It was perhaps only the advent of war in 1914 and the need for female doctors, especially at the front, that convinced many that women's competence equalled that of male physicians. Outside medical training, Oxford and Cambridge admitted female students in the 1870s but they did not award them degrees. In Warsaw the so-called Flying University established in 1884 offered lectures in secret to noblewomen, and by the 1900s the University for All in Warsaw and the provincial People's Universities provided public lectures accessible to the working classes but these were not degree-awarding institutions.[42] Cambridge did not grant women full university degrees until 1948. By 1900 the majority of European universities had opened their doors to women although not always on the same terms as male students. The last bastions of male-dominated learning were the Prussian and Austrian institutions, which held out until 1900 and much later in the case of the Austrian theological and law faculties.

By the end of the century the generation born in the 1860s and 1870s was emerging from secondary and higher education and changing the face of women's employment. Certainly, the old professions were not yet a level playing-field: female medical graduates encountered opposition in the prestigious hospitals so that they were forced to practise in the less prestigious and more poorly paid sectors such as asylums, poor law and women's hospitals, a situation that led many to leave the country to practise in the colonies.[43] In other professional spheres such as social work, women took the lead. In Germany, where there was still opposition to female doctors and secondary school teachers, educated women created their own professional sphere of social work, a respectable form of female employment which could be portrayed as a maternal profession and an apparent extension of women's natural predisposition to service and self-sacrifice and thus not a threat to men. By 1914, a system of professional training in social work had been established in schools run by women like the feminist Alice Salomon in Berlin.[44] Salomon, one of the first women to gain a doctorate from a German university, opened the Women's School of Social Work in 1908, the culmination of her efforts to improve girls' secondary education in order to encourage in them a sense of social responsibility based on women's special understanding of social problems. For Salomon, the female social worker undertook 'the assumption of duties for a wider circle which are usually performed by the mother at home.'[45] Similarly, in Belgium, women organised in the Christian women's movement moved into social work as an extension of 'spiritual mothering'.[46]

The professions were still the preserve of a tiny minority of educated women by the First World War, but many thousands of others did use their education as a stepping stone to jobs in the semi-professional and skilled white-collar sectors. It was acceptable for women with a decent secondary or higher education to take employment in a range of suitable occupations which included clerking in the civil service or private business, in banking and insurance, as well as teaching and nursing. Across Europe, female inspectors of girls' schools, women's prisons, reformatories for children and young women and in factories and workshops employing women, represented an admission by the state that there was a way of combining ideals of femininity with a place for women in the public sphere. Such women were standard-bearers of the feminist doctrine which wished to see woman's special influence in society increased and her special role enhanced and protected. In France, Aldona Sochazewska Juillerat, the first female member of the labour inspectorate in Rouen, cautioned against women aspiring to professional equality in the more demanding professions such as medicine and the law on the grounds of their 'natural' inclination to marriage and motherhood.[47]

However, with the exception of medicine which, to some extent, was being redefined as a suitable area of work for women, women's access to the professions requiring a university degree and extensive training was, by 1918, extremely limited. Women were filling office and retail jobs, but not professional ones. In Britain, for example, between 1881 and 1911 there were significant increases in the numbers of women employed in the white-collar sector. In 1881, 3216 women constituted 12.6 per cent of officers and clerks in the civil service; by 1911 there were more than 22,000 of them, or 26.5 per cent. Amongst commercial clerks female employees increased from just over

3 per cent of employees in 1881 to 24.5 per cent in 1911. By 1911 more than half of telegraphy workers were women, almost 13 per cent of journalists and 30 per cent of photographers.[48] On the other hand, very few gains at all were made in law, dentistry, architecture, accountancy and engineering and in academic posts in universities. Before 1914 the number of female lecturers in British universities was miniscule and 'professorial chairs, apparently, were designed to accommodate only the masculine frame'.[49] It was not until after the war that women would make significant progress in gaining positions in areas of professional work formerly the preserve of men, such as the more prestigious posts in the civil service and the law which was barred to women in Britain and Germany until 1919.

SOCIALIST SOLUTIONS

The feminist movement was both encouraged and disappointed by the development in the late nineteenth century of the European socialist movement. Socialism offered a new ideological umbrella for some streams of feminist thought, putting the subjugation of women on a par with the subjugation of the proletariat. But, socialism had the capacity to split feminism along class lines. How could the bourgeois and upper-class feminist continue to consort with the working-class feminist who supported the overthrow of capitalism as the route to both class and female emancipation?

The claims made by middle-class feminists for legal equality, access to higher education and the professions were sometimes criticised as irrelevant to the vast majority of working women for whom the daily struggle to put a meal on the table was a more pressing need. The so-called bourgeois feminists were castigated by Russian feminist and Bolshevik Aleksandra Kollontai (1872–1952) in 1923, for 'imagining themselves to be the advocates and spokesmen of the demands and aspirations of all women, believing themselves placed above all class differences, when in fact they were the very mouthpieces for the needs and interests of the women of the bourgeois class.'[50] Kollontai's words were harsh, but as a leading socialist writer and member of the Bolshevik Central Committee, she was hardly likely to pay even lip service to the achievements of middle-class feminists whose solution to the woman question stood in such stark contrast to her own position. For Kollontai and socialist women before her, the root of women's oppression was capitalism. The feminist demand for equal rights was a bourgeois solution to women's plight; only the overthrow of the capitalist social order would offer women a means of casting off their economic and political oppression. In the meantime, however, it was left to socialist women to work out a means of pursuing emancipation in the here and now.

The intellectual stimulus behind the development of a socialist women's movement was the work of Karl Marx (1818–83), Friedrich Engels (1820–95) and August Bebel (1840–1913). Strictly speaking, socialist feminism is something of a misnomer, since socialist women (and men) portrayed the feminist campaign for women's rights as bourgeois. For socialists, demands on behalf of a special group – women – were a distraction from the class struggle. The fundamental cause of women's subordination was capitalism, and only with the overthrow of the capitalist system would working-class women, along with working-class men, be emancipated. However, Engels and Bebel offered a gendered analysis of capitalism. Women's subordination was the consequence of the introduction of private property and monogamous marriage, resulting in the exclusion of women from public production. Only the full participation of women in waged labour and the destruction of private property and the family with the socialist revolution would lead to women's emancipation. However, links had to be made between theory and practice. Engels, in his *The Origin of the Family, Private Property and the State* published in 1884, advocated political rights for women as a means to achieving equality in the home and the workplace. But it was the German socialist August Bebel, in his tremendously popular book *Woman and Socialism* (1879), who provided the most tangible arguments for working-class women. Like the liberal John Stuart Mill, Bebel rejected notions about woman's destiny being rooted in her special nature, and like Mill he was supportive of liberal demands such as entry to universities, civil rights within marriage and so forth. And, like Mill, Bebel believed that women's emancipation – albeit as part of the emancipation of the working class as a whole – would be of benefit to society as a whole. 'A society in which all the means of production are the property of the community, a society which recognises the full equality of all without distinction of sex . . . which enrols as workers all those who are at present unproductive . . . raises the mental and physical condition of all its members to the highest attainable pitch.'[51] Just as Mill galvanised the 'liberal' feminist movement, so Bebel popularised the woman question within the labour movement and provided women on the left with an inspiration for action as socialists and feminists.

Bebel's book was read by thousands of German women and inspired many – but it took *female* activists who understood the oppression of working women, to put theory into practice. It was women like Clara Zetkin (1857–1933) in Germany, Hubertine Auclert in France, Adelheid Popp (1869–1939) in Austria and Anna Kuliscioff (c.1854–1925) in Italy, who tried to bring about a synthesis of two potentially conflicting ideologies: feminism and socialism. For the German socialist Clara Zetkin, the double oppression of working women by capitalist employers and by men required immediate attention because the leaders of the socialist parties were not about to take action despite their theoretical and much-trumpeted commitment to equality for women. European socialists accepted the reality of working-class women's oppression but were reluctant either to embrace an agenda determined by sex (seeing the woman question as a social or private as opposed to a political issue) or to endorse separate women's organisations. In a speech to a workers' congress in 1889, Zetkin spelled out her socialist-feminist vision which combined an advocacy of women's rights with a commitment to the proletarian revolution:

> As the worker is subjected to the capitalist, so is woman subjected to man; and she will remain subjected as long as she is economically dependent. Work is the essential condition upon which this economic independence of woman is based. If we wish women to be free human beings, to have the same rights as men in our society, women's work must neither be abolished nor limited.[52]

Thus Zetkin showed that she accepted the key tenet of the socialist position on the woman question articulated by Bebel. Women's participation in paid labour would lead to their full economic independence which would free them from their dependence upon men. 'Once women have attained their economic independence from men, there is no reason why they should remain socially dependent on them.' A woman who had achieved economic independence was man's equal.

Zetkin and her counterparts elsewhere in Europe battled to convince their respective parties that the woman question was not subordinate to the class question but intrinsic to it. 'I am truly afraid that human equality, as preached by every socialist school, will still mean the equality of men, and that women will be duped by the proletarian men just as the latter have been duped by the bourgeoisie', commented the French socialist Hubertine Auclert.[53] Socialist women did succeed in gaining commitments to female equality by socialist political parties, but such commitments were worth little in practice. In France, when the lifelong socialist Paule Mink (1839–1901) argued that working women should be educated in order that they might become more conscious of the revolutionary cause, stating that the working woman 'cannot go into the streets dressed only in her innocence', she was ridiculed by male activists who aspired to keep their womenfolk at home.[54] And her efforts to stand as a candidate in municipal elections were treated with contempt by her male socialist colleagues. In Italy, Anna Kuliscioff's commitment to universal suffrage was not shared by her party.[55] In Sweden the Social Democrats evidently thought little of their formal support for female suffrage since they refused to support either a female suffrage campaign or to allow women members to debate the decision.[56] In Britain, the Independent Labour Party expressed little more than lukewarm support for female suffrage until it introduced a bill to extend the suffrage to women on the same property basis as men in 1904. Across Europe it was left to female socialist activists in trade unions and local party organisations to convert Zetkin's theoretical position into practical improvements on the ground for ordinary working women.

The central plank of the socialist women's policy was the guarantee of women's right to work. Most working-class women most of their adult lives undertook paid labour of some kind and a woman's right to work was self-evident. It was a position that was to bring socialist women into conflict with male trade unionists and workers, many of whom regarded female workers as a threat to male jobs and to pay rates. French and German socialists were by the 1890s seeking the votes of male workers, and won support by promising protection for male jobs against feminist demands for equal pay for equal work and equal access to jobs.

There was no such thing as a socialist women's movement in Europe before the First World War, at least not in the sense of an organisation with agreed aims and a unity of purpose. The two manifestations of such a movement – the Socialist Women's International (the counterpart of the Second Socialist International) and International Women's Day on 8 March – were, by no stretch of the imagination expressions of a mass movement of proletarian women. At a national level, the German Social Democratic Women's Movement was the most successful in Europe with around 175,000 members by 1914, a party newspaper for women – *Die Gleichheit* (*Equality*) – and more than 400 party spokeswomen. Elsewhere the level of socialist representation for working women was lamentable. There was no socialist women's organisation in France until Elisabeth Renaud (1846–1932) and Louise Saumoneau (1875–1950) formed the Groupe Féministe Socialiste (Feminist Socialist Group) in 1899. In Britain, although the Women's Labour League was founded in 1906, it never achieved critical mass, partly perhaps because of the existence of a lively suffrage campaign at a time when the Independent Labour Party had not formally committed itself to the vote for women. Few working women belonged to either European socialist parties or trade unions. Yet at the grassroots, in the workplace, the socialist feminist agenda offered working women representation and a hope of material improvements in the immediate future. We can see this twin-track policy in operation in Scotland, where thousands of women were employed in the textile trades with little or no union representation. The Women's Trades Union League, a London-based organisation with branches in the main industrial centres, aimed to 'free working women from the yoke of middle-class patronage and to encourage their independent organisation'. In practice, its activists made successful attempts to speak to working women on their own terms. 'We are careful beforehand to find out something about the conditions at the factory', wrote the WTUL's Scottish secretary Mary MacArthur. 'It is no good talking generalities . . . They will not understand. You have got to talk to them about why they should be fined twopence or threepence a week or why the employer does not pay for the thread . . . Of course they are interested.'[57] In this way the League helped to promote union organisation amongst female workers and clearly also an understanding of the reasons for their exploitation. Similarly, in Italy Anna Kuliscioff toured factories to encourage women to join unions affiliated to the Italian Socialist Party because this way women could help themselves by amassing strike funds to enable them to resist the employers.[58] The socialist message was relayed to working women in a language that spoke to everyday experience.

The problem for socialist women had always been how to combine socialist and feminist platforms without alienating male workers and socialist colleagues. Clara Zetkin had achieved this marriage in a theoretical sense, but she had never really understood the double burden of working women – the difficulties of combining paid and domestic work. Zetkin's successor, Luise Zietz, was more acceptable to her male colleagues in arguing that protective legislation and maternity benefits would improve the condition of the woman worker, enabling her to carry out her domestic role more effectively. Perhaps the most integrated vision was formulated by the Frenchwoman and member of the Marxist Parti Ouvrier Français (French Workers' Party), Aline Valette (1850–99). For Valette, the key to the advancement of all workers, men and women, was social and sexual harmony, a view which accepted women's maternal role whilst insisting on women's equal right to work. The inscription on her headstone when she died in 1899 read, 'The emancipation of woman lies in emancipated labour (L'harmonie sociale)'.[59] Valette's acknowledgement of the need for equality in the labour market as well as recognition of the reality of most women's lives as wives and mothers brought her closer to the bourgeois feminists than most socialists would have countered.

In most European countries, socialist women never experienced the culmination of revolutionary ideology. In Russia and in Germany, though, the revolutions of 1917 and 1918 offered the prospect that sexual equality might be realised as part of the emancipation of the proletariat. Though the German Revolution of 1918–19 culminated in the murder of those on the radical left, including Rosa Luxemburg (1871–1919), it established the democratic Weimar Republic which recognised women as equals under the constitution and gave the vote to all women over the age of 18. In Russia, though, the revolutionaries seized control of the government and proceeded to carry out fundamental changes to state and society. In these circumstances, the potential for women's emancipation was far greater. There was probably a much stronger tradition of female radicalism in Russia than anywhere else in Europe, and Russian left intellectuals, including Lenin, had assumed the mobilisation of women would be crucial to the success of the revolution. In 1903, at Lenin's instigation, although probably influenced by his wife Nadezhda Krupskaya (1869–1939) who had recently published a pamphlet *The Woman Worker* (1900), the party programme of the Russian Social Democrats included a commitment to civil and political equality of the sexes.[60] During the revolutionary years 1905–17, a group of revolutionary women including Krupskaya, Inessa Armand (1874/5–1920) and Aleksandra Kollontai, set about organising proletarian women, weaning them away from bourgeois feminism and raising consciousness of exploitation through meetings and a newspaper, *Rabotnitsa* (*Woman Worker*). The February Revolution in 1917 was initiated by groups of war-weary Petrograd women who came out on to the streets on International Women's Day demanding bread and an end to the war. In the wake of the Czar's abdication Bolshevik women swung into action, mobilising women workers, and in July of that year the government granted women the right to vote and the right to equal pay. The October Revolution, which saw the Bolsheviks take control of the government, offered the opportunity for Bolshevik women to implement more far-reaching change. It was recognised by all Bolshevik activists, though, that this change could not happen overnight.

In 1918, Lenin, in a speech to the First All-Russian Congress of Women, reaffirmed the commitment of the Soviet government to women's emancipation:

The aim of the Soviet Republic is to abolish, in the first place, all restrictions of the rights of women . . . Up to the present the position of women has been such that it is called a position of slavery. Women are crushed by their domestic drudgery, and only socialism can relieve them from this drudgery, when we shall pass on from small household economy to social economy and to social tilling of the soil. Only then will women be fully free and emancipated.[61]

The first few months of the Soviet government had seen far-reaching reforms affecting women's lives. By December 1917, marriage had been made a civil contract, divorce was permitted on demand, and the laws on separate property and the rights of women to work and to equal pay were reformed in women's favour. By 1920, abortion was legalised and Kollontai, in her job as People's Commissar for Social Welfare, set in train policies to protect women workers and provide maternity care. The *Zhenotdel* or women's bureau, worked during the civil war to raise consciousness amongst women workers in the towns and the countryside, including those in the east where activists encountered serious opposition to their attempts to liberate women, particularly in Muslim communities. But family reforms aside, there was little commitment to change within the Bolshevik Party and the organisation of the state. Aside from a few prominent activist women such as Kollontai, Krupskaya, Armand, Elena Stasova (1873–1966), a professional revolutionary and secretary of the Bolshevik Party during the revolution, and Angelica Balabanova who had helped to organise the International Women's Socialist Conference in Berne in 1914, very few women found a place within the party hierarchy and even Kollontai lost influence. In 1922 she was sent to Norway to assist with trade negotiations following criticism of her writings on sex in a collection entitled *New Morality*. The absence of women, not only in positions of power in the Party hierarchy but also in the soviets and trade unions, almost certainly permitted the government to lose sight of the woman question by the 1920s when economic problems and political in-fighting took precedence over social reform and the woman question. Nevertheless, the short-lived Bolshevik experiment before the reaction of the 1920s and 1930s was the most visionary and theoretically radical anywhere in Europe, inspiring feminists elsewhere who visited Russia and who believed they were seeing a revolution in gender relations under way. Perhaps a more realistic assessment was made by Leon Trotsky in 1936, who wrote honestly that although the Soviet government granted women equal legal and political rights, it failed in its attempt to destroy the family and therefore women were still chained to household drudgery. The reason, according to Trotsky was that, 'The real resources of the state did not correspond to the plans and intentions of the Communist Party.' 'It is doubtful', he continued, 'if the resolution of the Communist International on the "complete and irrevocable triumph of socialism in the Soviet Union" sounds very convincing to the women of the factory districts!'[62]

WOMEN'S SUFFRAGE

By 1900, votes for women was an issue whose time had come. Political rights had been on the feminist agenda since the French Revolution, but it was not until the 1860s and 1870s that women organised specifically to achieve the vote. Hitherto the issue had been subordinated to competing claims such as access to higher education or legal reform. By 1900, though, there was agreement amongst feminists of all persuasions – equal rights, moderate and socialist – that female suffrage was a non-negotiable step needed in the democracies of Europe. Women's lack of political power was hindering further legislative change. The suffrage campaign was the expression of both frustration at the inability of women's groups to achieve their aims, and of a new-found confidence and radicalism amongst feminists who understood that tinkering around the edges of the legislative process was never going to be sufficient. The demand for enfranchisement, in essence a demand for freedom and equality, was, then, 'a direct strike at the very seat and symbolic locus of patriarchal power'.[63]

The suffrage campaign, then, did not emerge out of the blue. In northern Europe it is possible to trace a fairly seamless line from the temperance and social purity activism of the 1870s and 1880s to the demand for political representation in the 1900s. In Britain and in Germany, feminists had demonstrated their success on the ground by engaging in social and moral reform organisations. In Britain, many thousands of temperance activists drawn, for the most part, from the ranks of urban middle-class women, saw themselves first and foremost as moral reformers. But their day-to-day encounters with working-class families and their unsuccessful attempts to convince the government to introduce temperance legislation, provided both public political practice and a catalyst for some to become advocates of the vote, for it was only through granting women the parliamentary franchise that temperance campaigners could see their way to success.[64] Similarly, in Germany, where the majority of feminists within the moderate wing of the movement were initially hostile to a campaign for women's political rights, the campaign to abolish the state regulation of prostitution turned the majority in favour of suffrage in order that feminists and women in general might have a means of influencing government policy on matters affecting them, and in order that women's 'moral voice' might be heard on the political stage.[65]

The intransigence of the opposition to women's suffrage suggests that political rights were indeed the last bastion of separate spheres to be breached in the light of earlier successes in the fields of legal reform and educational opportunity. And indeed there is an inevitability about the resistance of the opposition and the eventual victory of the campaigners. Feminists had succeeded in connecting the personal with the political long before this slogan entered popular usage. Issues which had hitherto been designated as belonging in the private sphere and thus not within the purview of government, such as child custody and divorce legislation, had been brought to public attention and legislated on. Once measures such as the married women's property laws and laws affecting prostitutes were deemed to be within the jurisdiction of parliament, feminists could argue that there was no longer any justification for maintaining politics as an exclusively male privilege. In Britain, their argument was bolstered by the success of granting women the franchise in local and municipal elections as well as permitting them to stand for election to civic governing bodies such as school boards. Parliamentary franchise reform in New Zealand (1894), Western Australia (1899) and Finland (1906) demonstrated to the sceptics that female suffrage was an aid to political stability rather than an instigator of turmoil. By the first decade of the twentieth century, women's suffrage was no longer just another campaign issue. The franchise had become the most potent symbol of male dominance and it is this, along with the apparent likelihood of success, that helps explain why this issue united feminists of all persuasions and ignited some of the most passionate campaigning seen in Europe.

The story of the fight for the vote – particularly in Britain – is often dominated by the tactics of the militant Women's Social and Political Union (WSPU), the so-called suffragettes, formed in 1903. Frustrated with the constitutional approach of the National Union for Women's Suffrage Societies (NUWSS) – the suffragists – the suffragettes, led by Emmeline and Christabel Pankhurst, embarked upon a strategy of civil disobedience which drew massive public attention to the cause of votes for women, positive and negative. WSPU members across the country took the suffrage battle to the streets, the homes of politicians and the play parks of the rich. They dug up golf courses, set fire to theatres, poured tar into post boxes as well as made speeches, interrupted political meetings and marched with placards. Justifying militant tactics Emmeline Pankhurt remarked in 1908:

> We have tried to be womanly, we have tried to use feminine influence, and we have seen that it is of no use. Men have invariably got reforms for their impatience. And they have not our excuse for being impatient . . . it is because we realise that the condition of our sex is so deplorable that it is our duty even to break the law in order to call attention to the reasons why we do so.[66]

However, an exclusive focus on the actions of the minority (WSPU) detracts from the truly international character of the struggle for political rights, and risks ignoring the dogged and just as determined activities of the majority of feminists across Europe who mostly advocated peaceable and lawful campaigning. Only in Ireland, where nationalist women were engaged in the independence struggle, was such violent activity seen outside Britain. Elsewhere in Europe, suffrage campaigners addressed meetings, organised mass demonstrations and circulated petitions and pamphlets. Most suffrage associations rejected the militant tactics of the WSPU on the grounds that such methods would be counterproductive. Some found their antics distasteful, certainly unfeminine. In Germany, where suffragists legitimately feared the repressive power of the state so soon after the relaxation of legal restraints in 1908 which had forbidden Prussian and Saxon feminists from political association, militant tactics were condemned by moderate feminists as undignified, ridiculous, a sign of 'desperado politics'.[67] Conversely, French suffragists were accused of endangering the very existence of the Third Republic; female enfranchisement, it was argued, given women's 'innate' conservatism and Catholicism, would strengthen the forces of reaction and anti-republicanism. Although some individual feminists such as Madeleine Pelletier and Nelly Roussel did speak out against this notion and, in Pelletier's case, adopted tactics akin to those of the British suffragettes, the rights of women were subordinated to the need for the stability of the French state until 1945.

But tactical differences concealed a united aim, a fact acknowledged by Millicent Garrett Fawcett (1847–1929), president of the NUWSS. She condemned the use of physical violence but recognised that such 'novel and startling methods' had the effect of drawing 'a far larger amount of public attention to the claims of women to representation than ever had been given to the subject before.' Moreover, diversity in method, she argued, had contributed to the growth of the campaign across the country and 'however acute were the differences between the heads of the different societies, the general mass of suffragists throughout the country were loyal to the cause by whomsoever it was represented.'[68]

Across Europe, suffragists were joining in common cause. In 1913 the International Woman Suffrage Association met in Budapest. The mood was optimistic. French feminists were hopeful the municipal franchise would soon be reformed in favour of women; in Britain, suffragists were confident the government could hold out no longer. In her address to the international suffragists, the American Carrie Chapman Catt (1859–1947), reflected this confidence, stating: 'our movement has reached the last stage . . . Parliaments have stopped laughing at woman suffrage, and politicians have begun to dodge! It is the inevitable premonition of victory.'[69] The primacy of foreign policy and the outbreak of war just a few months later merely postponed the successful outcome of her prediction. Although the suffrage campaign was put on ice during the war, by 1918 a combination of the political process, war and revolution, and a realisation that women's votes would more likely lead to stability than not, resulted in the inclusion of women in the franchise of a swathe of European states from Russia to Britain. Their sisters in France and Italy were to be disappointed. Their struggle continued for another 30 years.

CONCLUSIONS

Feminism was one of the defining political movements of the nineteenth century. Feminists were humanitarians, seeking to improve not only the position of women but also relations between men and women. Across Europe they had begun to redefine the legal, economic, moral and political relations between the sexes through campaigns on property and marriage law, the right to an education and to gainful employment, on prostitution and the double-standard and finally on political representation. By improving the position of women, feminists believed that they were contributing to progressive social change.

The nineteenth-century feminist movement was remarkably successful in such a short period of time in terms of the concrete reforms it achieved and in its challenge to the ideology of separate spheres and female subordination. With the exception of the socialist women, feminists did not aim to overturn society but to work within it to achieve fundamental changes in the relations between the sexes based on a recognition of women's right to equal opportunity. Bearing in mind that feminist activism for the whole of the period before the war was undertaken outside the formal political sphere, and that women had virtually no political power, the achievements – improvements in education, access to the universities and the professions, greater recognition of women's rights within marriage, and, in many countries, the vote – changed women's lives, and gave women a language and a platform to change their own.

Chapter 11

◆

THE GREAT WAR

The Great War of 1914–18 marks, for most historians, the conclusion of the long nineteenth century which started with the French Revolution of 1789. For women's historians the war has become a key subject of critical debate. Did it mark the end of women's subordination and the beginning of women's long twentieth-century march to liberation? Conversely, did the war grant women limited and ineffectual rights in return for perpetuating their lives along old grooves and postponing the feminist challenge for another fifty years?

The idea of the war as a caesura, a defining moment in modern European history, stems in part from the very nature and scale of the conflict as much as from its political impact on the geopolitics of the continent. The First World War was a new type of war: a war waged not just on the battlefield but also on the home front. This war, unlike any war of the nineteenth century, dissolved the border between the home front and the field of conflict in both an ideological and a practical sense. The war was not something that was happening somewhere else. For non-combatants in the belligerent countries (Britain, France, Russia, Italy, Germany, Austria, Bulgaria and Turkey), the war was ever present in the lists of lost and fallen soldiers printed in the newspapers, in the letters sent home from soldier sweethearts, in the food shortages, and in the physical destruction wrought by air-raids on civilian populations and by advancing armies on local residents. Women were in the front line, literally and metaphorically. As war workers, mothers, lovers, mourners, servicewomen, nurses and victims of violence as well as the objects of government propaganda and emotional blackmail, women were participants in this war as never before.

The Great War has been made to bear a great deal of interpretative weight by historians of women. It comes at the end of a period of feminist activism and caps several decades of quite profound change in women's experience, and is easy to view as a turning point or a catalyst. Some women who lived through the war believed this to be the case. The suffragist Millicent Garrett Fawcett remarked of women in 1919 that the war had 'found [them] serfs and left them free'.[1] Others have stressed the continuities in gender roles through the war. This approach emphasises the temporary nature of shifts in the labour market and the continuing power of long-standing ideas about gender roles. This chapter examines the ways in which European women's identities and roles were affected by the exigencies of wartime, and asks whether the war marks a turning point for women in terms of individual and collective experience, considering their roles as civilians and combatants, as workers, as sexual beings and as patriots or pacifists.

THE HOME AT WAR

It was usual during the war years to represent the home and battle fronts as diametrically opposed, mirroring perceived gender roles. The home front was perceived as feminine, conveyed by the image of peaceful and stable home life and the absence of many men. The fighting front was indisputably male terrain, dominated by expressions of masculinity – violence, aggression and male camaraderie. It was a dichotomy used by governments desperate to maintain morale amongst the troops and stability at home, but it was also alluded to by feminists and pacifists for whom war was innately masculine in contrast to the more peaceful, conciliatory and life-affirming nature of woman. Yet, the experience of war did not fall neatly into two separate domains. The borders of each front were porous. The battle front was purveyed by scenes of domesticity; the home front was invaded by war.

Women were mobilised during the First World War as never before in wartime. As workers and as civilian service personnel they participated directly in the war machine. Mothers and potential mothers were urged to reproduce as part of their patriotic duty; motherhood became war work. As non-combatants they were subject to domestic legislation framed to meet military demands. This mobilisation of the home front made it more likely that the war would impinge directly on people's everyday lives. In Britain, France, Germany and the Low Countries, civilian populations were targeted by air-raids. The invasion and occupation of Belgium and France brought stories of atrocities perpetrated against civilians including the rape of women. In Britain, the presence of Commonwealth, and later American, soldiers brought the war into villages and towns hitherto untouched by the conflict. In Germany, the chronic food shortages as a result of the Allied blockade of German ports put housewives on a continuous war footing. In those countries where the war was physically being fought, civilian populations experienced the war on their doorstep: soldiers moving to and from the front, the retreat of the wounded, the sound of shells. In Freiburg in south-ern Germany, close to the border with France, the war was just 50 kilometres distant so that, when the westerly wind blew, windows in the town rattled from the roar of the heavy guns; 'no-one, no woman, no child could forget for one day that we were in a war', wrote an observer in 1917.[2] And the war was ever present in people's consciousness, brought home by letters from the front, lists of casualties in the newspapers and newsreel shown at the cinema. Women, then, were not innocent bystanders in this war. They were asked to fill a number of positions, all contingent upon the unique wartime conditions but at the same time informed by pre-existing ideas about woman's role. The nineteenth-century construction of woman as wife, mother, domestic man-ager and emotional anchor, allied to the more negative assumptions about her dangerous sexuality and her place in a wartime society where men were absent, informed the ways in which governments sought to control the home front. It was almost as if the disruption of wartime was used by governments to justify a return to values that women had just spent decades resisting.

The first women to experience the impact of war on their doorsteps were those living in the regions of Belgium and France invaded and then occupied by the German army. Almost immediately following the invasion in August 1914, so-called atrocity stories started to circulate in Britain and France, telling of the alleged rape and brutalisation of women and the murder of infants. Reports of outrages, including the rape of pregnant women and women having their breasts cut off, were difficult to evaluate, although in view of what we know about more recent conflicts (in the former Yugosla-via, for instance) it is entirely credible that the rape of women may have been an element of military campaigns in the past. The spreading of atrocity sto-ries was not the preserve of the Allied powers though. In Alsace, a contested region of France, German soldiers returning from combat told tales about the French cutting out the tongues of those who spoke ill of their presence.[3] Whether the reports were true or exaggerated, the uses to which the stories were put illustrates the dominant attitudes towards women in this particular conflict. It was no coincidence that Belgium was frequently portrayed as a female victim of a brutal rape which was subsequently 'milked' of her resources.[4] The representation of wartime atrocities in newspaper reports and poster campaigns 'bolstered an understanding of gender that aimed to preserve traditional notions of male and female behaviour as well as the divide between the sexes exemplified by the home front/war front split' in the face of evidence to the contrary, that is, that the war front had already infiltrated the home.[5] Stories of rape were used explicitly to mobilise men to defend their womenfolk and their home and to encourage women, who could not fight, to persuade men to volunteer. 'You have read what the Germans have done in Belgium', read one British recruitment poster; 'Have you thought what they would do if they invaded this Country?' The poster, though, was directed not at men but at women: 'Won't you help and send a man to join the Army today?'[6]

Notwithstanding the immediate shock value of the stories of rape and violence against women, the real propaganda value lay in the ways in which acts of violence against women were used to reinforce a number of influential discourses on woman during wartime. The first was the portrayal in British propaganda of women as (sexually) passive or helpless victims whom men had to defend. The second, which pervaded French discussion of rape, was the emphasis on women as mothers, as reproducers of the nation and the race. In both cases, concern for the rape victim was subordinated to issues of national survival. In Britain, atrocity stories were used to encourage men to join the armed forces; in France debate focused on the potential outcome of rape, the so-called *boche*-baby. In the light of shifting attitudes against interracial mixing in the colonies in the prewar years, it is not surprising that, in France, debates about the availability of abortion and what or who determined the nationality of any child born of rape, dominated discussion at the expense of concern about the violence perpetrated against women.[7] War was violent and rape was only the most obvious intrusion of that violence into everyday life.

In France and Belgium, the German invasion and occupation took the war into people's homes and into their psyches. Most women were not the victims of physical or sexual violence at the hands of the enemy, but they heard the stories from refugees or read them in the newspapers, and lived in a state of fear of those 'barbarians' who requisitioned their homes and food and, it was feared, their bodies. In Britain and Germany, women were largely spared the anticipatory terror of sexual violence, although those living along Germany's southern border with France were on constant alert fearing an imminent French invasion. But their femininity was compromised or threatened in different ways: by the destructive impact of air-raids and, in Germany, the effects of the British naval blockade which transformed women's role in the home as they strove to put food on the table. Aerial bombardment by planes and Zeppelin airships in the south of England and in the south-west of Germany took the war to civilians for the first time. In Freiburg, for instance, the population was totally unprepared for air attacks and was left to pray to God to protect them in the absence of any effective defence. 'Trembling and silent we sat downstairs in the hallway, the ceiling shook, the windows and chandeliers rattled, a thunderous noise rolled over the house as I had never experienced before', wrote Charlotte Herder in her diary after one French onslaught.[8] Civilians, women and children included, were now regarded as legitimate targets and those who had been bombed out of their homes were used by British propaganda to shame men into signing up and doing their duty for home and country. 'Innocent' women, who had found themselves caught up in the war, were feted as stalwart heroines, representative of the determination of the country as a whole to stand up to the enemy. Women workers in munitions factories, on the other hand, although much more at risk of death than their sisters in homes along the British south coast – owing to the frequent factory explosions and Zeppelin raids on industrial plants – were given little praise or even recognition for the risks they took. In fact, such explosions were rarely publicised for fear of affecting morale, and in one such event – at a shell-filling factory in Lancashire – the workers were shut in behind locked and guarded gates while the shells exploded inside.[9] In Germany, though, women were forthright in their criticisms of the authorities. In the spring of 1917 a group of women sent an anonymous letter to the town council of Freiburg cleverly making use of the familiar language of male protection, remarking that 'it is bad enough that our menfolk are out in danger, but we women and children must be better protected at home.'[10]

The most tangible impact of the war in German and, to a lesser extent, in British and French homes, was felt at the kitchen table. In Britain there were shortages of food staples such as tea and sugar, the supply of fresh food in the towns was affected by the submarine warfare of 1916–17, and by 1918 rationing of bread, meat, butter and bacon had been introduced. In France, requisitioning of food by German troops contributed to shortages and price rises. But the privations and inconveniences experienced by British and French housewives were nothing compared with those of their German counterparts who 'spent countless hours fighting the war from their own kitchens'.[11] In the absence of 9 million male 'breadwinners', provided with inadequate state assistance, and obliged to pay extortionate prices for basic foodstuffs, working-class women especially were forced to take paid work and to spend an inordinate amount of time and energy procuring and preparing food. By 1917, rations of meat, eggs and butter were less than 20 per cent of peacetime consumption levels, basic food prices had increased by 800 per cent, and millions only just survived on a fat- and protein-free diet.[12] Those in urban areas grew vegetables on any available space, and when these supplies were inadequate, women and children embarked upon 'hamstering' journeys to the countryside where they could buy or barter foodstuffs. In the towns, barter was the only other way to obtain food if one did not have the requisite ration cards or enough money to purchase items on the black market.

In this type of economy the role of housewife and household manager became crucial to survival and the result was the politicisation of women, who blamed the government for their plight. From the beginning of the war, housewives had been criticised for stockpiling food; as the food shortage intensified they were reproached for manipulating the ration system, for not managing the pitiful rations sensibly, and for obtaining from farms food which had been destined for the towns thus disrupting the government's food distribution system. From the point of view of the women trying to put a meal on the table, the state was an impediment. The so-called turnip winter of 1916–17 was a turning point in Germany. The winter that year was exceptionally cold and wet, the frost ruined the potato crop, there was a lack of fat, meat and dairy products, and people were forced to delve amongst rubbish heaps and alongside railway lines for fuel. The story of Berlin women rushing out of their homes when a horse collapsed and died in the street, tearing at it with knives and even collecting the blood in containers, relays the sheer desperation of urban inhabitants.[13] Urban suffering was endemic. Mortality rates rose as a result of an influenza epidemic as well as malnutrition, tuberculosis and other diseases of the poor and weak. In the light of rumours that the war was lost, food riots and demonstrations by women and young people became commonplace. 'It is the countless female workers who constantly agitate and stir things up', commented an official report from 1916.[14] The extension of the war into the kitchen transformed the role of housewife. According to Ute Daniel, 'The subversive strategies that, above all, working-class women developed during the war to fulfil their responsibility of providing for their families turned into strategies of subversion that, in the end, irrevocably destroyed the consensus of wartime society between the rulers and the ruled.'[15]

Hunger, air-raids, fear of invasion – all brought the war home to women. But the common experience for all women on both sides was loss. The massive loss of life and bodily mutilation amongst soldiers, first on the Western Front in France and Belgium and later in the war in the east in Russia, had an enormous impact on those left behind. The war generated awesome statistics: around 9 million people dead, 21 million seriously wounded, 5 million widows and 9 million orphaned children. Individual stories show how the war, in its sheer human devastation, destroyed families and forced women to reconfigure their lives as mourners, widows, and carers. Anna Eisenmenger, a middle-class Austrian wife and mother, graphically and movingly described her loss with hardly a trace of self-pity. In 1918 she wrote in her diary of the armistice and the end of 'the terrible massacre of human lives'.

> After four years that seemed as if they would never end, I have to mourn a terrible war sacrifice: my husband and Otto [son] dead, Erni [son] for the time being deprived of his sight; Rudi [son-in-law] a cripple with only half a leg; Karl [son] utterly changed owing to his head wound and perhaps not sane; Liesbeth [daughter] weak and ailing for lack of nourishing food, Aunt Bertha bedridden with bone-softening due to under nourishment . . . Five of my nephews and one of my nieces were sacrificed to the war fury . . . myself, still in health, but nervously overstrained and in need of a rest. Fully conscious of my heavy obligations, and firmly resolved to withstand the tempests of fate, and under these melancholy circumstances still to make the best of everything.[16]

Anna Eisenmenger's experience was shared by the women of the enemy nations. 'Before I had reached my twenty-first birthday', wrote the Englishwoman Barbara Wootton, 'I had experienced the deaths of my father, my brother, my favourite school friend and the husband to whom I had been married in theory for five weeks and in practice for something less than forty-eight hours . . . I do not think that anyone can live through such experiences without some significant and permanent marks remaining.'[17] The daily casualty lists, the constant fear that a loved one would not return, the fearful wait for the telegram, personalised the war for women. The letters received from the front brought the fighting home to those waiting. The most well-known female chronicler of the war, Vera Brittain (1893–1970), described how, upon receiving her dead fiancé Roland's mud-caked uniform, the smell of it vividly brought home to her the 'mortality & decay & corruption' of war.[18] Some of the bereaved asked if they could be told where their loved ones were buried since, at least in the British case, bodies were left close by the field of battle. Despite all of this, the overriding impression gained from personal memoirs is of stoic women doing their best to carry on. We know very little about those women who cracked under the strain. The story of a young German woman who 'went mad' upon hearing of the death of her husband can surely not be an isolated one.[19] From the point of view of those – the majority – who lost loved ones, the First World War represented a change of gear, a rupture in personal lives. For the woman whose husband was killed leaving her with children to bring up alone, and for the young girl who lost her betrothed, life in the future would be a far cry from what they had envisaged.

WOMEN AS THE ENEMY WITHIN

Women, it was said, 'had the hardest job' of the war. They had to stay at home.[20] It was hard to wait, and it was difficult to keep morale high. But women were repeatedly told by governments that their 'emotional and reproductive labour' was as important to the war effort as the combat role of men.[21] And precisely because of their crucial role at home they were also identified as potential internal enemies, capable of undermining the war effort if they did not conform to the image of the stoic housewife, if they failed to discipline themselves. Governments expected women to carry on their domestic work regardless of air-raids and food shortages and the unrelenting toll of casualties; and most did. However, the reverse side of the veneration of the mother and homemaker was fear of the consequences of the breakdown of patriarchal authority. Women whose menfolk were away could be seen as vulnerable to temptation. Those accused of sleeping with the enemy, prostituting themselves to occupying soldiers, making the most of foreign troops stationed in the vicinity, cheating on their fiancés and husbands or merely fitting the description of fun-loving or frivolous girls, were castigated for endangering the nation and for undermining the morale of those who were fighting on their behalf.

The bodies of civilian women became a focus of attention of a variety of groups during the war, and once again, just as during the 1870s and 1880s across Europe, women's sexuality was subjected to legal and moral discipline. The double-standard lived on and in some respects was reaffirmed during the war as soldiers were permitted considerable sexual freedom as a reward or release from the combat experience. On the other hand, all women, civilians and those in combat-support roles, were expected to eschew temptation in the name of patriotism and morale. In Britain, the Defence of the Realm Act 1914 resumed where the Contagious Diseases Acts had left off, permitting military curfews on women in order, supposedly, to prevent prostitution and the spread of venereal disease. And at the end of the war it was made illegal for any woman to have sex with a soldier if she was infected with VD. In Germany and in France, the official response to fears about women's immoral conduct was similar; surveillance and regulation were stepped up, and in Germany the military governors acted upon the assumption that 'almost all women who abandon themselves to extramarital sexual intercourse are infected with venereal disease'.[22] Any woman who appeared to be acting suspiciously could be apprehended by the morals police.

Ironically, though, wartime offered young women new forms of excitement and greater freedoms, especially in Britain. Unlike in occupied France and Belgium or blockaded Germany, women in Britain were spared many of the immediate horrors of war and could take advantage of the loosening of family constraints in the absence of many fathers. In the early months of the war, British towns became home to encampments of volunteer soldiers which were an obvious draw for young girls and boys. But whilst the boys could channel their excitement into joining up, girls had no 'patriotic outlet for their urge to participate in the great national effort', especially since the outbreak of war had been accompanied by large-scale female unemployment.[23] So they hung about the camps, flirted with the soldiers, invited them home for tea, accompanied them to pubs and, it was alleged, engaged in lewd sexual activity. These girls were accused of succumbing to an infection called 'khaki fever', a condition that made respectable girls 'lose their heads'. *The Times* newspaper in October 1914 noted that 'little imagination is needed to picture the evils which may arise when a young girl in a state of mental restlessness produced by the war finds herself at once unemployed . . . with a sudden and absorbing interest thrust upon her through the presence of a large number of troops stationed in her town, and with a desire to help with no ability to do so.'[24]

Girls stricken with khaki fever were not, however, regarded as innocent victims of circumstance but as little vixens exhibiting an active sexuality, causing a nuisance to soldiers who were loath to accept their advances, and presenting a moral danger to themselves. By January 1916, when conscription for men was introduced in Britain, there was an influx of women into factory and munitions work, raising new fears about the behaviour of women who were no longer constrained by patriarchal authority. The khaki fever panic was soon superseded by the identification of another internal enemy: the so-called amateurs in Britain, or wild prostitutes in Germany (that is women who had sex for fun). Munitions workers especially took advantage of their situation; living away from parents and with their own wages to spend, there were few constraints on their behaviour. It was this very public display of female sexuality accompanied by smoking, drinking and swearing that concerned critics who saw it as an expression of women's increasing independence from men and which seemed to indicate a rejection of the middle-class respectable morality of the 1880s and 1890s.

It was not only young, single women who attracted critical comment. War-wives and mothers also found themselves censured for all kinds of behaviour deemed inappropriate and damaging to stability at home and the war effort in general. Marriage and birth rates in all the belligerent countries fell during the war whilst the death rate was rising. In Germany, where politicians had already been expressing fears about the fertility decline before the war, there was almost a halving of marriages from more than 500,000 in 1913 to only 278,208 in 1915. Not surprisingly the birth rate also fell dramatically from 110 births per 1000 women of childbearing age in 1913 to a low-point of 53 in 1917. In Britain the rate fell from 97 per 1000 women in 1913 to 71 in 1918.[25] In response, procreation was promoted by governments as women's national service. The French adopted a pro-natalist policy that encompassed the recognition of illegitimate 'war babies' as well as support for pregnant women and mothers. In Britain, calls for reform of the bastardy laws fell on deaf ears, and when separation allowances were paid to wives of men in the armed forces and to some unmarried mothers, a debate commenced concerning the ends to which this money might be put. Checks were made on the recipients to ensure they were using the money for its intended purposes, but women were still accused of drinking, dancing and cavorting with soldiers whilst neglecting their children. This was a powerful argument at a time when the mother was represented in government and religious propaganda as the 'first line of defence'.[26] The morale and motivation of the fighting forces was predicated upon the notion of a man's instinct to defend his family. In Germany the tone of official propaganda was extremely harsh bearing in mind the extremely difficult conditions prevalent on the home front there. 'There are war wives who have forgotten about love, loyalty, discipline and morals and throw themselves at strange men while their own husbands are starving and bleeding at the front' railed a Prussian War Ministry leaflet.[27]

Fulfilling the role of the moral wife and fecund mother was a woman's national duty. Any woman who strayed from the ideal of the respectable wife at home was subject to censure. Women who drank were especially castigated, and alleged drunkenness amongst women was blamed for the rise in convictions of child neglect. The foremost child-saving charity in Scotland commented in 1917 that:

In the course of their work the Men Inspectors find that there is a determination amongst a large number of women to go their own way and live as they like in the absence of their husbands ... A common practice is for women to lock children in and take the key away so that the Inspectors cannot get access to the children. The early part of the night is spent in public houses, picture houses and theatres and it is often not till the early hours of the morning that they return home.[28]

The decline of the marriage and birth rates also drew attention to the so-called war babies phenomenon. These were children born out of wedlock, either as a consequence of prewar liaisons between women and men who then joined the forces or, as in France, the result of rape or consensual intercourse between French women and German soldiers. In Germany, women who engaged in relationships with enemy men, such as prisoners of war who had been assigned to work on farms, were not only prosecuted but publicly humiliated in the media who referred to them as 'dishonoured women' and as women who had no national pride.[29]

The official justifications for these attempts to control female sexuality in all of the participating countries were given as the need to prevent disease and the requirement to maintain morale. The fighting strength of the country was said to be influenced by not only the fitness of its soldiers but also soldiers' motivation to defend home and family. Both arguments were flawed in theory and in execution, not least because the military authorities were powerless to prevent soldiers using prostitutes and, recognising this, they put their efforts into trying to protect the men from disease. 'Every time that you have the weakness to be tempted by these women, don't neglect to use a rubber *préservatif*': these words warned French soldiers of unprotected sex with prostitutes yet implicitly condoned their actions whilst the women were positioned as the active seducers.[30] German soldiers were not so lucky. The military authorities there preferred to recommend chemical treatments for sexually transmitted diseases as well as implementing a novel idea to reduce the number of prostitutes. In Belgium, women were given employment knitting woollen underclothes for the forces in an attempt to keep them from destitution and therefore reducing the need for them to sell their bodies. But what governments were really concerned about was social stability. Female sexual promiscuity, allied with the decline in the marriage and birth rates, posed a threat to a society experiencing the upheaval of war – or so some wartime commentators seemed to believe. Female immorality could only hasten the weakening of the home front. Yet it was not female sexual behaviour that posed a threat to political stability at home but women's experiences as housewives and workers. The struggle to put food on the table, to keep a roof over the family's heads, and to combine paid work with child care, raised women's political consciousness and informed female political protest.

The war transformed the role of the family. The absence of men, often for years at a time, meant the family no longer fulfilled a reproductive function. Rather the function of the family was the production and consumption of goods. This shift in emphasis helps to explain why attempts to discipline women's sexual behaviour had little impact. In Germany it has been suggested that the state lost its moral legitimacy as women especially were forced to adopt subversive or illegal strategies in order simply to survive. Women who were working in the war industries and continuing to fulfil their familial obligations came to realise that the state was not on their side. Women, in Daniel's words, 'emancipated themselves from the system'.[31] When they demonstrated against food shortages, it was not the privation as such that prompted their protest, but a perception that inequalities in food distribution had been caused by iniquitous state measures. Street protests targeted the government for its perceived failure to stem profiteering and for its inability to engineer equitable distribution of food. Commenting upon disturbances in Vienna amongst women waiting for hours in a queue for a pathetic ration of horse-meat, Anna Eisenmenger regarded the 'patient apathy with which we housewives endure . . . blameworthy and incomprehensible.'[32] The war politicised Austrian and German women, not because these special circumstances permitted state intrusion into private matters which women resented, but because women themselves came to understand that the system (rather than the war) was at the root of their problems. By 1917, women were joining with strikers from munitions factories and demanding not just bread but peace and democratic reform. The enemy within was not the sexually promiscuous girl but the housewife.

Food shortages, price rises and war-weariness alongside long working hours and low wages for female war workers were the immediate causes of female unrest across Europe. From Glasgow to St Petersburg, ordinary women – women who had never been involved in politics – took to the streets, went on strike and took part in demonstrations, acts of sabotage and civil disobedience. Italian women workers in the industrial centre of Turin, angry at the food shortages, the long hours of work and the continuation of the war, marched through the streets to the city hall in August 1917 demanding food and an end to the war.[33] At the start of 1918, women workers in the Loire region of France marched in the streets shouting 'Down with the war! We want bread!' and singing the Internationale. 'It's no longer a question of extra pennies or the young class of conscripts', wrote one working mother to a relative in the trenches. 'It's peace that's important.'[34] Even in non-belligerent Spain the war had an impact, causing inflation and food short-ages. In cities across the country, women marched to demand reductions in the price of basic foodstuffs such as olive oil, fish and potatoes, and in Barce-lona during the harsh winter of early 1918 housewives and textile workers attacked coal trucks, went on strike, and demanded reductions in rents and prices to pre-war levels.[35] In Glasgow and other cities across Britain with a high proportion of rented accommodation, women reacted to rent increases imposed by landlords who were exploiting the high demand for rented housing from the influx of war industry workers. Tenants unable to pay were evicted. At a time when the home front was being exhorted to unify behind the war effort, tenants regarded landlords' actions as morally reprehensible. Crowds, mainly of women, gathered outside the homes of evicted families, and in 1915 tenants began a rent strike – a housewives' campaign which challenged not only the landlords but the state as well. A combination of kitchen cabinets, local committees and the Glasgow Women's Housing Association, none of whom were formally affiliated to any political move-ment, successfully managed this protest by working women and, by the end of 1915, the government had introduced legislation to limit rents.[36] This was not the end for Glasgow's women, however, who, whilst not engaging in revolutionary activity to compare with their sisters in Germany and Russia, were motivated to involve themselves in the peace movement and labour politics at the war's end.

Elsewhere, women's action had more immediate and far-reaching con-sequences. In Germany, working-class women's experiences had alienated them from the state. War-weariness and a desire for peace had been evident across the country since 1916, but housewives and war workers were rightly regarded as the most radically opposed to the continuation of the war. The starvation diet and the mistrust of the wartime authorities, allied with women's lack of identification with a state that did not recognise them as citizens, fuelled collective action. By 1918, working women had already eman-cipated themselves from the state; they laid the groundwork for the revolu-tion. In Russia, similar privations – food shortages, rising prices, low wages – plus anger at the government's inefficiency as well as the slaughter of men on the Eastern Front, fuelled working women's protests in St Petersburg and Moscow. Already by 1915 women were stoning and looting food markets and stores and engaging in strike action, but on 23 February 1917 (Russian calendar), International Women's Day, the food riots, strikes and the mass demonstration of women came together in the city of St Petersburg. 'The

Russian Revolution was begun by hungry women and children demanding bread and herrings', recorded one observer. 'They started by wrecking tram cars and looting a few small shops. Only later did they, together with workmen and politicians, become ambitious to wreck that mighty edifice the Russian autocracy.'[37] These were not organised or political women in any formal sense; they were workers and housewives, war-weary and tired of endless queues for food. As in Germany, their role was to destabilise the regime rather than to create a new one. The war had stimulated women's nascent political consciousness by asking them to play the role of producer and consumer but it gave them nothing in return.

WORKERS

War work has probably received more attention than any other aspect of women's wartime experience. The employment of women in the wartime industries drew attention to the female worker as never before. The independent wage-earner, the woman who stepped into a man's shoes – whether she be a tram conductor, a welder or a 'munitionette' – came to represent a new kind of female identity which would be both liberating (for women) and threatening (to men). Women workers symbolised the otherness of wartime in the transgression of gender boundaries. As workers, women were to be found in large numbers in hitherto male spaces – on the factory floor, at the wheel of a lorry or on the foot-plate of a tram. They even began to resemble men in their practical clothing of dungarees and overalls. And yet, despite the fact that it was almost universally recognised that women's labour was essential to the war effort, there existed a tension between this pragmatic understanding and concerns about woman's role as mother. It was these concerns that helped to counter demands for permanent change at the war's end.

Assessments of women's work experiences have formed the basis for far-reaching claims about the impact of the war on women's lives. For some historians, war work liberated women from the constraints of Victorian femininity and demonstrated to others that women were capable of carrying out 'men's jobs'. Others have argued that the war at best offered only limited progress, and at worst fuelled gender tensions that were to continue into the postwar years promoting a backlash against the woman worker. All are agreed, though, that the war years saw a significant shift in the kinds of jobs undertaken by women. On the other hand, it is clear that this structural change was not accompanied by a massive rise in the proportion of women in employment during the course of the war, nor did it result in a rise in the status of the woman worker. In Germany, for example, the percentage of women in paid work remained remarkably steady at around 35 per cent. There was some movement of women into traditionally male sectors of employment, but the vast majority were simply moving from other forms of work, that is there was no mass recruitment of 'war wives' or formerly non-working women.[38] In Bavaria, for instance, more than 40 per cent of female workers in the war industries had been factory workers before 1914; 28 per cent had not been previously employed but this figure included women just leaving education. Germany did not seriously begin to recruit women to munitions work until 1916. In Britain, where women constituted 38 per cent of the labour force in 1918 compared with 24 per cent in 1914, the movement of women workers away from domestic service and into a variety of employments was the most notable development early on. And in the first instance it was white-collar and service jobs that accommodated these women (accounting for 23 per cent of women entering employment since 1914), with munitions work some way behind with 14 per cent.[39] The most feminised sectors of the economy in 1918 were much the same as they had been in 1914: the clothing and textile trades, manufacturing, and teaching and nursing.[40] Many of the so-called new workers had previously been hidden in home work and the sweated trades, unnoticed and unrecognised; that is, they had been workers but invisible. Perhaps the greatest quantitative contribution of female workers to the war economy occurred in Russia, where the proportion of women in the workforce increased from 26 per cent at the beginning of the war to 43 per cent at its end. Yet in terms of patterns of employment and experiences of work, the position of Russian women workers was comparable to the situation farther west.[41]

At the war's outset women experienced high levels of unemployment as sectors deemed marginal to war production shed labour and domestic servants were let go in the name of releasing working-class girls for service to the nation. The consumer industries employing large numbers of female workers also declined. In August 1914, Louise Delétang, a Parisian seamstress, wrote in her diary that 'everywhere, there is a ceaseless chase for work . . . so many factories and boutiques have closed.'[42] The situation was no better for German women textile workers for whom survival was difficult in the absence of a male earner. Hence the scenes in Berlin in September 1914 on the occasion of work being made available to experienced seamstresses. 'The number of people applying for this work was unbelievable . . . The army of women and girls grew from hour to hour and filled the wide pavement . . . we saw between 7 to 8000 people standing there.'[43] By 1915–16, though, as serious labour shortages began to impact upon the war economy, women were brought in to fill industrial and public service jobs vacated by men sent to the front, and more especially they were employed en masse in munitions factories. Moreover, within certain sectors the kinds of jobs undertaken by women expanded. Women replaced men as weavers in the textile industry for example, and in the agricultural sector they virtually replaced men altogether. 'I had to do all the tasks the men used to do', recalled one Italian woman. 'I even had to unload the wheat, spread the wheatsheaves, help to thresh when the machine came around', all jobs traditionally undertaken by men.[44] Clearly the term 'war work' is something of a misnomer since so many women workers were doing jobs such as work in offices and transport not directly in the service of the war. But the demands of a war economy ensured that all female workers were assured that their work was in the national interest. By stepping into a man's shoes they were freeing him for the armed forces; by making armaments they were doing their bit to defeat the enemy.

War work was conceived of by governments and by some feminists as a woman's patriotic duty. 'Sex has nothing to do with patriotism or with the spirit of service', remarked the veteran suffrage campaigner Emmeline Pankhurst (1858–1928) in the summer of 1915. 'Women are just as eager to work for the nation as men are.' This was at a time when industry was desperate for workers to fulfil its contracts in the wake of the recruitment of Kitchener's volunteers and a munitions crisis.[45] For the president of the National Union of Women's Suffrage Societies, Millicent Garrett Fawcett, the state's dependence on women workers was a prime opportunity to show that women were 'worthy of citizenship'. German feminists adopted a similar line, advocating compulsory war service for women to complement the military service for men, but unlike their British counterparts, feminists such as Gertrud Bäumer (1873–1954) and Helene Lange emphasised women's special contribution in the field of welfare and social work which might be put to the service of the state. However, despite feminists' endorsement of patriotic service there is little evidence to suggest women flooded into the labour market motivated by patriotic fervour and a desire to serve their nation, let alone an expectation of political rights, with the exception perhaps of those amongst the wealthier classes who, in any case, preferred nursing to munitions work. Neither did legislation, where it was enacted, have any significant effect. German women proved remarkably resistant to the government's attempts to recruit them for auxiliary service, and when they did respond they preferred to do office work at home or to become 'rear-echelon helpers' behind the lines rather than to become munitions workers, largely on account of the better pay and the opportunities for greater independence.[46] Women worked during wartime because they had to. With their fathers and husbands away and government allowances inadequate to support a family, women needed to earn an income.

State propaganda valorised women workers, but attitudes of male workers and trade unionists were far less favourable, particularly in the skilled trades of traditional industries. Evidence from Britain, Germany and Russia shows that fears of substitution of male by female workers conditioned responses to women drafted into the engineering and shipbuilding industries. Nowhere was the stand-off between employers and the state on one side and trade unions on the other more protracted than on Clydeside near Glasgow. In order to enable women to fill jobs in the engineering and shipbuilding industries a process known as dilution of skill was introduced, the breaking down of skilled tasks into a number of smaller 'unskilled' ones, therefore enabling unskilled and untrained women to be employed on lower rates of pay. Male workers and their unions, perhaps correctly, saw this as a threat to traditional bastions of male employment which would result in an erosion of skilled trades and rates of pay at the war's end. In Germany, male workers offered similar resistance to the introduction of female co-workers in their reluctance to participate in the training of women. 'As trainers, men frequently make no effort to teach female replacement labour, whose competition they fear in the coming time of peace', remarked the Nuremberg War office in respect of mechanical engineering.[47] Women found themselves patronised by their foremen who were reluctant to accept that a fresh approach could be advantageous. 'Engineering mankind is possessed of the unshakeable opinion that no woman can have the mechanical sense', observed a British munitions worker.

> If one of us asks humbly why such and such an alteration is not made to prevent this or that drawback to a machine, she is told, with a superior smile, that a man has worked her machine before her for years, and that therefore if there were any improvement possible it would have been made. As long as we do exactly what we are told and do not attempt to use our brains, we give entire satisfaction . . . Any swerving from the easy path prepared for us by our males arouses the most scathing contempt in their manly bosoms.[48]

In Russia too, despite the Bolshevik entreaty to all workers, male and female, to work side by side in order to achieve the advancement of women, male workers showed a reluctance to accept women on equal terms. Huge numbers of women were employed in Russia's war industries but they were overwhelmingly concentrated in jobs designated as unskilled and thus paid less. The breadwinner ideology which had been so pervasive during the nineteenth century was hard to break down even in the extraordinary circumstances of wartime.[49]

Like the mill girl of the early industrial imagination who was perceived as disrupting notions of femininity, so the munitionette was constructed as a symbol of gender instabilities during wartime. Munitions workers were portrayed as predominantly young, single and working class, who revelled in the independence their wages gave them, and who had little thought of patriotic duty. They were prone to extravagance, amusement and inappropriate behaviour in wartime, and their practical clothing, coarse banter and their desire for equal wages prompted some to comment on the masculinisation of war workers. One young soldier pleaded with his fiancée: 'whatever you do, don't go in Munitions or anything in that line – just fill a woman's position and remain a woman – don't develop into one of those "things" that are doing men's work.'[50] 'When one looks at women these days', remarked a German government representative in 1917, 'one has to look closely in order to tell whether one is looking at a woman or a man.'[51] But of course there was no question of female war workers actually being treated as men, despite the fact that many of them were indeed breadwinners and heads of household. The perception that their role was temporary and subsidiary continued to determine the position of women workers in the war industries, a situation condemned by the British socialist and suffrage activist Sylvia Pankhurst (1882–1960). In addition to fair wages and satisfactory working conditions she further demanded that 'women who are enlisted as recruits in the National War Service shall have the Vote at once.'[52] Working women may have looked like men to some onlookers, and their work may have been regarded as a patriotic duty, but they were not treated like patriotic men; that is, they were still not regarded as equal citizens.

PATRIOTS AND PACIFISTS

In October 1914, just after the outbreak of war, a young upper middle-class English woman, Vera Brittain, wrote to her fiancé Roland Leighton who was about to be sent to France with his battalion. Vera had just gained a place at Oxford University.

> I don't know whether your feelings about war are those of a militarist or not. I always call myself a non-militarist, yet the raging of these elemental forces fascinates me, horribly, but powerfully, as it does you. You find beauty in it too; certainly war seems to bring out all that is noble in human nature, but against that you can say it brings out all the barbarous too. But whether it is noble or barbarous I am quite sure that had I

been a boy I should have gone off to take part in it long ago . . . Women get all the dreariness of war and none of its exhilaration.[53]

For Brittain and many others like her, the outbreak of war engendered feelings of patriotism and a desire to be involved. Few women were either wholeheartedly patriotic or ideologically pacifist, although by 1918 there were many more in the latter camp, Brittain included. Like many of her social contemporaries, Vera Brittain found an outlet for her patriotism in nursing. But her first-hand experience of war in Malta and then in France, coupled with the loss of so many of her young male friends including her fiancé, caused her to reflect in later years on her initial enthusiasm for war. 'Women are just as liable as men to be carried away by war-time emotion', she wrote in 1936, 'and deceived by the shining martial figure of patriotism'.[54]

In the first year or so of the war there were few means by which women could actively demonstrate their support for the war other than by releasing their menfolk to fight. In Britain there was an infamous white-feather campaign, whereby women attempted to shame men dressed in civilian clothing by sticking a white feather in their lapel. This symbolised one of the ways in which patriotism was gendered. According to Nicoletta Gullace, women were implicated in 'defining the perameters of male citizenship, while endowing women's traditional domestic, maternal and sexual roles with an openly expressed importance to the military state.'[55] However, many feminists argued that women's patriotic service to the nation should provide a justification for the widening of citizenship and specifically voting rights. In Britain, France, Germany and Austria, many of those who had been prominent in the suffrage struggle now called on feminists to demonstrate their loyalty to the nation. Feminist opposition to the war, on the other hand, was more widespread than some historians have given credit. Patriotism and pacifism were two sides of the same coin. Both stances gave women a platform upon which to proclaim their right to citizenship.

Nursing was one of the few front-line roles open to women during the war that was deemed acceptable despite nurses' proximity to combat and the horrors of war. Nursing, in contrast with factory work and military service, was characterised as a feminine vocation which incorporated the values associated with nineteenth-century womanliness: service and self-sacrifice in the guise of the 'angel of mercy' and the devoted mother. Nursing, particularly as it was promoted by the Red Cross in the years before 1914, was portrayed as requiring 'spirituality, self-abnegation and perfect submission to authority', ideally suited to women. Even the courage and heroism required of the military nurse were regarded as natural attributes of the mother. 'In truth', remarked César Legrand of the French Red Cross, 'what a tiny distance a woman must go to change herself into a nurse!'[56] However, prior to the First World War, female nurses had not been allowed to work in front-line medical units; during this war, though, they were mobilised alongside soldiers, they travelled to the front line with soldiers and they participated in the experiences of the battlefield.

The military nurse was the acceptable face of the patriotic woman who wanted to serve her country. Unlike the munitions workers and uniformed women in the auxiliary services, the nurse never compromised her femininity, or at least not in popular representations of her role. Indeed, nursing was the ultimate form of female national service, unthreatening to the masculinity of war and reaffirming women's duty to men. But those who volunteered regarded their work somewhat differently. Nursing was women's chance to contribute to their nation in its time of need, a means of expressing patriotism equal to that on offer to men. 'Defence was a man's job, and I, unfortunately, was a woman', wrote a British member of the Volunteer Aid Detachment (VAD), the military nursing service which provided nursing assistants for the professional medical services. 'And yet', she continued, 'the New Army of men would need a New Army of nurses. Why not go and learn to be a nurse while the Kitchener men were learning to be soldiers?'[57] 'This is a wild adventure I am on', wrote Ellie Rendel to her mother in 1916 from HMS *Huntspill*, having volunteered to serve with the Scottish Women's Hospital in Russia.[58] Similarly, German nurses expressed their patriotic desire to do their bit tinged with overtones of adventure and escape from a constrained and mundane existence, their accounts combining a sense of duty to serve with the excitement of the challenge ahead. 'My heart was thumping . . . it was a day of honour for us all', recalled one. 'Our faces were positively transfigured, all petty concerns forgotten.'[59]

However, the opportunity to serve alongside the military was compromised by the presumption that women's war service was an extension of domestic work and social duty. Such work was acceptable because it continued a tradition of middle-class women's philanthropic endeavour, albeit in quite different circumstances. Just as in the pre-war decades women had exported an ideology of domesticity to working-class homes, in wartime volunteer nurses, along with those who remained at home knitting socks and bandages and writing to pen-pal soldiers, were creating a kind of domesticity at the front. With few exceptions, nurses recorded their traumatic experiences tending to mutilated and dying men in terms of conventional family relations. They cast themselves in the roles of sisters and mothers to the young men – their brothers and sons – since often all they could do was comfort the wounded and dying. In their helplessness amidst the brutality, these young women reverted to the role they had been taught since childhood. The gap between their expectations of tending to heroic soldiers and their experiences of the reality of war forced many to fall back on the roles they knew so well. German nurses wrote in terms of comforting their children and singing lullabies to them as they died. It was a common reaction, as Mary Borden, an American writer and suffragette who financed a hospital in France, demonstrates in her observations of the nurse–invalid relationship: 'he awakes bewildered as children do, expecting, perhaps, to find himself at home with his mother leaning over him, and he moans a little and then lies still again. He is helpless, so we do for him what he cannot do for himself, and he is grateful.'[60]

For many of these nurses the experience of war was to mark them for the rest of their days. If we return to Vera Brittain we can witness a journey from youthful patriotism to more mature pacifism which was shared by many of her contemporaries and especially those who experienced the military hospitals. Brittain had volunteered to become a nurse so that she too could contribute to the war in an active way, just as her brothers and fiancé were doing. But her experience, especially in France, where as a VAD nurse she tended to wounded German prisoners, as well as her personal loss led her towards a pacifist position which she elucidated so well in her postwar autobiographical work *Testament of Youth* (1933). Brittain was not alone in having travelled this path. Surely expressing the sentiments of so many nurses, Helen Zenna Smith's fictional dramatisation of one woman's experience of war powerfully expressed how disillusionment could lead to an anti-war position:

> I have schooled myself to stop fainting at the sight of blood. I have schooled myself not to vomit at the smell of wounds and stale blood, but view these sad bodies with professional calm I shall never be able to. I may be helping to alleviate the sufferings of wretched men, but common sense rises up and insists that the necessity never should have arisen. I become savage at the futility. A war to end war my mother writes. Never . . .[61]

There was another, if less acceptable way, for a woman to demonstrate her patriotism, and that was by joining a paramilitary organisation or auxiliary service or, exceptionally, to engage in armed combat. By 1917, British women were recruited to auxiliary corps of the armed forces. Needless to say, members of the Women's Army Auxiliary Corps and the Women's Royal Naval Service and Air Force were not allowed anywhere near armed combat although British servicewomen were sent to the Western Front as drivers, signallers and clerical workers. The desire to 'do one's bit' was undoubtedly fuelled by patriotism in many cases, but women had other reasons for enlisting in the women's services, not least the perception that the wages would be better than factory work and an anticipation of adventure overseas.[62] The wearing of uniform by women in the British auxiliary services brought forth criticisms that they had not earned the right to wear it. Certainly for servicewomen, part of the attraction of uniform was its symbolic value, allowing women to appropriate male forms of war service. A second explanation for the unease with which females in uniform were greeted was the sense that dressing as a soldier symbolised a woman denying her femininity and questioning gender roles. Women's femininity entitled them to protection and it was the feminine woman who became the emblem of all that soldiers were fighting to defend. In Britain, khaki became the 'emblem of National Service', signifying sacrifice; women in uniform, at least until the end of the war, were regarded as dissimulators, assuming the badge of service whilst being unable to fulfil its demands (since they were forbidden to engage in combat) and thereby demeaning the soldier's role.[63] Whereas nurses were idealised as angels in white, cloaked in feminine garb and their heads modestly covered, the khaki-clad members of the British Women's Volunteer Reserve were dubbed Amazons by those who were uncomfortable about any association of women with the military. Ironically, though, these women were watched for unnecessary feminisation of their uniforms with jewellery, silk stockings and high-heeled shoes.[64] More seriously they were accused of being unpatriotic by wearing a uniform they did not deserve and thus pouring scorn on those who did wear it in the true defence of their country.

In Serbia and Russia, women did serve at the front, if in an unofficial capacity. It has been estimated that around 5000 Russian women, some in disguise, fought alongside men, continuing a tradition of female involvement in violence and unrest, and exploiting the Russian government's laxity in policing membership of the armed forces. Both upper-class and peasant women contributed to the Russian war effort in this way, but historians tend to argue that most did so for personal reasons; there was no agenda of equality underlying their actions. Indeed, the motivation of the most famous of female soldiers, Maria Bochkarëva, suggests that she was just as stirred by patriotism and a sense of duty as well as adventure as those who volunteered to be nurses. 'My soul was deeply stirred . . . "Go to war to help save the country!" a voice within me called . . . my heart yearned to be there in the seething cauldron of war, to be baptised in its fire and scorched in its lava.'[65]

Servicewomen and nurses embodied the contradictions of wartime. The uniformed paramilitaries, and even the 'Walküries in knickerbockers', as some nurses wearing boots and khaki were described, personified the breakdown of rigid gender divisions that assigned men to combat and women to the home front. These women were patriots, yet their work as nurses and as service auxiliaries drew them into fields of conflict not envisaged as the appropriate place for patriotic femininity. Their active engagement with the war forced many to re-evaluate their own identities, and in this sense the First World War must be seen as a crucible of change.

For other women the appropriate response to the war was opposition to war itself. Feminist pacifists, although standing at the opposite end of the ideological spectrum to patriotic servicewomen, came to be seen as a greater danger despite their use of the language of gender difference. Indeed, it was the pacifists' association of femininity with peace (and masculinity with war) that led them into conflict with the state because wartime governments were actively trying to reshape femininity as patriotic, expressed in service to the nation. The fact that feminist pacifism was internationalist, uniting women from the aggressor states, did little to enhance its reputation during the war. Perhaps even more threatening, though, was the feminist pacifist critique of male politics and the assertion that war was man-made. The logical conclusion to be drawn from this analysis was that the enfranchisement of women would change the way political disputes were handled. Pacifists, like patriots, were staking a claim to citizenship.

Pacifist women opposed war from a number of standpoints. Socialist feminists like Clara Zetkin opposed this war, like all wars, as a capitalist war that oppressed all working people, men and women. The majority of feminist pacifists, though, used moral arguments based on the belief in gender difference, emphasising women's role as mothers, as the moral sex, and as the victims of war. Drawing on Olive Schreiner's analysis of women's relationship to war in her *Woman and Labour* (1911), the British feminist Helene Swanwick (1864–1939) set out what has come to be seen as the feminist pacifist position:

[Women] are the life-givers and the home-makers. War kills or maims the children born of woman and tended by her; war destroys 'woman's place' – the home . . . Militarist states always tend to degrade women to the position of breeders and slaves . . . Women, whose physical force is specialised for the giving and nurture of life will never be able to oppose men with destructive force. If destructive force is to continue to dominate the world, then man must continue to dominate woman, to his and her lasting injury.[66]

Governments which listened to women's needs and which gave women a political voice would think twice before going to war. For Swanwick and others like the German feminists Anita Augsburg (1857–1943) and Lida Gustava Heymann (1867–1943), war exemplified male physical force both symbolically and actually. Heymann, echoing the atrocity stories that were rife in the early months of the war, drew attention to the physical violence of war in a vivid and brave acknowledgement of wartime rape. 'We do not want statements saying that we women are protected by war. No, we are being raped by war!'[67]

Feminist pacifism has been described as 'the creed of a minority, of a tiny band of courageous and principled women on the far-left fringes of bourgeois-liberal feminism.'[68] It is certainly true that many, indeed probably most, feminists supported their governments and suspended their campaigning during wartime. Pacifism split the feminist movement everywhere, not least in Britain where Swanwick and other leading suffrage activists like Maude Royden, Kate Courtney and Catherine Marshall, left the NUWSS in order to join hands with their pacifist sisters outside Britain. The significance of feminist pacifism goes further than a focus on the small band of activists would suggest. Anti-militarism had a broad base of support, especially amongst feminist and socialist women but also amongst women who merely recognised that war would achieve little. In the mill towns of north-west England, for example, there existed considerable grassroots support for the call for an end to the war and a mechanism to prevent war in the future. Furthermore, feminist pacifism was international; it crossed national borders and united women from aggressor states. 'We feel strongly that at a time when there is so much hatred among nations, we women must show that we can retain our solidarity and that we are able to maintain a mutual friendship', stated the Dutch feminist Dr Aletta Jacobs to an audience of women at an international women's peace congress in The Hague in 1915.[69] Their internationalism was a source and symbol of strength, of unity of purpose as women and as feminists, but it made them dangerous to national governments at a time of conflict. The British government tried to prevent women travelling to the Netherlands; in Germany, Clara Zetkin was jailed for her anti-war activity; and in France, all anti-war activity by women was closely monitored on the grounds that the apparent benign nature of women's pacifism was in fact all the more dangerous on account of the importance to the nation of women's morale. Louise Saumoneau was arrested and jailed for publicising her pacifist stance in the pages of her journal *La Femme Socialiste*.

The arrest and trial of the French socialist schoolteacher Hélène Brion (1882–1962) for so-called defeatism in 1918, was a defining moment for the history of women during this war, not only because of her spirited defence of her position – 'I am first and foremost a *feminist* . . . And it is because of my feminism that I am an enemy of war'[70] – but because of the way Brion was characterised as the antithesis of the good patriotic woman during wartime. But it was not only as an anti-militarist or 'defeatist' that Brion was on trial, but as a woman, a feminist, and as an alleged Malthusian, a supporter of birth control. Her defenders, sister feminists like Nelly Roussel, were moved to speak out on her behalf. 'I am proud of her as a Frenchwoman because the glory of a people is made not only by the warlike valour of soldiers but . . . also by the greatness of soul and generosity of heart'. She continued, 'Hélène Brion brings honour to France; she is a pure and true *Française*.'[71] For the French state, though, Brion was a traitor to France and to French women. She spent four months in prison and, although found guilty of treason, received a suspended sentence.

Women's pacifism, like their patriotism, was the ideological expression of an engagement with the war and with politics at a time when women had no political rights. The all-encompassing impact of this war in particular, coming after a period of sustained feminist campaigning for the vote, gave some women a new vigour leading them to question the government's definition of the female contribution to the war effort and forcing them to come to their own understanding of their position. Furthermore, feminist pacifism demanded a role for women in politics for they believed that only female enfranchisement would force a shift in the way politics was done. Indeed, both pacifists and patriots used the war to protest their exclusion from the privileges of citizenship and to demonstrate, in different ways, why they should be incorporated into national political life. For Hélène Brion, her arrest and trial provided the opportunity to make public the absurdity of the exclusion of women from politics when they were being asked to contribute so much to the nation.[72]

Many countries, including Germany, Austria, Czechoslovakia and Britain (limited to women over the age of 30), did enfranchise women at the end of the war, rewarding them for their sacrifices and their contribution to the war effort. Poland and Hungary did so in 1921 and 1925, respectively. By 1920 only France, Italy and Portugal amongst the belligerent nations had not taken this step. Only a small number of educated Portuguese women were enfranchised by the authoritarian Salazar regime in 1933. Although in France and Italy suffrage bills had been approved by parliament after the war, women had to wait until the end of another war for a chance to cast their votes.

CONCLUSIONS

The gender system which had been so painstakingly constructed over the course of the nineteenth century was not 'a casualty of war' but neither did it survive completely unscathed.[73] Both governments and women themselves contributed to the destabilising of gender identities, the former as a consequence of the need to maintain the war effort and the latter as a response to the demands and freedoms experienced in wartime conditions. Patterns of life were disrupted during the war years but traditional discourses on women's roles remained unquestioned and sometimes even were reinforced. So women were asked to make a significant contribution to the labour force but were castigated for spending their earnings freely. They were recruited as auxiliary servicewomen but criticised for wearing their patriotism. They were asked to be patriots but limits were placed on ways they might express their support for their nation. The sacrificial, silent, hardworking woman was far preferable to the independent-minded, sexually liberated woman who questioned her government or who exploited the conditions of wartime for her own pleasure or self-advancement. In these circumstances the gap between discourse and reality became unhinged for some women. The state never compromised on ways in which respectable femininity was configured, and yet it was unable to maintain a grip on women's changing sense of self. Whilst governments tried to discipline women's sexuality and became obsessed with morale they lost sight of changes in women's political consciousness fuelled by economic concerns. The temporary cessation of the feminist campaign for the vote concealed a more fundamental grassroots feminist consciousness emerging amongst many different groups of women and expressed in a variety of ways. Some used patriotism to escape the confines of a middle-class home and discover themselves as nurses or auxiliary servicewomen. Others, worn down by the dual burdens of work and family for four long years, resorted to direct action. A few expressed their feminism in pacifist activity.

Women were not the victors of this war because they made few concrete gains as a direct result of the conflict. Rather we should see the Great War as a time when the values of the previous century were reaffirmed whilst women were anticipating a future in which they played a greater role in national political and economic life. One of the causes of this partial collapse of gender roles was the blurring of the borders between the home front and the battlefield. Separate spheres, which had been the guiding principle for relations between the sexes since the French Revolution, was subject to immense strain during this war, but whilst governments and many men struggled to hold the line against women's incursions into male terrain, they were unable to prevent women developing a sense of self which demanded the recognition of their rightful place within the body politic.

NOTES

———◆———

Introduction

1. Marion Reid, *A Plea for Woman* (Edinburgh, 1843; this edition Edinburgh, 1988), p.29.
2. Ibid., pp.90–1.
3. J.F. McCaffrey, *Scotland in the Nineteenth Century* (Basingstoke, 1998), p.116.
4. Maïté Albistur quoted in G. Bock, 'Women's history and gender history: aspects of an international debate', *Gender and History* 1 (1989), pp.7–30, here p.7.
5. See T. Hareven, 'Family time and historical time', *Daedelus* 106 (1977), pp.57–70.
6. O. Hufton, *The Prospect Before Her. A History of Women in Western Europe*, Vol. 1, *1500–1800* (London, 1997); Bonnie G. Smith, *Changing Lives. Women in European History since 1700* (Lexington, MA, 1989).
7. Amanda Vickery, 'Golden age to separate spheres? A review of the categories and chronology of English women's history', *Historical Journal* 36 (1993), pp.383–414.
8. Judith M. Bennett, 'Confronting continuity', *Journal of Women's History* 9 (1997), pp.73–92, here p.76.
9. Ibid., p.83.
10. Hufton, *The Prospect Before Her*, p.488.
11. Hufton, 'Women in history: early modern Europe', *Past and Present* 101 (1983), pp.125–41.
12. Bennett, 'Confronting continuity', p.78.
13. Amanda Vickery, *The Gentleman's Daughter. Women's Lives in Georgian England* (New Haven and London, 1998), Introduction.
14. J.W. Scott, *Gender and the Politics of History* (New York, 1988), p.48.
15. G. Pomata, 'History particular and universal: on reading some recent women's history textbooks', *Feminist Studies* 19 (1993), pp.7–50, here p.42.
16. Maxine Berg, 'What difference did women's work make to the industrial revolution?', *History Workshop Journal* 35 (1993), pp.22–44.

Chapter 1: Body, Mind and Spirit

1. Jane Rendall, *The Origins of Modern Feminism* (Basingstoke, 1985), p.7.
2. On salon culture see Dena Goodman, 'Enlightenment salons: the convergence of female and philosophic ambitions', *Eighteenth Century Studies* 22 (1989), pp.329–50.
3. Dena Goodman, 'Women and the Enlightenment', in R. Bridenthal, S. Stuard and M. Wiesner, eds., *Becoming Visible: Women in European History* (3rd edn, Boston, MA, 1998), pp.233–64, here p.242.
4. Madame de Beaumer quoted in Karen Offen, *European Feminisms 1700–1950: A Political History* (Stanford, CA, 2000), p.39.

5. Margaret Ives, 'In praise of marriage: reflections on a poem by Gabrielle Baumberg (1766–1839)', in *Women Writers in the Age of Goethe*, Vol. VII (Lancaster, 1995), pp.3–17.

6. Patricia Meyer Spacks, ed., *Selections from the Female Spectator by Eliza Haywood* (Oxford, 1999), pp.123–4.

7. Jean-Jacques Rousseau, *Émile* (orig. 1762; London, 1993), p.388.

8. Quoted in Lyndal Roper, *Oedipus and the Devil. Witchcraft, Sexuality and Religion in Early Modern Europe* (London, 1994), p.191.

9. Thomas Laqueur, *Making Sex: Body and Gender from the Greeks to Freud* (Cambridge MA, 1995), p.150.

10. See Michel Foucault, *A History of Sexuality: An Introduction* (Harmondsworth, 1978).

11. Galen quoted in Thomas Laqueur, 'Orgasm, generation, and the politics of reproductive biology', in R. Shoemaker and M. Vincent, eds., *Gender and History in Western Europe* (London, 1998), pp.111–48, here p.115.

12. C. Bauhin (1605) quoted in Laqueur, 'Orgasm', pp.122–3.

13. Anthony Fletcher, *Gender, Sex and Subordination in England 1500–1800* (New Haven, CT, 1995), p.71.

14. See Cynthia Eagle Russett, *Sexual Science: The Victorian Construction of Womanhood* (Harvard, 1989).

15. Ludmilla Jordanova, *Sexual Visions: Images of Gender in Science and Medicine Between the Eighteenth and Twentieth Centuries* (London, 1989), p.40.

16. Elizabeth Fox-Genovese, 'Women and the Enlightenment', in R. Bridenthal, C. Koonz and S. Stuard, eds., *Becoming Visible: Women in European History* (2nd edn, Boston, 1987), pp.251–77, here p.268.

17. Barbara Duden, *The Woman Beneath the Skin: A Doctor's Patients in Eighteenth Century Germany* (London and Cambridge, MA, 1991), p.20.

18. Barbara Duden, *Der Frauenleib als öffentliche Ort* (Hamburg and Zurich 1991), translated as *Disembodying Women: Perspectives on Pregnancy and the Unborn* (Cambridge, MA, 1993).

19. Jane Ussher, *Women's Madness. Misogyny or Mental Illness?* (London 1991), p.69.

20. Quoted in Janet Beizer, *Ventriloquized Bodies: Narratives of Hysteria in Nineteenth Century France* (London, 1994), p.37.

21. Michelet quoted in Patricia Vertinsky, *The Eternally Wounded Woman* (Manchester, 1990), p.49.

22. Ibid.

23. Barbara Ehrenreich and Deirdre English, *For Her Own Good:150 Years of the Experts' Advice to Women* (London, 1979), p.94.

24. Dr Barnes quoted in Vertinsky, *Eternally Wounded Woman*, p.91.

25. Quoted ibid., p.62, note 41.

26. Quoted in Beizer, *Ventriloquized Bodies*, p.49.

27. The reference to over-exalted dreams is drawn from the experience of Emma Bovary in Gustave Flaubert's *Madame Bovary* (1856–57).

28. On the rest cure see Charlotte Perkins Gilman, *The Yellow Wallpaper* (orig. 1899; New York, 1973).

29. Elaine Showalter, *The Female Malady: Women, Madness and English Culture, 1830–1980* (London, 1987), p.128.

30. See Ruth Harris, *Murders and Madness. Medicine, Law and Society in the Fin de Siècle* (Oxford, 1989).

31. Ornella Moscucci, *The Science of Woman: Gynaecology and Gender in England 1800–1929* (Cambridge, 1990).

32. Isaac Baker Brown (1866) in Sheila Jeffreys, ed., *The Sexuality Debates* (London, 1987), pp.16–17.

33. Quoted in Ehrenreich and English, *For Her Own Good*, p.112.

34. Roper, *Oedipus and the Devil*, p.17.

35. Kathleen Canning, 'Feminist history after the linguistic turn: historicizing discourse and experience', *Signs* 19 (1994), pp.368–404, here pp.385–6.

36. Quoted in Edward Shorter, *Women's Bodies: A Social History of Women's Encounter with Health, Ill-health, and Medicine* (New Brunswick, NJ, 1991), p.287.

37. Ulinka Rublack, 'The public body: policing abortion in early modern Germany', in L. Abrams and E. Harvey, eds., *Gender Relations in German History: Power, Agency and Experience from the Sixteenth to the Twentieth Century* (London, 1996), pp.57–79.

38. See Lindsay Wilson, *Women and Medicine in the French Enlightenment: The Debate over 'Maladies des Femmes'* (Baltimore, 1993).

39. Isabel Hull, 'The body as historical experience; review of recent works by Barbara Duden', *Central European History* 28 (1995), pp.73–9, here p.74.

40. Shetland Archives: AD 22/2/38/42, Precognition, Robina Ritch or Pennant, 14 June 1903.

41. See Catherine Fouquet, 'The unavoidable detour: must a history of women begin with the history of their bodies?', in M. Perrot, ed., *Writing Women's History* (Oxford, 1984), pp.51–60.

42. Stephen Wilson, *The Magical Universe. Everyday Ritual and Magic in Pre-modern Europe* (London, 2000), pp.156–60.

43. Quoted in Shorter, *Women's Bodies*, p.104.

44. David Cressy, *Birth, Marriage and Death. Ritual, Religion, and the Life-cycle in Tudor and Stuart England* (Oxford, 1997), pp.197–229; Wilson, *The Magical Universe*, pp.253–7.

45. Shorter, *Women's Bodies*, p.239.

46. Rousseau, *Émile*, p.385.

47. Quoted in Roper, *Oedipus and the Devil*, p.19.

48. Gervase Markham, *The English Housewife*, ed. M. Best (orig.1615; Montreal, 1986), p.8. *The Day Star*, 1855.

49. *Free Church Magazine* (1844).

50. *The Day Star*, Vol. X (1854), pp.301–5.

51. Mary Wollstonecraft, *A Vindication of the Rights of Woman* (orig. 1792; London, 1985), p.68.

52. Rousseau, *Émile*, p.393.

53. Wollstonecraft, *Vindication*, p.69.

54. Ibid., pp.181–2.

55. Ibid., p.69.

56. Tombstone in North Walsham parish church, Norfolk, England.

57. Quoted in Lee Davidoff and Catherine Hall, *Family Fortunes. Men and Women of the English Middle Class, 1780–1850* (London, 1987), p.114.

58. Marina Warner, *Alone of All Her Sex: The Myth and the Cult of the Virgin Mary* (London, 1976), pp.334–5.

59. John Angell James quoted in Hugh McLeod, *Religion and Society in England 1850–1914* (Basingstoke, 1996), p.161.

60. Barbara Welter, 'The cult of true womanhood: 1820–1860', *American Quarterly* 18 (1966), pp.151–74.

61. Barbara Taylor, *Eve and the New Jerusalem: Socialism and Feminism in the Nineteenth Century* (London, 1983), p.127.

62. G. Malmgreen, ed., *Religion in the Lives of English Women 1760–1930* (London, 1986), p.3.

63. Quoted in Heide Wunder, 'Gender norms and their enforcement in early modern Germany', in Abrams and Harvey, eds., *Gender Relations in German History*, pp.39–56, here p.42.

64. Fletcher, *Gender, Sex and Subordination*, p.363.

65. Hugh McLeod, *Religion and the People of Western Europe 1789–1989* (Oxford, 1997), p.28.

66. Ralph Gibson, *A Social History of French Catholicism 1789–1914* (London, 1989), pp.180–1.

67. Hugh McLeod, *Piety and Poverty: Working-class Religion in London, Berlin and New York 1870–1914* (New York, 1996), p.163.

68. Callum G. Brown, *The Death of Christian Britain: Understanding Secularisation 1800–2000* (London, 2000), p.156.

69. McLeod, *Piety and Poverty*, pp.158–64.

70. Pirjo Markkola, 'Introduction: the Lutheran context of Nordic women's history', in Markkola, ed., *Gender and Vocation. Women, Religion and Social Change in the Nordic Countries, 1830–1940* (Helsinki, 2000), pp.9–25, here pp.16–17.

71. McLeod, *Piety and Poverty*, p.162.

72. Bonnie Smith, *Ladies of the Leisure Class: The Bourgeoisie of Northern France in the Nineteenth Century* (Princeton, NJ, 1981), pp.99–101.

73. Gibson, *Social History of French Catholicism*, p.153.

74. David Blackbourn, *The Marpingen Visions. Rationalism, Religion and the Rise of Modern Germany* (London 1995), p.28.

75. Gibson, *Social History of French Catholicism*, pp.146–7.

76. Blackbourn, *Marpingen Visions*, pp.293–5.

77. Smith, *Ladies of the Leisure Class*, pp.95–6.

78. Deborah Valenze, *Prophetic Sons and Daughters: Female Preaching and Popular Religion in Industrial England* (Princeton, NJ, 1985), p.9.

79. Anna Clark, *The Struggle for the Breeches: Gender and the Making of the British Working Class* (London, 1995), pp.108–9.

80. E. Baumann (1880) quoted in McLeod, *Piety and Poverty*, pp.165–6.

81. See Callum G. Brown, *Religion and Society in Scotland since 1707* (Edinburgh, 1997), pp.196–8.

82. Rendall, *Origins of Modern Feminism*, p.73.

83. Gibson, *Social History of French Catholicism*, pp.106–7.

84. Quoted in McLeod, *Religion and Society in England*, p.161.

85. Catherine M. Prelinger, 'Prelude to consciousness. Amalie Sieveking and the Female Association for the Care of the Poor and the Sick', in J. Fout, ed., *German Women in the Nineteenth Century: A Social History* (New York and London, 1984), pp.118–32.

86. See Judith Rowbotham, '"Soldiers of Christ"? Images of female missionaries in late nineteenth-century Britain: issues of heroism and martyrdom', *Gender and History* 12 (2000), pp.82–106.

87. H. Goldschmidt cited in Ann Taylor Allen, *Feminism and Motherhood in Germany 1800–1914* (New Brunswick, NJ, 1991), p.95.

88. Rev. Binney quoted in Davidoff and Hall, *Family Fortunes*, p.118.

Chapter 2: Learning to be a Woman

1. Merry E.Wiesner, 'Guilds, male bonding and women's work in early modern Germany', in M.E. Wiesner, *Gender, Church and State in Early Modern Germany* (London, 1998), pp.163–77, here p.168.

2. Wunder, 'Gender norms and their enforcement', p.43.

3. L. Davidoff, 'Catching the greased pig: domesticity and feminist history', in A. Petó and M. Pittaway, eds., *Women in History – Women's History: Central and Eastern European Perspectives* (Budapest, 1994), pp.11–19, here p.14.

4. Smith, *Ladies of the Leisure Class*, p.17.

5. A. Clark, review of Vickery, *The Gentleman's Daughter*, in *Reviews in History*, www.ihrinfo.ac.uk/reviews (1998).

6. Rousseau, *Émile*, p.399.

7. See Barbara Corrado Pope, 'The influence of Rousseau's ideology of domesticity', in M.J. Boxer and J.H. Quataert, eds., *Connecting Spheres. European Women in a Globalizing World* (Oxford, 1987), pp.136–43, here p.143.

8. In U. Frevert, *Women in German History. From Bourgeois Emancipation to Sexual Liberation* (Oxford, 1989), p.34.

9. C.M. Wieland, 'Die ideale Gattin', in A. van Dülmen, ed., *Frauen: Ein historisches Lesebuch* (Munich, 1995), p.90.

10. Ibid.

11. *The General Baptist Repository and Missionary Observer*, February 1840, No.14, p.34.

12. Catherine Hall, 'The early formation of Victorian domestic ideology', in Shoemaker and Vincent, eds., *Gender and History in Western Europe*, pp.181–96.

13. More, 'Strictures on the Modern System of Female Education' (1799), in S.G. Bell and K.M. Offen, eds., *Women, the Family, and Freedom*, Vol. 1 (Stanford, CA, 1983), p.88.

14. S. Stickney Ellis, 'The Wives of England' (1843), ibid., pp.193–4.

15. Rendall, *Origins of Modern Feminism*, p.115.

16. Pirjo Markkola, 'The calling of women: gender, religion and social reform in Finland, 1860–1920', in Markkola, ed., *Gender and Vocation*, pp.113–45.

17. Vicomte de Bonald, 'De l'éducation des femmes' (1802), in Bell and Offen, eds., *Women, the Family, and Freedom*, Vol. 1, pp.90–1.

18. Rev. John Gregg, 'Women: A lecture delivered in Trinity Church' (1856), in M. Luddy, ed., *Women in Ireland 1800–1918* (Cork, 1995), p.14.

19. S. La Roche, 'Tageslauf', in van Dülmen, ed., *Frauen*, pp.107–8. See also Frevert, *Women in German History*, p.50.

20. S. Meyer, 'The tiresome work of conspicuous leisure: on the domestic duties of the wives of civil servants in the German Empire (1871–1918)', in Boxer and Quataert, eds., *Connecting Spheres* (2nd edn, Oxford, 2000), pp.185–93.

21. Clark, *Struggle for the Breeches*, p.178.

22. *L'Atelier* (1844) in Bell and Offen, eds., *Women, the Family and Freedom*, Vol. 1, pp.230–1.

23. Staatsarchiv Hamburg: N 1729, 1860; P II B 542, 19 Jan. 1860. See Lynn Abrams, 'Restabilisierung der Geschlechterverhältnisse: Die Konstruktion und Repräsentation von Männlichkeit und Weiblichkeit in Scheidungsprozessen des 19. Jahrhunderts', *Westfälische Forschungen* 45 (1995), pp.9–25.

24. *Patriot* (1804) quoted in J. Tovrov, 'Mother–child relationships among the Russian nobility', in D.L. Ransel, ed., *The Family in Imperial Russia* (Urbana, IL, 1976), pp.15–43, here p.34.

25. Smith, *Ladies of the Leisure Class*, pp.166–7.

26. Barbara Caine, *Destined to be Wives. The Sisters of Beatrice Webb* (Oxford, 1986), p.31.

27. See Carole Dyhouse, 'Mothers and daughters in the middle-class home, c.1870–1914', in Jane Lewis, ed., *Labour and Love* (Oxford, 1986), pp.38–40.

28. K. Milde, 'Der deutschen Jungfrau Wesen und Wirken' (1888), quoted in I. Schraub, *Zwischen Salon und Mädchenkammer. Frauen in Biedermeier und Kaiserzeit* (Hamburg, 1992), p.32.

29. Braun quoted in Y. Schütze, 'Mutterliebe–Vaterliebe. Elternrolle in der bürgerlichen Familie des 19. Jahrhunderts', in U. Frevert, ed., *Bürgerinnen und Bürger* (Göttingen, 1988), pp.118–33, here p.125.

30. Power Cobbe, 'The Duties of Women' (1881), quoted in John Gillis, *A World of Their Own Making: A History of Myth and Ritual in Family Life* (Oxford, 1997), p.123.

31. Quoted ibid., p.125.

32. Ellen Ross, *Love and Toil: Motherhood in Outcast London 1870–1918* (Oxford, 1993); Anna Davin, *Growing Up Poor: Home, School and Street in London 1870–1914* (London, 1996).

33. Colin Heywood, 'On learning gender roles during childhood in nineteenth century France', *French History* 5 (1991), pp.451–66, here pp.459–60.

34. Quoted in John Burnett, ed., *Destiny Obscure. Autobiographies of Childhood, Education and Family from the 1820s to the 1920s* (London, 1982), p.226.

35. Quoted in John Fout, 'The woman's role in the German working-class family in the 1890s from the perspective of women's autobiographies', in Fout, ed., *German Women in the Nineteenth Century* (New York and London, 1984), pp.295–319, here p.311.

36. Ross, *Love and Toil*, p.154.

37. Ellen Ross, 'Survival networks: women's neighbourhood sharing in London before World War One', *History Workshop Journal* 15 (1983), pp.4–27.

38. Hogg, 'Schoolchildren as wage earners' (1897), quoted in Davin, *Growing Up Poor*, p.173.

39. Lynn Jamieson, 'Limited resources and limiting conventions: working-class mothers and daughters in urban Scotland c.1890–1925', in Lewis, ed., *Labour and Love*, pp.49–69.

40. Lynn Jamieson and Clare Toynbee, *Country Bairns: Growing Up 1900–1930* (Edinburgh, 1992).

41. Smith, *Ladies of the Leisure Class*, p.168.

42. Quoted in Pat Jalland, *Women, Marriage and Politics, 1860–1914* (Oxford, 1986), p.12.

43. Quoted in Barbara Alpern Engel, 'Mothers and daughters: family patterns and the female intelligentsia', in Ransel, ed., *The Family in Imperial Russia*, pp.44–59, here p.51.

44. Quoted in Frevert, *Women in German History*, p.34.

45. Renate Möhrmann, ed., *Frauenemanzipation im deutschen Vormärz* (Stuttgart, 1978), p.15; Frevert, *Women in German History*, p.36.

46. Quoted in Jalland, *Women, Marriage and Politics*, p.12.

47. Wollstonecraft, *Vindication*, p.32.

48. Ibid., p.164.

49. Aimé-Martin in Bell and Offen, eds., *Women, the Family, and Freedom*, Vol. 1, p.166.

50. Hamilton, 'Letters on the Elementary Principles of Education' (1803), quoted in Rendall, *Origins of Modern Feminism*, p.111.

51. Napoleon I (1807), in Bell and Offen, eds., *Women, the Family, and Freedom*, Vol. 1, p.95.

52. Quoted in James C. Albisetti, *Schooling German Girls and Women: Secondary and Higher Education in the Nineteenth Century* (Princeton, NJ, 1988), pp.6, 13.

53. Albisetti, *Schooling German Girls*, p.12; Sharif Gemie, *Women and Schooling in France, 1815–1914. Gender, Authority and Identity in the Female Schooling Sector* (Keele, 1995), pp.60–7.

54. Quoted in D. Ladj-Teichmann, 'Weibliche Bildung im 19. Jahrhundert: Fesselung von Kopf, Hand und Herz?', in I. Brehmer *et al.*, eds., *Frauen in der Geschichte IV* (Düsseldorf, 1983), p.229.

55. S. Alberg, 'Briefe über Mädchenbildung' (1852), in Brehmer *et al.*, eds., *Frauen in der Geschichte*, p.230.

56. Quoted in Danuta Rzepniewska, 'Women of the landowning class in the Polish Kingdom in the 19th century', *Acta Poloniae Historica* 74 (1996), pp.97–120, here pp.100–1.

57. Laura S. Strumingher, 'L'ange de la maison. Mothers and daughters in nineteenth century France', *International Journal of Women's Studies* 2 (1979), pp.51–61, here p.54.

58. Francinet (1869) cited in Laura S. Strumingher, *What were Little Girls and Boys Made of? Primary Education in Rural France, 1830–1880* (Albany, NY,1983), p.28.

59. Elisabeth Meyer-Renschhausen, *Weibliche Kultur und Sozialer Arbeit: eine Geschichte der Frauenbewegung am Beispiel Bremens 1810–1927* (Cologne, 1989), pp.20–1.

60. Allen, *Feminism and Motherhood*, pp.32–3.

61. Albisetti, *Schooling German Girls,* pp.18–20.

62. Davidoff and Hall, *Family Fortunes*, pp.289–93.

63. Quoted in Gemie, *Women and Schooling in France*, p.76.

64. Quoted in Linda L. Clark, 'The primary education of French girls: pedagogical prescriptions and social realities, 1880–1940', *History of Education Quarterly* 21 (1981), pp.411–28, here p.411.

65. 'Reading Book for the Use of Female Schools' (Dublin, 1846), in Luddy, *Women in Ireland*, pp.98–9.

66. Carol Dyhouse, *Girls Growing Up in Late Victorian and Edwardian England* (London, 1981), p.83.
67. See Annemarie Turnbull, 'Learning her womanly work: the elementary school curriculum, 1870–1914', in F. Hunt, ed., *Lessons for Life: The Schooling of Girls and Women, 1850–1950* (Oxford, 1987), pp.83–100, here pp.88–92.
68. E. Sellers (1911) quoted in Carol Dyhouse, 'Towards a "feminine" curriculum for English schoolgirls: the demands of ideology 1870–1963', *Women's Studies International Quarterly* 1 (1978), pp.297–311, here p.300.
69. Elizabeth Roberts, 'Learning and living – socialisation outside school', *Oral History* 3 (1975), p.14–28.
70. Linda L. Clark, 'The socialization of girls in the primary schools of the Third Republic', *Journal of Social History* 15 (1981–2), pp.685–97, here p. 690.
71. Tod, 'On the education of girls of the middle classes' (1874), in Luddy, *Women in Ireland*, pp.108–9.
72. Quoted in Albisetti, *Schooling German Girls*, p.148.
73. Albisetti, *Schooling German Girls*, pp.99–104.
74. Dyhouse, *Girls Growing Up*, pp.165–9.
75. S. Mitchell, 'The forgotten women of the period: penny weekly family magazines of the 1840s and 1850s', in M. Vicinus, ed., *A Widening Sphere* (Bloomington, IN, 1977), pp.29–51; Margaret Beetham, *A Magazine of her Own? Domesticity and Desire in the Woman's Magazine 1800–1914* (London, 1996).
76. S.R. Williams, 'The true "Cymraes": images of women in women's nineteenth century Welsh periodicals', in A.V. John, ed., *Our Mothers' Land: Chapters in Welsh Women's History, 1830–1939* (Cardiff, 1991), pp.69–92, p.74.
77. Strumingher, *What Were Little Girls and Boys Made Of?*, pp.49ff.
78. Deborah Gorham, 'The ideology of femininity and reading for girls, 1850–1914', in Hunt, ed., *Lessons for Life*, pp.39–59, here pp.43–5; L.L. Clark, *Schooling the Daughters of Marianne* (New York, 1984), pp.46–8.
79. Judith Rowbotham, *Good Girls Make Good Wives: Guidance for Girls in Victorian Fiction* (Oxford, 1989), ch.1.
80. E. Harvey, 'Private fantasy and public intervention: girls' reading in Weimar Germany', in J. Birkett and E. Harvey, eds., *Determined Women. Studies in the Construction of the Female Subject, 1900–90* (Basingstoke, 1991), pp.38–67, here pp.42–50.
81. Rowbotham, *Good Girls make Good Wives*, pp.21–2.
82. See Brown, *Death of Christian Britain*, pp.69–87.
83. Clark, *Schooling the Daughters of Marianne*, p.37.
84. Cowper quoted in Rowbotham, *Good Girls make Good Wives*, pp.15–17.
85. Gorham, 'The ideology of femininity', pp.48–52.
86. See Rowbotham, *Good Girls Make Good Wives*, pp.33–40.
87. D.Grenz, '"Das eine sein und das andere auch sein . . ." Über die Widerspruchlichkeit des Frauenbildes am Beispiel der Mädchenliteratur', in Brehmer *et al.*, eds., *Frauen in der Geschichte*, pp.291–2.
88. See J. Jacobi-Dittrich, 'Growing up female in the nineteenth century', in Fout, ed., *German Women in the Nineteenth Century*, pp.197–217, here pp.204–5.
89. Strumingher, 'L'ange de la maison', pp.54–5.

Chapter 3: Marriage

1. Jalland, *Women, Marriage and Politics*, p.47.
2. See Lynn Abrams, 'The personification of inequality: challenges to gendered power relations in the nineteenth-century divorce court', *Archiv für Sozialgeschichte* 38 (1998), pp.41–55.
3. Quoted in Frevert, *Women in German History*, p.40.
4. Davidoff and Hall, *Family Fortunes*, p.322.
5. R.J. Evans, 'Family and class in the Hamburg grande bourgeoisie 1815–1914', in D. Blackbourn and R.J. Evans, eds., *The German Bourgeoisie* (London, 1991), pp.115–39.
6. Jane Austen, *Pride and Prejudice* (orig. 1813; Ware, 1992,), p.10.
7. Caine, *Destined to be Wives*, p.72.
8. Quoted in P. Borscheid, 'Romantic love or material interest: choosing marriage partners in nineteenth century Germany', *Journal of Family History* 11 (1986), pp.157–68, here p.160.
9. L. Aston, 'Meine Emancipation, Verweisung und Rechtfertigung' (1846), in Möhrmann, ed., *Frauenemanzipation im deutschen Vormärz*, pp.68–9.
10. Staatsarchiv Hamburg: N 1226, 1850; Lynn Abrams, 'Women writers and the "problem of marriage" in early 19th century Germany', in *Women Writers in the Age of Goethe: VII* (Lancaster, 1995), pp.18–31.
11. A.G. Meyer, 'The radicalization of Lily Braun', in Fout, ed., *German Women in the Nineteenth Century*, pp.218–33.
12. J. Knodel, 'Law, marriage and illegitimacy in nineteenth-century Germany', *Population Studies* 20 (1967), pp.279–94, here p.282.
13. J. Hajnal, 'European marriage patterns in perspective', in D.V. Glass and D.E.C. Eversley, eds., *Population in History: Essays in Historical Demography* (Chicago, 1965), pp.101–43.
14. Martine Segalen, *Love and Power in the Peasant Family: Rural France in the Nineteenth Century* (Oxford, 1983), p.17.
15. Miriam Cohen, *Workshop to Office. Two Generations of Italian Women in New York City, 1900–1950* (Ithaca, NY, 1992), p.20.
16. Borscheid, 'Romantic love', p.165.
17. John Gillis, *For Better, For Worse. British Marriages, 1600 to the Present* (Oxford, 1985), pp.113–14.
18. Barbara W. Robertson, 'In bondage: the female farm worker in south east Scotland', in E. Gordon and E. Breitenbach, eds., *The World is Ill Divided* (Edinburgh, 1990), pp.117–35.
19. Gillis, *For Better, For Worse*, pp.121–2.
20. See Gillis, *World of Their Own Making*, pp.134–51.
21. From the Commonplace book of Mary Young (1828), in Davidoff and Hall, *Family Fortunes*, p.397.
22. See Karin Hausen, '". . . eine Ulme für das schwanke Efau". Ehepaare im Bildungsbürgertum. Ideale und Wirklichkeiten im späten 18. und 19. Jahrhundert', in Frevert, ed., *Bürgerinnen und Bürger*, pp.85–117. Hausen traces the image to an

1855 publication, *Aus dem Frauenleben* although it was a common trope in the early decades of the century in England. See Davidoff and Hall, *Family Fortunes*, p.325, for another example.

23. Quoted in S. Foster, *Victorian Women's Fiction: Marriage, Freedom and the Individual* (London, 1985), p.51.
24. In Bell and Offen, eds., *Women, the Family, and Freedom*, Vol. 1, p.31.
25. Ibid., pp.39–40.
26. Ibid., p.33.
27. Quoted in Robert Shoemaker, *Gender in English Society 1650–1850* (London, 1998), p.102.
28. Judith Bennett, 'Medieval women, modern women: across the great divide', in D. Aers, ed., *Culture and History 1350–1600: Essays in English Communities, Identities and Writing* (London, 1992), pp.147–76, here p.154.
29. A.J. Hammerton, *Cruelty and Companionship: Conflict in Nineteenth Century Married Life* (London, 1992), p.2.
30. See Fletcher, *Gender, Sex and Subordination*, pp.190–1.
31. See, for example, Nancy Tomes, 'A "torrent of abuse": crimes of violence between working-class men and women in London, 1840–1875', *Journal of Social History* 11 (1978), pp. 328–45; Ellen Ross, '"Fierce questions and taunts": married life in working-class London, 1870–1914', *Feminist Studies* 8 (1982), pp.575–602.
32. Staatsarchiv Hamburg: PII B583: Burmeister, 1850.
33. Hammerton, *Cruelty and Companionship*, pp.83–9.
34. Ibid., p.89.
35. Ibid., p.89. See also the case of Frances and John Curtis described at pp.91–4. John was said by his wife to carry 'the idea of his authority to a mania'.
36. David W. Sabean, *Property, Production and Family in Neckarhausen, 1700–1870* (Cambridge, 1990), pp.166–74.
37. See Lynn Abrams, 'Whores, whore-chasers and swine: the regulation of sexuality and the restoration of order in the nineteenth-century German divorce court', *Journal of Family History* 21 (1996), pp.267–80.
38. Hauptstaatsarchiv Düsseldorf: Cleve Landgericht, Rep. 7/254: 6 May 1842.
39. Hammerton, *Cruelty and Companionship*, p.101.
40. Quoted in O. Kenyon, ed., *800 Years of Women's Letters* (Stroud, 1992), p.111.
41. Peter Gay, *The Bourgeois Experience. Victoria to Freud, Vol.1, Education of the Senses* (London, 1984), p.458.
42. Jalland, *Women, Marriage and Politics*, p.73.
43. G.E. Jensen, 'Henriette Schleiermacher. A woman in a traditional role', in Fout, ed., *German Women in the Nineteenth Century*, pp.88–103.
44. Quoted in Jalland, *Women, Marriage and Politics*, pp.127–9.
45. Quoted in A-C. Trepp, 'Gender relations in bourgeois marriages between 1770 and 1850: limits and possibilities', unpublished paper 1997, p.16.
46. Ibid., p.20.
47. James F. McMillan, *Housewife or Harlot: The Place of Women in French Society 1870–1940* (Brighton, 1981), p.35.

48. Quoted in Frevert, *Women in German History*, p.134.

49. Quoted in Trepp, 'Gender relations', p.23.

50. L. Davidoff, M. Doolittle, J. Fink and K. Holden, *The Family Story: Blood, Contract and Intimacy, 1830–1960* (London, 1998), p.120.

51. E. Shorter, *The Making of the Modern Family* (London, 1977).

52. See J.M. Phayer, *Sexual Liberation and Religion in Nineteenth Century Europe* (London, 1977).

53. Shetland Archives: SC 12/6/1884/55, 28 Oct. 1884.

54. Shetland Archives: SC 12/6/1867/2, 4 Jan. 1867. For similar cases see Ginger S. Frost, *Promises Broken. Courtship, Class and Gender in Victorian England* (Charlottesville, VA, 1995).

55. Quoted in Clark, *Struggle for the Breeches*, p.65.

56. Staatsarchiv Hamburg: P II, B 235: Berott, 1845/6.

57. Leah Leneman, *Alienated Affections: the Scottish Experience of Divorce and Separation, 1684–1830* (Edinburgh, 1998), p.13.

58. *Statistisches Jahrbuch für das Deutsche Reich* 28 (1907), p.22; 42 (1921–2), p.48.

59. Lawrence Stone, *Road to Divorce. England 1530–1987* (Oxford, 1990), p.435, table 13.1.

60. Thomas Erskine quoted in Stone, *Road to Divorce*, p.231.

61. Staatsarchiv Hamburg: P II C 73: 2 May 1835.

62. D.A. Kent, '"Gone for a Soldier": Family breakdown and the demography of desertion in a London parish, 1750–91', *Local Population Studies* 45 (1990), pp.27–42.

63. Roderick Phillips, *Untying the Knot: A Short History of Divorce* (Cambridge, 1991), p.172.

64. Clark, *Struggle for the Breeches*, p.70.

65. Ibid., p.71.

66. Hauptstaatsarchiv Düsseldorf: Cleve Landgericht, Rep. 7/225: 7 May 1853.

67. See Abrams, 'Whores, whore-chasers and swine'; Sabean, *Property, Production and Family*, pp.124–46.

68. S. Möhle, *Ehekonflikte und sozialer Wandel. Göttingen 1740–1840* (Frankfurt-am-Main, 1997).

69. Clarke, *Struggle for the Breeches*, p.79.

70. Regina Wecker, *Zwischen Ökonomie und Ideologie: Arbeit im Lebenszusammenhang von Frauen im Kanton Basel-Stadt 1870–1910* (Zurich, 1997), pp.228–92. See also Lynn Abrams, 'Martyrs or matriarchs? Working-class women's experience of marriage in Germany before the First World War', *Women's History Review* 1 (1992), pp.357–76.

71. Ross, 'Fierce questions and taunts', pp.575–6.

72. Maryanne Kowaleski, 'Singlewomen in medieval and early modern Europe. The demographic perspective', in J.M. Bennett and A.M. Froide, eds., *Singlewomen in the European Past 1250–1800* (Philadelphia, 1999), pp.38–81, here pp.52–3.

73. Olwen Hufton, 'Women without men: widows and spinsters in Britain and France in the eighteenth century', *Journal of Family History* 9 (1984)', pp.355–76, here p.358.

74. Slater quoted in Pamela Sharpe, 'Dealing with love: the ambiguous independence of the single woman in early modern England', *Gender and History* 11 (1999), pp.209–32, here p.210.

75. Hufton, 'Women without men', p.356.
76. Quoted in A.M. Froide, 'Marital status as a category of difference. Singlewomen and widows in early modern England', in Bennett and Froide, eds., *Singlewomen*, pp.236–69, here p.236.
77. See Martha Vicinus, *Independent Women: Work and Community for Single Women 1850–1920* (London, 1985); Davidoff *et al.*, *The Family Story*, pp.221–43.
78. Margaret R. Hunt, 'The sapphic strain: English lesbians in the long eighteenth century', in Bennett and Froide, eds., *Singlewomen*, pp.270–96, here pp.277–80.
79. Vicinus, *Independent Women*, pp.3–4.
80. Quoted ibid., p.13.
81. *Girl's Own Paper*, 10 July 1886, p.644.
82. Joanna Bourke, *Husbandry to Housewifery. Women, Economic Change, and Housework in Ireland, 1890–1914* (Oxford, 1993).
83. Hufton, 'Women without men', p.361.
84. Richard Wall, 'The residence patterns of elderly English women in comparative perspective', in L. Botelho and P. Thane, eds., *Women and Ageing in British Society since 1500* (London, 2001), pp.139–65, here p.142; Susannah Ottaway, 'The old woman's home in eighteenth-century England', ibid., pp.111–38, here pp.114–16.
85. E. Gordon and G. Nair, 'The economic role of middle-class women in Victorian Glasgow', *Women's History Review* 9 (2000), pp.791–814, here pp.807–8.
86. Davidoff and Hall, *Family Fortunes*, pp.314–15.
87. Quoted ibid., p.315.
88. Gordon and Nair, 'Economic role of middle-class women', p.796.
89. L. Gunga, *'Zimmer frei'. Berliner Pensionswirtinnen im Kaiserreich* (Frankfurt-am-Main, 1995). See also Lee Davidoff, 'The separation of home and work? Landladies and lodgers in nineteenth- and twentieth-century England', in Lee Davidoff, *Worlds Between: Historical Perspectives on Gender and Class* (Cambridge, 1995), pp.151–77.
90. C.G. Brown, 'Residential differentiation in nineteenth-century Glasgow', (ESRC Award Report, R00023 2733, 1993), p.29.
91. Davidoff *et al.*, *The Family Story*, p.222.
92. Alice Jay was the author's great-grandfather's sister.
93. *Girls' Favourite* (1927) quoted in Penny Tinkler, 'Women and popular literature', in J. Purvis, ed., *Women's History: Britain, 1850–1945* (London, 1995), pp.131–56, here p.148.
94. Peter N. Stearns, *Old Age in European Society. The Case of France* (London, 1977), p.120.
95. Gay L. Gullickson, *Spinners and Weavers of Auffay. Rural Industry and the Sexual Division of Labor in a French Village, 1750–1850* (Cambridge, 1986), p.167.
96. Gillis, *For Better, For Worse*, p.123.
97. See B. Todd, 'The remarrying widow: a stereotype reconsidered', in M. Prior, ed., *Women in English Society 1500–1800* (London, 1985), pp.54–92; Shoemaker, *Gender in English Society*, pp.135–40.
98. Natalie Zemon Davis, *Women on the Margins. Three Seventeenth Century Lives* (Cambridge, MA, 1995), pp.8–15.

99. Gordon and Nair, 'Economic role of middle-class women', p.805.

100. Pamela Sharpe, 'Survival strategies and stories: poor widows and widowers in early industrial England', in S. Cavallo and L. Warner, eds., *Widowhood in Medieval and Early Modern Europe* (London, 1999), pp.220–39. here p.224.

101. Stearns, *Old Age in European Society*, p.52.

102. Jill S. Quadagno, *Ageing in Early Industrial Society. Work, Family, and Social Policy in Nineteenth-century England* (New York, 1982), p.153.

103. P. Bairoch, T. Deldycke, H. Gelders and J.-M. Limbor, *The Working Population and its Structure* (Brussels, 1968), pp.133, 169, 185. The figures for Germany and Britain include divorced women.

104. Pat Thane, 'Old women in twentieth-century Britain', in Botelho and Thane, eds., *Women and Ageing*, pp.207–31, here p.210.

105. Gullickson, *Spinners and Weavers of Auffay*, pp.170–3.

106. Sharpe, 'Survival strategies and stories', pp.220–39.

107. Shetland Archives: SC 12/6/1891/45, 11 Aug. 1891.

108. Quoted in Davidoff and Hall, *Family Fortunes*, p.327.

Chapter 4: Mothers and Children

1. Quoted in A. Martynova, 'Life of the pre-revolutionary village as reflected in popular lullabies', in Ransel, ed., *The Family in Imperial Russia*, p.172.

2. See Davidoff *et al.*, *The Family Story*, pp.221–43.

3. Ross, *Love and Toil*, p.92.

4. Quoted in Smith, *Changing Lives*, p.104.

5. Lynn Hunt, *The Family Romance of the French Revolution* (Berkeley and London, 1992), pp.89–123.

6. Yvonne M. Ward, 'The womanly garb of Queen Victoria's early motherhood, 1840–42', *Women's History Review* 8 (1999), pp.277–94.

7. R. Wortman, 'The Russian empress as mother', in Ransel, ed., *The Family in Imperial Russia*, pp.60–74.

8. A. Taylor Gilbert, 'My Mother' (1802), quoted in Davidoff and Hall, *Family Fortunes*, p.459.

9. Rousseau, *Émile*, pp.15 and 31.

10. S. Tillyard, *Aristocrats. Caroline, Emily, Louisa and Sarah Lennox 1740–1832* (London, 1995), pp.240–8.

11. A. Dally, *Inventing Motherhood. The Consequences of an Ideal* (London, 1982), p.17.

12. See Allen, *Feminism and Motherhood*, pp.22–7.

13. Quoted ibid., p.17.

14. Wollstonecraft, *Vindication*, p.197.

15. Allen, *Feminism and Motherhood*, p.42.

16. Ibid., p.47.

17. N.M. Frieden, 'Child care: medical reform in a traditionalist culture', in Ransel, ed., *The Family in Imperial Russia*, pp.236–59, here p.249.

18. Caleb Salleby in Deborah Dwork, *War is Good for Babies and Other Young Children: A History of the Infant and Child Welfare Movement in England 1889–1918* (London, 1987), p.151.

19. Quoted in E. Ross, 'Good and bad mothers: lady philanthropists and London housewives before World War I', in D.O. Helly and S.M. Reverby, eds., *Gendered Domains. Rethinking Public and Private in Women's History* (Ithaca, NY, 1992), pp.199–216, here p.201.

20. Ross, *Love and Toil*, p.203.

21. Eileen Janes Yeo, 'The creation of "motherhood" and women's responses in Britain and France, 1750–1914', *Women's History Review* 8 (1999), pp.201–17, here p.203.

22. Quoted in Ross, *Love and Toil*, p.197.

23. Davidoff and Hall, *Family Fortunes*, pp.335–8.

24. M. Anderson, *Approaches to the History of the Western Family 1500–1914* (Basingstoke, 1980), pp.19–20.

25. Shetland Archives: AD 22/2/28/5, Precognition against Margaret Johnston, 1893.

26. Shetland Archives: AD 22/2/6/4, Precognition against Laura Scott, 1862.

27. M. Llewelyn Davies, ed., *Maternity. Letters from Working Women* (1915), p.44.

28. Ibid., p.64.

29. Ibid., p.39.

30. Amanda Foreman, *Georgiana Duchess of Devonshire* (London, 1999), pp.107–8.

31. W.L. Mackenzie, *Report on the Physical Welfare of Mothers and Children*, Vol. 3, *Scotland* (Dunfermline, 1917), p.485.

32. Davies, ed., *Maternity*, pp.22–3.

33. Ibid., p.61.

34. Ibid., p.166.

35. Ibid., p.44.

36. Foreman, *Georgiana*, caption to plate of Georgiana and Lady Georgiana (n.p.).

37. Ross, *Love and Toil*, p.102.

38. Davies, ed., *Maternity*, pp.27–8.

39. Ibid., p.25.

40. See Rublack, 'The public body', pp.61–6.

41. Davies, ed., *Maternity*, p.38.

42. Cressy, *Birth, Marriage and Death*, p.55.

43. Foreman, *Georgiana*, pp.121–2.

44. Mackenzie, *Report on the Physical Welfare*, p.490.

45. I. Loudon, *Death in Childbirth. An International Study of Maternal Care and Maternal Mortality 1800–1950* (Oxford, 1992), pp.176–7.

46. Davies, ed., *Maternity*, p.115.

47. Anne Løkke, 'The "antiseptic" transformation of Danish midwives, 1860–1920', in H. Marland and A.M. Rafferty, eds., *Midwives, Society and Childbirth: Debates and Controversies in the Modern Period* (London, 1997), pp.102–33, here pp.110–13.

48. Christina Romlid, 'Swedish midwives and their instruments in the eighteenth and nineteenth centuries', in Marland and Rafferty, eds., *Midwives, Society and Childbirth*, pp.38–60.

49. Frieden, 'Child care', p.236, n.1.

50. S.C. Ramer, 'Childbirth and culture: midwifery in the nineteenth-century Russian countryside', in Ransel, ed., *The Family in Imperial Russia*, pp.218–35.

51. Loudon, *Death in Childbirth*, p.427.

52. Shorter, *History of Women's Bodies*, p.157.
53. Loudon, *Death in Childbirth*, tables 1 and 9, appendix 6, pp.542–3, 555–6. See also Hilary Marland, 'The midwife as health missionary: the reform of Dutch childbirth practices in the early twentieth century', in Marland and Rafferty, eds., *Midwives, Society and Childbirth*, pp.153–79.
54. Loudon, *Death in Childbirth*, pp.221–2.
55. Løkke, 'The "antiseptic" transformation of Danish midwives', pp.110–13.
56. I. Loudon, 'Midwives and the quality of maternal care', in Marland and Rafferty, eds., *Midwives, Society and Childbirth*, pp.180–200, here pp.184–5.
57. B.A. Engel, *Between the Fields and the City. Women, Work and Family in Russia, 1861–1914* (Cambridge, 1996), pp.47–9.
58. Elizabeth Badinter, *The Myth of Motherhood: An Historical View of the Maternal Instinct* (London, 1981), pp.xix–xx.
59. Shorter, *Making of the Modern Family*, pp.191–9. For a convincing critique of this position see S. Wilson, 'The myth of motherhood a myth: the historical view of European child-rearing', *Social History* 9 (1984), pp.181–98.
60. Rousseau, *Émile*, p.12.
61. Alford (1810–71) quoted in Linda A.Pollock, *Forgotten Children. Parent–Child Relations from 1500 to 1900* (Cambridge, 1983), p.215.
62. G.D. Sussman, 'The end of the wet-nursing business in France, 1874–1914', in R. Wheaton and T.K. Hareven, eds., *Family and Sexuality in French History* (Philadelphia, 1980), pp.224–52.
63. M.L. Arnot, 'Infant death, child care and the state: the baby-farming scandal and the first infant life protection legislation of 1872', *Continuity and Change* 9 (1994), pp.271–311.
64. Ross, *Love and Toil*, pp.141–2.
65. R.J. Evans, *Death in Hamburg* (Oxford, 1987), pp.445–50.
66. Wilson, *The Magical Universe*, p.279.
67. K. Russell (1824–74) quoted in Pollock, *Forgotten Children*, p.225.
68. Ross, *Love and Toil*, pp.184–6.
69. L. Stone, *The Family, Sex and Marriage in England 1500–1800* (London, 1977), pp.54–9, 264–7.
70. Quoted in Pollock, *Forgotten Children*, p.139.
71. Martynova, 'Life of the pre-revolutionary village', p.172.
72. Quoted in Davin, *Growing Up Poor*, p.20.
73. Davies, ed., *Maternity*, p.32.
74. See J. Fink and K. Holden, 'Pictures from the margins of marriage: representations of spinsters and single mothers in the mid-Victorian novel, inter-war Hollywood melodrama and British film of the 1950s and 1960s', *Gender and History* 11 (1999), pp.233–55.
75. Regina Schulte, *The Village in Court. Arson, Infanticide, and Poaching in the Court Records of Upper Bavaria, 1848–1910* (Cambridge, 1994), pp.98–100.
76. A. Blaikie, *Illegitimacy, Sex and Society: Northeast Scotland 1750–1900* (Oxford, 1993).
77. O. Gardarsdóttir, 'The implications of illegitimacy in late nineteenth-century Iceland', *Continuity and Change* 15 (2000), pp.435–61.

78. See Lynn Abrams, *The Orphan Country: Children of Scotland's Broken Homes, 1845 to the Present Day* (Edinburgh, 1998), pp.11–12.

79. M. Weber, *Ehefrau und Mutter in der Rechtsentwicklung* (Tübingen, 1907), p.508.

80. R. Fuchs, *Abandoned Children. Foundlings and Child Welfare in Nineteenth-century France* (Albany, NY, 1984), p.87.

81. D. Symonds, *Weep Not For Me. Women, Ballads and Infanticide in Early Modern Scotland* (Pennsylvania, 1997).

82. Shetland Archives: SC 12/43/3, *Shetland News*, 26 Oct. 1895.

83. D.L. Ransel, *Mothers of Misery. Child Abandonment in Russia* (Princeton, NJ, 1988), p.19.

84. D. Kertzer, *Sacrificed for Honor: Italian Infant Abandonment and the Politics of Reproductive Control* (Boston, 1993).

85. Fuchs, *Abandoned Children*, pp.66–79. Many cities in Belgium, Spain, Portugal and Italy had abolished the *tour* by the 1870s.

86. Quoted in Ransel, *Mothers of Misery*, p.174.

87. Quoted in I. Levitt, *Government and Social Conditions in Scotland 1845–1919* (Edinburgh, 1988), p.51.

88. Barbara Littlewood and Linda Mahood, 'Prostitutes, magdalenes and wayward girls: dangerous sexualities of working-class women in Victorian Scotland', *Gender and History* 3 (1991), pp.160–75.

89. Anna Cova, 'French feminism and maternity: theories and policies 1890–1918', in G. Bock and P. Thane, eds., *Maternity and Gender Policies. Women and the Rise of the European Welfare States 1880s–1950s* (London, 1991), pp.119–37, here p.121.

90. Quoted in Allen, *Feminism and Motherhood*, p.180.

91. G. Bock and P. Thane, Editor's introduction, in Bock and Thane, eds., *Maternity and Gender Policies*, pp.1–20, here p.7.

92. Ann-Sofie Ohlander, 'The invisible child? The struggle for a social democratic family policy in Sweden, 1900–1960s', in Bock and Thane, eds., *Maternity and Gender Policies*, pp.60–72, here p.60.

93. Cova, 'French feminism and maternity', pp.126–9.

94. Annarita Buttafuoco, 'Motherhood as a political strategy: the role of the Italian women's movement in the creation of the *Cassa Nazionale di Maternità*', in Bock and Thane, eds., *Maternity and Gender Policies*, pp.178–95.

95. Frieden, 'Child care', pp.257–8.

96. Ross, *Love and Toil*, p.205.

97. Sîan Reynolds, *France Between the Wars: Gender and Politics* (London, 1996), p.34.

98. Davies, ed., *Maternity*, pp.209–12.

99. Jane Lewis, 'Models of equality for women: the case of state support for children in twentieth-century Britain', in Bock and Thane, eds., *Maternity and Gender Policies*, pp.73–92, here p.77.

100. Quoted in Bock and Thane, Editor's introduction, p.8.

101. Offen, *European Feminisms*, p.239.

102. Marie Baum quoted in Allen, *Feminism and Motherhood*, p.190.

Chapter 5: Home, Kinship and Community

1. See for example, Gisela Bock, 'Challenging dichotomies: perspectives on women's history', in K. Offen, R.R. Pierson and J. Rendall, eds., *Writing Women's History:*

International Perspectives (Bloomington, IN, 1991), pp.1–21; Vickery, 'Golden age to separate spheres?'; S.M. Reverby and D.O. Helly, 'Converging on history', in Helly and Reverby, eds., *Gendered Domains. Rethinking Public and Private in Women's History* (Ithaca, NY, 1992), pp.1–26; Lee Davidoff, 'Regarding some "old husband's tales": public and private in feminist history', in Davidoff, *Worlds Between*, pp.227–76.

2. M. Rosaldo, 'The use and abuse of anthropology: reflections on feminism and cross-cultural understanding', *Signs* 5 (1980), pp.389–417, here p.400.

3. Segalen, *Love and Power*, p.108.

4. Quoted in Gillis, *A World of Their Own Making*, p.123.

5. Ibid., p.116.

6. Annik Pardailhé-Galabrun, *The Birth of Intimacy. Privacy and Domestic Life in Early Modern Paris* (Philadelphia, 1988), pp.145–73.

7. Ross, 'Fierce questions and taunts', pp.582–3.

8. Elizabeth Roberts, *A Woman's Place* (2nd edn, Oxford, 1995), p.129.

9. L. Davidoff, 'The rationalization of housework', in Davidoff, *Worlds Between*, pp.73–102, here p.74.

10. On long-term developments see Catherine Hall, 'The history of the housewife', in Hall, *White, Male and Middle Class* (Oxford, 1992), pp.43–71.

11. Donna Gabaccia, 'In the shadows of the periphery: Italian women in the nineteenth century', in Boxer and Quataert, eds., *Connecting Spheres* (2nd edn, Oxford, 2000), pp.194–203, here pp.200–1.

12. Bourke, *Husbandry to Housewifery*; Davidoff and Hall, *Family Fortunes*, p.385; Deborah Simonton, *A History of European Women's Work, 1700 to the Present* (London, 1998), p.94.

13. Lynn Abrams, 'Companionship and conflict: the negotiation of marriage relations in the nineteenth century', in Abrams and Harvey, eds., *Gender Relations in German History*, pp.101–20, here pp.111–14.

14. E. Warren, *A Young Wife's Perplexities* (1886), quoted in Gillis, *A World of Their Own Making*, pp.120–1.

15. Smith, *Ladies of the Leisure Class*, pp.74–5.

16. Quoted in Meyer, 'The tiresome work of conspicuous leisure', p.190.

17. Smith, *Ladies of the Leisure Class*, pp.74–92.

18. I. Beeton, *Book of Household Management* (1861).

19. Ibid.

20. Nancy Reagin, 'The imagined *Hausfrau*: national identity, domesticity, and colonialism in Imperial Germany', *Journal of Modern History* 73 (2001), pp.54–86.

21. E. Gaskell in Kenyon, ed., *800 Years of Women's Letters*, p.134.

22. Quoted in J. Bourke, '"The best of all home rulers": the economic power of women in Ireland 1880–1914', *Irish Economic and Social History* XVIII (1991), pp.34–47, here p.41.

23. J. Bourke, *Working-class Cultures in Britain 1890–1960* (London, 1994), pp.68–9.

24. Cissie Fairchilds, *Domestic Enemies. Servants and their Masters in Old Regime France* (Baltimore, 1984), pp.35–6.

25. Theresa M. McBride, *The Domestic Revolution: The Modernisation of Household Service in England and France 1820–1920* (London, 1976), p.45.

26. Quoted in Davidoff and Hall, *Family Fortunes*, p.274.

27. Quoted in Rendall, *Origins of Modern Feminism*, p.196.
28. Mrs X.3 born 1906 quoted in J.D. Stephenson and C.G. Brown, 'The view from the workplace: women's memories of work in Stirling, c.1910–c.1950', in Gordon and Breitenbach, eds., *The World is Ill Divided*, pp.7–28, here p.14.
29. Quoted in Hall, 'History of the housewife', p.66.
30. See Davidoff *et al.*, *The Family Story*, pp.77–83.
31. J. Dubisch, 'Gender, kinship and religion: reconstructing the anthropology of Greece', quoted in D. Sabean, *Kinship in Neckarhausen 1700–1870* (Cambridge, 1998), p.11.
32. Ibid., p.364.
33. Timothy Rees, 'Women on the land: household and work in the southern countryside, 1875–1939', in V.L. Enders and P.B. Radcliff, eds., *Constructing Spanish Womanhood: Female Identity in Modern Spain* (Albany, NY, 1999), pp.173–94, here pp.179–80.
34. See Sabean, *Kinship in Neckarhausen*, chapter 23. See also Carroll Smith-Rosenberg, 'The female world of love and ritual: relations between women in nineteenth century America', *Signs* 1 (1975), pp.1–29.
35. See Gillis, *A World of Their Own Making*, pp.77–80; Sabean, *Kinship in Neckarhausen*, pp.500–1.
36. Quoted in G-F. Budde, *Auf dem Weg ins Bürgerleben. Kindheit und Erziehung in deutschen und englischen Bürgerfamilien 1840–1914*, (Göttingen, 1994), p.191.
37. Quoted in Sabean, *Kinship in Neckarhausen*, p.505.
38. Davidoff and Hall, *Family Fortunes*, pp.280–1.
39. Tillyard, *Aristocrats*.
40. Roberts, *A Woman's Place*, p.169.
41. Budde, *Auf dem Weg*, pp.181–2; Smith, *Ladies of the Leisure Class*, pp.132–4.
42. Kristin Gager, *Blood Ties and Fictive Ties. Adoption and Family Life in Early Modern France* (Princeton, NJ, 1996).
43. Ross, 'Survival networks'.
44. Roberts, *A Woman's Place*, chapter 5.
45. See R. Phillips, 'Gender solidarities in late eighteenth-century urban France: the example of Rouen', *Histoire Sociale – Social History* 13 (1980), pp.325–37; Lynn Abrams, 'Crime against marriage? Wife-beating, divorce and the law in nineteenth-century Hamburg', in M.L. Arnot and C. Usborne, eds., *Gender and Crime in Modern Europe* (London, 1999), pp.118–36, here pp.123–7.
46. Ross, *Love and Toil*, pp.91–106.
47. Temma Kaplan, 'Female consciousness and collective action: the case of Barcelona, 1910–18', in *Signs* 7 (1982), pp.545–66, here p.566.
48. S. Rowbotham, *Women, Resistance and Revolution* (Harmondsworth, 1974).
49. Gay L. Gullickson, *Unruly Women of Paris: Images of the Commune* (Ithaca, NY, 1996), p.39.
50. Kaplan, 'Female consciousness', pp.553–9.
51. Allen, *Feminism and Motherhood*, p.80.
52. Smith, *Ladies of the Leisure Class*, pp.138, 140–1.
53. Glasgow Sabbath School Union, annual report 1896.
54. Meyer-Renschhausen, *Weibliche Kultur und soziale Arbeit*, pp.51–6.

55. Clare Midgley, 'Ethnicity, "race" and empire', in Purvis, ed., *Women's History*, pp.247–76. See also Marion Kaplan, *The Making of the Jewish Middle Class: Women, Family, and Identity in Imperial Germany* (New York, 1991).
56. Vicinus, *Independent Women*, p.212.
57. Rendall, *Origins of Modern Feminism*, p.265.
58. Allen, *Feminism and Motherhood*, p.88.
59. Ross, *Love and Toil*, pp.205–6.
60. Quoted in Ross, *Love and Toil*, p.206.
61. Rendall, *Origins of Modern Feminism*, p.255.
62. Clara Lucas Balfour, 'Woman and the Temperance Reformation' (1849), quoted in Rendall, *Origins of Modern Feminism*, p.256.

Chapter 6: Sex and Sexuality

1. Susan Kingsley Kent, *Sex and Suffrage in Britain, 1860–1914* (London, 1995), p.32.
2. Lesley A. Hall, *Sex, Gender and Social Change in Britain since 1880* (Basingstoke, 2000), p.16.
3. Acton, 'The functions and disorders of the reproductive organs' (1861), quoted in Lucy Bland, *Banishing the Beast: English Feminism and Sexual Morality 1885–1914* (London, 1995), p.55.
4. Keith Thomas, 'The double standard', *Journal of the History of Ideas* 20 (1959), pp.195–216.
5. Laura Gowing, *Domestic Dangers: Women, Words and Sex in Early Modern London* (Oxford, 1996), pp.60–1.
6. Clark, *Struggle for the Breeches*, pp.52–3.
7. Abrams, 'Whores, whore-chasers and swine'.
8. Sabean, *Property, Production and Household*, p.144.
9. P. Morris, 'Defamation and sexual reputation in Somerset, 1733–1850', PhD thesis, University of Warwick, 1985, quoted in Clark, *Struggle for the Breeches*, p.56.
10. M. Foucault, *The History of Sexuality*. Vol. 1 (New York, 1990), pp.103–14.
11. *The Lancet* (1885), quoted in Bland, *Banishing the Beast*, p.58.
12. Lynn Abrams, *Workers' Culture in Imperial Germany: Leisure and Recreation in the Rhineland and Westphalia* (London, 1992), p.100.
13. Paul Göhre (1895), quoted Abrams, *Workers' Culture*, p.105.
14. Quoted in Linda Mahood, 'The wages of sin: women, work and sexuality in the nineteenth century', in Gordon and Breitenbach, eds., *The World is Ill Divided*, pp.29–48, here p.32.
15. On 'treating' see Kathy Peiss, '"Charity girls" and city pleasures: historical notes on working-class sexuality 1880–1920', in A. Snitow, C. Stansell and S. Thompson, eds., *Power of Desire: The Politics of Sexuality* (New York, 1983), pp.74–87.
16. Judith R. Walkowitz, *City of Dreadful Delight. Narratives of Sexual Danger in Late Victorian London* (London, 1992), chapter 3.
17. Ibid., p.21.
18. Ibid., p.22.
19. On the symbolism of the prostitute see Lynda Nead, *Myths of Sexuality: Representations of Women in Victorian Britain* (Oxford, 1988).

20. See Judith R. Walkowitz, *Prostitution and Victorian Society: Women, Class and the State* (Cambridge, 1980); Mary Gibson, *Prostitution and the State in Italy, 1860–1915* (New Brunswick, NJ, 1986); Jill Harsin, *Policing Prostitution in Nineteenth Century Paris* (Princeton, NJ, 1985); Richard J. Evans, 'Prostitution, state and society in Imperial Germany', *Past and Present* 70 (1976), pp.106–29; Lynn Abrams, 'Prostitutes in Imperial Germany, 1870–1914: working girls or social outcasts?', in R.J. Evans, ed., *The German Underworld* (London, 1988), pp.189–209; Laura Engelstein, *The Keys to Happiness: Sex and the Search for Modernity in Fin-de-Siècle Russia* (Ithaca, NY, 1992).

21. T. Henderson, *Disorderly Women in Eighteenth Century London: Prostitution and Control in the Metropolis, 1730–1830* (London, 1999), p.171.

22. See A. Corbin, *Les Filles de Noce: Misère sexuelle et prostitution au 19e et 20e siècles* (Aubier, 1978); McMillan, *Housewife or Harlot*, pp.21–5.

23. Quoted in Kent, *Sex and Suffrage*, p.62.

24. Quoted in Engelstein, *Keys to Happiness*, p.135.

25. Flexner (1914), quoted in Walkowitz, *Prostitution and Victorian Society*, p.15.

26. Walkowitz, *Prostitution and Victorian Society*, pp.20–1; Engel, *Between the Fields and the City*, pp.184–5.

27. Abrams, 'Prostitutes in imperial Germany', p.193.

28. Richard Stites, *The Women's Liberation Movement in Russia: Feminism, Nihilism and Bolshevism, 1860–1930* (Princeton, NJ, 1991), pp.224–5.

29. Linda Mahood, *The Magdalenes: Prostitution in the Nineteenth Century* (London, 1990).

30. Mahood, 'The wages of sin', p.37.

31. Engel, *Between the Fields and the City*, p.188.

32. Walkowitz, *City of Dreadful Delight*, p.133.

33. Quoted in Kent, *Sex and Suffrage*, p.78.

34. Ibid., p.68.

35. Harsin, *Policing Prostitution*, pp.324–7.

36. Meyer-Renschhausen, *Weibliche Kultur und Soziale Arbeit*, pp.304–5.

37. Walkowitz, *City of Dreadful Delight*, p.134.

38. Quoted in Kent, *Sex and Suffrage*, p.102.

39. Ruth Brandon, *The New Women and the Old Men. Love, Sex and the Woman Question* (London, 1991), p.30.

40. Tristan, 'L'Union ouvrière', in Bell and Offen, eds., *Women, the Family and Freedom*, Vol. 1, p.213.

41. McMillan, *Housewife or Harlot*, p.80.

42. M. Pelletier, 'L'Emancipation sexuelle de la femme', in J. Waelti-Walters and S.J. Hause, eds., *Feminisms of the Belle Epoque* (Lincoln, NB, 1994), p.185.

43. Quoted in Brandon, *The New Women*, p.26.

44. E. Marx and E. Aveling, 'The woman question: from a socialist point of view' (1886), in Bell and Offen, eds., *Women, the Family, and Freedom*, Vol. 2, *1880–1950* (Stanford, CA, 1983), p.86.

45. M. Pelletier, 'L'Education féministe des filles' (1914), in Waelti-Walters and Hause, eds., *Feminisms of the Belle Epoque*, pp.112–13.

46. Bland, *Banishing the Beast*, p.256.

47. E. Key, 'The woman movement', in Sheila Jeffreys, *The Sexuality Debates* (London, 1987), p.574.
48. Ibid., p.574.
49. E. Key, 'Love and marriage' (1904), in Bell and Offen, eds., *Women, the Family, and Freedom*, Vol. 2, p.197.
50. Bland, *Banishing the Beast*, p.286.
51. I. Leatham (1912), quoted in Bland, *Banishung the Beast*, p.197.
52. See Allen, *Feminism and Motherhood*, pp.193–4.
53. Mary Nash, 'Un/contested identities: motherhood, sex reform and the modernization of gender identity in early twentieth century Spain', in Enders and Radcliff, eds., *Constructing Spanish Womanhood*, pp.25–50, here pp.37–8.
54. Stites, *Women's Liberation Movement in Russia*, p.180.
55. Roussel, 'Le Droit des vierges' (1904), in Bell and Offen, eds., *Women, the Family, and Freedom*, Vol. 2, p.178.
56. On Vickery see Bland, *Banishing the Beast*, pp.207–9 and 212–13.
57. See Allen, *Feminism and Motherhood*, p.189.
58. It was estimated that up to half a million illegal abortions were carried out in Germany every year by 1915. Cornelie Usborne, *The Politics of the Body in Weimar Germany* (London, 1992), p.28.
59. On the birth strike see Usborne, *The Politics of the Body*, pp.8–9.
60. Quoted in McLaren, *Sexuality and Social Order: The Debate over the Fertility of Women and Workers in France, 1770–1920* (New York, 1983), p.165.
61. Sanger, 'Family limitation' (1914), in Jeffreys, ed., *The Sexuality Debates*, pp.534–5.
62. Margaret Jackson, *The Real Facts of Life. Feminism and the Politics of Sexuality c.1850–1914* (London, 1994), p.129.
63. Lesley A. Hall, *Hidden Anxieties: Male Sexuality, 1900–1950* (London, 1991).
64. Lilian Faderman, *Surpassing the Love of Men. Romantic Friendship and Love between Women from the Renaissance to the Present* (London, 1991), pp.16–19.
65. Elizabeth Susan Wahl, *Invisible Relations. Representations of Female Intimacy in the Age of Enlightenment* (Stanford, CA, 1999), pp.94–102.
66. See Rosenberg, 'The female world of love and ritual'.
67. Faderman, *Surpassing the Love of Men*, pp.147–54.
68. Margaret Fuller (1855), quoted ibid., p.160.
69. Quoted ibid., pp.226–7.
70. Ibid., pp.205–18.
71. Havelock Ellis, 'Studies in the psychology of sex', quoted in Bland, *Banishing the Beast*, p.262.
72. Sheila Jeffreys, *The Spinster and her Enemies: Feminism and Sexuality, 1880–1930* (London, 1985).
73. Havelock Ellis quoted in N. Miller, *Out of the Past. Gay and Lesbian History from 1869 to the Present* (London, 1995), p.26.
74. See Bland, *Banishing the Beast*, pp.290–6.
75. Francesca Canadé Sautman, 'Invisible women: lesbian working-class culture in France, 1880–1930', in J. Merrick and B.T. Ragan, J., eds., *Homosexuality in Modern France* (Oxford, 1996), pp.177–201, here pp.179–80.

76. Quoted in Miller, *Out of the Past*, p.76.

77. Collette, 'The pure and the unpure', quoted in Miller, *Out of the Past*, p.82.

78. Sautman, 'Invisible women', p,196.

79. Faderman, *Surpassing the Love of Men*, pp.176–7.

80. Quoted in Bland, *Banishing the Beast*, p.21.

81. Nash, 'Un/contested identies', p.39.

Chapter 7: Working for a Living

1. Judith Bennett, 'History that stands still: women's work in the European past', *Feminist Studies* 14 (1988), pp.269–83, here p.278.

2. See K. Honeyman and J. Goodman, 'Women's work, gender conflict, and labour markets in Europe, 1500–1900', *Economic History Review* 44 (1991), pp.608–28.

3. Ibid., p.615.

4. Clark, *Struggle for the Breeches*, p.265. This view is elaborated by Katrina Honeyman, *Women, Gender and Industrialisation in England, 1700–1870* (Basingstoke, 2000).

5. Simonton, *European Women's Work*, p.137.

6. P. Hudson and W.R. Lee, 'Women's work and the family economy in historical perspective', in P. Hudson and W.R. Lee, eds., *Women's Work and the Family Economy in Historical Perspective* (Manchester, 1990), pp.2–47, here p.33.

7. R.L. Glickman, *Russian Factory Women. Workplace and Society, 1880–1914* (Berkeley, CA, 1984), p.2.

8. See E. Higgs, *Making Sense of the Census. The Manuscript Returns for England and Wales, 1801–1901* (London, 1989).

9. I. Blom, '"Hun er den Raadende over Husets økonomiske Angliggender"? Changes in women's work and family responsibilities in Norway since the 1860s', in Hudson and Lee, eds., *Women's Work*, pp.157–82, here p.163; Hudson and Lee, 'Women's work', p.21; Glickman, *Russian Factory Women*, p.95.

10. Frevert, *Women in German History*, p.329.

11. All figures from Bairoch *et al.*, *Working Population*, pp.132 and 184.

12. Ivy Pinchbeck, *Women Workers and the Industrial Revolution* (London, 1930 and 1981), pp.317–21.

13. Bairoch, *Working Population*, pp.174 and 190.

14. Robertson, 'In bondage', pp.117–35.

15. Smith, *Changing Lives*, p.149.

16. Ibid., p.277.

17. Kathleen Canning, *Languages of Labor and Gender: Female Factory Work in Germany, 1850–1914* (Ithaca, NY, 1996), chapter 2.

18. J. McDermid and A. Hillyer, *Women and Work in Russia 1880–1930* (London, 1998), p.87; Simonton, *European Women's Work*, pp.138–9.

19. Quoted in Canning, *Languages of Labor*, p.44.

20. Hauptstaatsarchiv Münster: Oberlandesgericht Hamm, Appellationsgericht 43: 14 June 1855.

21. Michelet, 'La femme' (1860), quoted in Smith, *Changing Lives*, p.138.

22. Maxine Berg, 'What difference did women's work make to the industrial revolution?', in Sharpe, ed., *Women's Work*, pp.149–72, here p.157.

23. Ibid., p.162.
24. Smith, *Changing Lives*, p.178.
25. On discontinuity see Pinchbeck, *Women Workers and the Industrial Revolution*. For a more recent analysis see Bridget Hill, 'Women's history: a study in change, continuity, or standing still?', *Women's History Review* 2 (1993), pp.78–94.
26. M. Mitterauer, 'Geschlechtsspezifische Arbeitsteilung in vorindustrieller Zeit', *Beiträge historische Sozialkunde* (1981), pp.77–87, here p.77.
27. Engel, *Between the Fields and the City*, pp.13–15.
28. Lynn Abrams, '"The best men in Shetland": women, gender and place in peripheral communities', in P. Payton, ed., *Cornish Studies: Eight* (Exeter, 2000), pp.97–114.
29. O. Lofgren, 'Arbeitsteilung und Geschlechterrollen', *Ethnologia Scandinavica* (1975), pp.49–71, here p.49.
30. Simonton, *European Women's Work*, p.121.
31. Pamela Sharpe, *Adapting to Capitalism: Working Women in the English Economy, 1700–1850* (Basingstoke, 1996); Rees, 'Women on the land', pp.183–4.
32. Hudson and Lee, 'Women's work', p.8.
33. Lofgren, 'Arbeitsteilung und Geschlechterrollen', p.49.
34. K.D.M. Snell, 'Agricultural seasonal unemployment, the standard of living, and women's work, 1690–1860', in Sharpe, ed., *Women's Work*, pp.73–121, here p.104.
35. R. Pederson, 'Die Arbeitsteilung zwischen Frauen und Männern in einem marginalen Ackerbaugebiet – Das Beispiel Norwegen', *Ethnologia Scandinavica* (1975), pp.37–48, here pp.42–3.
36. L. Sommestad, 'Education and de-feminization in the Swedish dairy industry', *Gender and History* 4 (1992), pp.34–48; Sommestad, 'Gendering work, interpreting gender: the masculinization of dairy work in Sweden, 1850–1950', *History Workshop Journal* 37 (1994), pp.57–75.
37. B.K. Hansen, 'Rural women in late nineteenth-century Denmark', *Journal of Peasant Studies* 9 (1981), pp.225–40.
38. Quoted in Sharpe, *Adapting to Capitalism*, p.97.
39. Quoted in Jane Rendall, *Women in an Industrializing Society: England 1750–1880* (Oxford, 1990), p.17.
40. T.P. Liu, 'What price a weaver's dignity? Gender inequality and the survival of home-based production in industrial France', in L.L. Frader and S.O. Rose, eds., *Gender and Class in Modern Europe* (Ithaca, NY, 1986), pp.57–76.
41. Gullickson, *Spinners and Weavers of Auffay*, pp.96–102.
42. A. Cento Bull, 'The Lombard silk-spinners in the nineteenth century: an industrial workforce in a rural setting', in Z.G. Baranski and S.W. Vinall, eds., *Women and Italy. Essay on Gender, Culture and History* (Basingstoke, 1991), pp.11–42.
43. Engel, *Between the Fields and the City*, pp.37–44.
44. Ibid., p.51.
45. Blom, 'Hun er den Raadende', p.160.
46. M.J. Boxer, 'Women in industrial homework: the flowermakers of Paris in the belle epoque', *French Historical Studies* 12 (1982), pp.401–23; Barbara Franzoi, *At the Very Least She Pays the Rent: Women and German Industrialization, 1871–1914* (Westport, CT, 1985), chapter 6.

47. B. Franzoi, '"...with the wolf always at the door ...": women's work in domestic industry in Britain and Germany', in Boxer and Quataert, eds., *Connecting Spheres* (2nd edn), pp.164–73, here p.166.
48. Ibid., p.169.
49. Louise A. Tilly, *Politics and Class in Milan 1881–1901* (Oxford, 1992), p.40.
50. Berg, 'What difference did women's work make?', pp.167–8.
51. Royal Commission on Poor Laws, 1909, quoted in Alice J. Albert, 'Fit work for women: sweated home-workers in Glasgow, c.1875–1914', in Gordon and Breitenbach, eds., *The World is Ill-Divided*, pp.158–77, here p.160.
52. Ibid.
53. Liu, 'What price a weaver's dignity?', p.74.
54. Judith G. Coffin, 'Consumption, production, and gender: the sewing machine in nineteenth century France', in Frader and Rose, eds., *Gender and Class in Modern Europe*, pp.111–41. See also Karin Hausen, 'Technical progress and women's labour in the nineteenth century: the social history of the sewing machine', in G. Iggers, ed., *The Social History of Politics* (Leamington Spa, 1985), pp.259–81.
55. Sonya O. Rose, *Limited Livelihoods: Gender and Class in Nineteenth-century England* (London, 1992), p.88.
56. 'Im Kampf uns Dasein' (c.1880), quoted in M.J. Maynes, *Taking the Hard Road: Life Course in French and German Workers' Autobiographies in the Era of Industrialization* (Chapel Hill, NC, 1995), p.72.
57. Edith Hogg (1900) quoted in Davin, *Growing Up Poor*, p.193.
58. British Parliamentary Papers, Cd. 555, 1872 Truck Enquiry, p.426. See L.G. Fryer, *Knitting by the Fireside and on the Hillside* (Lerwick, 1995), chapter 3.
59. Franzoi, *At the Very Least*, p.139.
60. Simonton, *European Women's Work*, p.151.
61. Rose, *Limited Livelihoods*, p.85.
62. Respondent to Select Commission on Homework (1908), in Rose, *Limited Livelihoods*, p.95.
63. Quoted in S. Pennington and B. Westover, *A Hidden Workforce. Homeworkers in England, 1850–1985* (Basingstoke, 1989), p.107.
64. Angela V. John, *By the Sweat of their Brow. Women Workers at Victorian Coal Mines* (London, 1984); Sharron P.Schwartz, '"No place for a woman": gender at work in Cornwall's metalliferous mining industry', in Payton, ed., *Cornish Studies: Eight*, pp.69–96.
65. Clark, *Struggle for the Breeches*, p.270.
66. Alice Clark, *Working Life of Women in the Seventeenth Century* (1919; 3rd edn, London, 1992), p.235.
67. Peter Earle, 'The female labour market in London in the late seventeenth and early eighteenth centuries', in Sharpe, ed., *Women's Work*, pp.121–49, here pp.132, 138.
68. Canning, *Languages of Labor*, p.81.
69. Clark, *Struggle for the Breeches*, p.3.
70. J.W. Scott, 'On language, gender, and working class history', in J.W. Scott, *Gender and the Politics of History*, p.64.

71. Quoted in Bell and Offen, eds., *Women, the Family and Freedom*, Vol. 1, p.206.

72. Bridget Hill, *Women, Work, and Sexual Politics in Eighteenth-century England* (Oxford, 1989), p.259.

73. F. Bettio, *The Sexual Division of Labour: The Italian Case* (Oxford, 1988), pp.128–32.

74. Ibid., p.141.

75. H.H. Chanut, 'The gendering of skill as an historical process: the case of the French knitters in industrial Troyes, 1880–1939', in Frader and Rose, eds., *Gender and Class*, pp.77–107, here pp.88–9.

76. (N.d.) quoted in Rose, *Limited Livelihoods*, p.27.

77. Sîan Reynolds, *Britannica's Typesetters. Women Compositors in Edwardian Edinburgh* (Edinburgh, 1989), pp.70–1.

78. G. de Groot and M.Schrover, *Women Workers and Technological Change in Europe in the Nineteenth and Twentieth Centuries* (London, 1992), p.284.

79. A. Phillips and B. Taylor, 'Sex and skill: notes towards a feminist economics', in Feminist Review, ed., *Waged Work: A Reader* (London, 1986), pp.54–66, here p.55.

80. Eleanor Gordon, *Women and the Labour Movement in Scotland 1850–1914* (Oxford, 1991), p.152.

81. Canning, *Languages of Labor*, pp.56 and 78.

82. Mary Lynn Stewart, *Women, Work and the French State. Labour Protection and Social Patriarchy, 1879–1919* (Kingston, 1989), p.203.

83. Ibid., p.162.

84. Ibid., p.9.

85. Quoted in Schwartz, 'No place for a woman', p.78.

86. S.O. Rose, 'Protective labor legislation in nineteenth-century Britain: gender, class and the liberal state', in Rose and Frader, eds., *Gender and Class*, pp.193–210, here p.202.

87. Canning, *Languages of Labor*, pp.129–30; Stewart, *Women, Work and the French State*, chapter 8; Rose, 'Protective labor legislation', pp.205–9; see also McDermid and Hillyar, *Women and Work in Russia*, pp.43–4.

88. Quoted in Canning, *Languages of Labor*, p.139.

89. Stewart, *Women, Work and the French State*, p.15.

90. Gordon, 'Women, work and collective action: Dundee jute workers 1870–1906', *Journal of Social History* 21 (1987), pp.27–48, here p.31.

91. Stephenson and Brown, 'The view from the workplace', p.26.

92. Judy Lown, *Women and Industrialization. Gender at Work in Nineteenth Century England* (Oxford, 1990), pp.109–16, 124–31.

93. Patricia Hilden, *Working Women and Socialist Politics in France 1880–1914* (Oxford, 1986), p.119.

94. Canning, *Languages of Labor*, p.221.

95. Ibid., p.220.

96. Ibid., p.258.

97. Mrs G.1 (1924) quoted in Stephenson and Brown, 'View from the workplace', p.20.

98. Reynolds, *Britannica's Typesetters*, p.138.

99. Heynrichs (1866) quoted in E.S. Riemer and J.C. Fout, eds., *European Women: A Documentary History 1789–1945* (New York, 1980), p.53.

100. Canning, *Languages of Labor*, p.260.

101. Rosa Maria Capel Martinez, 'Life and work in the tobacco factories: female industrial workers in the early twentieth century', in Enders and Radcliff, eds., *Constructing Spanish Womanhood*, pp.131–50, here p.135.

102. Roger Magraw, *History of the French Working Class*, Vol. 2, *Workers and the Bourgeois Republic* (Oxford, 1992), p.69.

103. D.J. O'Connor, 'Representations of women workers: tobacco strikers in the 1890s', in Enders and Radcliff, eds., *Constructing Spanish Womanhood*, pp.151–72.

104. See Pamela Radcliff, 'Elite women workers and collective action: the cigarette makers of Gijón, 1890–1930', *Journal of Social History* 27 (1993), pp.85–108.

105. Quoted in Riemer and Fout, eds., *European Women*, pp.20–3.

106. Tilly, *Politics and Class in Milan*, p.136.

107. Stites, *The Women's Liberation Movement*, p.244.

108. Glickman, *Russian Factory Women*, p.192.

109. Tilly, *Politics and Class in Milan*, p.171.

110. Canning, *Languages of Labor*, pp.261–7.

111. Gordon, *Women and the Labour Movement*, pp.172–6.

112. Ibid., p.177.

113. Magraw, *History of the French Working Class*, pp.67, 69.

114. Canning, *Languages of Labor*, p.266.

115. Quoted in McDermid and Hillyer, *Women and Work in Russia*, p.45.

116. Gordon, *Women and the Labour Movement*, p.210.

117. Smith, *Changing Lives*, p.304.

118. Frevert, *Women in German History*, pp.99–100.

119. Glickman, *Russian Factory Women*, p.196.

120. Canning, *Languages of Labor*, p.315.

121. Deborah Thom, *Nice Girls and Rude Girls: Women Workers in World War I* (London, 1998), p.140.

122. Quoted in B.S. Anderson and J.P. Zinsser, *A History of Their Own: Women in Europe from Prehistory to the Present*, Vol. II (London, 1988), pp.291–2.

123. Hilden, *Working Women*, p.131.

124. Quoted in Glickman, *Russian Factory Women*, p.208.

125. Ibid., p.200.

126. Union of Tailoresses, Dressmakers and Allied Trades (1903) in Riemer and Fout, eds., *European Women*, pp.27–8.

127. Bairoch, *The Working Population*, pp.83–4, 96.

128. Ellen Jordan, *The Women's Movement and Women's Employment in Nineteenth Century Britain* (London, 1999), p.79.

129. Ibid., p.195.

130. Ursula Nienhaus, *Vater Staat und seine Gehilfinnen. Die Politik mit den Frauenarbeit bei der deutsche Post (1864–1945)* (Frankfurt-am-Main, 1995).

131. Report to Parliament (1871) quoted in Jordan, *The Women's Movement*, pp.12–13.

132. Theresa M. McBride, 'A woman's world: department stores and the evolution of women's employment, 1870–1920', *French Historical Studies* 10 (1978), pp.664–83.

133. Quoted in Stephenson and Brown, 'The view from the workplace', p.17.

134. Simonton, *European Women's Work*, p.249.

135. See Shani D'Cruze, 'Imperfect workers – imperfect answers: recent publications on the history of women and work', *Urban History* 26 (1999), pp.257–67, here p.260.

Chapter 8: Politics, Nation and Identity

1. Quoted in Hunt, *Family Romance*, p.116.

2. H.B. Applewhite and D.G. Levy, Introduction, in Applewhite and Levy, eds., *Women and Politics in the Age of Democratic Revolution* (Ann Arbor, MI, 1990), p.2.

3. Ann McLintock, *Imperial Leather: Race, Gender and Sexuality in the Colonial Conquest* (New York, 1995), pp.24–5.

4. Quoted in B. Gray and L. Ryan, 'The politics of Irish identity and the interconnections between feminism, nationhood and colonialism', in R.R. Pierson and N. Chaudhuri, eds., *Nation, Empire, Colony: Historicizing Gender and Race* (Bloomington, IN, 1998), pp.121–38, here p.121.

5. Condorcet, 'Plea for the citizenship of women' (1790), in Bell and Offen, eds., *Women, the Family, and Freedom*, Vol. 1, p.99.

6. De Gouge, 'Les Droits de la femme' (1791), ibid., pp.104–5.

7. Demoulin (1793) quoted in Offen, *European Feminisms*, p.62.

8. D. Godineau, 'Masculine and feminine political practice during the French Revolution, 1793–Year III', in Applewhite and Levy, eds., *Women and Politics*, pp.61–80, here p.61.

9. Ibid., p.62.

10. See D.G. Levy and H.B. Applewhite, 'Women and political revolution in Paris', in Bridenthal, Koonz and Stuard, eds., *Becoming Visible* (2nd edn), pp.279–306.

11. D.G. Levy and H.B. Applewhite, 'Women, radicalization, and the fall of the French monarchy', in Applewhite and Levy, eds., *Women and Politics*, pp.81–107, here p.81.

12. J. Bohstedt, 'The myth of the feminine food riot: women as proto-citizens in English community politics, 1790–1810', in Applewhite and Levy, eds., *Women and Politics*, pp.21–60.

13. Godineau, 'Masculine and feminine political practice', p.65.

14. Levy and Applewhite, 'Women, radicalization', p.102.

15. James F. McMillan, *France and Women 1789–1914: Gender, Society and Politics* (London, 2000), p.25.

16. Applewhite and Levy, Introduction, p.6.

17. See Joan Landes, *Women and the Public Sphere in the Age of the French Revolution* (Ithaca, NY, 1988).

18. Chaumette quoted in McMillan, *France and Women*, pp.30–1.

19. W.Ph. te Brake, R.M. Dekker and L.C. van de Pol, 'Women and political culture in the Dutch revolutions', in Applewhite and Levy, eds., *Women and Politics*, pp.109–46.

20. Smith, *Changing Lives*, p.120.

21. Clark, *Struggle for the Breeches*, p.153.

22. Quoted in Rendall, *Origins of Modern Feminism*, p.235.

23. Clark, *Struggle for the Breeches*, p.172.

24. L.S. Struminger, 'Looking back: women of 1848 and the revolutionary heritage of 1789', in Applewhite and Levy, eds., *Women and Politics*, pp.269–73.

25. Jane Rendall, 'The citizenship of women and the Reform Act of 1867', in C. Hall, K. McLelland and J. Rendall, *Defining the Victorian Nation: Class, Race, Gender and the Reform Act of 1867* (Cambridge, 2000), pp.121–8.

26. 'Address of the Female Political Union of Newcastle Upon Tyne to their fellow countrywomen' (1839), in Bell and Offen, eds., *Women, the Family and Freedom*, Vol. 1, p.228.

27. 'Address to the Women of England' (1841), quoted in Jane Rendall, 'Claiming citizenship: women's politics in Britain 1780–1870', in *Major Themes in Women's History from the Enlightenment to the Great War* ([CD-ROM] Glasgow History Course-ware Consortium, 1998).

28. *L'Atelier* (1844), in Bell and Offen, eds., *Women, the Family and Freedom*, Vol. 1, pp.230–1.

29. M. Mylne (1872) quoted in Hall, McLelland and Rendall, *Defining the Victorian Nation*, p.29.

30. Quoted in S. Zucker, 'German women and the revolution of 1848: Kathinka Zitz-Halein and the Humania Association', *Central European History* 13 (1980), pp.237–54, here p.245.

31. J.W. Scott, *Only Paradoxes to Offer: French Feminists and the Rights of Man* (Cambridge, MA, 1996), p.81.

32. Schraub, *Zwischen Salon und Mädchenkammer*, pp.124–6.

33. Zucker, 'German women and the revolution of 1848', p.244.

34. Smith, *Changing Lives*, p.238.

35. Quoted in W. Walton, *Eve's Proud Descendants. Four Women Writers and Republican Politics in Nineteenth-century France* (Stanford, CA, 2000), p.228.

36. Ibid., p.230.

37. Quoted in Scott, *Only Paradoxes to Offer*, p.70.

38. Ibid., p.71.

39. Quoted in Schraub, *Zwischen Salon und Mädchenkammer*, pp.136–7.

40. Quoted in Walton, *Eve's Proud Descendants*, pp.178–9.

41. Hedwig Dohm, *Woman's Nature and Privilege*, trans. C. Campbell (Westport, CT, 1976), p.125.

42. J. Deroin and P. Roland (1851) in Bell and Offen, eds., *Women, the Family, and Freedom*, Vol. 1, p.289.

43. V. Woolf, *Three Guineas* (London, 1938), p.197.

44. Nira Yuval-Davis quoted in Gray and Ryan, 'Politics of Irish identity', p.123. See also Yuval-Davis, *Gender and Nation* (London, 1997).

45. Sarah L. White, 'Liberty, honor, order: gender and political discourse in nineteenth-century Spain', in Enders and Radcliff, eds., *Constructing Spanish Womanhood*, pp.233–57, here pp.236–40.

46. A. McLintock, 'Family feuds: gender, nationalism and the family', *Feminist Review* 44 (1993), pp.61–80, here p.66.

47. R.R. Pierson, Introduction, in Pierson and Chaudhuri, eds., *Nation, Empire, Colony*, p.4.

48. Linda Colley, *Britons. Forging the Nation 1707–1837* (London, 1992), pp.263–7; Karen Hagemann, 'A valorous *Volk* family', in I. Blom, K. Hagemann and C. Hall, eds., *Gendered Nations: Nationalisms and Gender Order in the Long Nineteenth Century* (Oxford, 2000), pp.179–206, here pp.183–6.

49. Colley, *Britons*, p.275.

50. John Lawrence Tone, 'Spanish women in the resistance to Napoleon, 1808–1814', in Enders and Radcliff, eds., *Constructing Spanish Womanhood*, pp.259–82.

51. Pieter M. Judson, 'The gendered politics of German nationalism in Austria, 1880–1900', in D.F. Good, M. Grandner and M.J. Maynes, eds., *Austrian Women in the Nineteenth and Twentieth Centuries* (Oxford, 1996), pp.1–17.

52. Hagemann, 'A valorous *Volk* family', p.192.

53. Ida Blom, 'Gender and nation in international comparison', in Blom, Hagemann and Hall, eds., *Gendered Nations*, pp.3–26, here pp.11–14; I.D. Björnsdottir, 'Nationalism, gender and the body in Icelandic nationalist discourse', *NORA, Nordic Journal of Women's Studies* 5 (1997), pp.3–13.

54. Nancy Reagin, 'The imagined *Hausfrau*', pp.74–9.

55. Irina Novikova, 'Constructing national identity in Latvia: gender and representation during the period of national awakening', in Blom, Hagemann and Hall, eds., *Gendered Nations*, pp.311–34, here p.325.

56. Ida Blom, 'Nation–class–gender: Scandinavia at the turn of the century', *Scandinavian Journal of History* 21 (1996), pp.1–16, here pp.3–4.

57. See Rendall, *Origins of Modern Feminism*, pp.34–42.

58. Jitka Malecková, 'Nationalising women and engendering the nation: the Czech national movement', in Blom, Hagemann and Hall, eds., *Gendered Nations*, pp.293–310, here p.296. Also Sharon L. Wolchik, 'Czech and Slovak women and political leadership', *Women's History Review* 5 (1996), pp.525–38.

59. Andrea Feldman, 'Yugoslavia imagined: women and the ideology of Yugoslavism (1918–1939)', in S. Kemlein, J. Gehmacher and E. Harvey, eds., *Zwischen Kriegen – Nationen, Nationalismen und Geschlechterverhältnisse in Mittel- und Osteuropa, 1918–1939* (forthcoming, 2002).

60. Anna Zarnowska, 'Education of working class women in the Polish Kingdom', *Acta Poloniae Historica* 74 (1996), pp.137–59, here p.144.

61. A. Szwarc, 'Women among the creators of intellectual and artistic culture in Poland', *Acta Poloniae Historica* 74 (1996), pp.245–6.

62. Quoted in B. Lorence-Kot, 'Klementyna Tanska Hoffmanowa, cultural nationalism and a new formula for Polish womanhood', *History of European Ideas* 8 (1987), pp.435–50, here p.437.

63. Malgorzata Fidelis, '"Participation in the creative work of the nation": Polish women intellectuals in the cultural construction of female gender roles, 1864–1890', *Women's History Review* 13 (2000), pp.108–31, here p.111.

64. Lorence-Kot, 'Klementyna Tanska Hoffmanowa', p.445.

65. Fidelis, 'Participation in the creative work', pp.115–18.

66. Quoted in Bell and Offen, eds., *Women, the Family and Freedom*, Vol. 1, pp.175–6.

67. On the Czechs see Malecková, 'Nationalising women', pp.296–7; for Bulgaria, K. Daskalova, 'Women and nationalism, old and new, in Bulgaria', unpublished paper, Oslo, 2000, and Tatyana Nestorova, 'Between tradition and modernity: Bulgarian women during the development of modern statehood and society, 1878–1945', *Women's History Review* 5 (1996), pp.513–24.

68. E. Varikas, 'Gender and national identity in *fin de siècle* Greece', *Gender and History* 5 (1993), pp.269–83, here p.272.

69. R. Chickering, '"Casting their gaze more broadly": women's patriotic activism in Imperial Germany', *Past and Present* 32 (1988), pp.156–85, here p.162.

70. Ibid., p.170.

71. Angelika Schaser, 'Women in a nation of men: the politics of the League of German Women's Associations (BDF) in Imperial Germany, 1894–1914', in Blom, Hagemann and Hall, eds., *Gendered Nations*, pp.249–68, here p.258.

72. Quoted ibid., p.262.

73. Lynn Abrams, 'Feminists–citizens–mothers: debates about citizenship, national identity and motherhood in nineteenth-century Germany', in T. Brotherstone, D. Simonton and O. Walsh, eds., *Gendering Scottish History: An International Approach* (Glasgow, 1999), pp.186–98.

74. Quoted in Margaret Ward, *Unmanageable Revolutionaries: Women and Irish Nationalism* (London, 1983), p.69.

75. Margaret Ward, 'The Ladies' Land League and the Irish Land War 1881/1882: defining the relationship between women and nation', in Blom, Hagemann and Hall, eds., *Gendered Nations*, pp.229–48, here p.244.

76. Gray and Ryan, 'The politics of Irish identity', p.127.

77. Blom, 'Gender and nation', p.17.

78. Geoff Eley, 'Culture, nation and gender', in Blom, Hagemann and Hall, eds., *Gendered Nations*, pp.27–40, here p.33.

79. G.L. Gullickson, *Unruly Women of Paris: Images of the Commune* (Ithaca, NY, 1996), p.3.

Chapter 9: Women's Mission to Empire

1. McLintock, *Imperial Leather*, p.6.

2. Ibid., p.34.

3. Quoted in Susan Thorne, *Congregational Missions and the Making of an Imperial Culture in 19th-century England* (Stanford, CA, 1999), p.85.

4. See Anna Davin, 'Imperialism and motherhood', *History Workshop Journal* 5 (1978), pp.9–65.

5. Rev. T. Matheson (1890) quoted in Thorne, *Congregational Missions*, p.97.

6. Ibid., p.98.

7. Clare Midgley, 'Anti-slavery and the roots of "imperial feminism"', in C. Midgley, ed., *Gender and Imperialism* (Manchester, 1998), pp.161–79, here p.165.

8. Reid, *A Plea for Woman*, p.2.

9. Midgley, *Women Against Slavery: The British Campaigns 1780–1870* (London, 1992), pp.97–8.

10. Quoted ibid., p.99.

11. Ibid., pp.60–2.
12. Antoinette Burton, 'Women and "domestic" imperial culture: the case of Victorian Britain', in Boxer and Quataert, eds., *Connecting Spheres* (2nd edn), pp.174–84, here p.176.
13. Clare Midgley, 'Female emancipation in an imperial frame: English women and the campaign against sati (widow burning) in India, 1813–30', *Women's History Review* 9 (2000), pp.95–121.
14. Quoted ibid., p.100.
15. Ibid., p.112.
16. Burton, 'Women and "domestic" imperial culture', p.177.
17. Midgley, *Women Against Slavery*, pp.87–91.
18. See Himani Bannerji, 'Age of consent and hegemonic social reform', in Midgley, ed., *Gender and Imperialism*, pp.21–44.
19. Burton, 'Women and "domestic" imperial culture', p.176.
20. McLintock, *Imperial Leather*, p.31.
21. Ibid., pp.210–19.
22. Yvette Abrahams, 'Images of Sara Bartman. Sexuality, race and gender in early-nineteenth-century Britain', in Pierson and Chaudhuri, eds., *Nation, Empire, Colony*, pp.220–36, here p.227.
23. Quoted in J.R. Horne, 'In pursuit of greater France: visions of empire among musée social reformers, 1894–1931', in J. Clancy-Smith and F. Gouda, eds., *Domesticating the Empire. Race, Gender and Family Life in French and Dutch Colonialism* (Charlottesville, VA, 1998), pp.21–42, here p.36.
24. Ibid., p.38.
25. Nancy R. Reagin, *A German Women's Movement. Class and Gender in Hanover, 1880–1933* (Chapel Hill, NC, 1995), pp.181–2.
26. Quoted in Julia Bush, '"The right sort of woman": female emigrators and emigration to the British Empire', *Women's History Review* 3 (1994), pp.385–409, here p.390.
27. Quoted in Jane Haggis, 'White women and colonialism: towards a non-recuperative history', in Midgley, ed., *Gender and Imperialism*, pp.45–75, here p.53.
28. David W. Savage, 'Missionaries and the development of a colonial ideology of female education in India', *Gender and History* 9 (1997), pp.201–21.
29. Haggis, 'White women and colonialism', p.58.
30. Elizabeth Robertson, *Mary Slessor. The Barefoot Missionary* (Edinburgh, 2001), p.27.
31. Bush, 'The right sort of woman', pp.385–6.
32. A.F. Walls, 'Mary Slessor', in *Dictionary of Scottish Church History and Theology* (Edinburgh, 1993), pp.778–9.
33. Burton, 'Women and "domestic" imperial culture', p.177.
34. Margaret Strobel, 'Gender, race and empire in nineteenth and twentieth-century Africa and Asia', in Bridenthal, Koonz and Stuard (eds.), *Becoming Visible* (3rd edn), pp.389–414, here p.395.
35. Quoted in Helen Callaway, *Gender, Culture and Empire: European Women in Colonial Nigeria* (Basingstoke, 1987), p.38.
36. www.channel4.com/plus/victorians/2_empire.html (accessed 7 August 2001).

37. Lora Wildenthal, 'Race, gender, and citizenship in the German colonial empire', in F. Cooper and A.L. Stoler, eds., *Tensions of Empire. Colonial Cultures in a Bourgeois World*, (Berkeley, 1997), pp.263–83.

38. P. Pattynama, 'Secrets and danger: interracial sexuality in Louis Couperus's *The Hidden Force* and Dutch colonial culture around 1900', in Clancy-Smith and Gouda, eds., *Domesticating the Empire*, pp.84–107, here p.99.

39. A.L. Conkin, 'Redefining "Frenchness": citizenship, race regeneration, and imperial motherhood in France and West Africa, 1914–40', in Clancy-Smith and Gouda, eds., *Domesticating the Empire*, pp.65–83, here pp.76–82.

40. P. Edwards, 'Womanizing Indochina: fiction, nation and cohabitation in colonial Cambodia, 1890–1930', in Clancy-Smith and Gouda, eds., *Domesticating the Empire*, pp.108–30, here p.118.

41. Conklin, 'Redefining "Frenchness"', pp.81–2.

42. Edwards, 'Womanizing Indochina', pp.113–6.

43. E. Locher-Scholten, 'So close and yet so far: the ambivalence of Dutch colonial rhetoric on Javanese servants in Indonesia, 1900–1942', in Clancy-Smith and Gouda, eds., *Domesticating the Empire*, pp.131–53.

44. See Pattynama, 'Secrets and danger', p.100.

45. A phrase coined by Mary Elisabeth Oake when she found herself the only white woman in British Cameroon, quoted in Callaway, *Gender, Culture and Empire*, p.5.

46. General Daumas quoted in J. Clancy-Smith, 'Islam, gender, and identities in the making of French Algeria, 1830–1962', in Clancy-Smith and Gouda, eds., *Domesticating the Empire*, pp.154–74, here p.163.

47. Midgley, 'Female emancipation', p.111.

48. The terms 'good' and 'bad patriarchy' are used by Midgley, 'Female emancipation', p.112.

49. Haggis, 'White women and colonialism'.

50. Burton, 'Women and "domestic" imperial culture', p.179.

51. R. Smith Kipp, 'Emancipating each other: Dutch colonial missionaries' encounter with Karo women in Sumatra, 1900–1942', in Clancy-Smith and Gouda, eds., *Domesticating the Empire*, pp.211–35.

52. Strobel, 'Gender, race and empire', p.403.

53. A. Burton, 'Women and "domestic" imperial culture', p.181.

54. McLintock, *Imperial Leather*, p.35.

55. See Midgley, 'Anti-slavery', pp.166–73.

56. Midgley, 'Female emancipation', p.108.

57. Midgley, *Women Against Slavery*, p.203.

58. Catherine Hall, 'The nation within and without', in Hall, McClelland and Rendall, *Defining the Victorian Nation*, pp.179–82.

59. Catherine Hall, *White, Male and Middle Class: Explorations in Feminism and History* (Cambridge, 1992), p.207.

60. Antoinette Burton, *Burdens of History: British Feminists, Indian Women and Imperial Culture, 1865–1915* (Chapel Hill, NC, 1994).

61. Clancy-Smith, 'Islam, gender, and identities', p.170.

62. Quoted ibid., p.171.

63. Strobel, 'Gender, race and empire', p.407.

64. See J.M. Bowlan, 'Civilizing gender relations in Algeria: the paradoxical case of Marie Bugéga, 1919–39', in Clancy-Smith and Gouda, eds., *Domesticating the Empire*, pp.175–92, and Barbara Bush, '"Britain's conscience on Africa": white women, race and imperial politics in inter-war Britain', in Midgley, ed., *Gender and Imperialism*, pp.200–23.

Chapter 10: First-Wave Feminism

1. Karen Offen, 'Liberty, equality, and justice for women: the theory and practice of feminism in nineteenth-century Europe', in Bridenthal, Koonz and Stuard, eds., *Becoming Visible*, 2nd edn, pp.335–74, here pp.337–9.

2. On the etymology of the terms see Offen, *European Feminisms*, pp.183–8.

3. Offen, 'Liberty, equality, and justice for women', p.339.

4. See Kathryn Gleadle and Sarah Richardson, eds., *Women in British Politics, 1760–1860: The Power of the Petticoat* (Basingstoke, 2000); Midgley, *Women Against Slavery*; F. Gordon and M. Cross, eds., *Early French Feminisms, 1830–1940* (Cheltenham, 1996).

5. Stites, *Women's Liberation Movement*, pp.68–74.

6. See Richard J. Evans, *The Feminists. Women's Emancipation Movements in Europe, America and Australasia 1840–1920* (London, 1977), chapter 1.

7. Offen, *European Feminisms*, p.31.

8. In Bell and Offen, eds., *Women, the Family and Freedom*, Vol. 1, pp.252–5.

9. Danuta Rzepniewska, 'Women of the landowning class in the Polish Kingdom during the 19th century', *Acta Poloniae Historica* 74 (1996), pp.97–120, here pp.112–16.

10. M.L. Mikhailov, 'Women: their education and significance in the family and society' (1860); N.G. Chernyshevsky, 'What is to be Done' (1863), in Bell and Offen, eds., *Women, the Family and Freedom*, Vol. 1, pp.350–7; Stites, *Women's Liberation Movement*, pp.38–63.

11. J.S. Mill, 'The Subjection of Women' (1869), in Bell and Offen, eds., *Women, the Family and Freedom*, Vol. 1, p.392.

12. Evans, *The Feminists*, p.30.

13. Reagin, *A German Women's Movement*, pp.30, 133.

14. Fidelis, 'Participation in the creative work of the nation', pp.109–10.

15. M. Oliphant, 'The laws concerning women' (1856), in Bell and Offen, eds., *Women, the Family and Freedom*, Vol. 1, p.306.

16. B. Leigh Smith, 'A Brief Summary, in Plain Language of the Most Important Laws Concerning Women' (1854); C. Norton, 'The Separation of Mother and Child' (1838), both ibid., pp.161–3, 300–5.

17. A.M. Mozzoni, 'La donna e i suoi rapporti sociali in occasione della revisione del codice civile italiano' (1864), ibid., pp.447–8.

18. Dohm, *Der Frauen Natur und Recht*, p.165.

19. In Bell and Offen, eds., *Women, the Family and Freedom*, Vol. 1, p.453.

20. Hedwig Dohm, 'Der Jesuitismus im Hausstande' (1873), ibid., p.506.

21. J. Hirsch, 'Hedwig Dohm: Der Jesuitismus im Hausstande' (1873–4), ibid., p.509.

22. Quoted in Kent, *Sex and Suffrage*, p.141.

23. Wollstonecraft, *Vindication*, p.183.

24. Quoted in M. Bryant, *The Unexpected Revolution: A Study in the History of Education of Woman and Girls in the Nineteenth Century* (London, 1979), p.22.

25. Otto-Peters (1847) in Bell and Offen, eds., *Women, the Family, and Freedom*, Vol. 1, pp.177–9.

26. Harlor (1900) in Waelti-Walters and Hause, eds., *Feminisms of the Belle Epoque* (Lincoln, NB, 1994), p.77.

27. Ibid., p.78.

28. M. Pelletier, 'L'Education féministe des filles' (1914) in Waelti-Waters and Hause, eds., *Feminisms of the Belle Epoque*, p.110.

29. Reagin, *A German Women's Movement*, pp.101–13.

30. Sarah J. Smith, 'Retaking the register: women's higher education in Glasgow and beyond, c.1796–1845', *Gender and History* 12 (2000), pp.310–35, here p.323.

31. Clarke (1873) in Bell and Offen, eds., *Women, the Family and Freedom*, Vol. 2, pp.427–31.

32. Quoted in W. Heindl and M. Tichy, eds., *'Durch Erkenntnis zu Freiheit und Glück . . .' Frauen an der Universität Wien (ab 1897)* (Vienna, 1993), pp.27–35.

33. Maudsley, 'Sex in Mind and Education' (1874), quoted in E.S. Eschbach, *The Higher Education of Women in England and America 1865–1920* (New York, 1993), p.84.

34. Garrett Anderson, 'Sex in mind and education' (1874), in Bell and Offen, eds., *Women, the Family, and Freedom*, Vol. 1, p.435.

35. Ferry (1870) ibid., pp.440–2.

36. Sée (1880) ibid., pp.443–4.

37. J. Crouzet-Benaben (1911) in Bell and Offen, eds., *Women, the Family and Freedom*, Vol. 2, pp.170–1.

38. Linda Clark, *The Rise of Professional Women in France. Gender and Public Administration since 1830* (Cambridge, 2000), pp.44–5.

39. McMillan, *Housewife or Harlot*, pp.52–3.

40. Davies, 'Special systems of education for women' (1868), in Bell and Offen, eds., *Women, the Family, and Freedom*, Vol. 1, pp.417–22.

41. Claire Jones, 'Grace Chisolm Young: gender and mathematics around 1900', *Women's History Review* 9 (2000), pp.675–92.

42. Rzepniewska, 'Women of the landowning class', p.115; Zarnowska, 'Education of working-class women', p.152.

43. Wendy Alexander, 'Early Glasgow women medical graduates', in Gordon and Breitenbach, eds., *The World is Ill Divided*, pp.70–94.

44. Reagin, *A German Women's Movement*, pp.112–16.

45. Salomon quoted in Allen, *Feminism and Motherhood*, p.212.

46. Ria Christens, 'Sociaal geëngageerd en ongehuwd: sociale werksters in Vlaanderen in de jaren 1920–1930', *Cahiers d'Histoire du Temps Présent/Bijdragen tot de Eigentijdse Geschiedenis* 4 (1998), pp.65–82.

47. Clark, *Rise of Professional Women in France*, pp.118–19.

48. Figures in Jordan, *The Women's Movement*, pp.78–9.

49. Quoted in Carol Dyhouse, *No Distinction of Sex: Women in British Universities, 1870–1939* (London, 1995), p.134.

50. Kollontai (1923) in Bell and Offen, eds., *Women, the Family and Freedom*, Vol. 2, pp.287–8.

51. Bebel, 'Woman under socialism', ibid., p.85.

52. Zetkin (1889) ibid., p.87.

53. Quoted in Offen, *European Feminisms*, p.169.

54. M.J. Boxer, 'Socialism faces feminism: the failure of synthesis in France, 1879–1914', in M.J. Boxer and J.H. Quataert, eds., *Socialist Women. European Socialist Feminism in the Nineteenth and Early Twentieth Centuries* (New York, 1978), pp.75–111, here p.85.

55. B. Tanner Springer, 'Anna Kuliscioff: Russian revolutionist, Italian feminist', in J. Slaughter and R. Kern, eds., *European Women on the Left. Socialism, Feminism, and the Problems faced by Political Women, 1880 to the Present* (Westport, CT, 1981), pp.13–28.

56. Evans, *The Feminists*, p.169.

57. Quoted in Gordon, *Women and the Labour Movement*, p.228.

58. C. LaVigna, 'The Marxist ambivalence toward women: between socialism and feminism in the Italian Socialist party', in Boxer and Quataert, eds., *Socialist Women*, pp.146–81, here pp.156–7.

59. Boxer, 'Socialism faces feminism', p.91.

60. Stites, *Women's Liberation Movement*, p.242.

61. Lenin (1918) in Bell and Offen, eds., *Women, the Family, and Freedom*, Vol. 2, p.288.

62. Trotsky (1936) ibid., p.402.

63. Kent, *Sex and Suffrage*, p.13.

64. Megan Smitley, 'Inebriates, "heathens", templars and suffragists: Scotland and imperial feminism 1870–1914', *Women's History Review* (forthcoming 2002).

65. See R.J. Evans, *The Feminist Movement in Germany 1894–1933* (London, 1976), pp.76–7.

66. E. Pankhurst (1908) in Bell and Offen, *Women, the Family and Freedom*, Vol. 2, p.237.

67. H. Lange (1913) ibid., pp.243–4.

68. M. Garrett Fawcett (1912) ibid., pp.239–40.

69. C. Chapman Catt (1913) ibid., p.245.

Chapter 11: The Great War

1. Quoted in Thom, *Nice Girls and Rude Girls*, p.1.

2. Quoted in C. Geinitz, *Kriegsfurcht und Kampfbereitschaft. Das Augusterlebnis in Freiburg. Eine Studie zum Kriegsbeginn 1914* (Essen, 1997), pp.333–4.

3. Ibid., p.336.

4. Jay Winter, 'Some paradoxes of the First World War', in R. Wall and J. Winter, eds., *The Upheaval of War. Family, Work and Welfare in Europe, 1914–1918* (Cambridge, 1988), pp.9–42, here p.11.

5. Susan R. Grayzel, *Women's Identities at War: Gender, Motherhood and Politics in Britain and France during the First World War* (Chapel Hill, NC, 1999), p.51.

6. Ibid., p.64.

7. Ibid., pp.52–63; Ruth Harris, '"The child of the barbarian": rape, race and nationalism in France during the First World War', *Past and Present* 141 (1993), pp.170–206.

8. Quoted in Geinitz, *Kriegsfurcht*, p.356.
9. Angela Woollacott, *On Her Their Lives Depend. Munitions Workers in the Great War* (Berkeley, CA, 1994), pp.84–8.
10. Quoted in Geinitz, *Kriegsfurcht*, pp.382–3.
11. Frevert, *Women in German History*, p.153.
12. Belinda J. Davis, *Home Fires Burning: Food, Politics and Everyday Life in World War I Berlin* (Chapel Hill, NC, 2000), pp.180–1.
13. The story was told by Asta Nielson, a Danish visitor to Berlin, in Davis, *Home Fires Burning*, pp.180–1.
14. Quoted in Ute Daniel, *The War from Within: German Working-class Women in the First World War* (Oxford, 1997), p.249.
15. Ibid., p.207.
16. Quoted in Y.M. Klein, ed., *Beyond the Home Front. Women's Autobiographical Writing of the Two World Wars* (Basingstoke, 1997), pp.121–2.
17. Barbara Wootton (1917) in J. Marlow, ed., *The Virago Book of Women and the Great War 1914–18* (London, 1998), pp.199–200.
18. Vera Brittain ibid., p.195.
19. Dr Bartsch ibid., p.51.
20. This phrase from May Sinclair's *The Tree of Heaven* (1917), quoted in Grayzel, *Women's Identities at War*, p.20.
21. Grayzel, *Women's Identities at War*, p.27.
22. Quoted in Daniel, *War from Within*, p.143.
23. Angela Woollacott, '"Khaki fever" and its control: gender, class, age and sexual morality on the British homefront in the First World War', *Journal of Contemporary History* 29 (1994), pp.325–47, here p.328.
24. *The Times* (Oct. 1914) quoted in G.J. de Groot, *Blighty. British Society in the Era of the Great War* (London, 1996), p.231.
25. Daniel, *War from Within*, pp.132, 136; B.R. Mitchell and P. Deane, eds., *Abstract of British Historical Statistics* (Cambridge, 1962), p.300.
26. C.G. Brown, 'Piety, gender and war in Scotland in the 1910s', in C.M.M. Macdonald and E.W. McFarland, eds., *Scotland and the Great War* (East Linton, 1999), pp.173–91, here p.173.
27. Quoted in Daniel, *War from Within*, p.144.
28. National Archives of Scotland: GD 409/1/5: SNSPCC, Edinburgh District Minute Book, 1 July–30 Sept. 1917.
29. Daniel, *War from Within*, pp.145–7.
30. Grayzel, *Women's Identities at War*, p.141.
31. Daniel, *War from Within*, pp.273–4.
32. Quoted in Smith, *Changing Lives*, p.377.
33. Kaplan, 'Women and communal strikes in the crisis of 1917–1922', in Bridenthal, Koonz and Stuard, eds., *Becoming Visible* (2nd edn), pp.429–49, here pp.438–40.
34. Quoted in Magraw, *History of the French Working Class*, pp.171–2.
35. Kaplan, 'Women and communal strikes', pp.441–4; Kaplan, 'Female consciousness and collective action', pp.545–66.

36. J.J. Smyth, 'Rents, peace, votes: working-class women and political activity in the First World War', in E. Breitenbach and E. Gordon, eds., *Out of Bounds. Women in Scottish Society 1800–1945* (Edinburgh, 1992), pp.174–96.
37. P. Sorokin quoted in Stites, *Women's Liberation Movement*, pp.289–90.
38. Daniel, *War from Within*, pp.38–49.
39. Ibid., pp.48–9.
40. Thom, *Nice Girls and Rude Girls*, pp.46–7.
41. McDermid and Hillyer, *Women and Work in Russia*, pp.144–5.
42. L. Delétang quoted in Marlow, ed., *Women and the Great War*, p.29.
43. *Vorwärts* (10 Sept. 1914) ibid., p.33.
44. Quoted in Anna Bravo, 'Italian peasant women and the First World War', in A. Marwick, C. Emsley and W. Simpson, eds., *Total War and Historical Change: Europe 1914–1955* (Buckingham, 2001), p.88.
45. Pankhurst in Marlow, ed., *Women and the Great War*, pp.86–97, here p.84.
46. Daniel, *War from Within*, pp.82–4.
47. Quoted ibid., p.99.
48. N. Loughnan quoted in Marlow, ed., *Women and the Great War*, p.167.
49. McDermid and Hillyer, *Women and Work in Russia*, pp.144–8.
50. Quoted in Janet K. Watson, 'Khaki girls, VAD's, and Tommy's sisters: gender and class in First World War Britain', *The International History Review* 19 (1997), pp.32–51, here p.49.
51. Quoted in Daniel, *War from Within*, p.101.
52. Sylvia Pankhurst (1915) in Bell and Offen, eds., *Women, the Family and Freedom*, Vol. 2, p.281.
53. V. Brittain to Roland Leighton, 1 Oct. 1914, in A. Bishop and M. Bostridge, eds., *Letters from a Lost Generation: First World War Letters of Vera Brittain and Four Friends* (London, 1999), p.31.
54. Quoted in Deborah Gorham, *Vera Brittain: A Feminist Life* (Oxford, 1996), p.183.
55. N.F. Gullace, 'White feathers and wounded men: female patriotism and the memory of the Great War', *Journal of British Studies* 36 (1997), pp.178–206, here p.183.
56. Quoted in Margaret H. Darrow, 'French volunteer nursing and the myth of war experience in World War One', *American Historical Review* 101 (1996), pp.80–106, here p.88.
57. O. Dent (1917) quoted in Watson, 'Khaki girls', p.32.
58. F.E. Rendel in Marlow, ed., *Women and the Great War*, p.231.
59. Regina Schulte, 'The sick warrior's sister: nursing during the First World War', in Abrams and Harvey, eds., *Gender Relations in German History*, pp.121–41, here p.127.
60. M. Borden in Marlow, ed., *Women and the Great War*, p.331.
61. Smith ibid., p.325.
62. Krisztina Robert, 'Gender, class, and patriotism: women's paramilitary units in First World War Britain', *The International History Review* 19 (1997), pp.52–65.
63. See Susan R. Grayzel, '"The outward and visible sign of her patriotism": women, uniforms and national service during the First World War', *Twentieth Century British History* 8 (1997), pp.145–64.

64. Ibid., p.159.
65. Bochkarëva quoted in McDermid and Hillyar, *Women and Work in Russia*, p.141.
66. H. Swanwick (1915) quoted in Bell and Offen, eds., *Women, the Family and Freedom*, Vol. 1, p.270.
67. Quoted in Offen, *European Feminisms*, p.260.
68. Richard J. Evans, 'Women's peace, men's war?', in R.J. Evans, ed., *Comrades and Sisters: Feminism, Socialism and Pacifism in Europe 1870–1945* (London, 1987), p.130.
69. Quoted in Offen, *European Feminisms*, p.259.
70. Quoted in Bell and Offen, eds., *Women, the Family and Freedom*, Vol.2, p.274.
71. Quoted in Grayzel, *Women's Identities at War*, p.181, and see pp.165–86 for a full discussion of the trial of Brion.
72. See Gordon and Cross, eds., *Early French Feminisms*, chapter 7, pp.189–227.
73. Grayzel, *Women's Identities at War*, p.246.

FURTHER READING

———— ◆ ————

ull references to all the materials used in this text can be found in the Notes. What follows is a guide to further reading, not a comprehensive bibliography.

General Works

Anderson, B.S. and J.P. Zinsser, *A History of Their Own. Women in Europe from Prehistory to the Present*, 2 volumes (London, 1990).

Bell, S.G. and K.M. Offen, eds., *Women, the Family, and Freedom. The Debate in Documents*. Vol. 1, *1750–1880*; Vol. 2, *1880–1950* (Stanford, CA, 1983).

Boxer, M.J. and J.H. Quataert, eds., *Connecting Spheres: European Women in a Globalizing World. 1500 to the Present* (Oxford, 1987; 2nd edn, 2000).

Bridenthal, R., C. Koonz and S. Stuard, eds., *Becoming Visible: Women in European History* (2nd edn, Boston, 1987).

Bridenthal, R., S.M. Stuard and M.E. Wiesner, eds., *Becoming Visible: Women in European History* (3rd edn, Boston, 1998).

Caine, B. and G. Sluga, *Gendering European History 1780–1920* (Leicester, 2000).

Duby, G. and M. Perrot, eds., *A History of Women in the West*, 5 vols (Cambridge, MA, 1984).

Hannam, J., K. Holden, H. Meller and P. Summerfield, *Major Themes in Women's History from the Enlightenment to the Great War* [CD ROM] (Glasgow History Courseware Consortium, 1998).

McMillan, J.F., *Enfranchising Women: The Politics of Women's Suffrage in Europe, 1789–1945* [CD ROM] (Glasgow History Courseware Consortium, 1998).

Rendall, J., *The Origins of Modern Feminism: Women in Britain, France and the United States, 1780–1860* (Basingstoke, 1985).

Shoemaker, R. and M. Vincent, eds., *Gender and History in Western Europe* (London, 1998).

Smith, B.G., *Changing Lives: Women in European History since 1700* (Lexington, MA, 1989).

National Histories

Abrams, L. and E. Harvey, eds., *Gender Relations in German History: Power, Agency and Experience from the Sixteenth to the Twentieth Century* (London, 1996).

Baranski, Z.G. and S.W. Vinall, eds., *Women and Italy. Essay on Gender, Culture and History* (Basingstoke, 1991).

Breitenbach, E. and E. Gordon, eds., *Out of Bounds. Women in Scottish Society 1800–1945* (Edinburgh, 1992).

Enders, V.L. and P.B. Radcliff, eds., *Constructing Spanish Womanhood. Female Identity in Modern Spain* (Albany, NY, 1999).

Engel, B.A., *Between the Fields and the City: Women, Work and Family in Russia, 1861–1914* (Cambridge, 1996).

Frevert, U., *Women in German History: From Bourgeois Emancipation to Sexual Liberation* (Leamington Spa, 1989).

Good, D.F., M. Grandner and M.J. Maynes, eds., *Austrian Women in the Nineteenth and Twentieth Centuries* (Oxford, 1996).

John, A.V. ed., *Our Mothers' Land: Chapters in Welsh Women's History, 1830–1939* (Cardiff, 1991).

Luddy, M. ed., *Women in Ireland 1800–1918* (Cork, 1995).

McMillan, J.F., *France and Women 1789–1914: Gender, Society and Politics* (London, 2000).

Purvis, J., ed., *Women's History in Britain, 1850–1945: An Introduction* (London, 1995).

Ransel, D.L. ed., *The Family in Imperial Russia* (Urbana, IL, 1976).

Shoemaker, R.B., *Gender in English Society 1650–1850: The Emergence of Separate Spheres* (London, 1988).

'Women in Central and Eastern Europe', special issue, *Women's History Review* 5 (1996).

Women's History, Theory and Historiography

Bock, G., 'Women's history and gender history: aspects of an international debate', *Gender and History* 1 (1989), pp.7–30.

Davidoff, L., *Worlds Between: Historical Perspectives on Gender and Class* (Cambridge, 1995).

Hall, C., *White, Male and Middle Class: Explorations in Feminism and History* (Cambridge, 1992).

Offen, K.M., R. Roach Pierson and J. Rendall, eds., *Writing Women's History: International Perspectives* (Bloomington, IN, 1991).

Scott, J.W., *Gender and the Politics of History* (New York, 1988).

Vickery, A., 'Golden age to separate spheres? A review of the categories and chronology of English women's history', *Historical Journal* 36 (1993), pp.383–414.

Body, Mind and Spirit

Ehrenreich, B. and D. English, *For Her Own Good: 150 years of the Experts' Advice to Women* (London, 1979).

Jalland, P. and J. Hooper, eds., *Women from Birth to Death: The Female Life Cycle in Britain 1830–1914* (Brighton, 1986).

Jordanova, L., *Sexual Visions: Images of Gender in Science and Medicine Between the Eighteenth and Twentieth Centuries* (London, 1989).

Laqueur, T., *Making Sex: Body and Gender from the Greeks to Freud* (Cambridge, MA, 1995).

Malmgreen, G., ed., *Religion in the Lives of English Women 1760–1930* (London, 1986).

Markkola, P., ed., *Gender and Vocation. Women, Religion and Social Change in the Nordic Countries, 1830–1940* (Helsinki, 2000).

Moscucci, O., *The Science of Woman: Gynaecology and Gender in England 1800–1929* (Cambridge, 1990).

Shorter, E., *Women's Bodies: A Social History of Women's Encounter with Health, Ill-health, and Medicine* (New Brunswick, NJ, 1991).

Showalter, E., *The Female Malady: Women, Madness and English Culture, 1830–1980* (London, 1987).

Vertinsky, P., *The Eternally Wounded Woman* (Manchester, 1990).

Femininity and Domesticity

Albisetti, J.C., *Schooling German Girls and Women: Secondary and Higher Education in the Nineteenth Century* (Princeton, NJ, 1988).

Clark, L.L., *Schooling the Daughters of Marianne: Textbooks and the Socializing of Girls in Modern France 1848–1870* (New York, 1984).

Davin, A., *Growing Up Poor: Home, School and Street in London 1870–1914* (London, 1996).

Dyhouse, C., *Girls Growing Up in Late Victorian and Edwardian England* (London, 1981).

Gemie, S., *Women and Schooling in France, 1815–1914. Gender, Authority and Identity in the Female Schooling Sector* (Keele, 1995).

Hall, C., 'The early formation of Victorian domestic ideology', in Hall, ed., *White, Male and Middle Class*, pp.75–93.

Hausen, K., 'Family and role-division: the polarisation of sexual stereotypes in the nineteenth century – an aspect of the dissociation of work and family life', in R.J. Evans and W.R. Lee, eds., *The German Family* (London, 1981), pp.51–83.

Hunt, F., ed., *Lessons for Life: The Schooling of Girls and Women, 1850–1950* (Oxford, 1987).

Rowbotham, J., *Good Girls Make Good Wives: Guidance for Girls in Victorian Fiction* (Oxford, 1989).

Strumingher, L.S., *What were Little Girls and Boys Made of? Primary Education in Rural France, 1830–1880* (Albany, NY, 1983).

Marriage, Spinsters and Widows

Bennett, J.M. and A.M. Froide, eds., *Singlewomen in the European Past 1250–1800* (Philadelphia, 1999).

Botelho, L. and P. Thane, eds., *Women and Ageing in British Society since 1500* (London, 2001).

Gillis, J., *For Better, For Worse. British Marriages, 1600 to the Present* (Oxford, 1985).

Hammerton, A.J., *Cruelty and Companionship: Conflict in Nineteenth Century Married Life* (London, 1992).

Hufton, O., 'Women without men: widows and spinsters in Britain and France in the eighteenth century', *Journal of Family History* 9 (1984), pp.355–76.

Jalland, P., *Women, Marriage and Politics, 1860–1914* (Oxford, 1986).

Phillips, R., *Untying the Knot: a Short History of Divorce* (Cambridge, 1991).

Segalen, M., *Love and Power in the Peasant Family: Rural France in the Nineteenth Century* (Oxford, 1983).

Vicinus, M., *Independent Women: Work and Community for Single Women 1850–1920* (London, 1985).

Motherhood

Allen, A.T., *Feminism and Motherhood in Germany 1800–1914* (New Brunswick, NJ, 1991).

Badinter, E., *The Myth of Motherhood: an Historical View of the Maternal Instinct* (London, 1981).

Bock, G. and P. Thane, eds., *Maternity and Gender Policies. Women and the Rise of the European Welfare States 1880s–1950s* (London, 1991).

Fuchs, R., *Abandoned Children: Foundlings and Child Welfare in Nineteenth-Century France* (Albany, NY, 1984).

Loudon, I., *Death in Childbirth: An International Study of Maternal Care and Maternal Mortality 1800–1950* (Oxford, 1992).

Marland, H. and A.M. Rafferty, eds., *Midwives, Society and Childbirth: Debates and Controversies in the Modern Period* (London, 1997).

Pollock, L.A., *Forgotten Children. Parent–Child Relations from 1500 to 1900* (Cambridge, 1983).

Ransel, D.L., *Mothers of Misery. Child Abandonment in Russia* (Princeton, NJ, 1988).

Ross, E., *Love and Toil: Motherhood in Outcast London 1870–1918* (Oxford, 1993).

Home, Household, Community

Bourke, J., *Husbandry to Housewifery: Women, Economic Change and Housework in Ireland, 1890–1914* (Oxford, 1993).

Clark, A., *The Struggle for the Breeches: Gender and the Making of the British Working Class* (London, 1995).

Davidoff, L. and C. Hall, *Family Fortunes. Men and Women of the English Middle Class, 1780–1850* (London, 1987).

Gillis, J., *A World of Their Own Making: A History of Myth and Ritual in Family Life* (Oxford, 1997).

Kaplan, T., 'Female consciousness and collective action: the case of Barcelona, 1910–18', *Signs* 7 (1982), pp.545–66.

McBride, T.M., *The Domestic Revolution: The Modernisation of Household Service in England and France 1820–1920* (London, 1976).

Roberts, E., *A Woman's Place: An Oral History of Working-class Women* (Oxford, 1984; 2nd edn, 1995).

Rowbotham, S., *Women, Resistance and Revolution* (Harmondsworth, 1974).

Smith, B., *Ladies of the Leisure Class: The Bourgeoisie of Northern France in the Nineteenth Century* (Princeton, NJ, 1981).

Sexuality

Bland, L., *Banishing the Beast: English Feminism and Sexual Morality 1885–1914* (London, 1995).

Engelstein, L., *The Keys to Happiness: Sex and the Search for Modernity in Fin-de-Siècle Russia* (Ithaca, NY, 1992).

Faderman, L., *Surpassing the Love of Men. Romantic Friendship and Love between Women from the Renaissance to the Present* (London, 1991).

Gibson, M., *Prostitution and the State in Italy, 1860–1915* (New Brunswick, NJ, 1986).

Harsin, J., *Policing Prostitution in Nineteenth Century Paris* (Princeton, NJ, 1985).

Jackson, M., *The Real Facts of Life. Feminism and the Politics of Sexuality c.1850–1914* (London, 1994).

Jeffreys, S., ed., *The Sexuality Debates* (London, 1987).

Kent, S.K., *Sex and Suffrage in Britain, 1860–1914* (London, 1995).

Walkowitz, J.R., *Prostitution and Victorian Society: Women, Class and the State* (Cambridge, 1980).

Walkowitz, J.R., *City of Dreadful Delight. Narratives of Sexual Danger in Late Victorian London* (London, 1992).

Work

Canning, K., *Languages of Labor and Gender: Female Factory Work in Germany, 1850–1914* (Ithaca, NY, 1996).

De Groot, G. and M. Schrover, *Women Workers and Technological Change in Europe in the Nineteenth and Twentieth Centuries* (London, 1992).

Frader, L.L. and S.O. Rose, eds., *Gender and Class in Modern Europe* (Ithaca, NY, 1986).

Glickman, R.L., *Russian Factory Women. Workplace and Society, 1880–1914* (Berkeley, CA, 1984).

Gordon, E., *Women and the Labour Movement in Scotland 1850–1914* (Oxford, 1991).

Hilden, P., *Working Women and Socialist Politics in France 1880–1914* (Oxford, 1986).

Honeyman, K., *Women, Gender and Industrialisation in England, 1700–1870* (Basingstoke, 2000).

Hudson, P. and W.R. Lee, eds., *Women's Work and the Family Economy in Historical Perspective* (Manchester, 1990).

McBride, T.M., 'A woman's world: department stores and the evolution of women's employment, 1870–1920', *French Historical Studies* 10 (1978), pp.664–83.

McDermid, J. and A. Hillyer, *Women and Work in Russia 1880–1930* (London, 1998).

Rose, S.O., *Limited Livelihoods: Gender and Class in Nineteenth-century England* (London, 1992).

Sharpe, P., ed., *Women's Work: the English Experience 1650–1914* (London, 1998).

Simonton, D., *A History of European Women's Work, 1700 to the Present* (London, 1998).

Stewart, M.L., *Women, Work and the French State. Labour Protection and Social Patriarchy, 1879–1919* (Kingston, 1989).

Tilly, L.A., *Politics and Class in Milan 1881–1901* (Oxford, 1992).

Tilly, L. and J. Scott, *Women, Work and Family* (New York, 1978).

Politics and Nationalism

Applewhite, H.B. and D.G. Levy, eds., *Women and Politics in the Age of Democratic Revolution* (Ann Arbor, MI, 1990).

Blom, I., K. Hagemann and C. Hall, eds., *Gendered Nations: Nationalisms and Gender Order in the Long Nineteenth Century* (Oxford, 2000).

Gullickson, G.L., *Unruly Women of Paris: Images of the Commune* (Ithaca, NY, 1996).

Hall, C., K. McLelland and J. Rendall, *Defining the Victorian Nation: Class, Race, Gender and the Reform Act of 1867* (Cambridge, 2000).

Scott, J.W., *Only Paradoxes to Offer: French Feminists and the Rights of Man* (Cambridge, MA, 1996).

Shafer, D.A., 'Plus que des ambulancières: women in articulation and defence of their ideals during the Paris Commune (1871)', *French History* 7 (1993), pp.85–101.

Ward, M., *Unmanageable Revolutionaries: Women and Irish Nationalism* (London, 1983).

Empire

Burton, A., *Burdens of History: British Feminists, Indian Women and Imperial Culture, 1865–1915* (Chapel Hill, NC, 1994).

Callaway, H., *Gender, Culture and Empire: European Women in Colonial Nigeria* (Basingstoke, 1987).

Chaudhuri, N. and M. Strobel, *Western Women and Imperialism: Complicity and Resistance* (Bloomington, IN, 1992).

Clancy-Smith, J. and F. Gouda, eds., *Domesticating the Empire. Race, Gender and Family Life in French and Dutch Colonialism* (Charlottesville, VA, 1998).

McLintock, A., *Imperial Leather: Race, Gender and Sexuality in the Colonial Conquest* (New York, 1995).

Midgley, C., *Women Against Slavery: the British Campaigns 1780–1870* (London, 1992).

Midgley, C. ed., *Gender and Imperialism* (Manchester, 1998).

Pierson, R.R. and N. Chaudhuri, eds., *Nation, Empire, Colony: Historicizing Gender and Race* (Bloomington, IN, 1998).

Strobel, M., 'Gender, race and empire in nineteenth and twentieth-century Africa and Asia', in Bridenthal, Koonz and Stuard, eds., *Becoming Visible* (3rd edn), pp.389–414.

Feminism

Boxer, M.J. and J.H. Quataert, eds., *Socialist Women. European Socialist Feminism in the Nineteenth and Early Twentieth Centuries* (New York, 1978).

Edmondson, L., *Feminism in Russia, 1900–1917* (Stanford, CA, 1984).

Evans, R.J., *The Feminists. Women's Emancipation Movements in Europe, America and Australasia 1840–1920* (London, 1977).

Gordon, F. and M. Cross, eds., *Early French Feminisms, 1830–1940: A Passion for Liberty* (Cheltenham, 1996).

Offen, K., *European Feminisms 1700–1950: A Political History* (Stanford, CA, 2000).

Reagin, N.R., *A German Women's Movement. Class and Gender in Hanover, 1880–1933* (Chapel Hill, NC, 1995).

Slaughter, J. and R. Kern, eds., *European Women on the Left. Socialism, Feminism, and the Problems Faced by Political Women, 1880 to the Present* (Westport, CT, 1981).

Stites, R., *The Women's Liberation Movement in Russia: Feminism, Nihilism and Bolshevism, 1860–1930* (Princeton, NJ, 1991).

Waelti-Walters, J. and S.C. Hause, eds., *Feminisms of the Belle Epoque: A Historical and Literary Anthology* (Lincoln, NB, 1994).

First World War

Bravo, A., 'Italian peasant women and the First World War', in A. Marwick, C. Emsley and W. Simpson, eds., *Total War and Historical Change: Europe 1914–1955* (Buckingham, 2001), pp.86–97.

Braybon, G., *Women Workers in the First World War: The British Experience* (London, 1981).

Daniel, U., *The War from Within: German Working-class Women in the First World War* (Oxford, 1997).

Davis, B.J., *Home Fires Burning: Food, Politics and Everyday Life in World War I Berlin* (Chapel Hill, NC, 2000).

Grayzel, S.R., *Women's Identities at War: Gender, Motherhood and Politics in Britain and France during the First World War* (Chapel Hill, NC, 1999).

Marlow, J., ed., *The Virago Book of Women and the Great War 1914–18* (London, 1998).

Thom, D., *Nice Girls and Rude Girls: Women Workers in World War I* (London, 1998).

Wall, R. and J. Winter, eds., *The Upheaval of War. Family, Work and Welfare in Europe, 1914–1918* (Cambridge, 1988).

INDEX